FIRE APPARATUS FIGHTING FIRES II

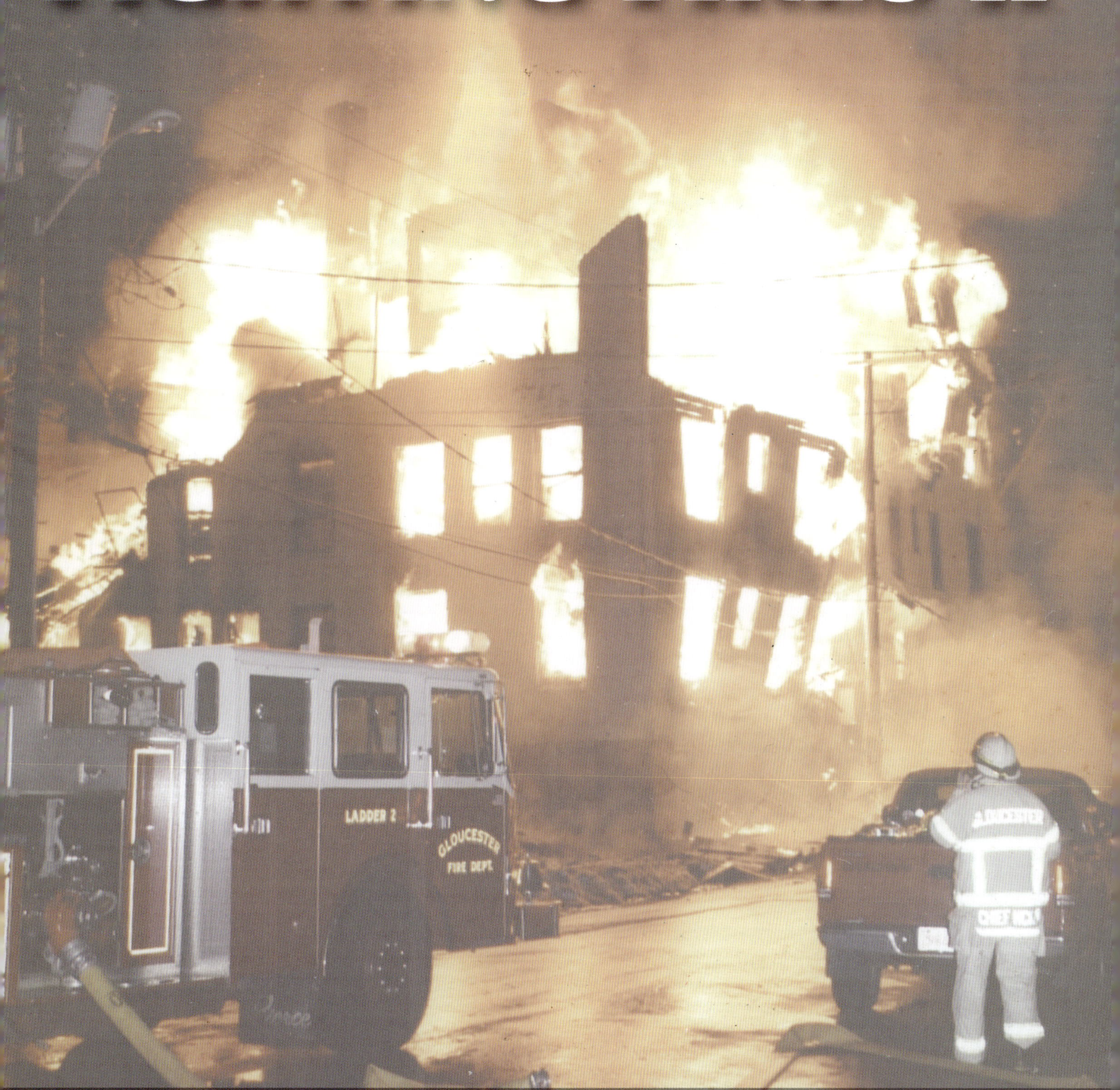

by PETER ALOISI

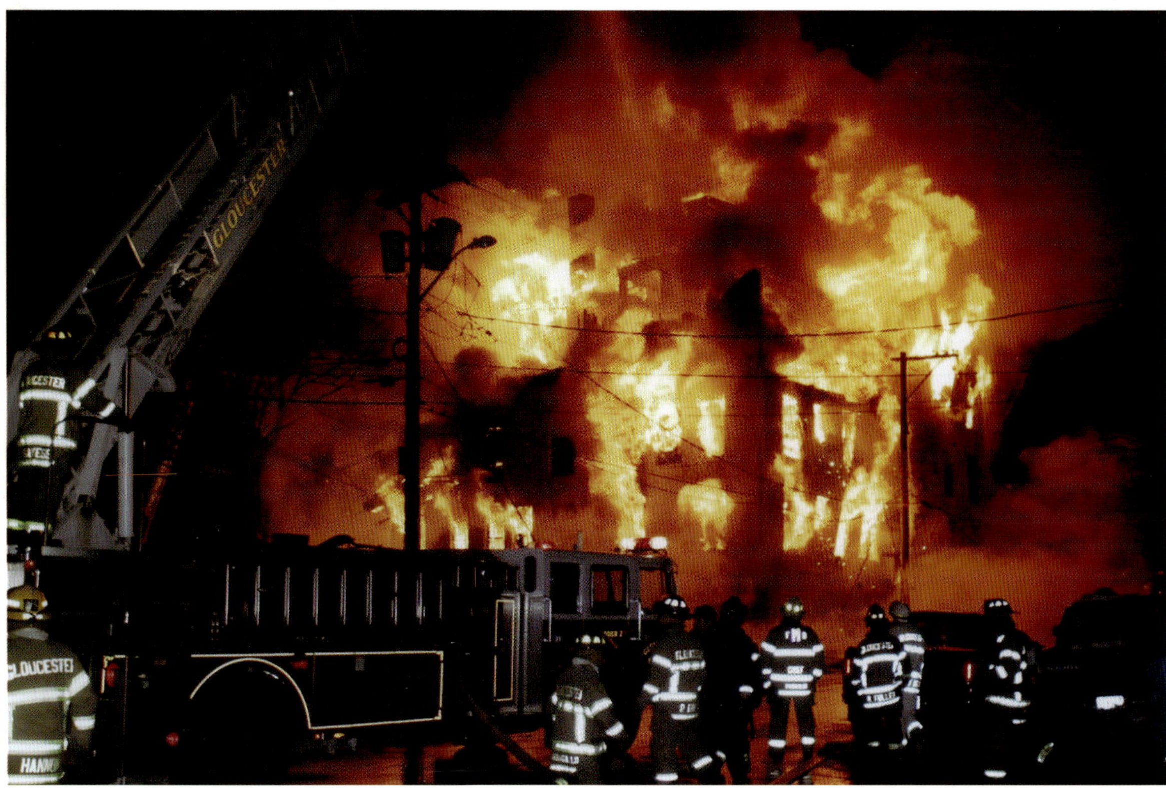

Shortly before midnight on December 14, 2007, a fire was reported at The Lorraine Apartment Building at 80 Middle Street, in downtown Gloucester, MA. The building was located across the street from fire headquarters and occupied by 23 residents. The fire spread rapidly throughout the building due to balloon construction and quickly involved the adjacent Temple Ahavat Achim Synagogue. 8 alarms were sounded, however both buildings burned to the ground, and one resident died in the fire.

ALL PHOTOGRAPHS BY THE AUTHOR

ISBN: 978-0-9841287-4-7

Published by:

Chariot Publishing Co., Inc.
210 Broadway
Lynnfield, MA 01940

781-581-7541

www.chariotpublishing.net

Printed in China

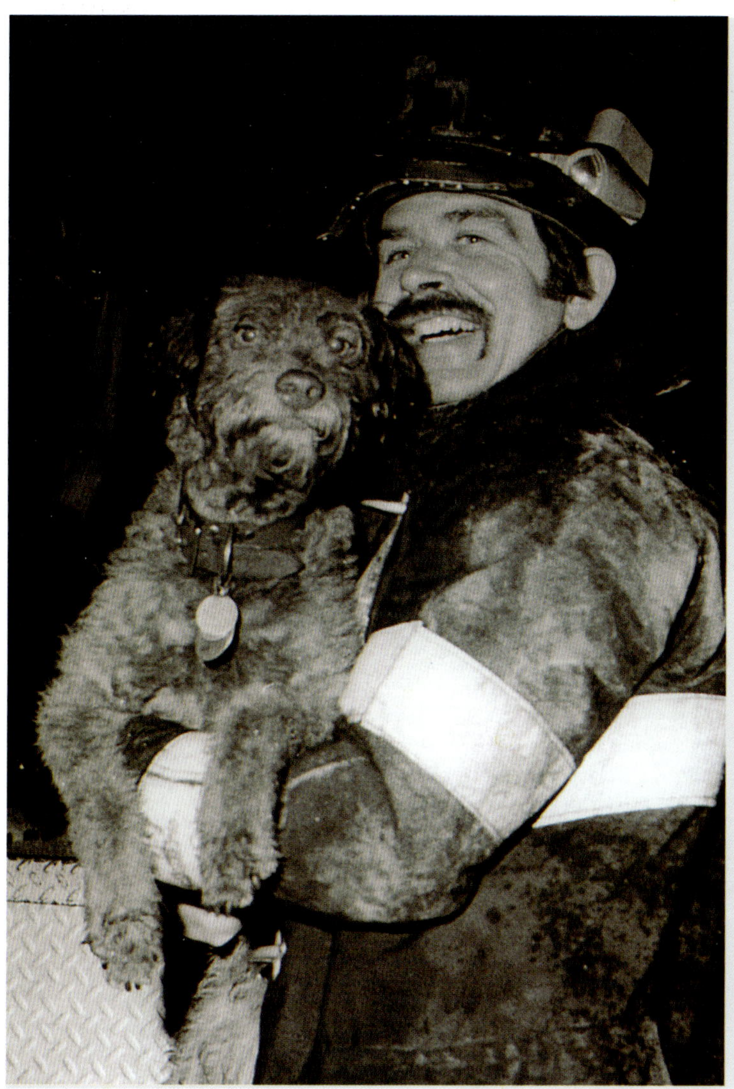

DEDICATION

This book is dedicated to the memory of Franklin Arthur (Artie) O'Leary. Artie was a long-time member of The Boston Fire Department, who died unexpectedly on June 17, 1999. He was 56 years old. In 1991 he rescued a fellow firefighter who collapsed while fighting a fire in a six story apartment building, for which he received the John E. Fitzgerald Medal for the Most Meritorious Act. He made many other rescues during his career and was highly decorated for bravery. Artie was a firefighter 24/7, always ready to go to a fire and sometimes helping out to fight the "Red Devil". He was also an avid fire buff, traveling the Country, attending firematic shows, conventions and funerals for firefighters who died in the line of duty. Artie sponsored me into the Firefighting Brotherhood, something I am forever grateful for.

ABOUT THE AUTHOR

Peter Aloisi has been photographing fires and fire apparatus across the Country for 40 years. He is the photographer for The Lynnfield, Massachusetts Fire Department and a member of Revere, Massachusetts Emergency Management. He has published three books: *Fire Apparatus Fighting Fires* (1990), *Apparatus and Fires Across America* (1994) and *Fire Buffs* (2009). His photographs have appeared in many publications. He has produced ten fire-ground videos, which have been used for training by many fire departments. Since 1999, he has published a fire-ground calendar. He is an Honorary Battalion Chief, FDNY, Honorary Member of The Connecticut Fire Photographers Association, and The Massachusetts Antique Fire Apparatus Association. He is a life member of The Box 52 Association and member of The 100 Club of Massachusetts.

TABLE OF CONTENTS

FDNY 5

BOSTON FIRE 18

CLASSICS 29

APPARATUS ACROSS AMERICA 42

TILLERS 51

SECOND CAREER APPARATUS 56

MASSACHUSETTS FIRES 66

FIRES ACROSS AMERICA 104

WINTER FIREFIGHTING 112

TRUCK WORK 118

GROUPS 122

MEMORIALS 126

GONE BUT NOT FORGOTTEN 128

NO WORDS ARE NEEDED 134

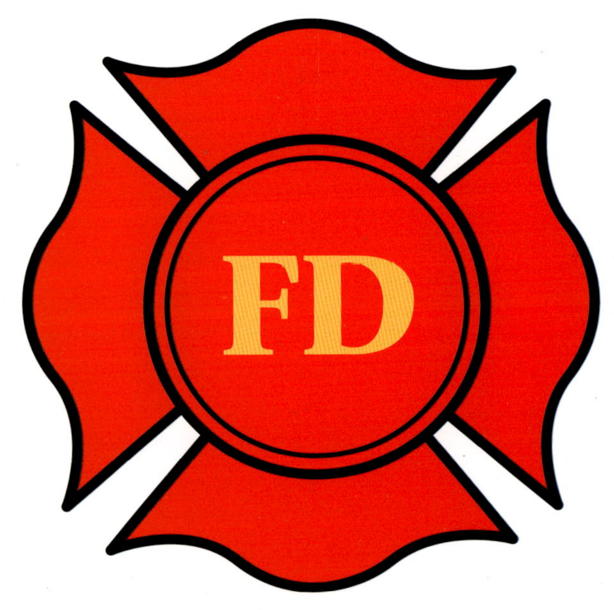

FDNY

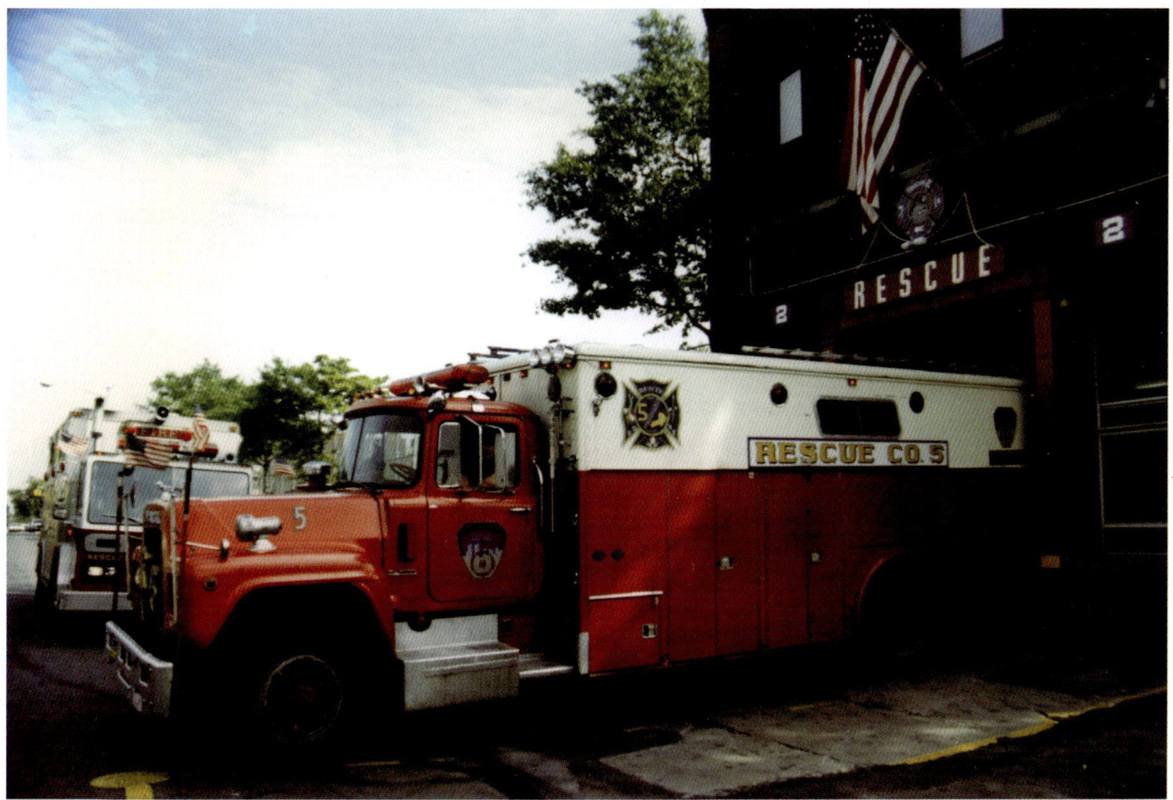

Rescue 5, disbanded in 1962 and re-established in 1984, 1976 Mack/Hamerly, former Rescue 2. Rescue 5 had been relocated to Rescue 2 for the day tour.

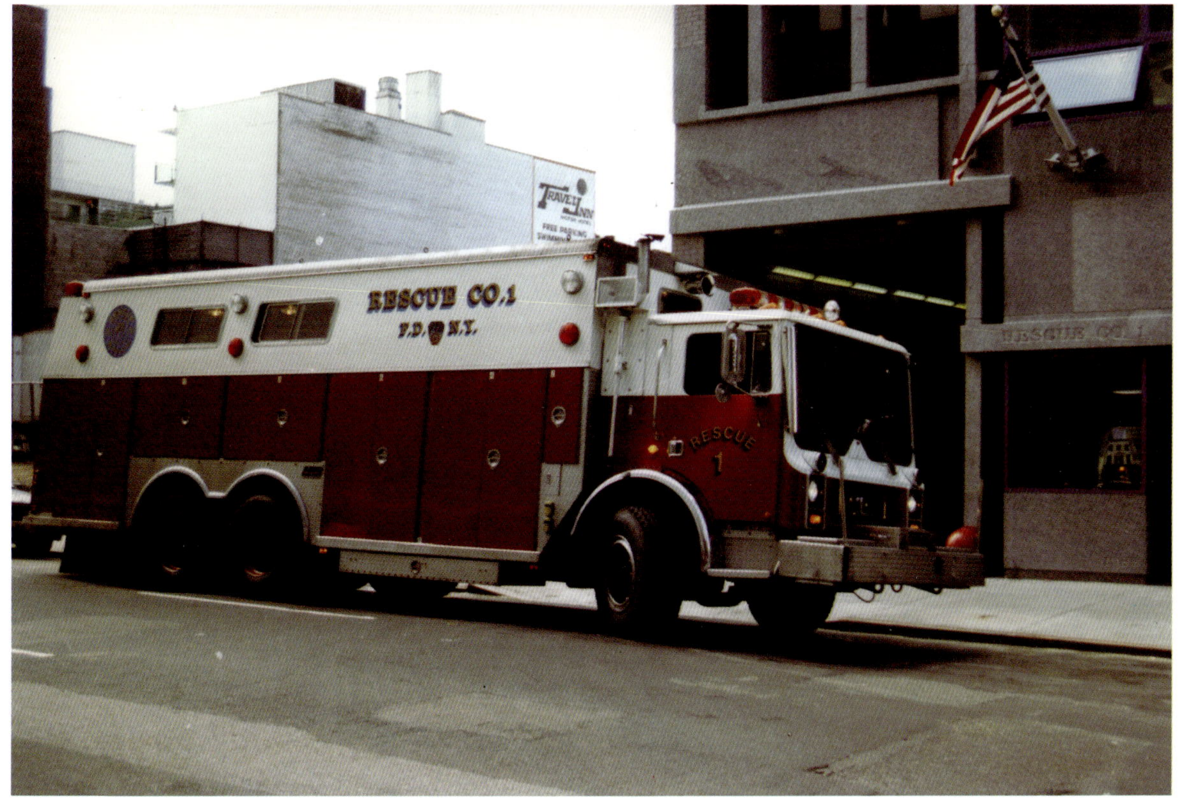

Rescue 1, 1985 Mack/Saulsbury.

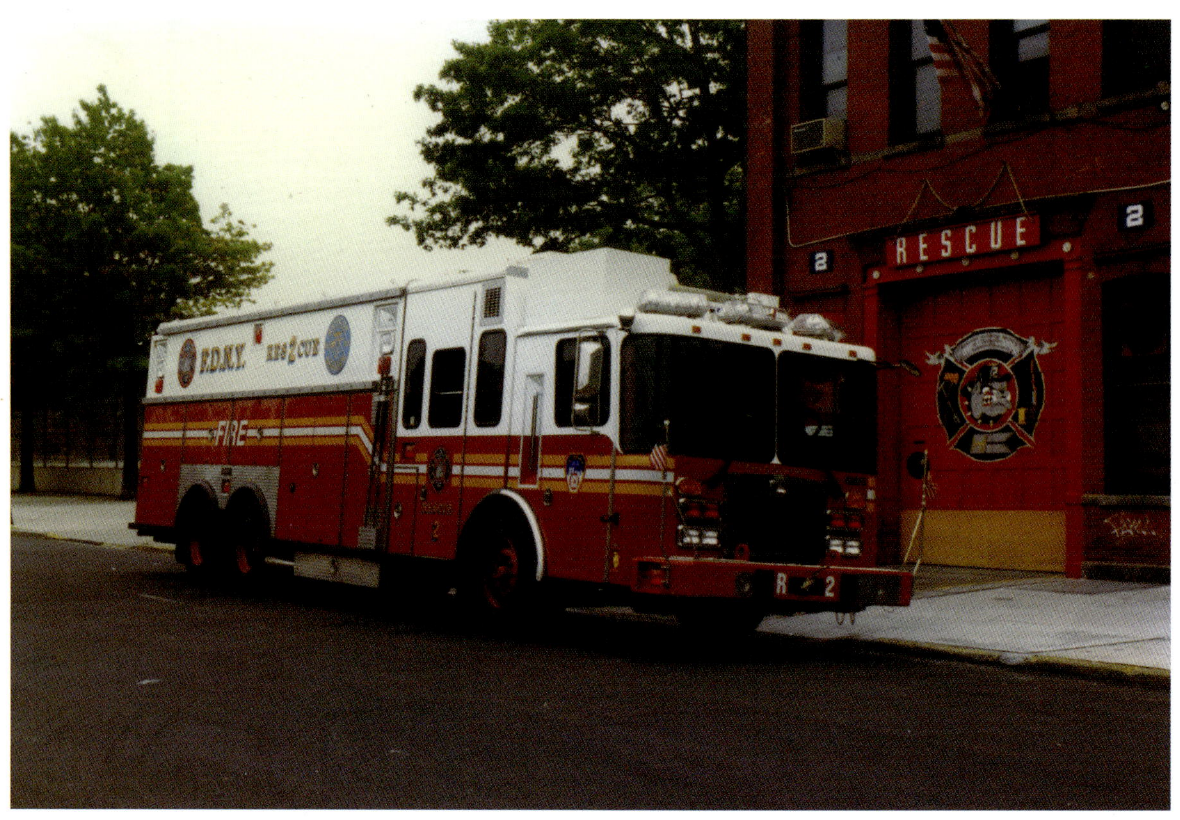

Rescue 2, 1996 HME/Saulsbury, which was destroyed on September 11, 2001.

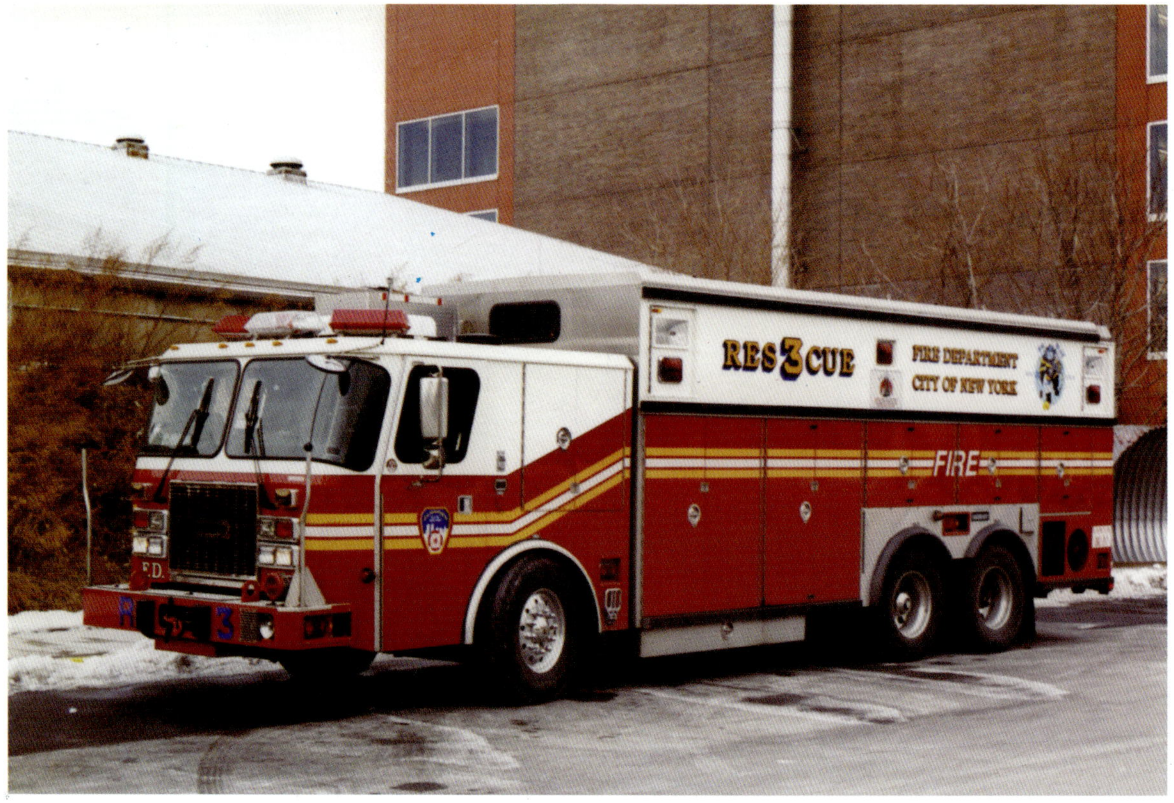

Rescue 3, 2002 Emergency-One, Cyclone II.

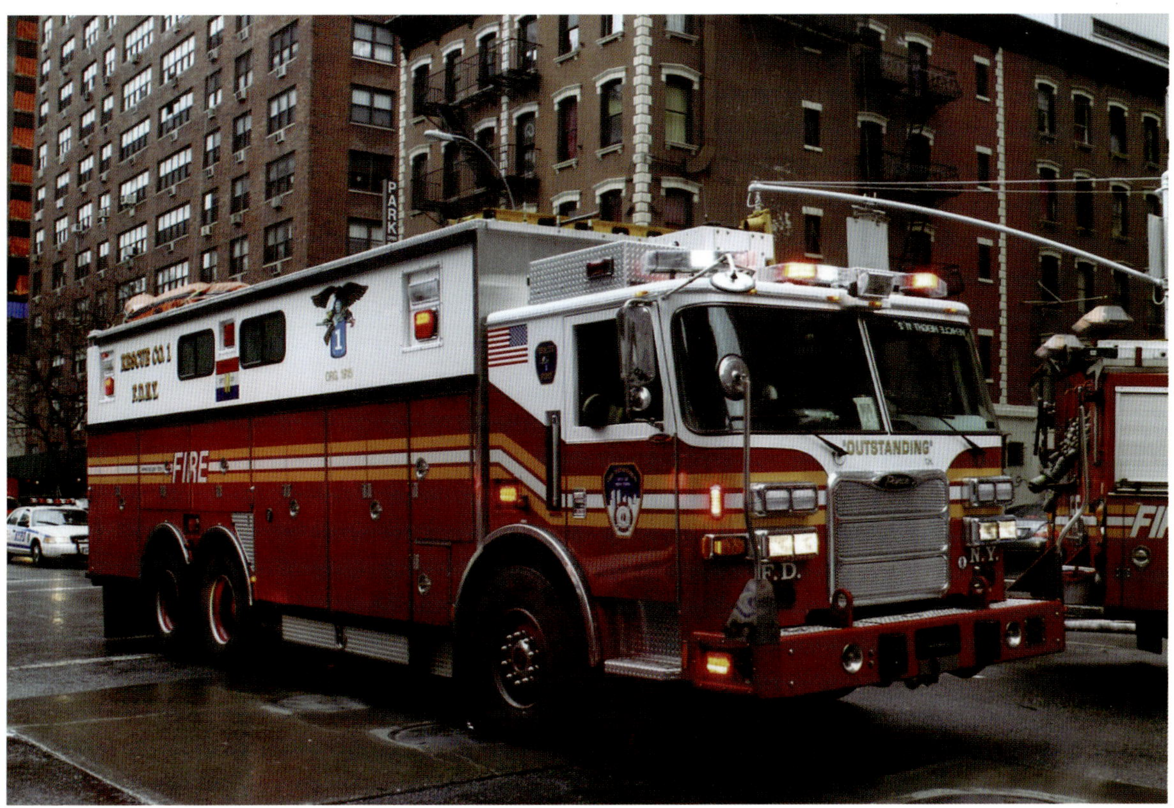

Rescue 1, 2006 Pierce, Arrow, XT donated by Airbus.

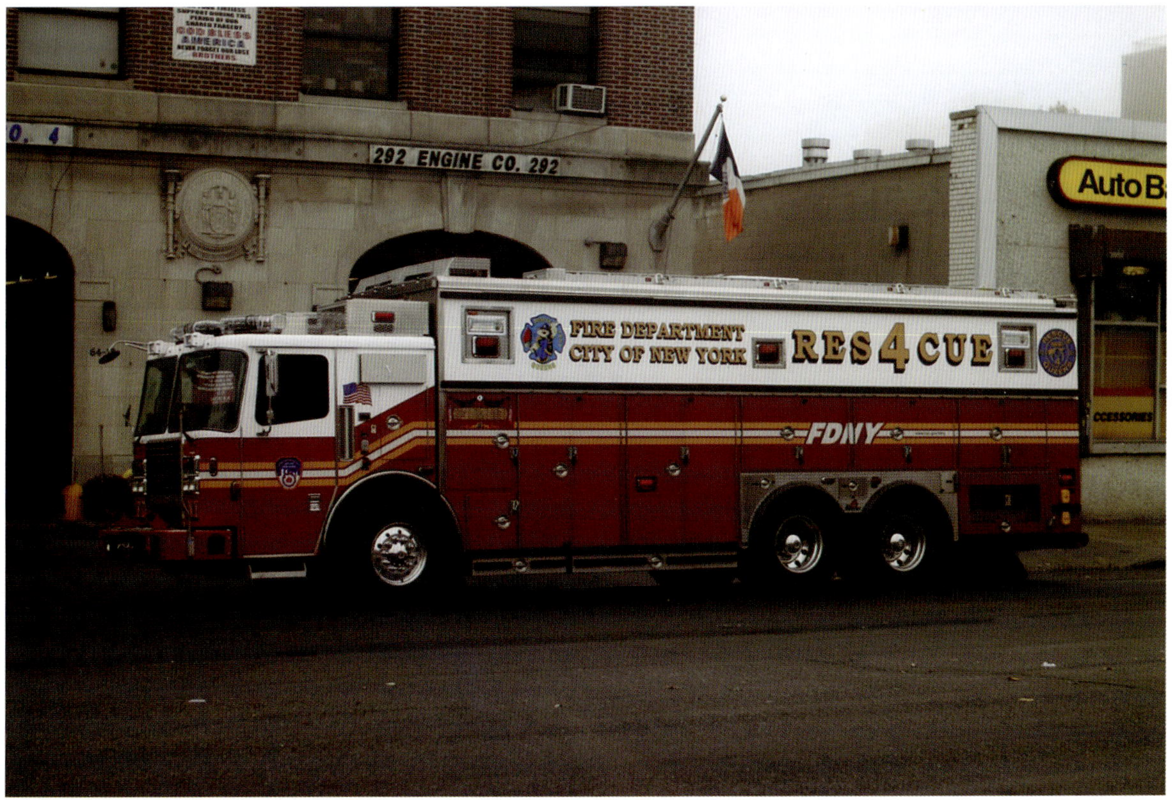

Rescue 4, 2011 Ferrara, Igniter.

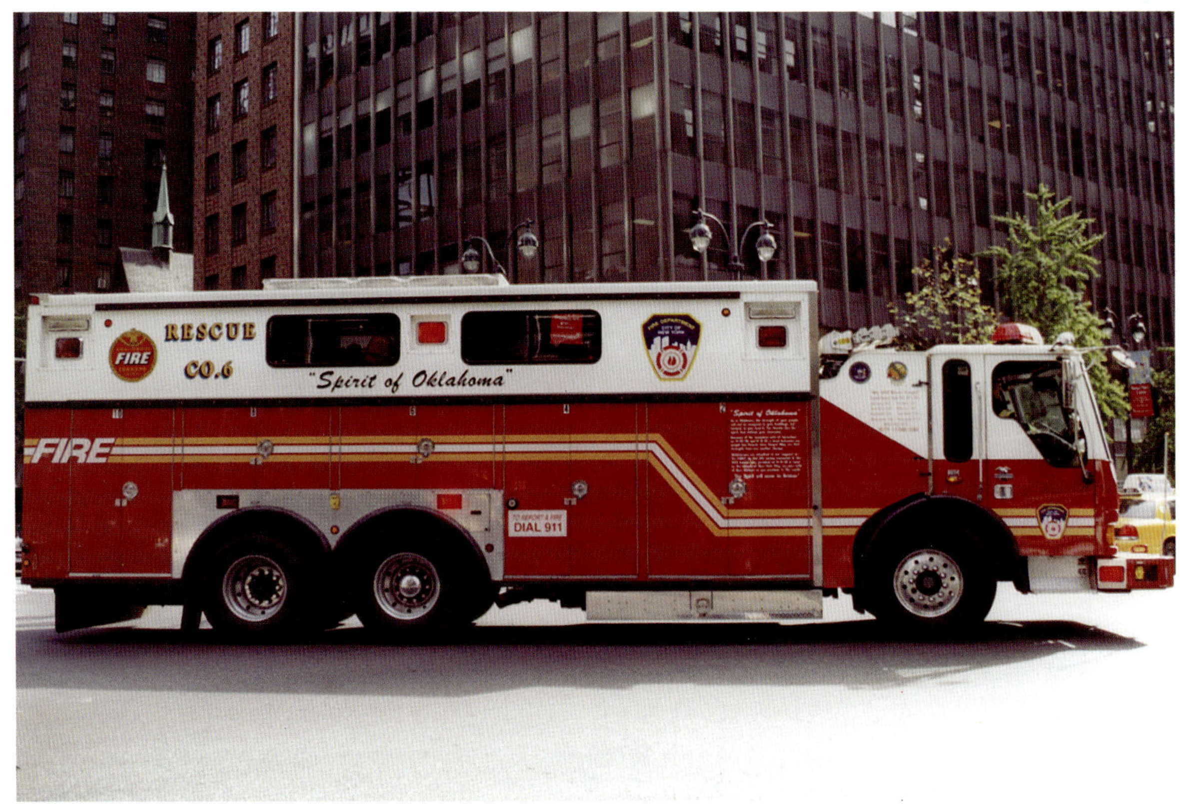

Rescue 6, 2002 Freightliner/ALF donated by Oklahoma City. Rescue 6 was organized on August 2, 2004 and quartered with Ladder 20 in Lower Manhattan. It was disbanded on November 3, 2004, the day after the presidential election.

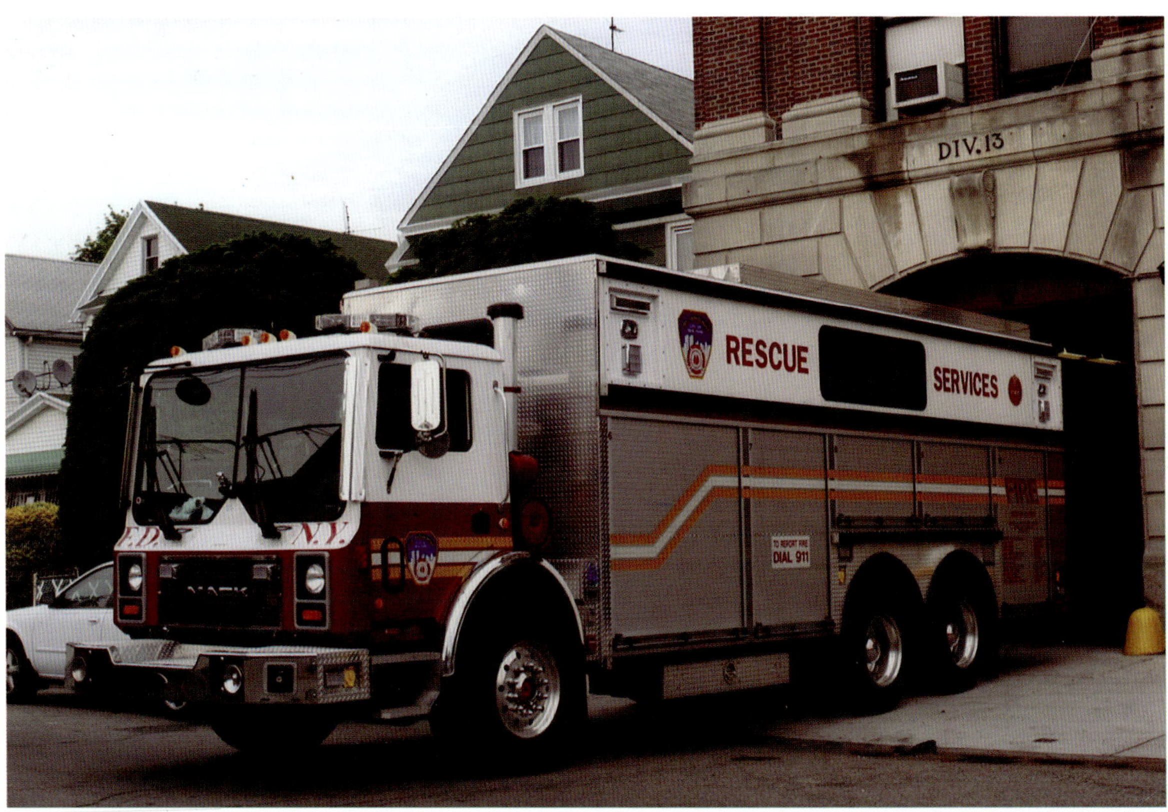

Rescue 7, 2002 Mack, MR/General Safety /Rosenbauer. Donated by Mack and was never put in service, but kept as a reserve.

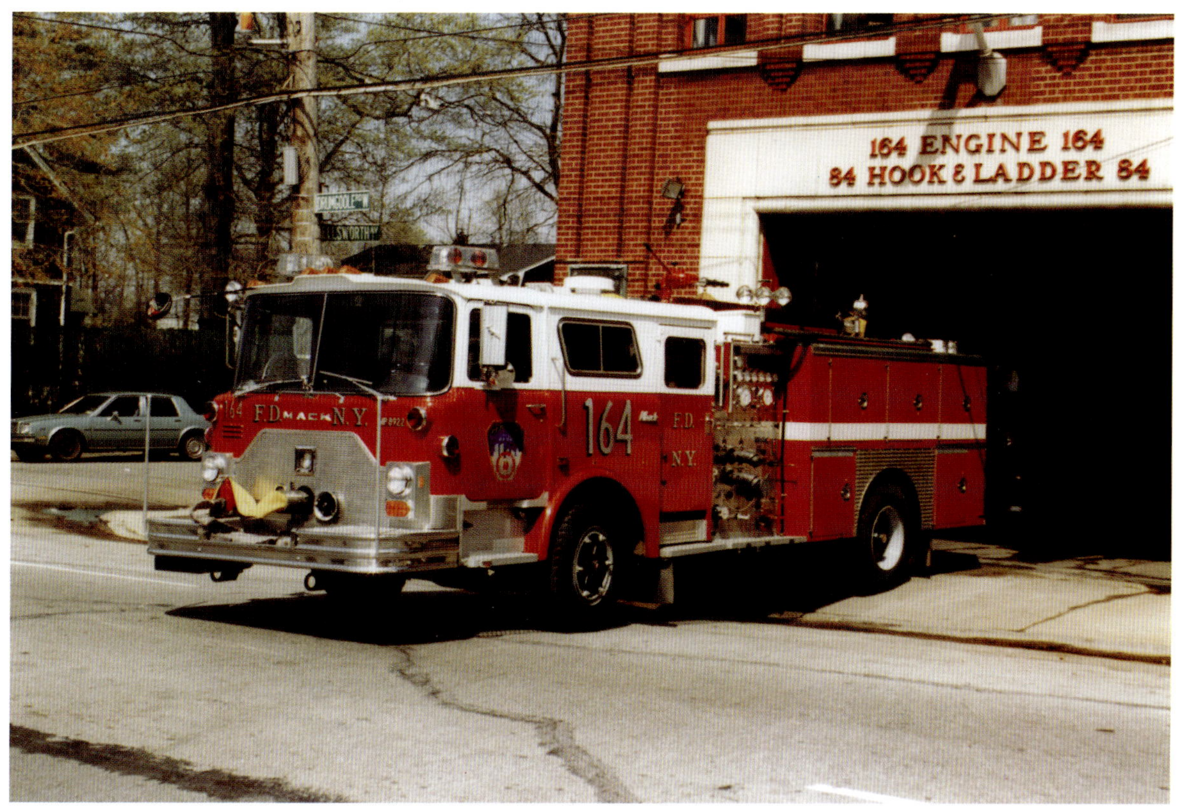

Engine 164, The last Mack/CF Pumper in front line service, 1989 Mack/Ward 79.

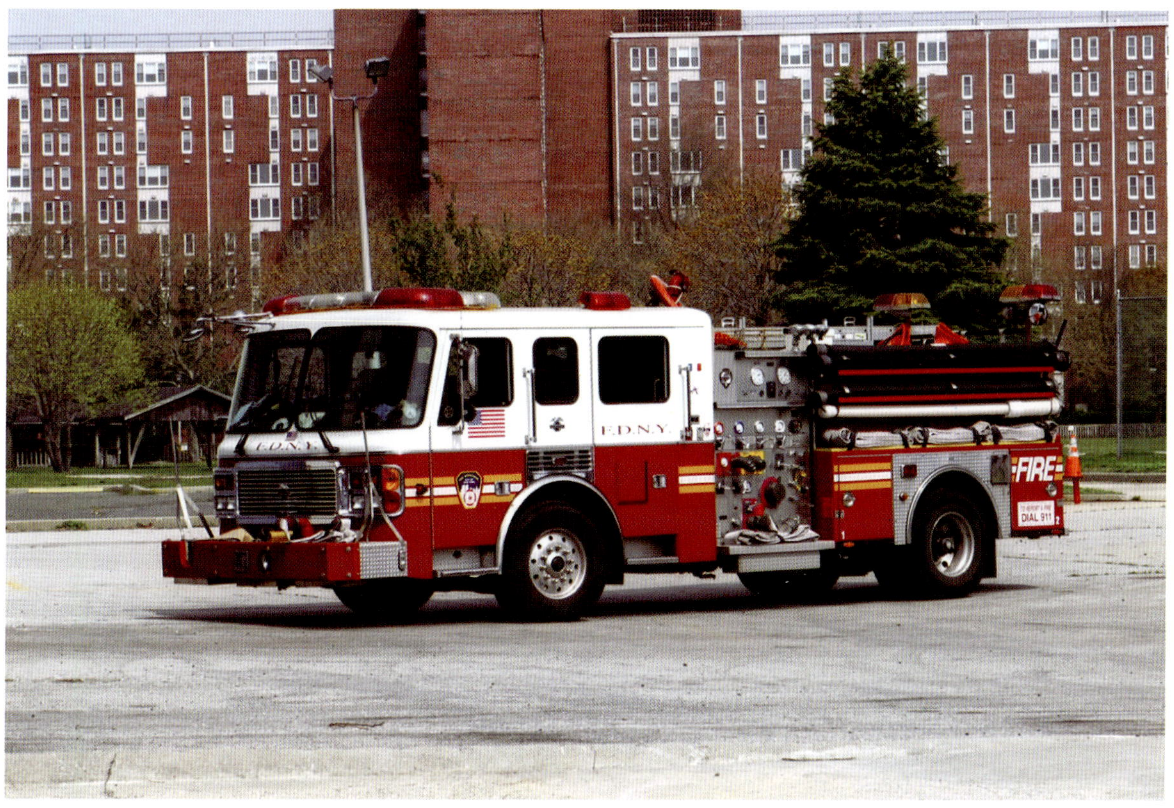

Former Engine 34, 2001 American LaFrance, Eagle, on loan for evaluation and was purchased after September 11, 2001. Shipped to Paris for The Bastille Day Parade on July 14, 2002. Now in reserve on Governor's Island.

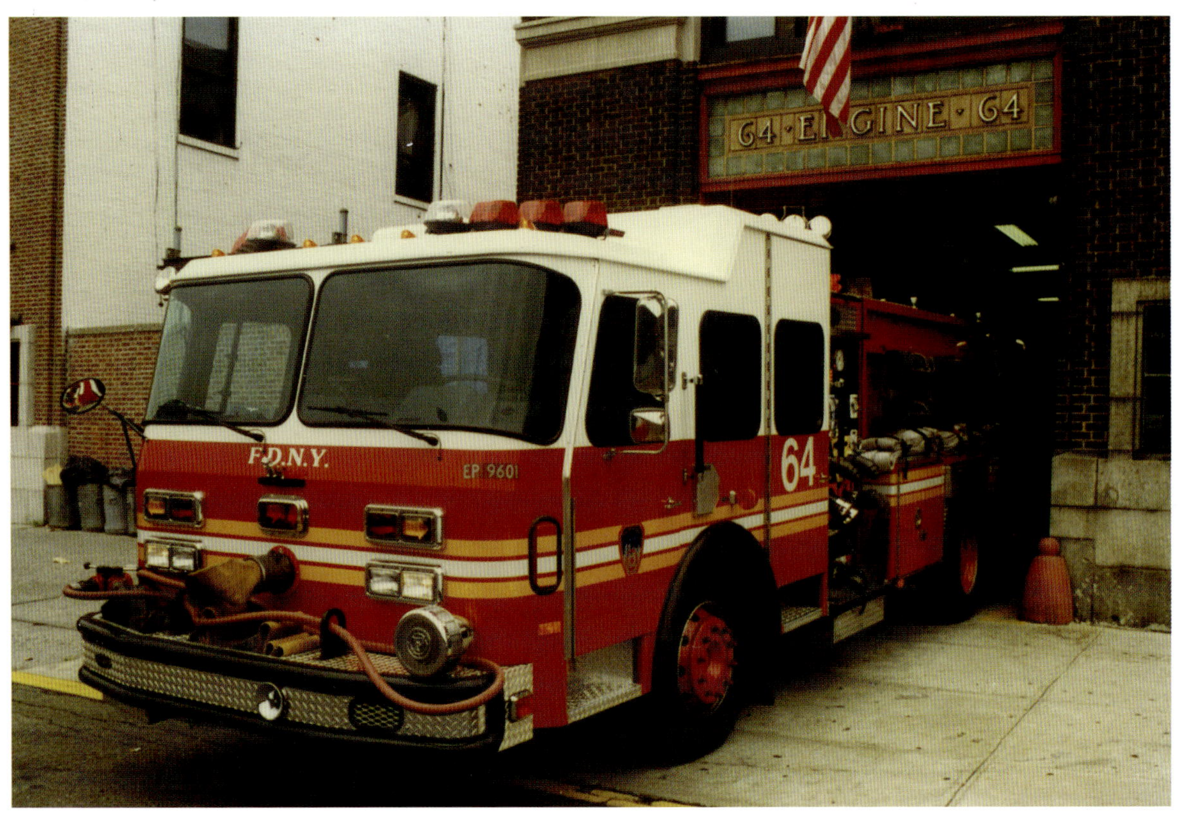

The first and only Emergency One pumper, a 1995 Hush demonstrator, on loan for evaluation. It served as Engine 8, 64, 275 and 290.

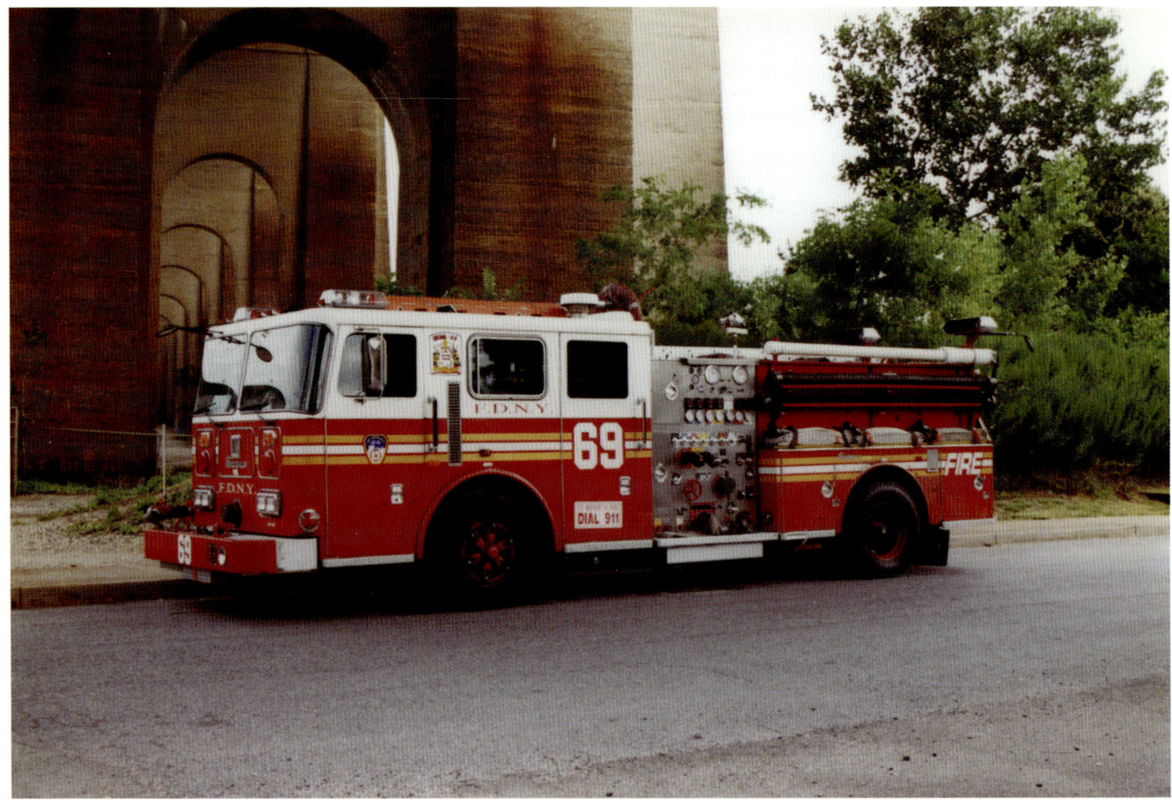

Engine 69, 1992 Seagrave, 1,000 GPM, one of twelve purchased and the first Seagrave Pumpers since 1934.

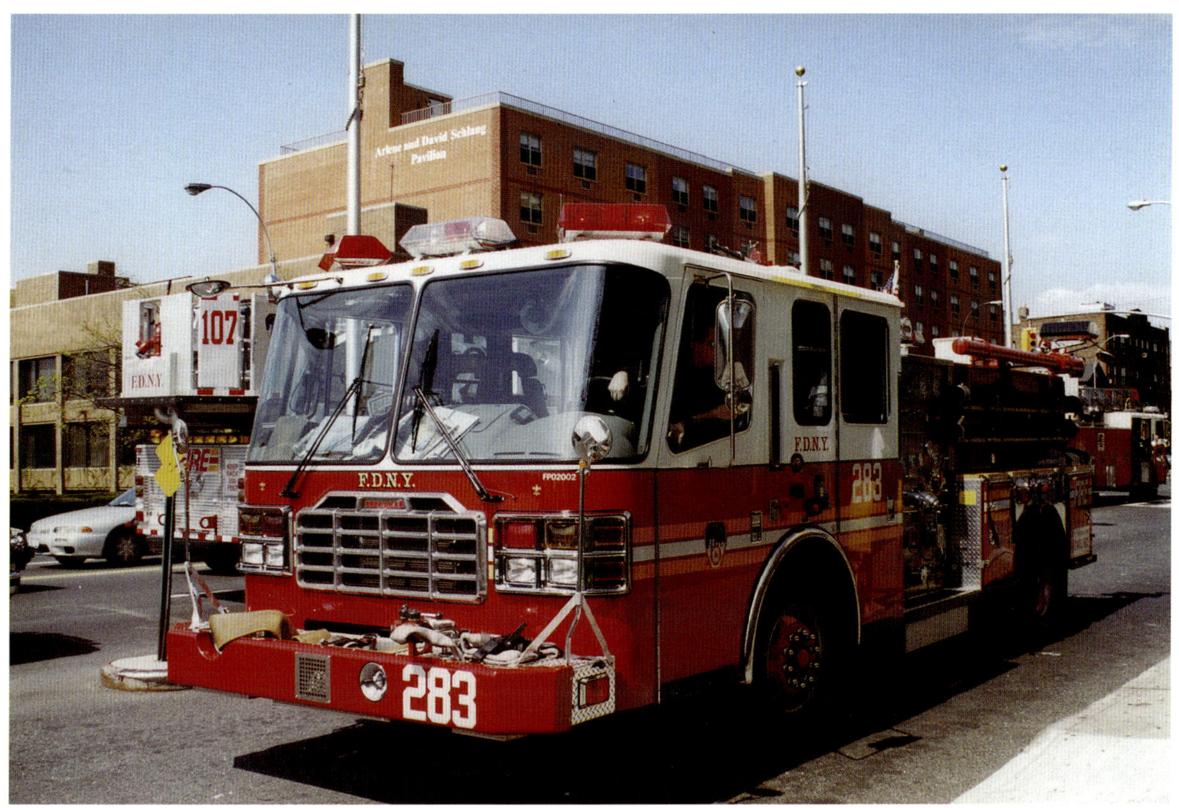

Engine 283, 2002 Ferrara, Inferno, donated by the State of Louisiana and the first Ferrara Engine. It was returned following Hurricane Katrina, where it saw service in New Orleans. It came back to New York (Long Beach, Long Island) after Hurricane Sandy in 2012.

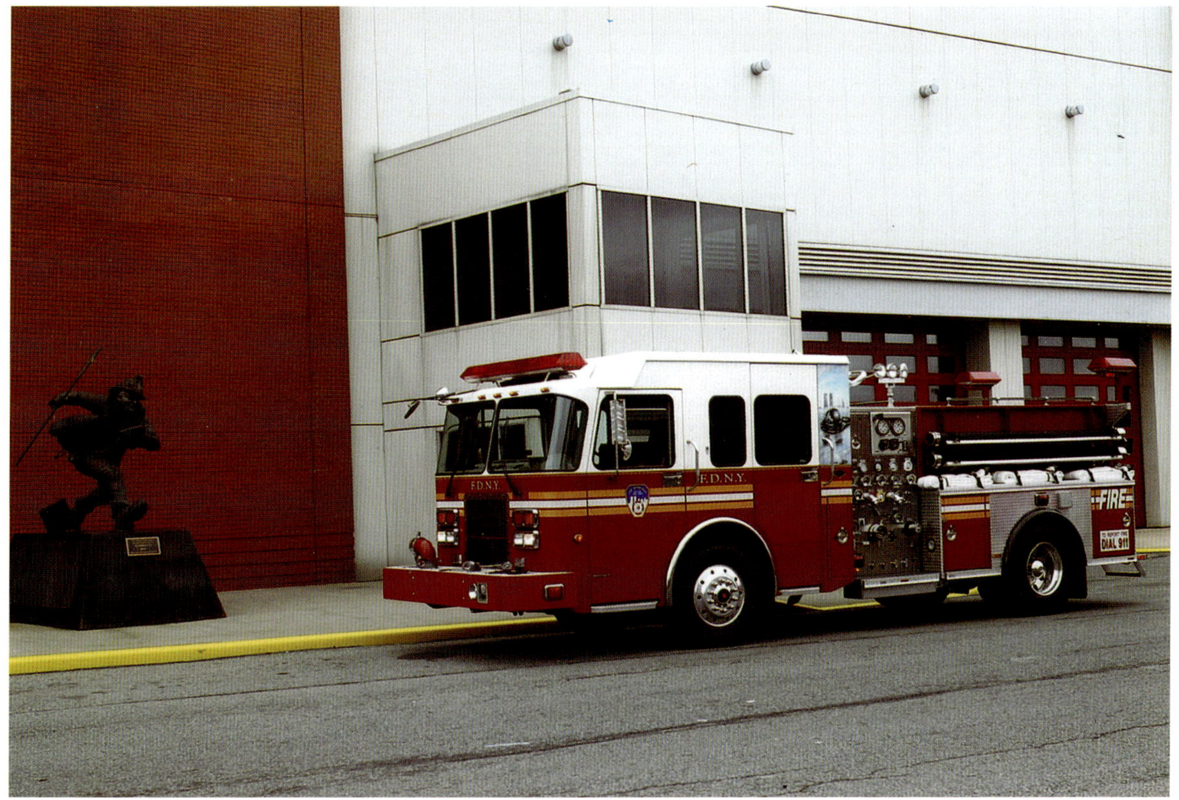

2002 Luverne donated by Luverne, used as the funeral caisson, and will never see fire duty.

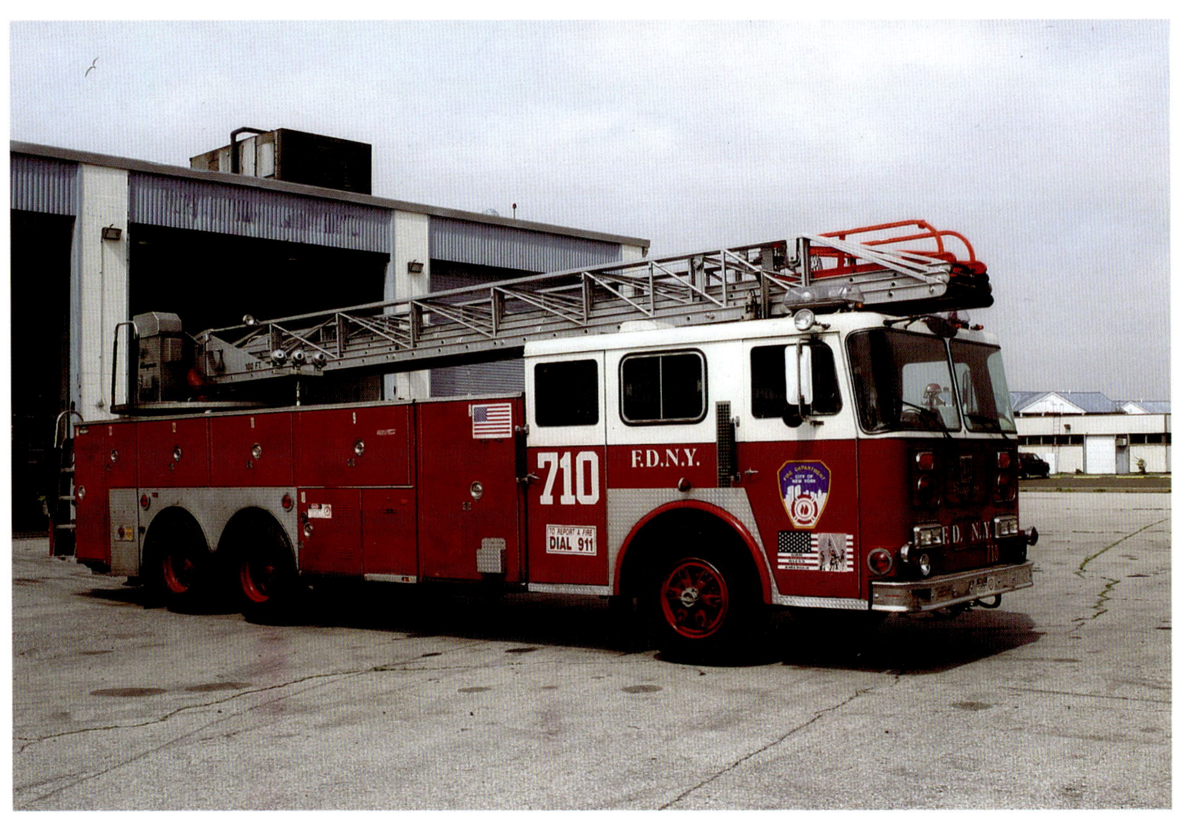

Reserve Ladder 710, 1991 Seagrave, former Ladder 56.

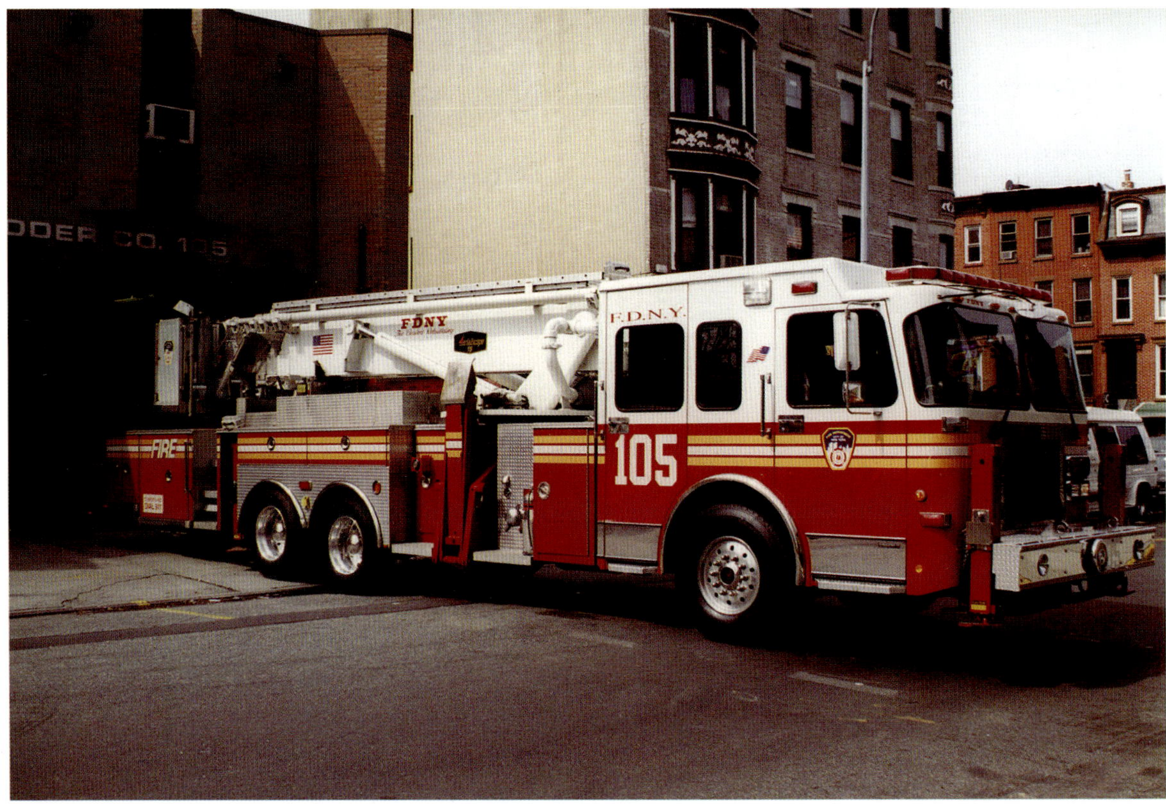

Tower Ladder 105, 2001 Spartan/Aerialscope. The only tower ladder built on a Spartan chassis. It has been reassigned to Tower Ladder 53 on City Island, Bronx.

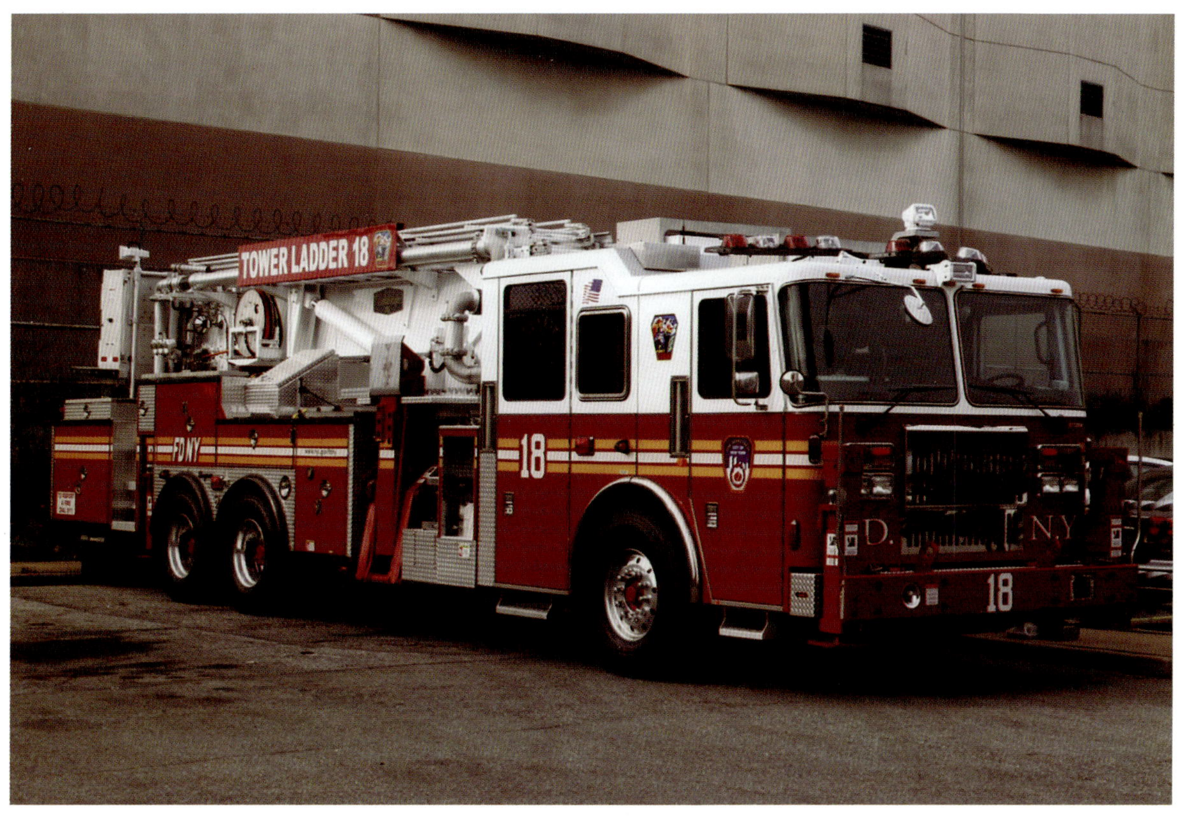

Tower Ladder 18, 2012 75 foot Seagrave/Aerialscope.

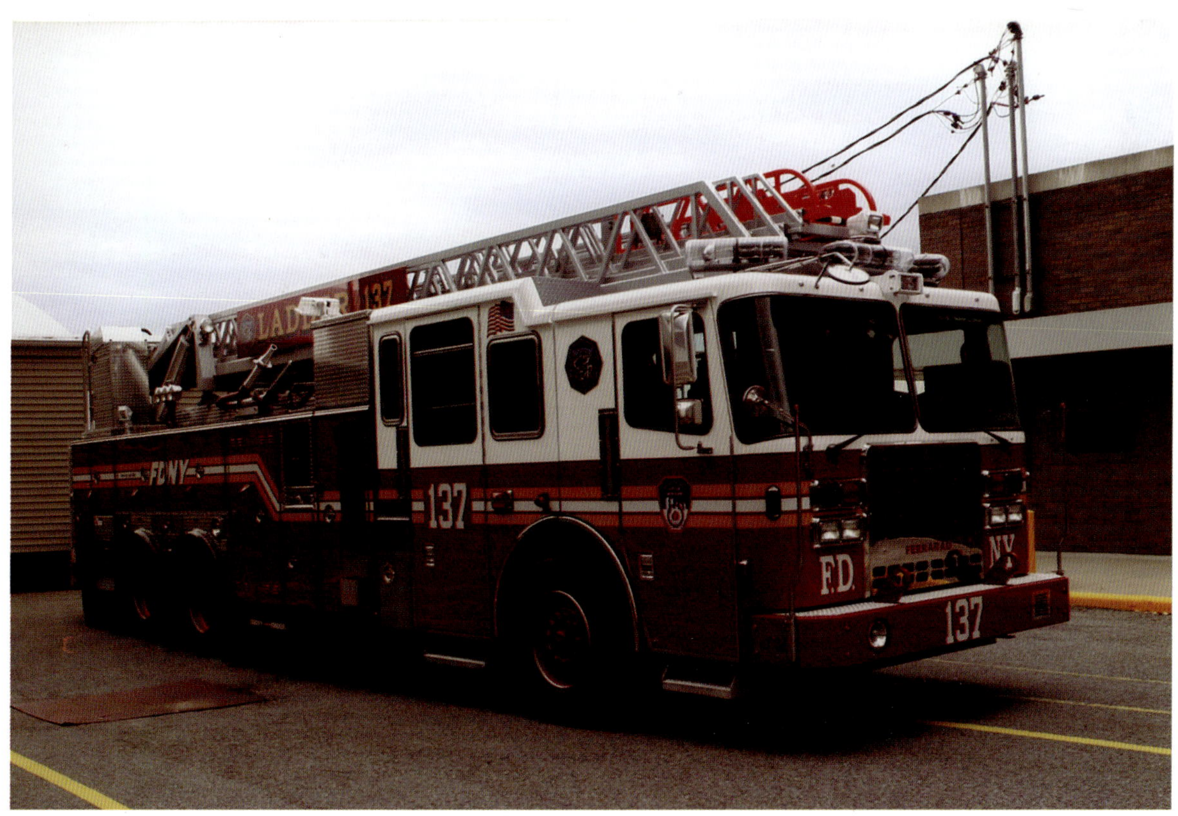

Ladder 137, 2011 Ferrara 100 foot rear-mount and the first Ferrara Ladder delivered. A year later, it was destroyed by Hurricane Sandy's flood waters.

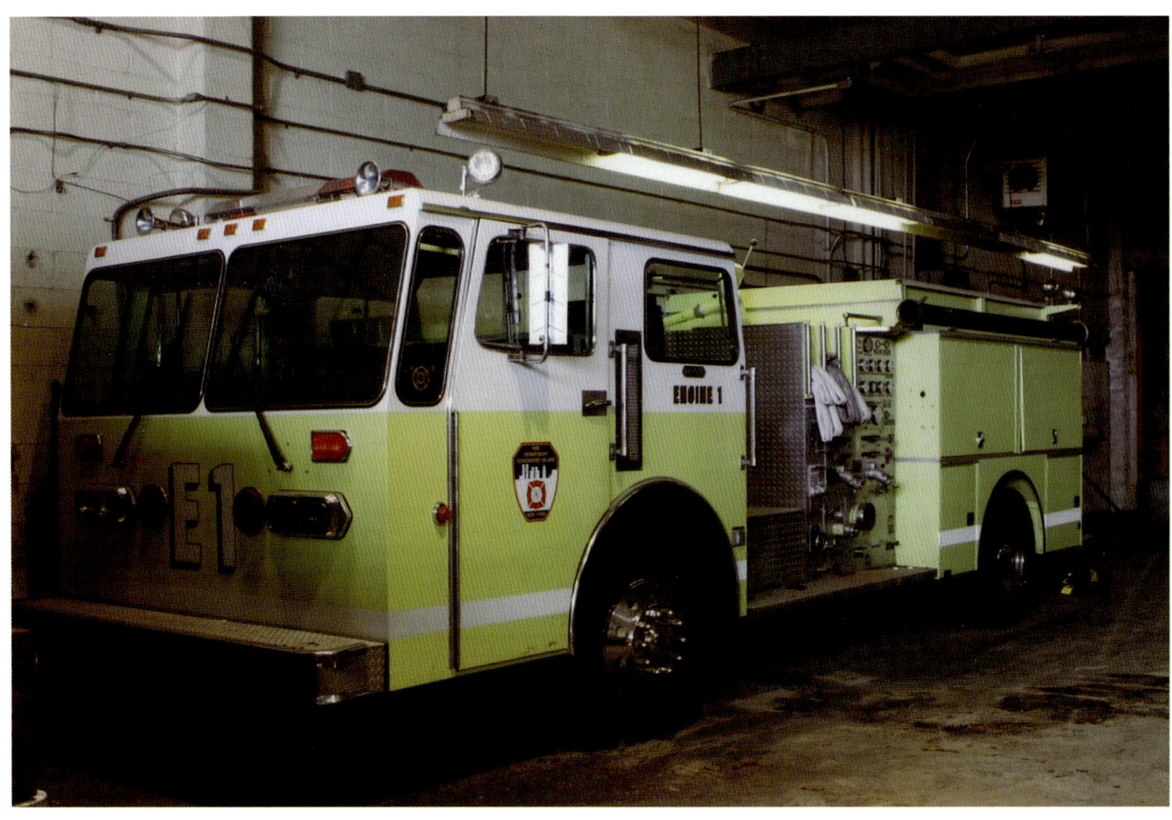

The Federal Fire Department was disbanded when the US Coast Guard left Govenor's Island on September 30, 2003. Engines 1 and 2 were 1984 Walter /Duplex's.

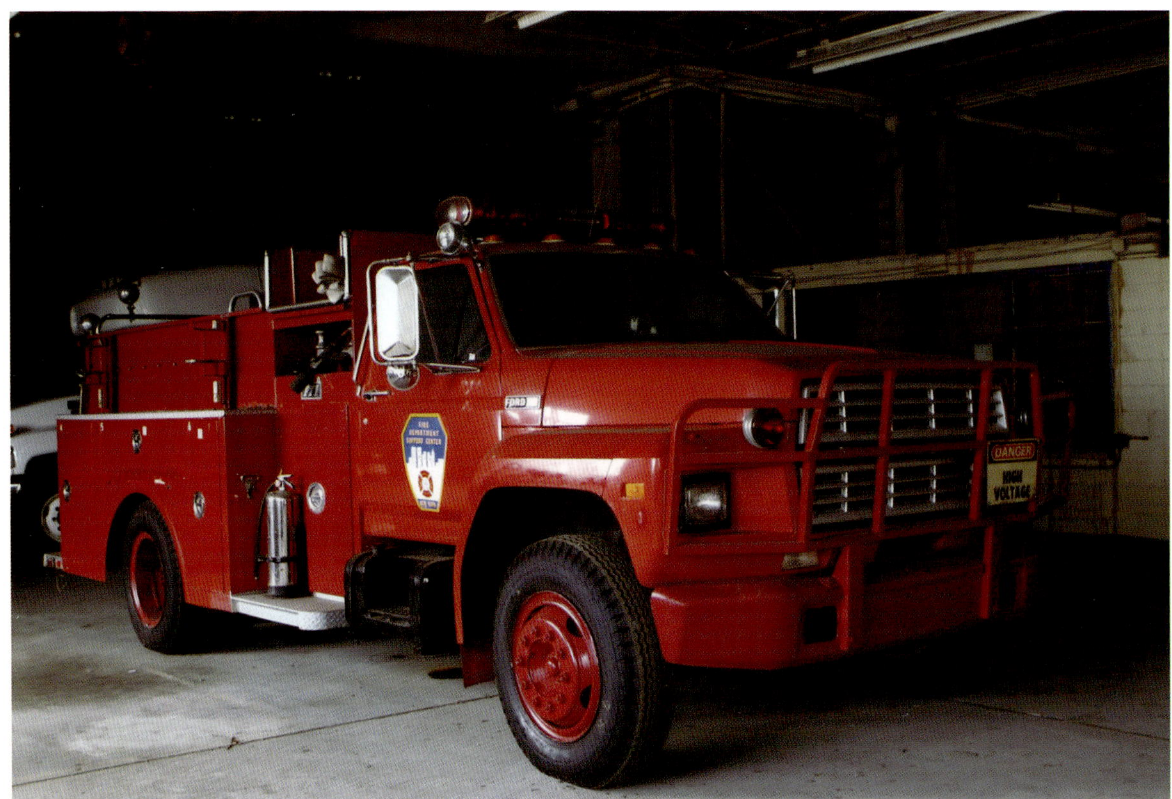

Engine 3 was a 1982 Ford/FireTech 300/30 foam with 150 lbs of dry chemical.

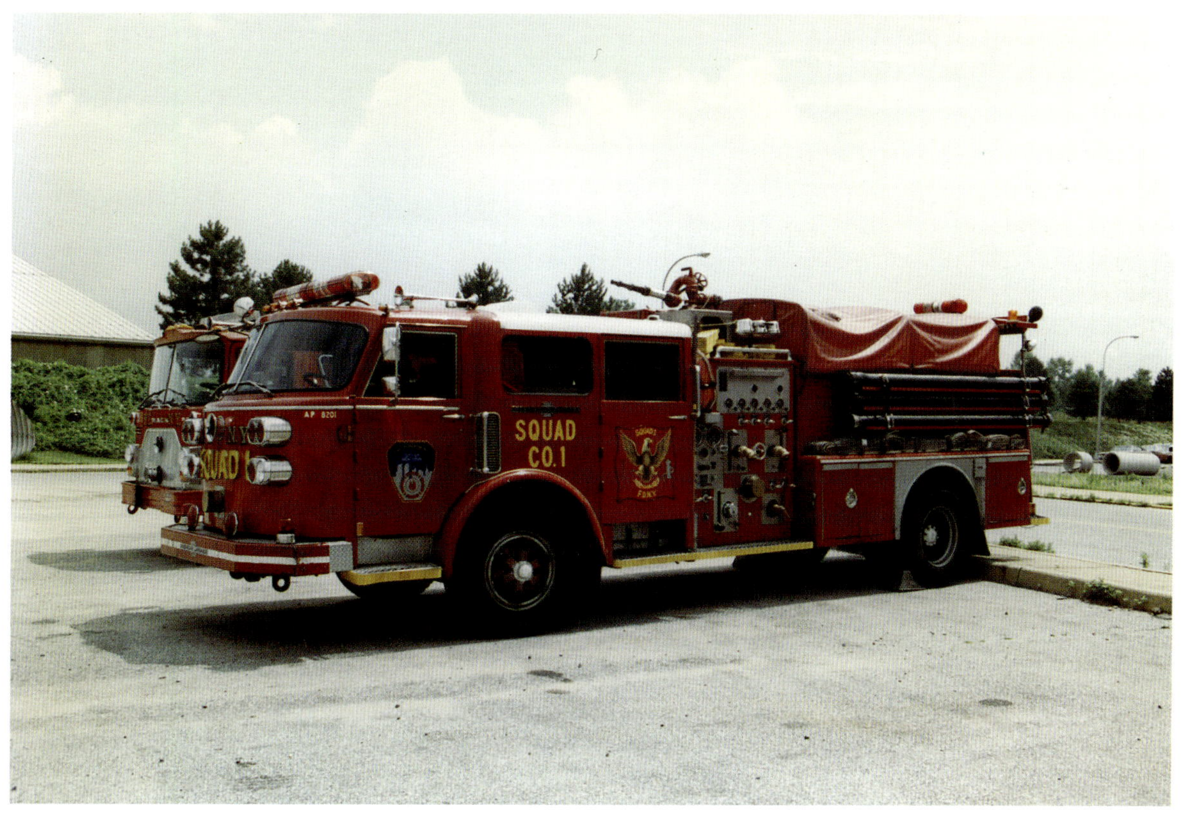

Squad Company 1, Brooklyn, 1982 American LaFrance.

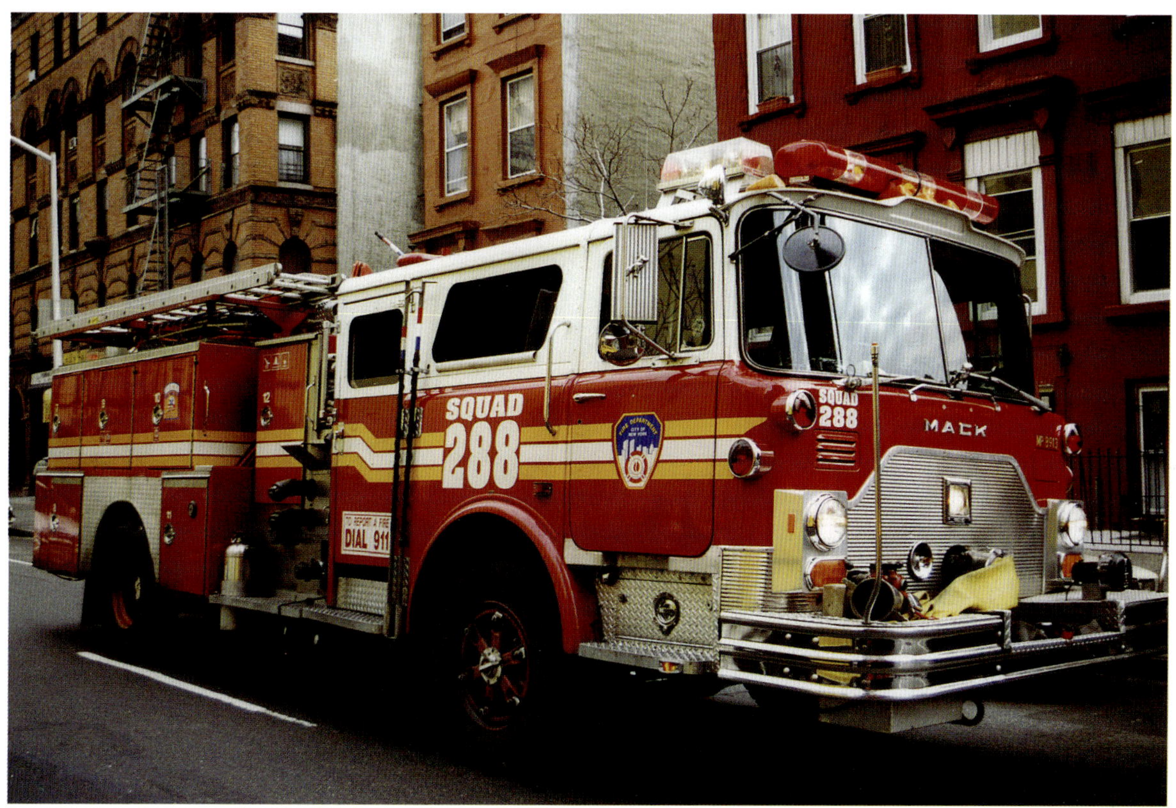

Squad 288, 1989 Mack/Ward 79. Effective July 1, 1998, Engine Companies 18, 41, 61, 252, 270 and 288 were designated Squad Companies in addition to Squad 1.

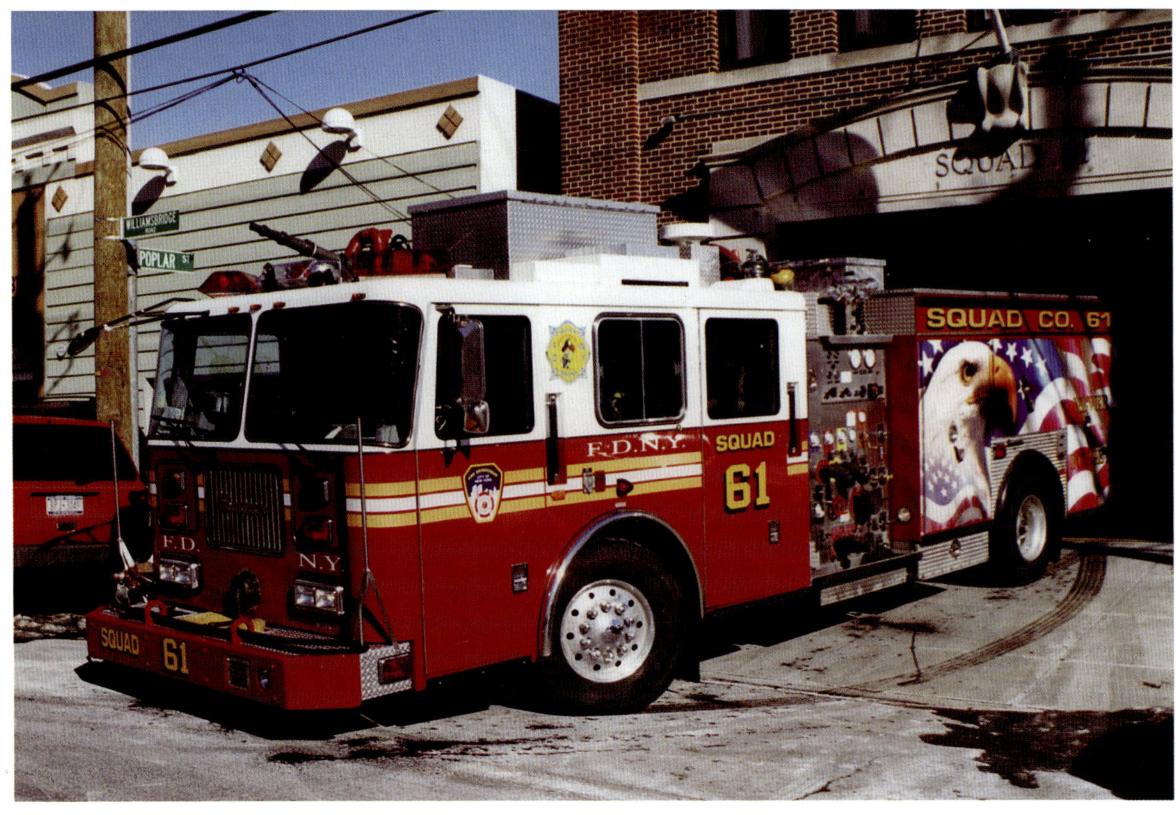

Squad 61, 2003 Seagrave, Commander II, donated by Seagrave and their employees.

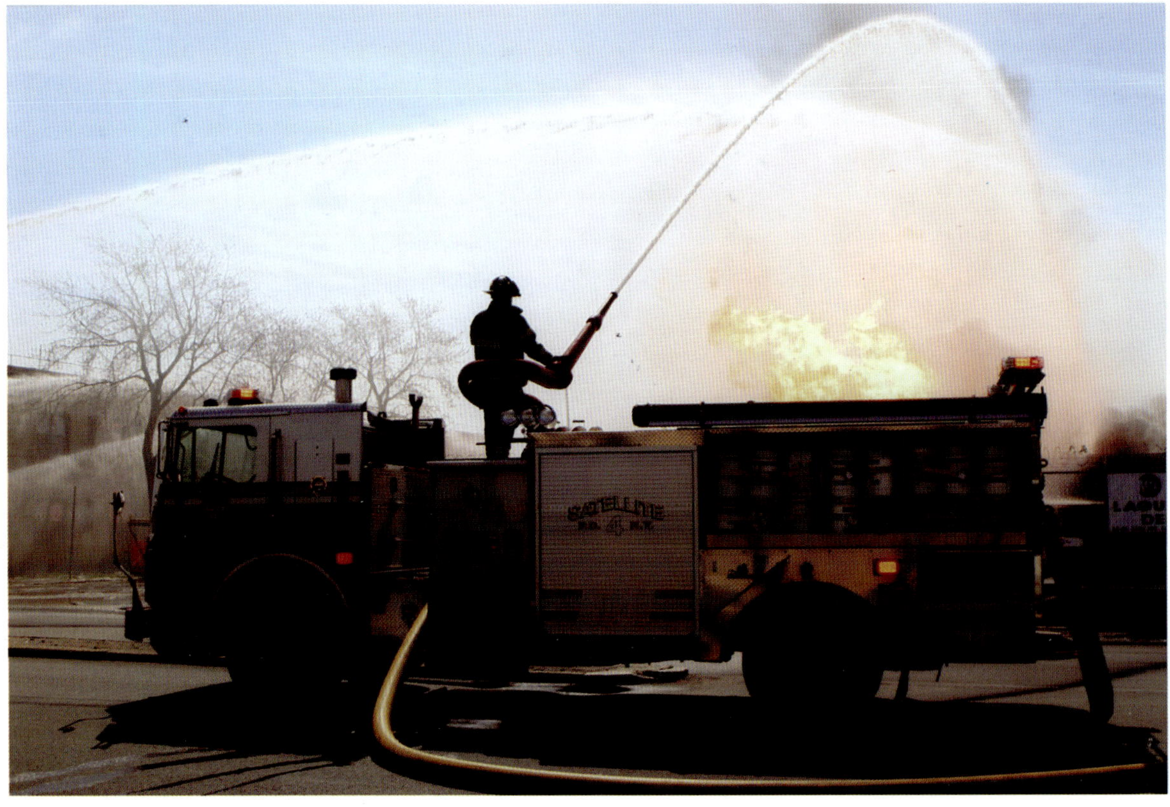

Satellite 4, 2006 Mack MR/Ferrara.

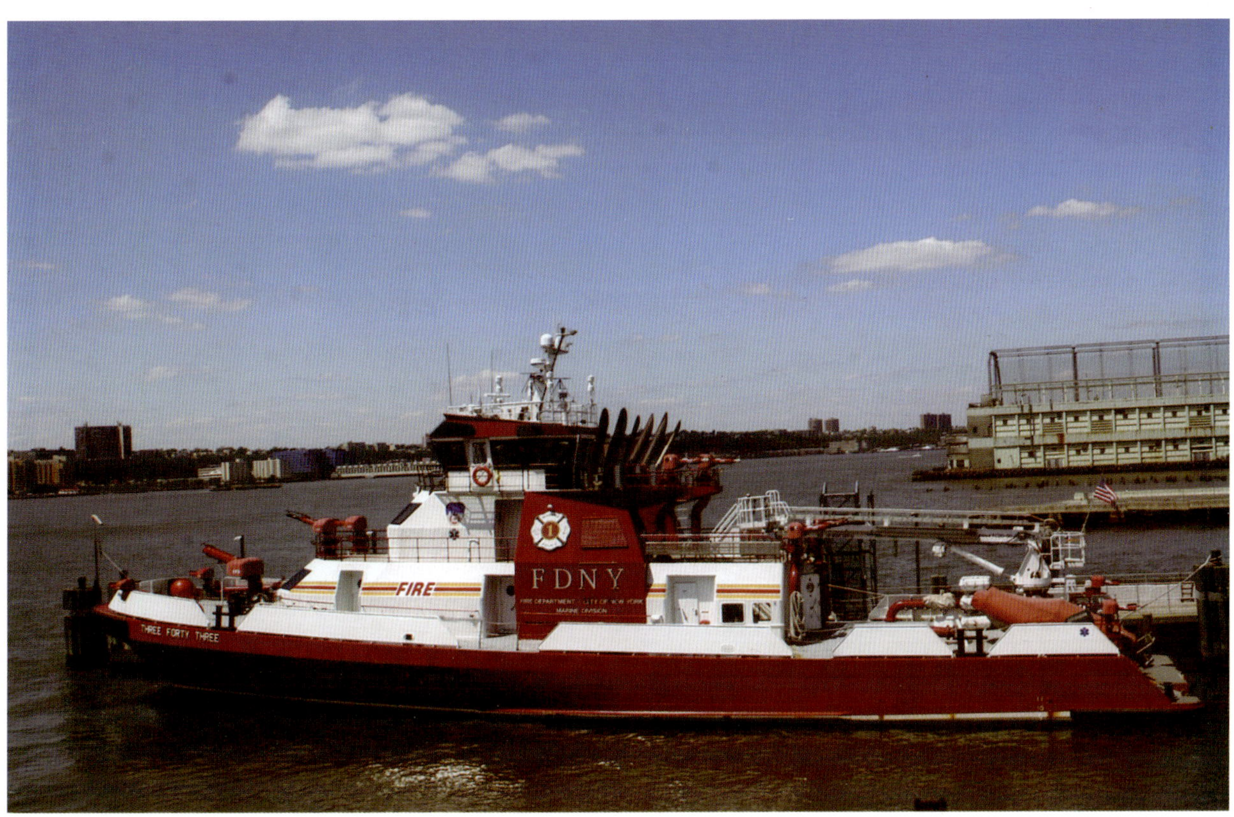

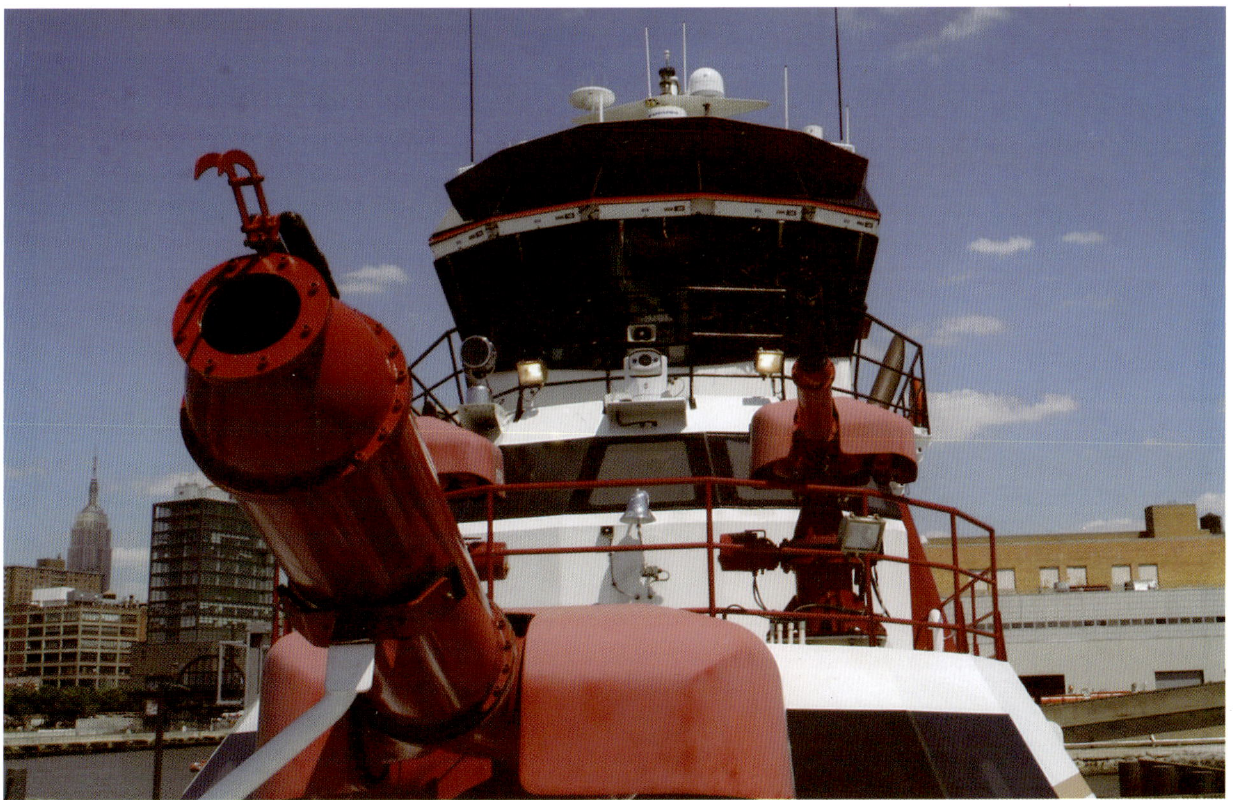

Marine 1, The "343" went into service on May 26, 2010 at Pier 53, Manhattan. It operates with a 7-man crew, but is designed to respond with as many as 27 land based firefighters. The command room contains remote cameras and state of the art communications equipment. The crew is protected in a pressurized area with its own filtered air supply. It has 9 deck guns and has the capacity of pumping 50,000 gallons per minute. It's sister ship, FireFighter II, is assigned to Marine 9 on Staten Island.

BOSTON FIRE

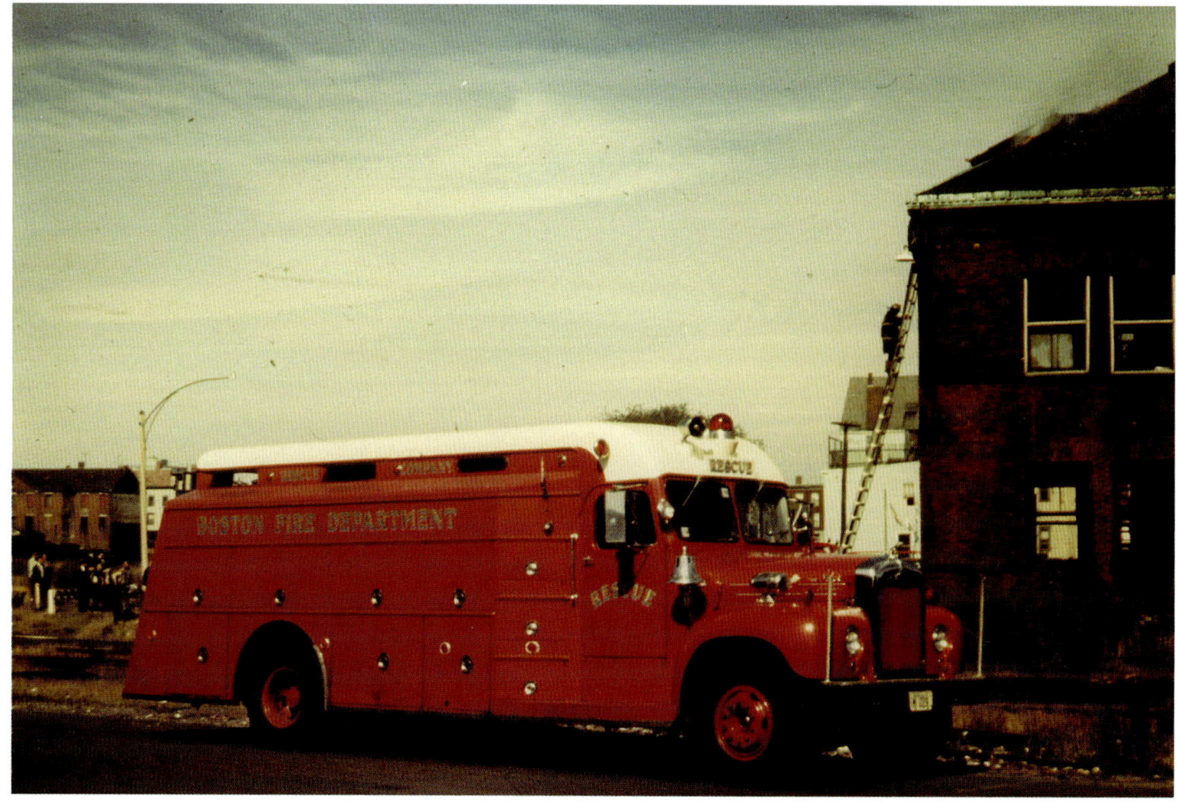

The Rescue Company 1964 Mack/Gerstenslager. It became Rescue 1 in 1972.

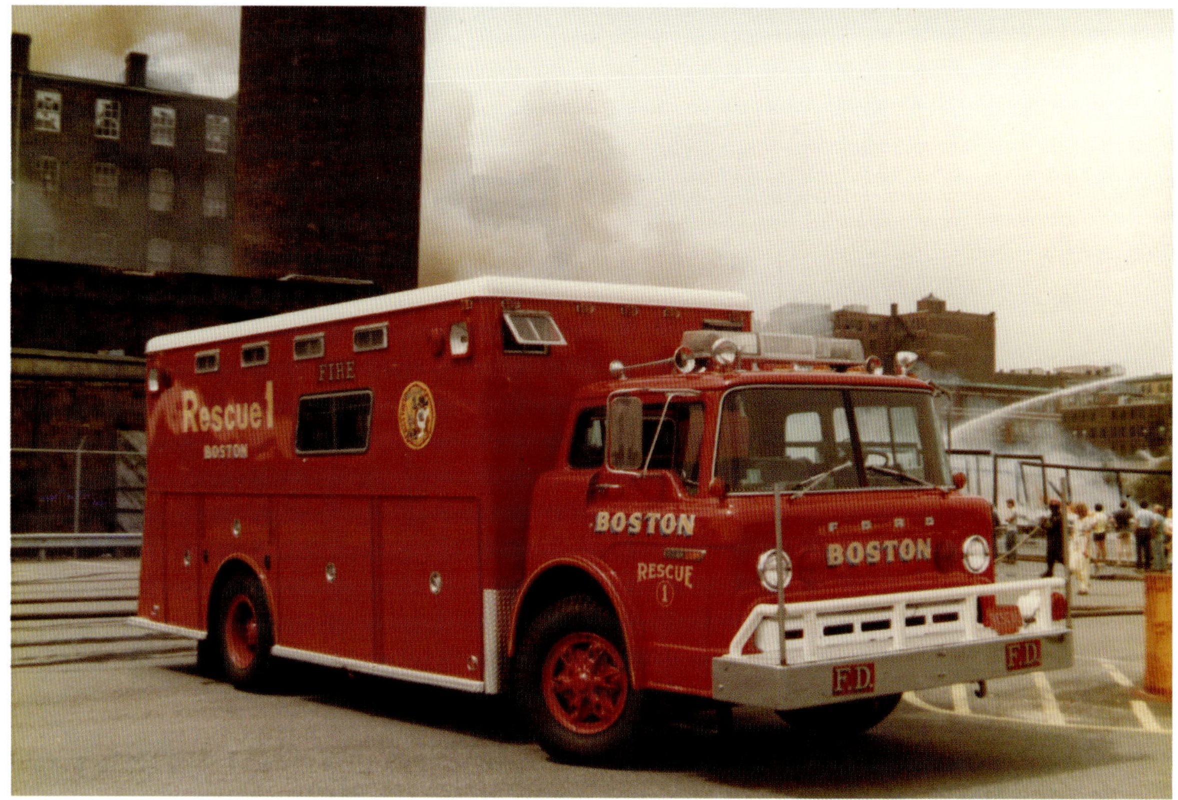

Rescue 1, 1977 Ford/Providence.

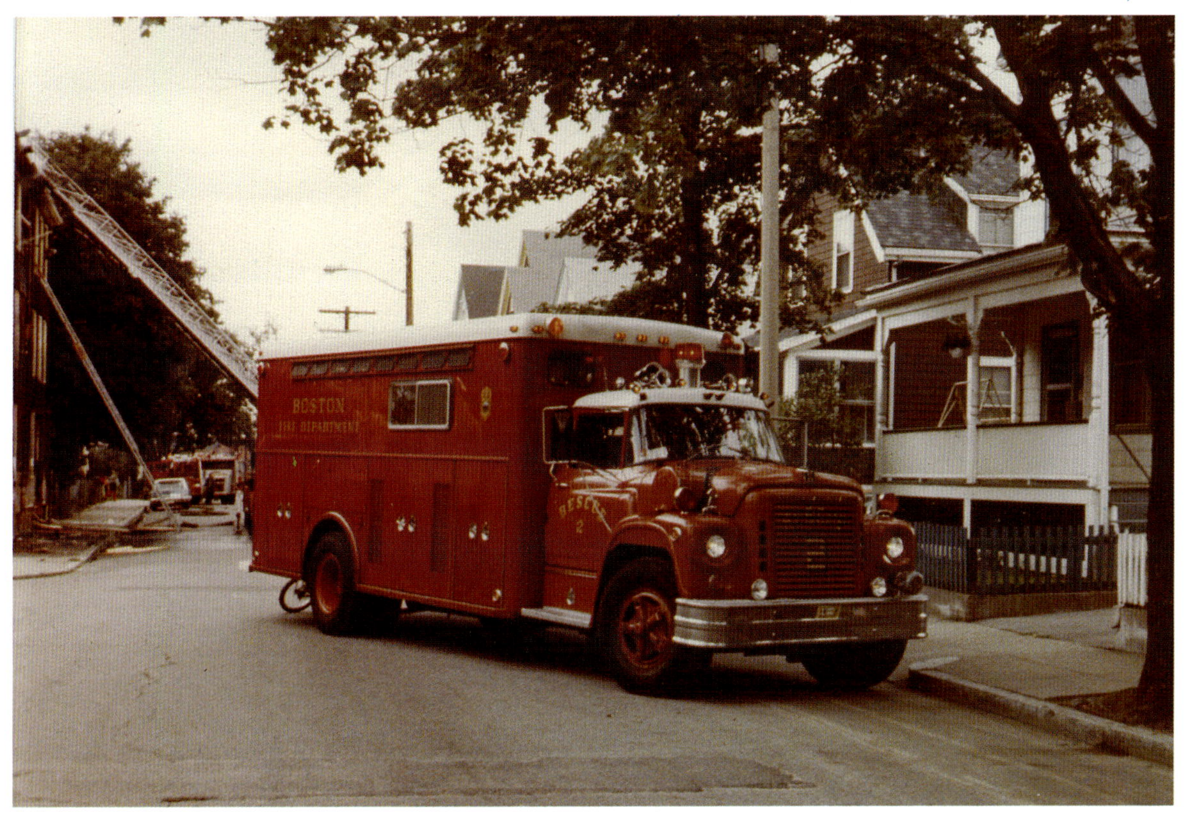

Rescue 2, 1972 International/Gerstenslager.

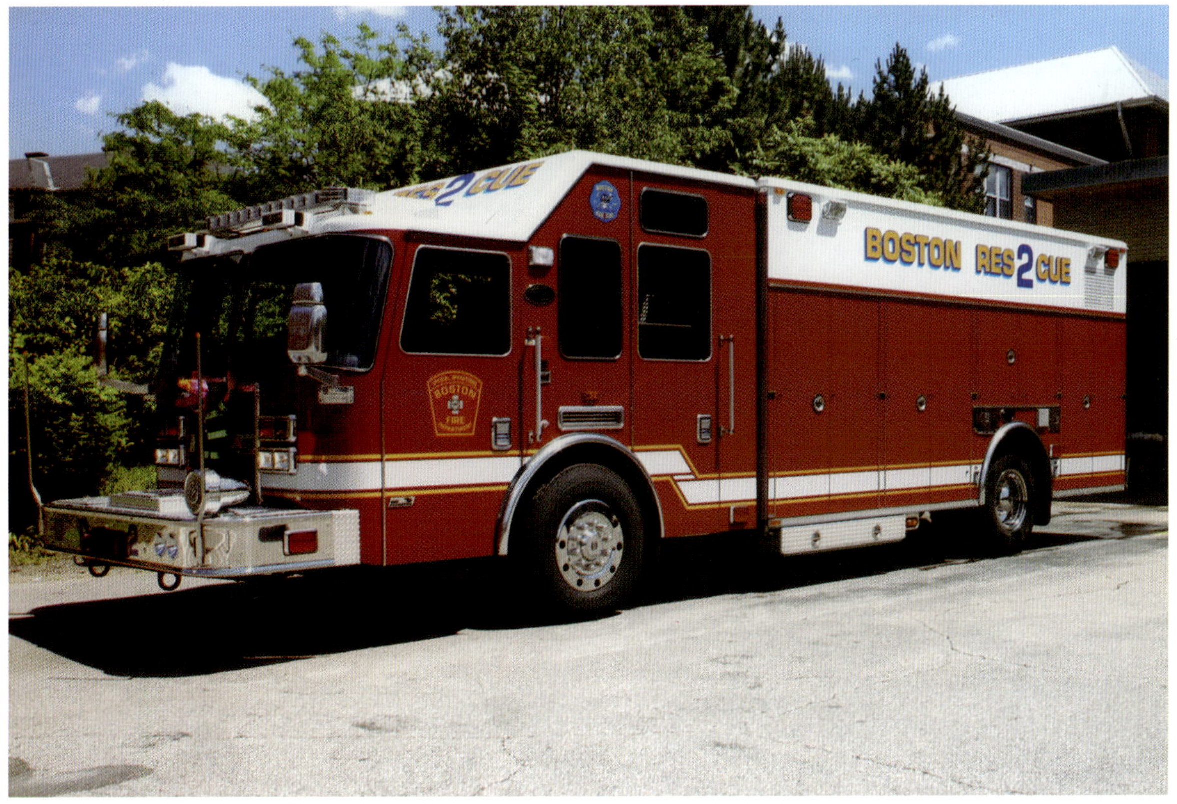

Rescue 2, 2009 KME Predator.

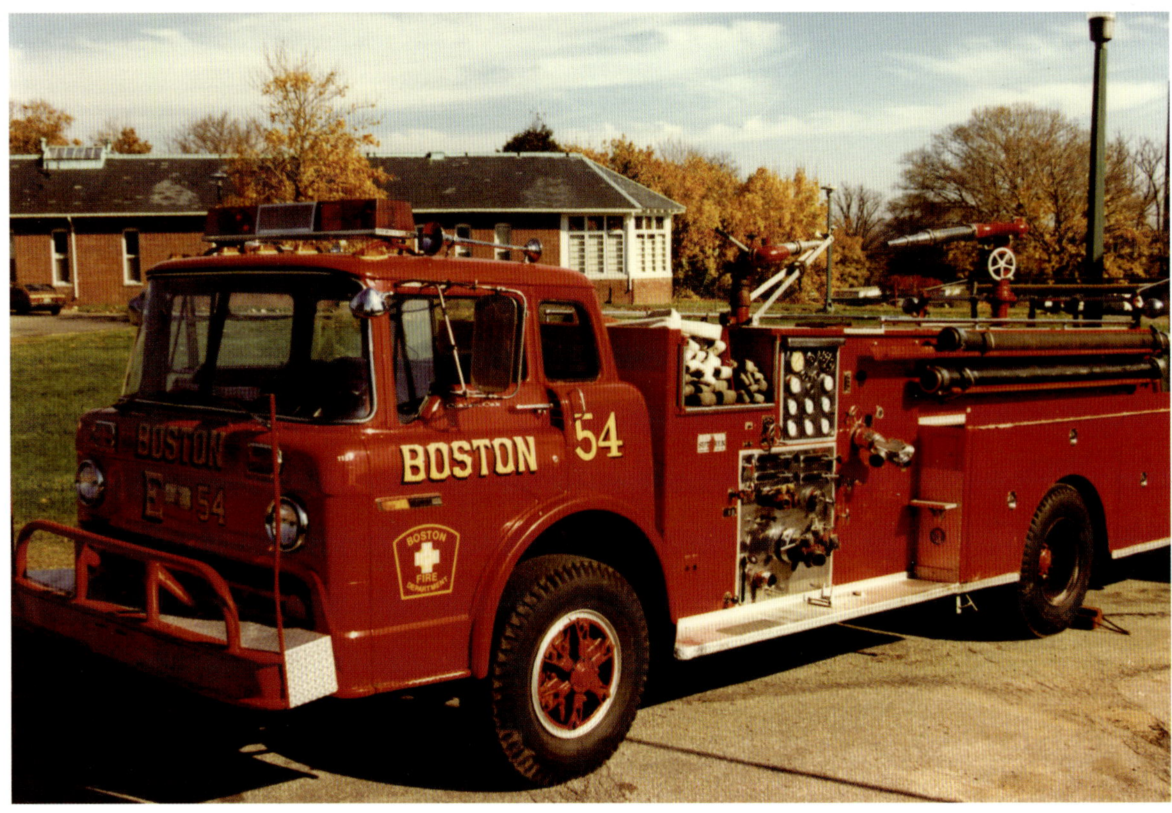

Engine 54, 1979 Sutphen high pressure hose wagon, formerly Engine 4 and protecting The Long Island Hospital in Boston Harbor.

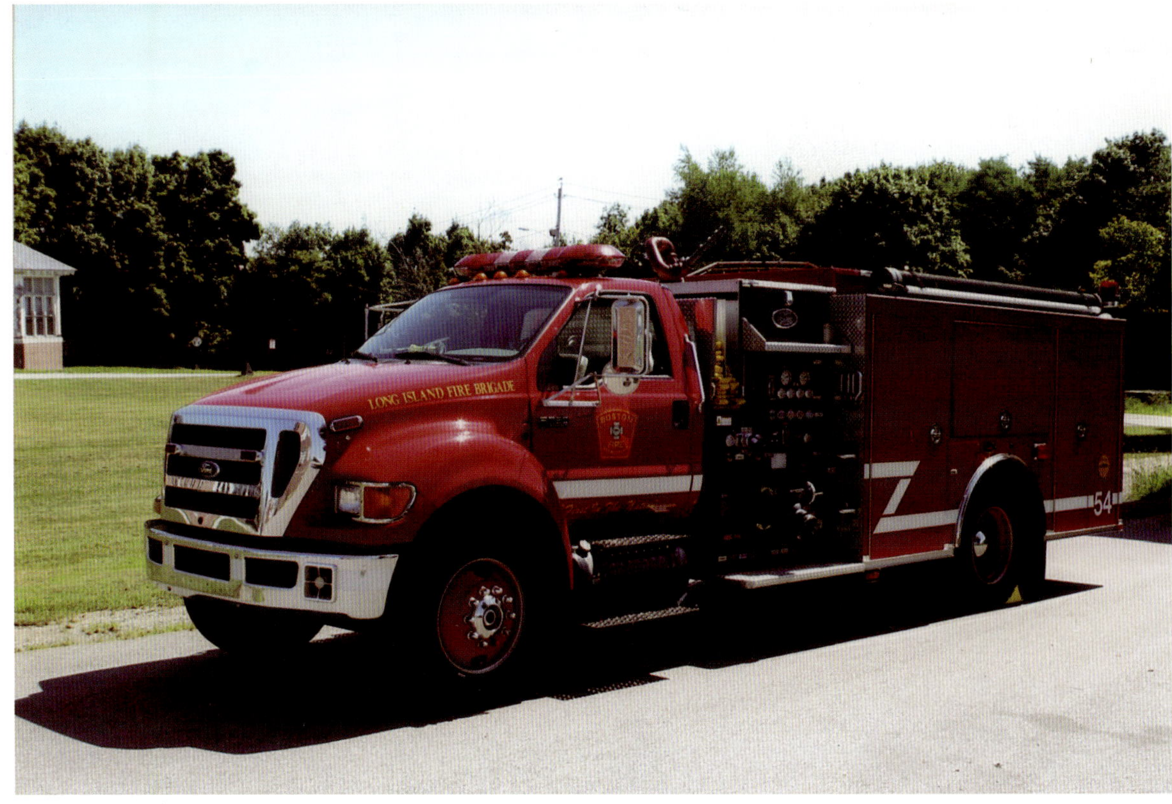

Now known as The Long Island Fire Brigade, 2009 KME/Ford, F-750 (purchased in 2010).

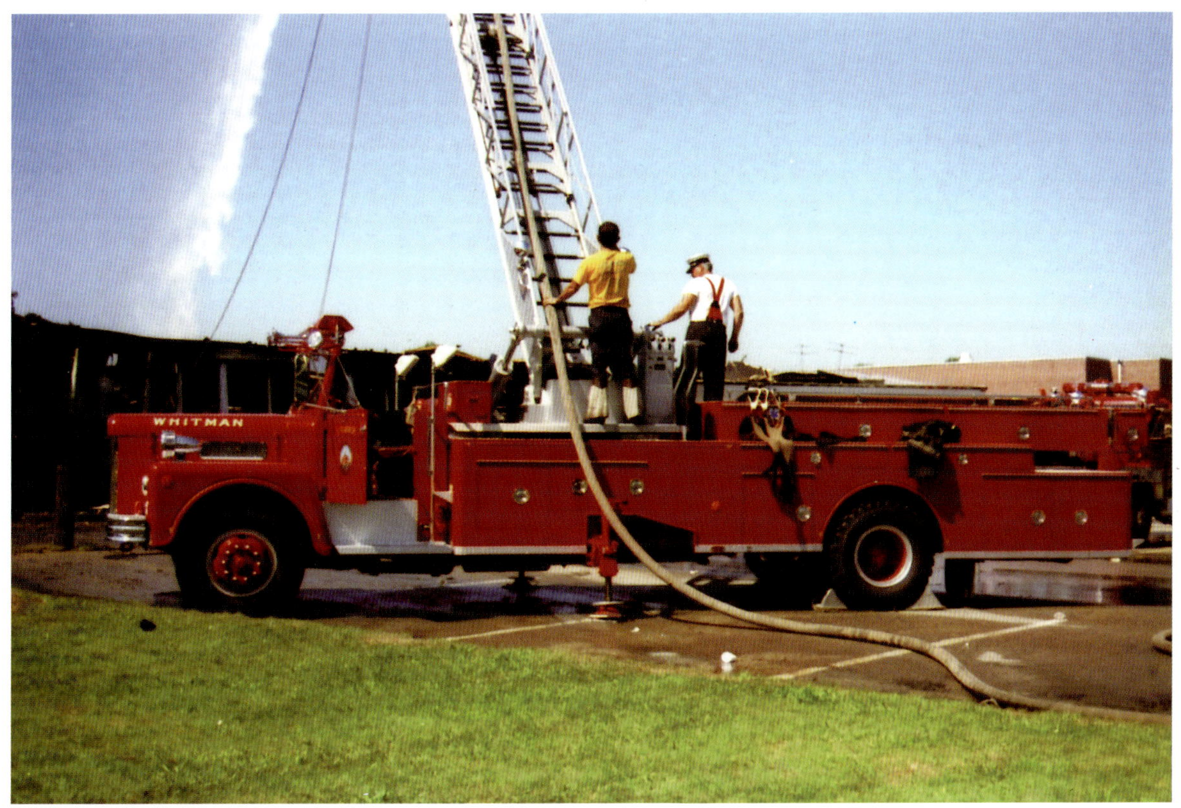

Whitman, MA Ladder 1, 1974 Maxim "S" Model, mid-mount. It was rebuilt in 1996 with a roof and the aerial was shortened to 75 feet.

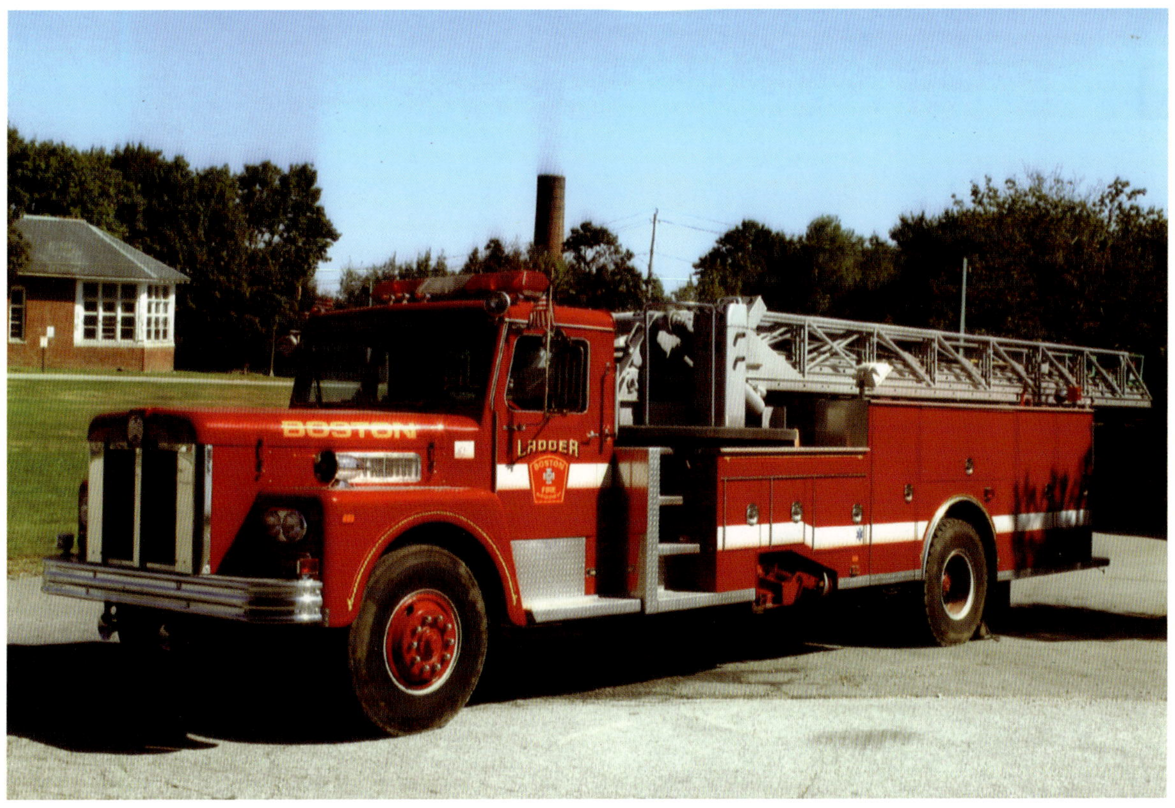

Now the second section of The Long Island Fire Brigade (formerly known as Ladder 31).

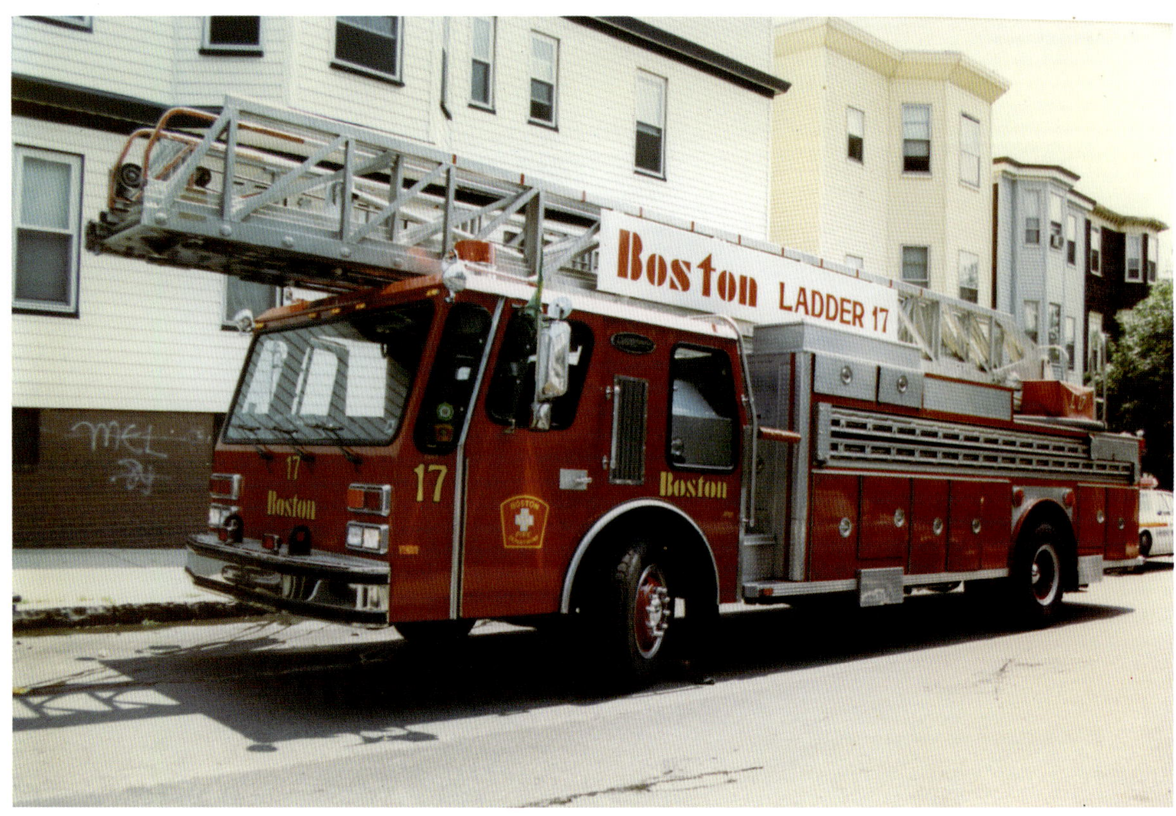

Ladder 17, 1984 Emergency-One, Hurricane 110 foot aerial and Boston's first Emergency-One Ladder.

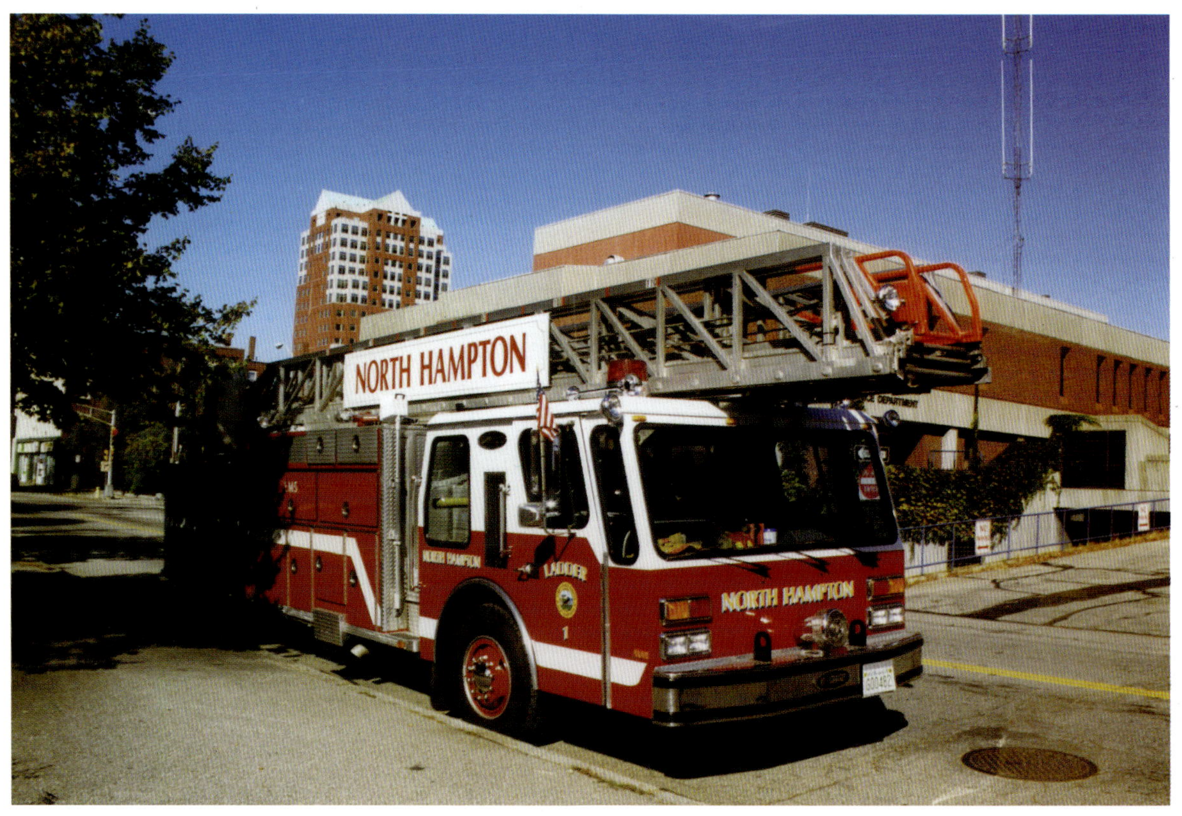

Now Ladder 1, North Hampton, NH.

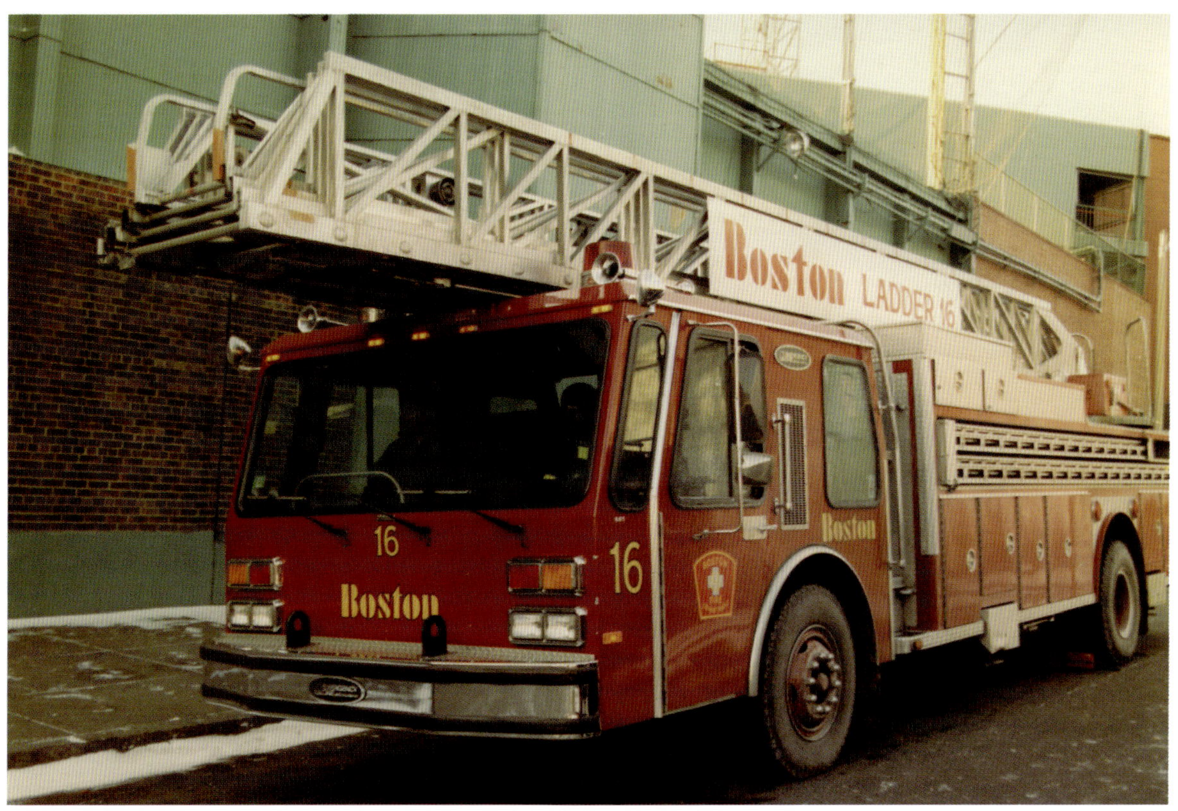

Ladder 16, 1984 Emergency-One, Hurricane, sold to Weymouth, MA in 1997, when a four door cab was added.

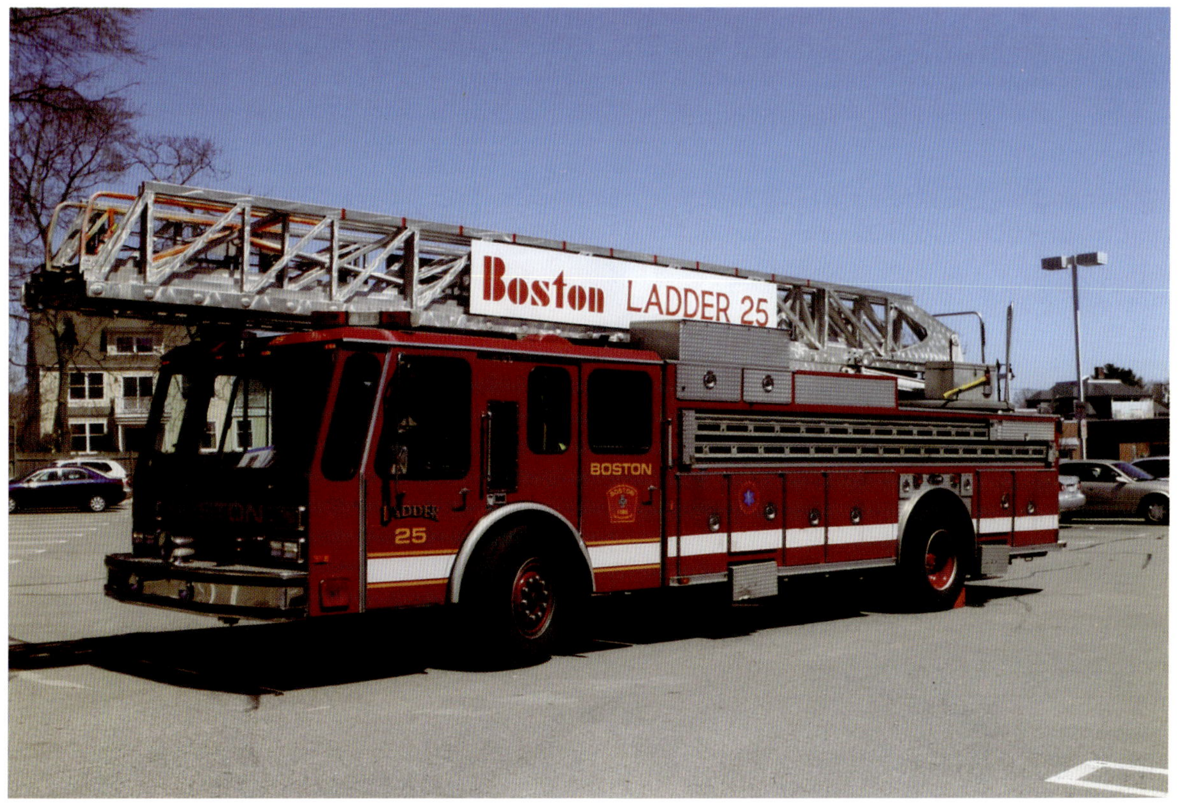

When Ladder 25's, 1990 Emergency-One cab needed to be replaced, Weymouth had traded in former Ladder 16. Boston purchased the cab and installed it on Ladder 25.

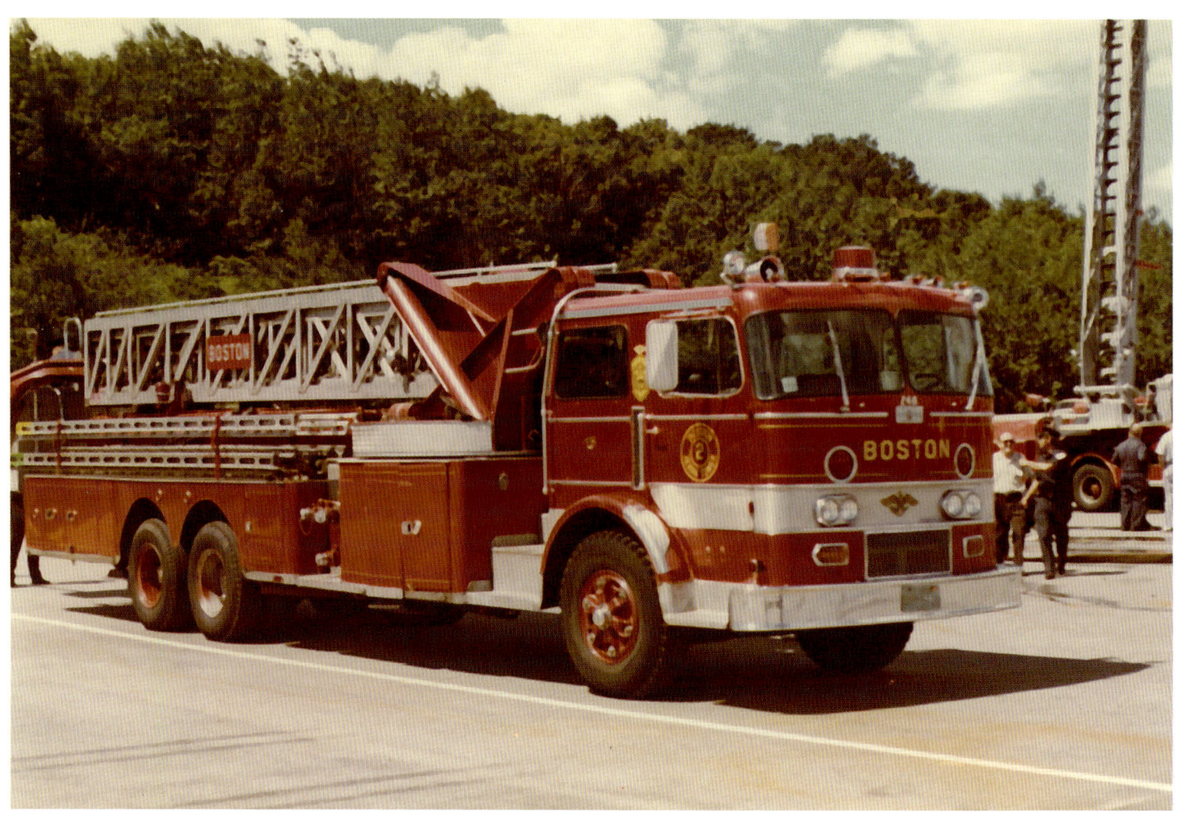

Aerial Tower 2, 1970 Sutphen 85 foot Aerial Tower assigned to ladder 26's quarters. It also served as Aerial Tower 1 and as the Tower Unit in the early 80's.

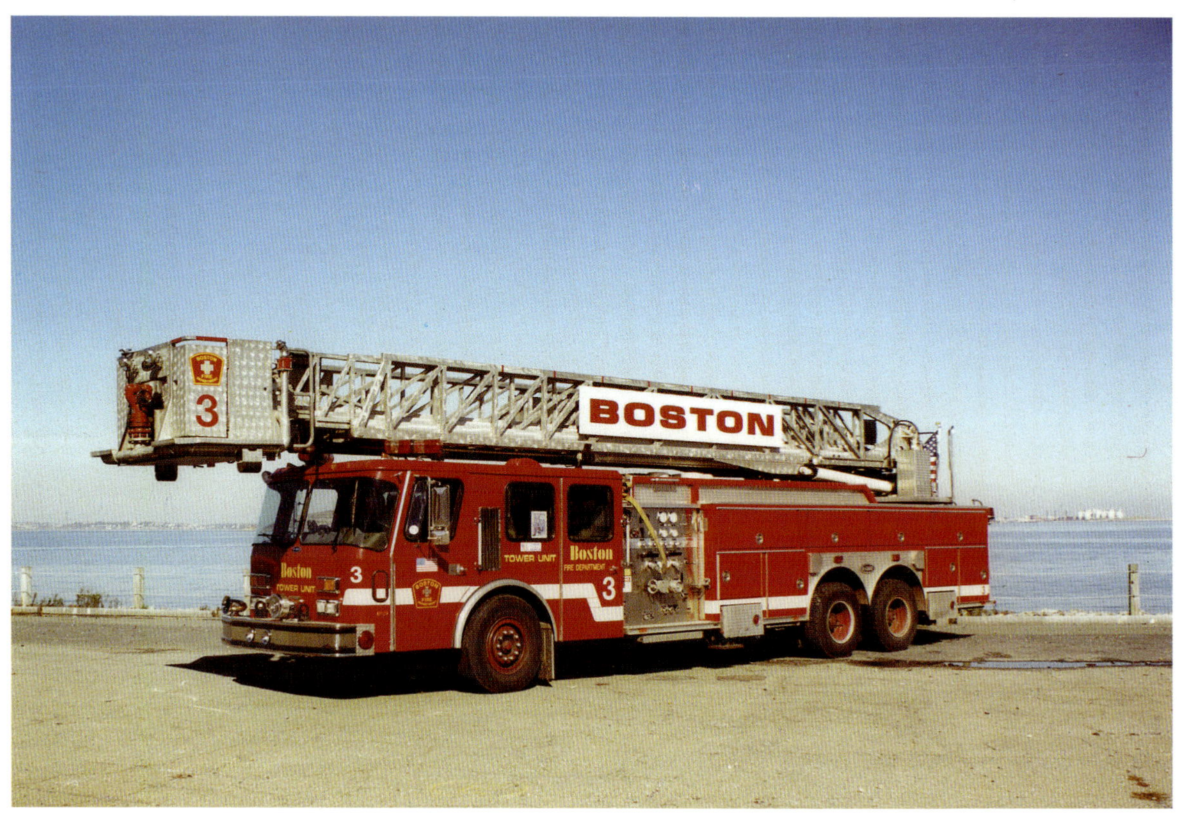

Tower Ladder 3, 1992 Emergency-One 95 foot Tower 1500/300 formerly known as the Tower Unit.

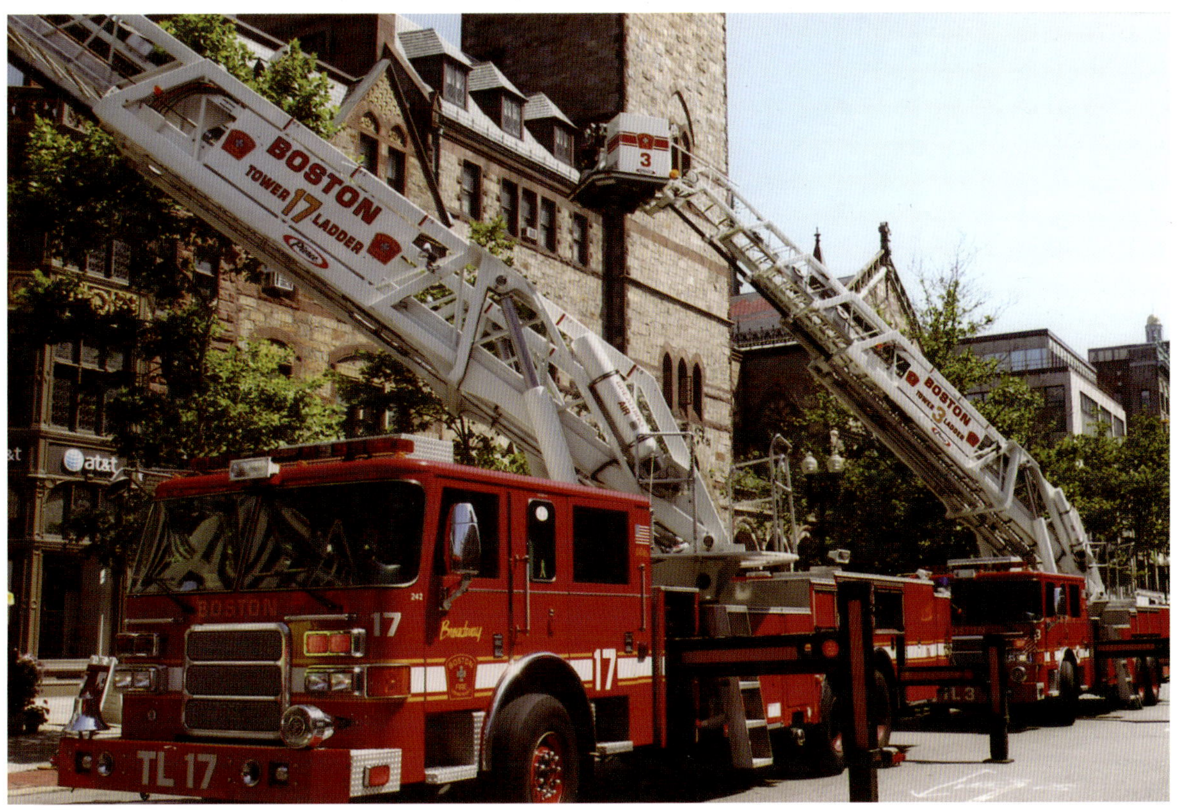

Boston's Twin Towers 17 and 3, 2005 Pierce, Dash, mid-mount, 5 section 95 foot Towers.

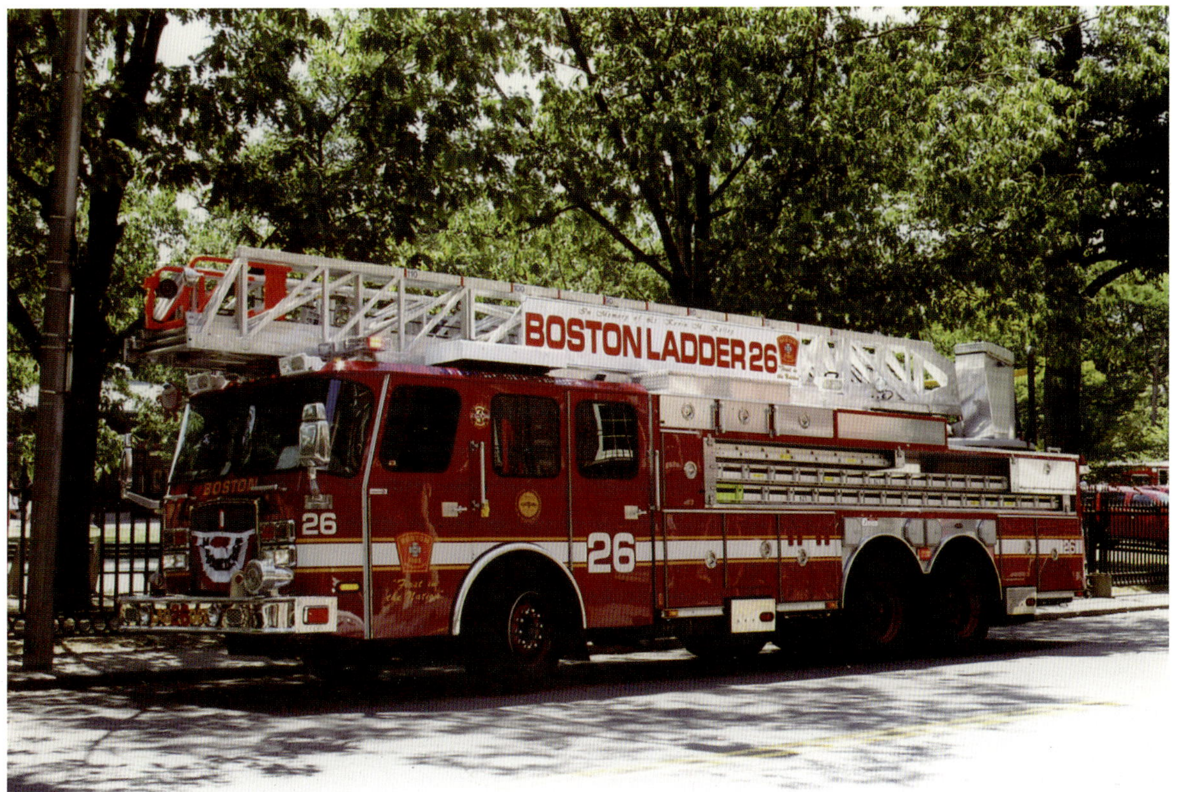

Ladder 26, 2009 Emergency-One, Cyclone II dedicated to the memory of LT. Kevin M. Kelley who died in the line of duty.

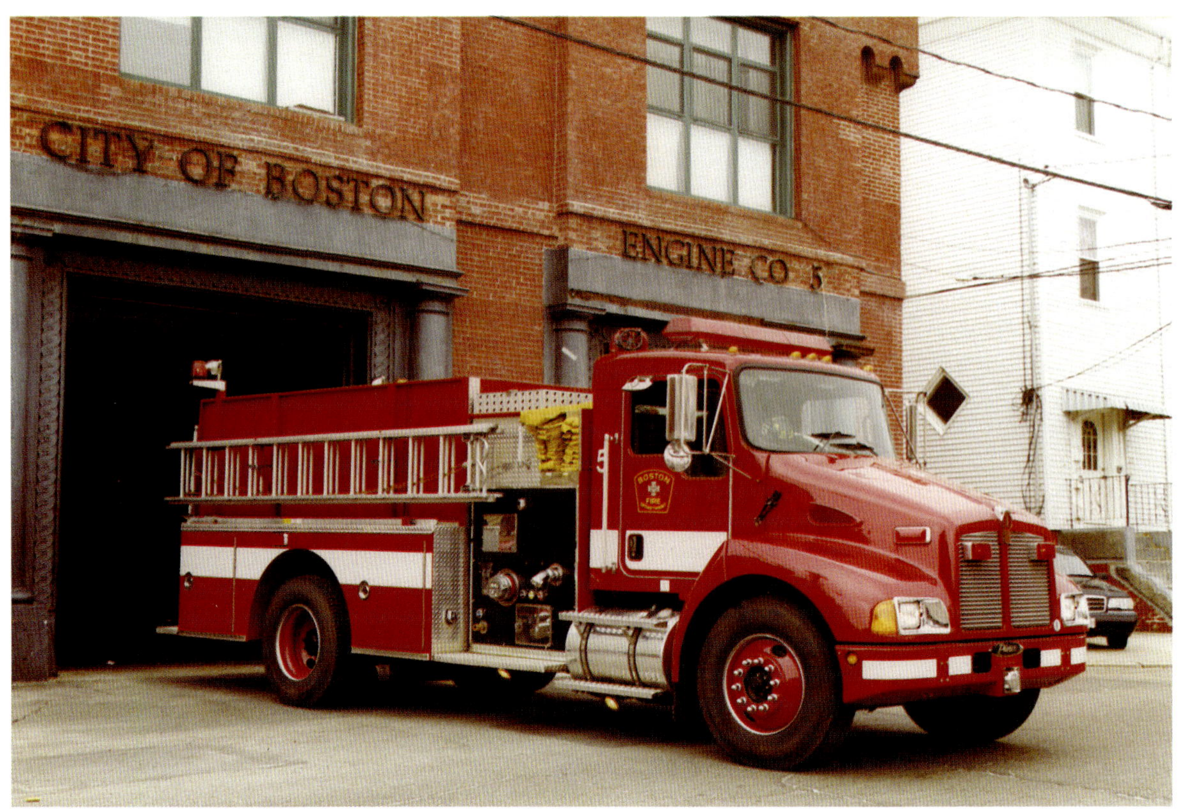

Engine 5, 2002 Kenworth/Pierce 1250/1000/40 foam.

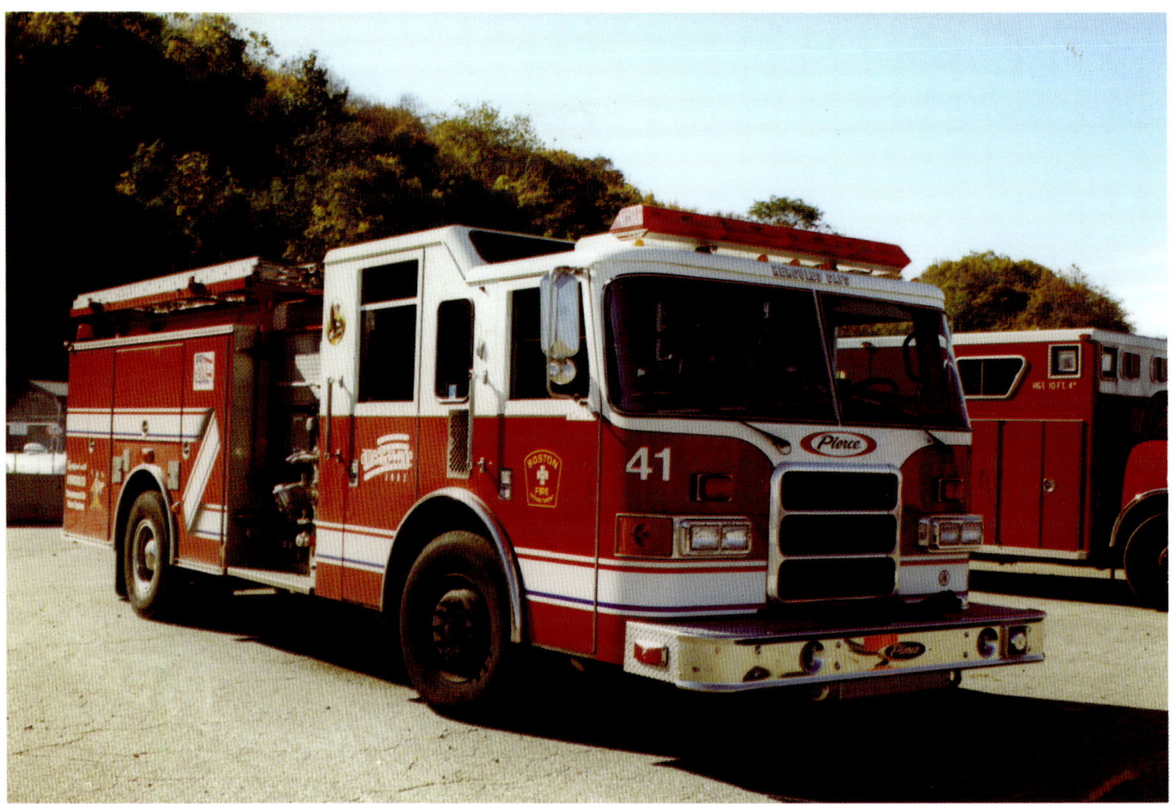

Engine 41, 2002 Pierce, Enforcer 1500/750/30 foam. Both units were leased, for a short period, in order that the O'Neil Tunnel (Big Dig) could open on time.

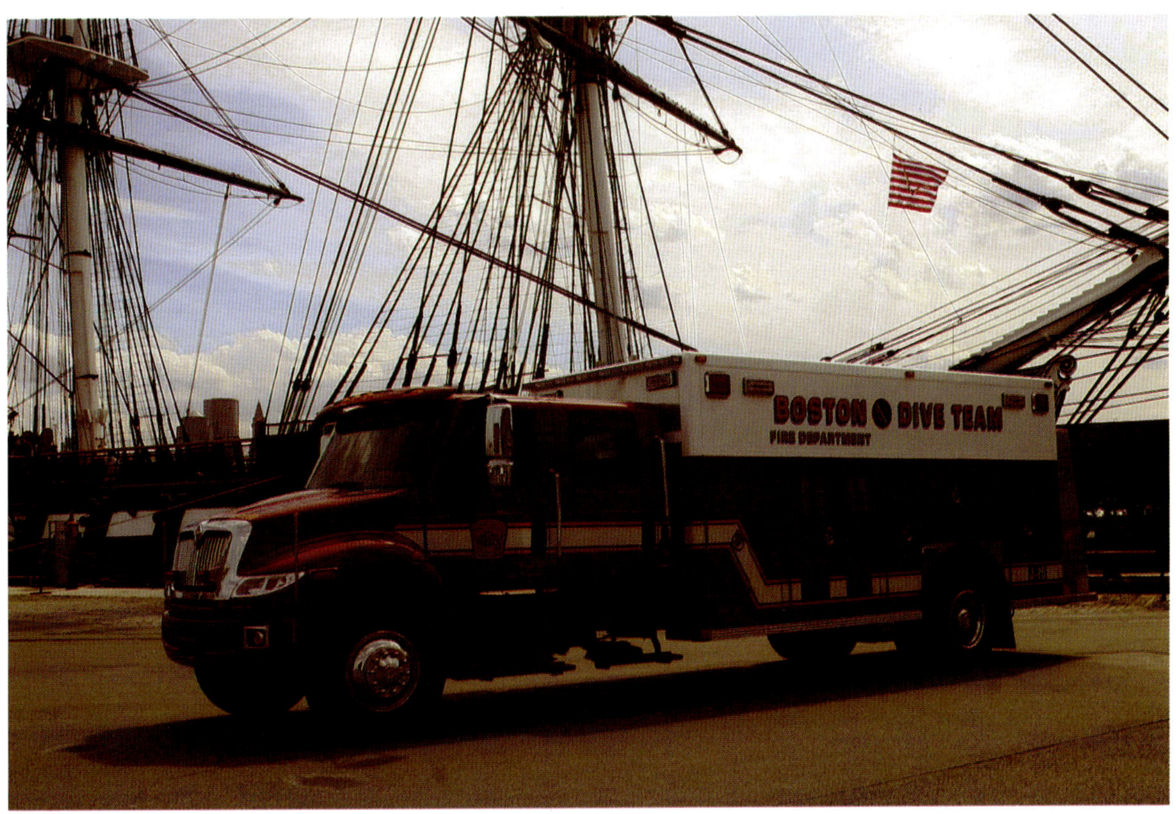

Dive Team Support Truck, 2011 International with former Rescue One's rebuilt 1986 Emergency-One Box.

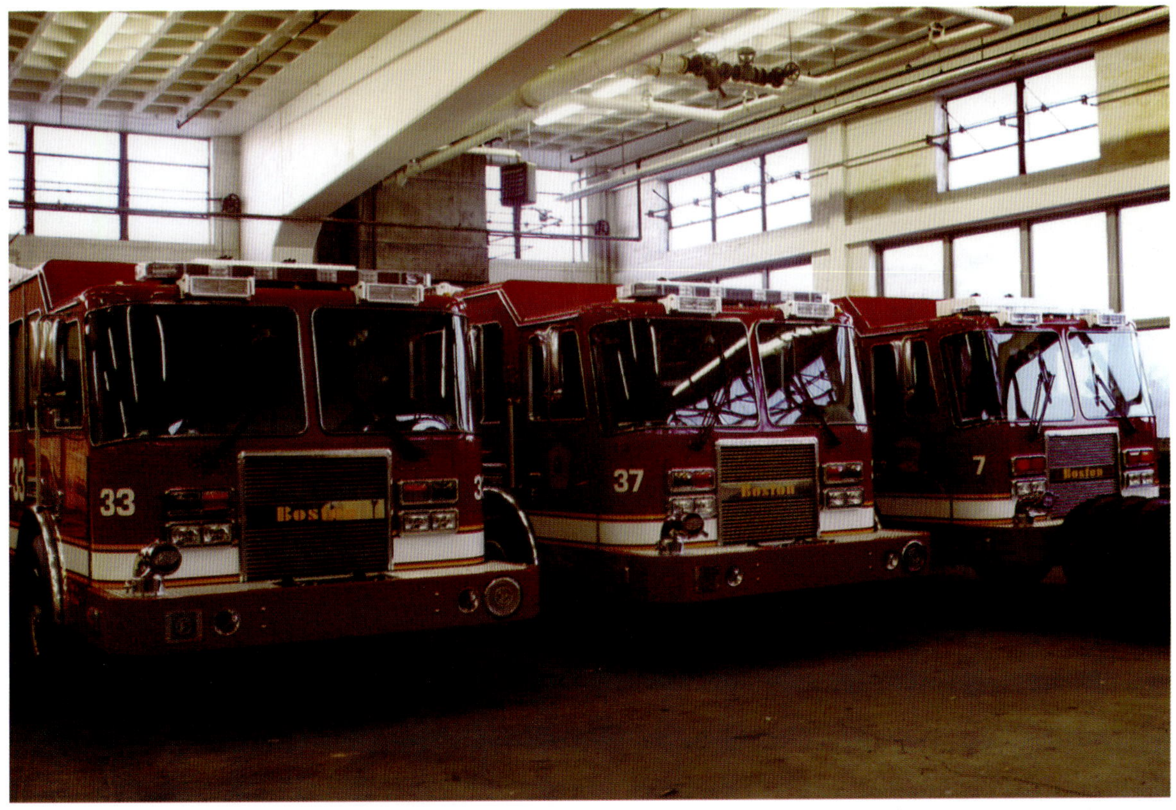

Boston's first KME Engines, 2010 Predators. Shortly after going into service, Engine 33 was reassigned to Engine 14 and Engine 7 was reassigned to Engine 42.

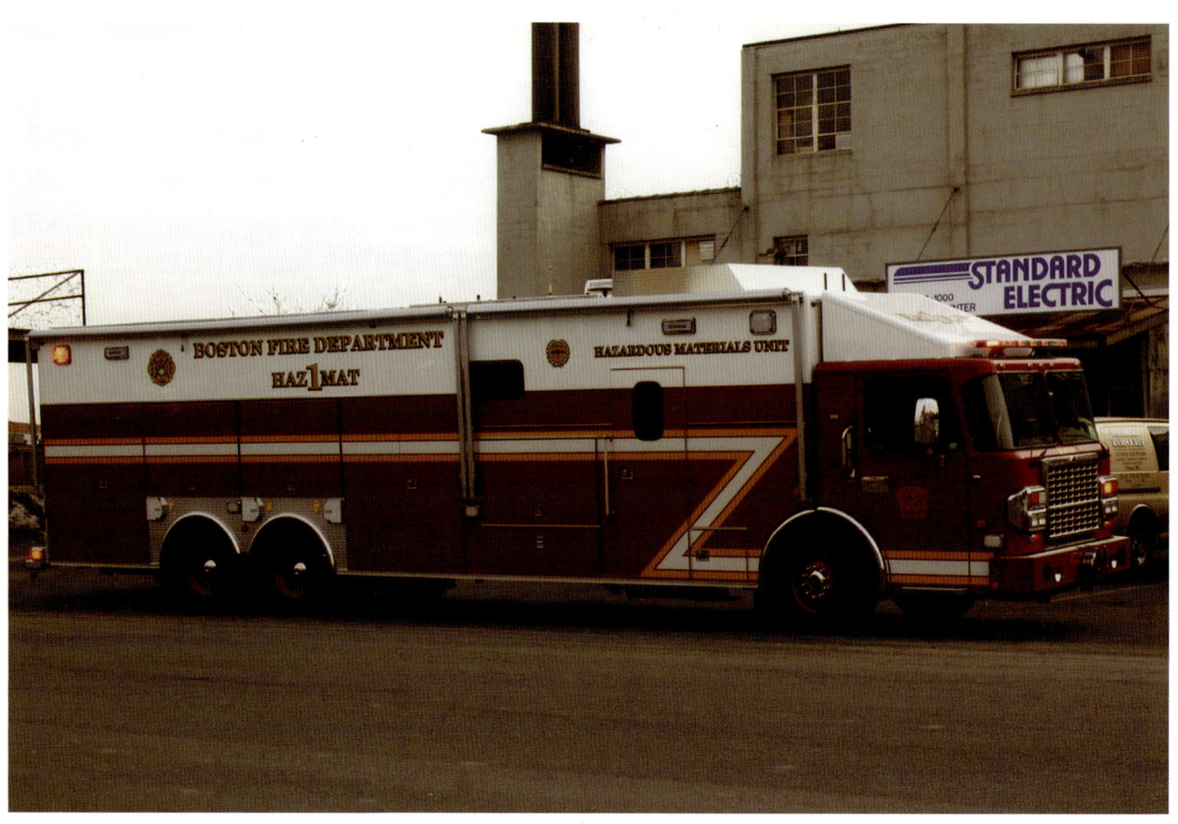

2012 Spartan MetroStar/EVI 42 foot Hazmat/Command Unit

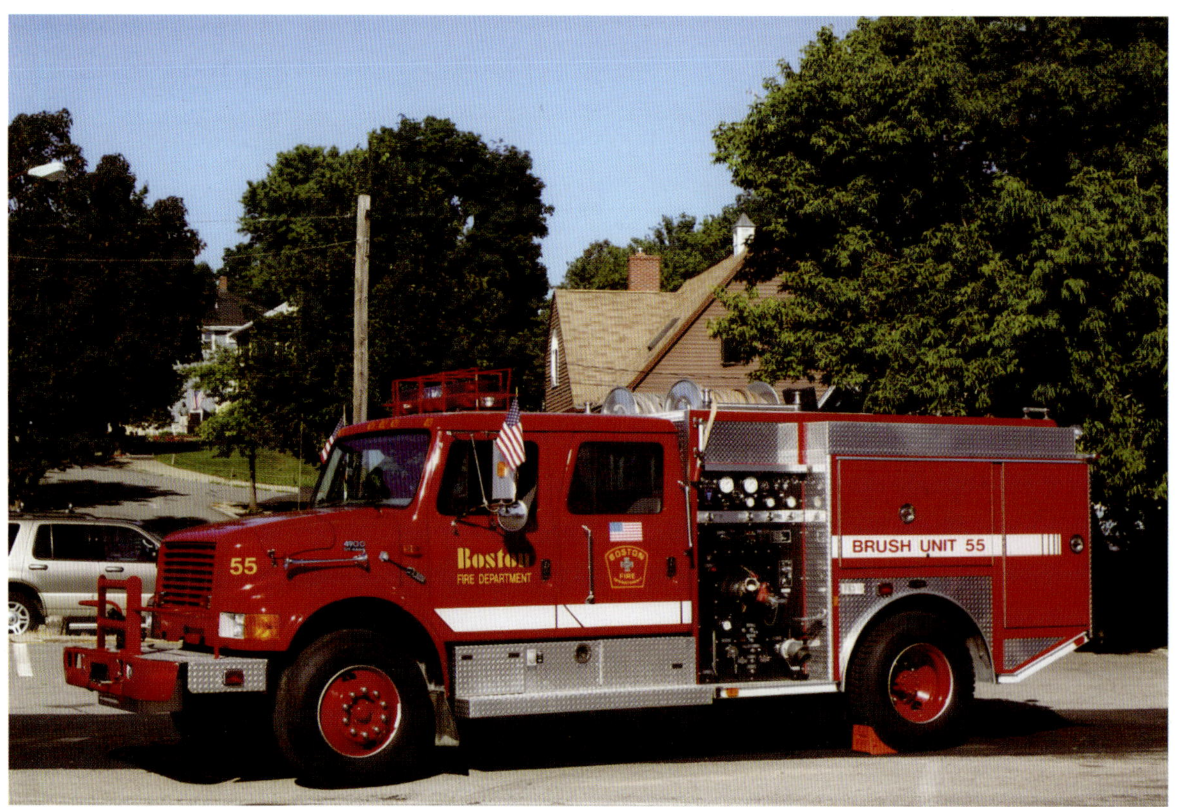

Engine 55's Brush Truck, 1998 International/Emergency-One 650/500/50.

CLASSICS

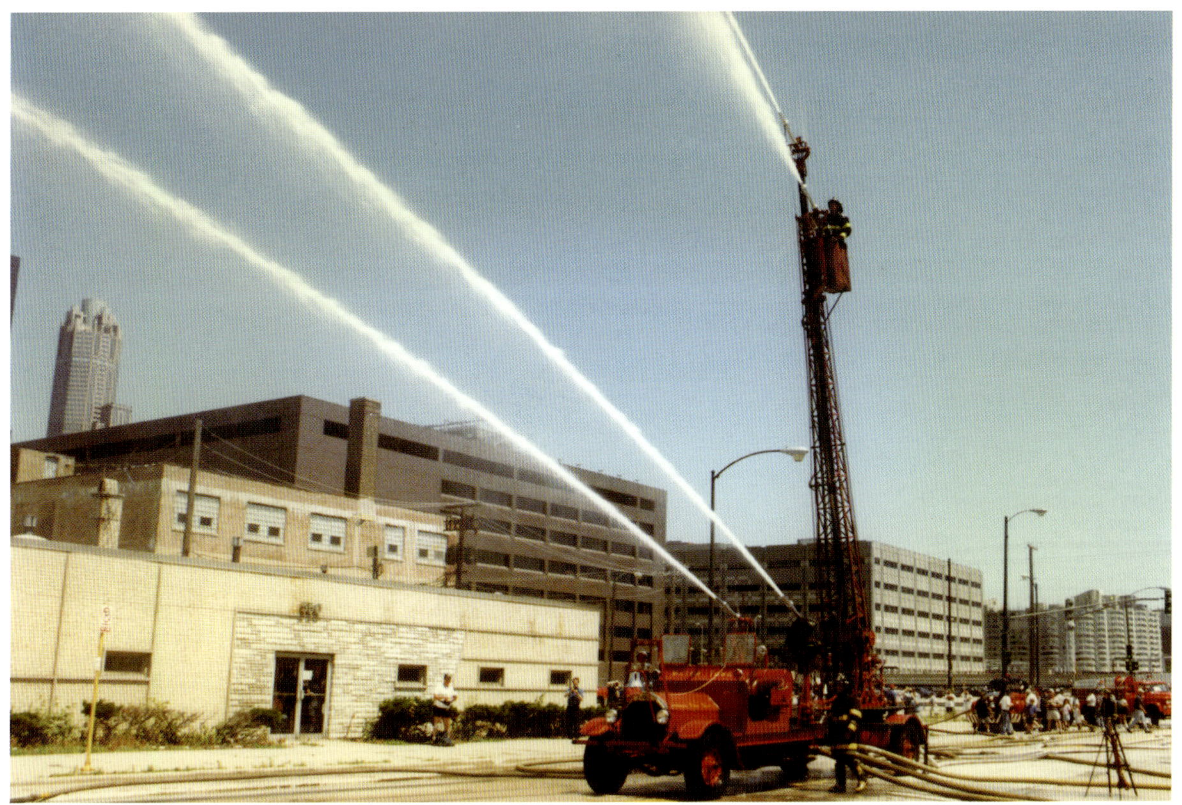

Chicago Water Tower 2, 1925 Seagrave, 65 foot Tower.

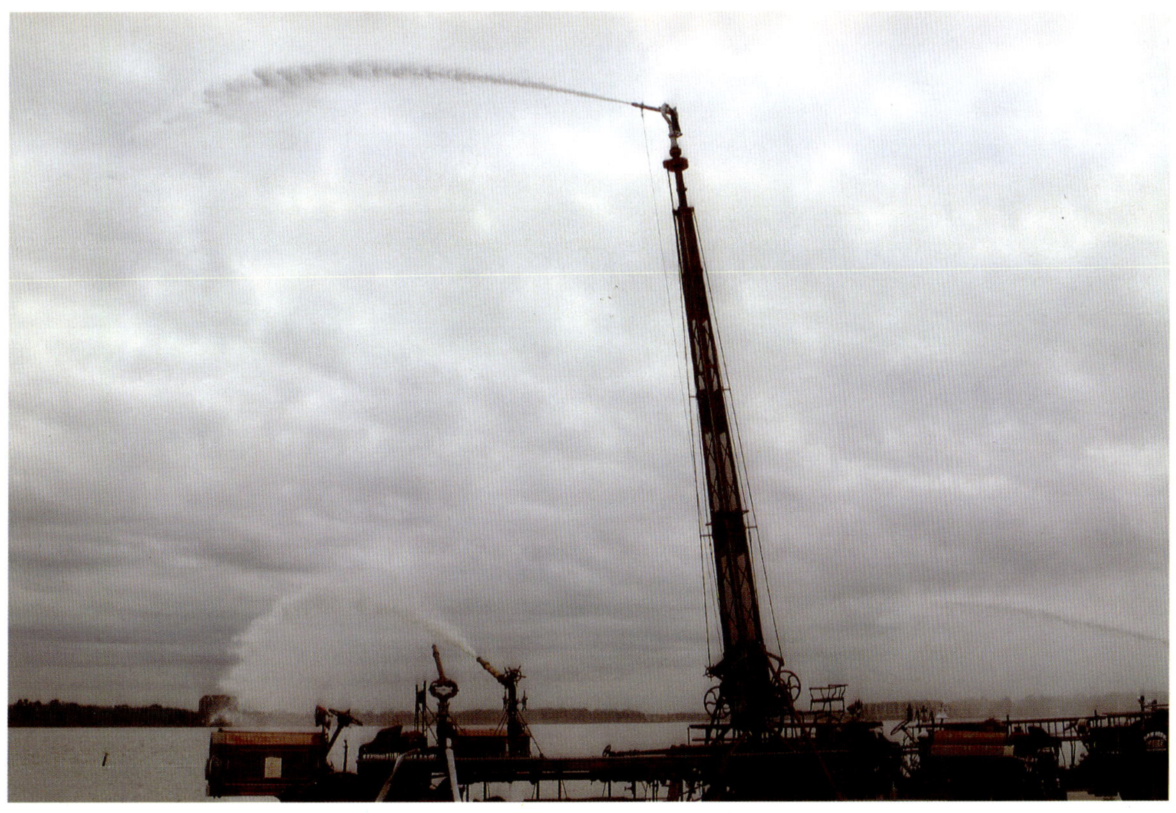

Houston Water Tower 1, 1912 American Automatic, 65 foot Tower, originally horsedrawn, before a 1923 American LaFrance cab was added. In service until 1960.

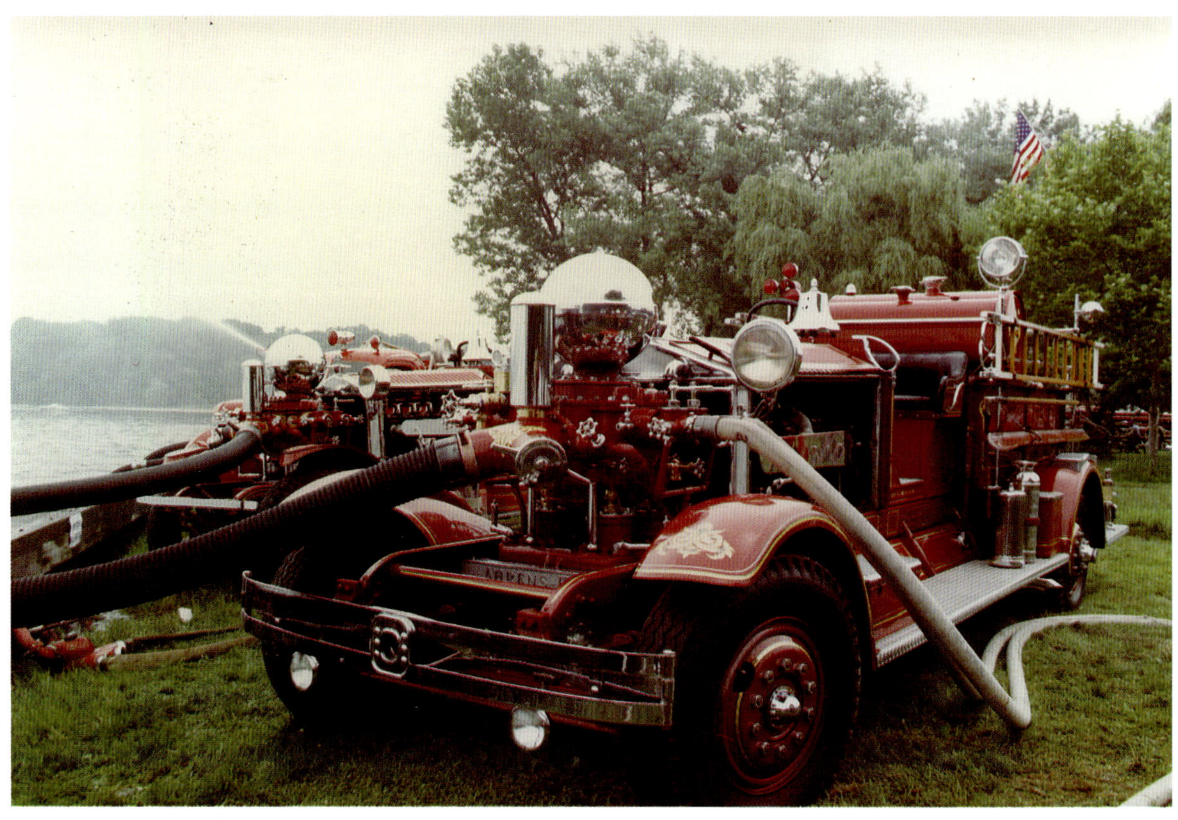

Ahrens Fox's drafting at Croton-on-Hudson, NY Muster.

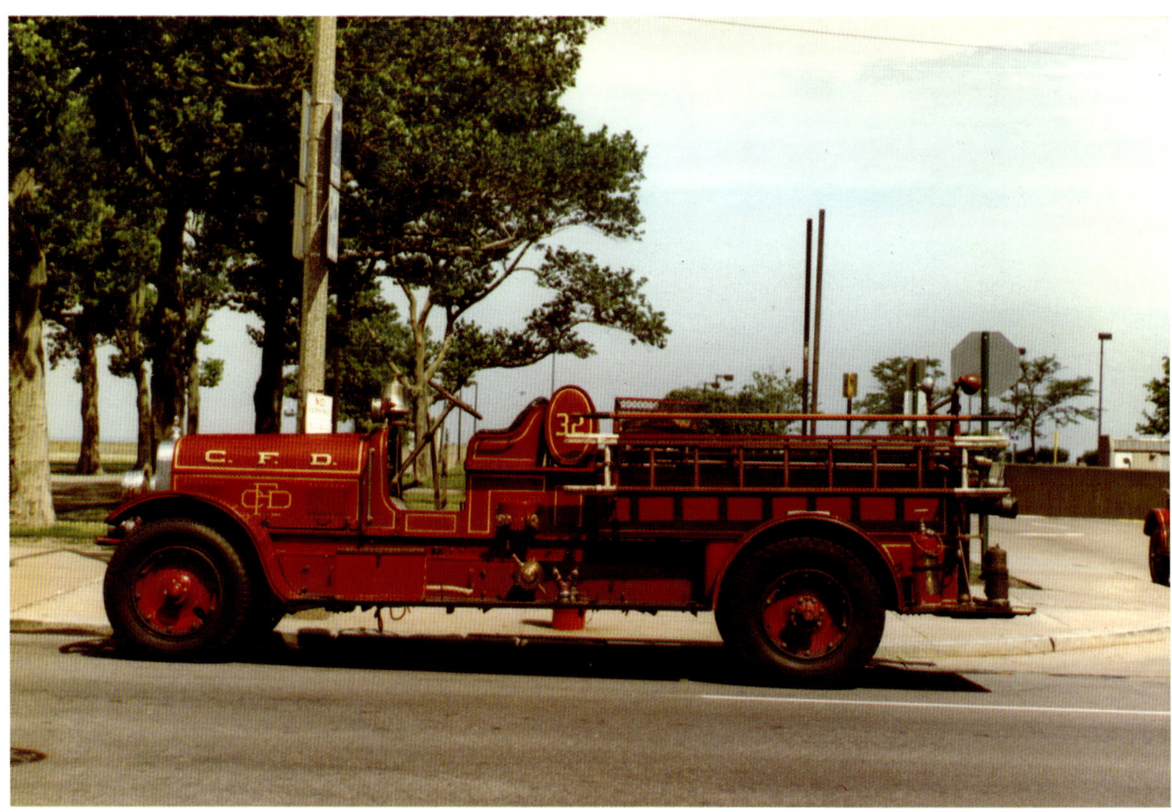

Cleveland Engine 32, 1925 Seagrave, 1000 GPM and the last open cab apparatus in Cleveland.

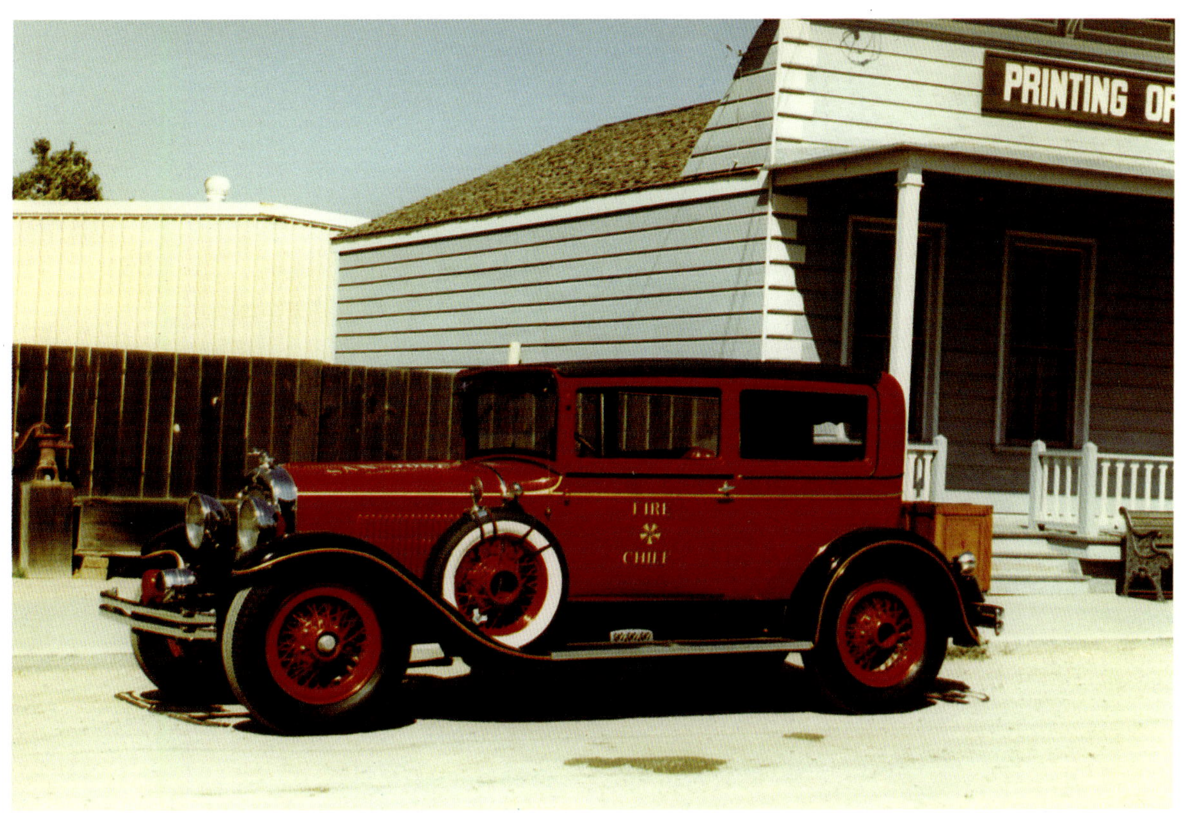

San Jose, CA 1929 Reo Chief's car.

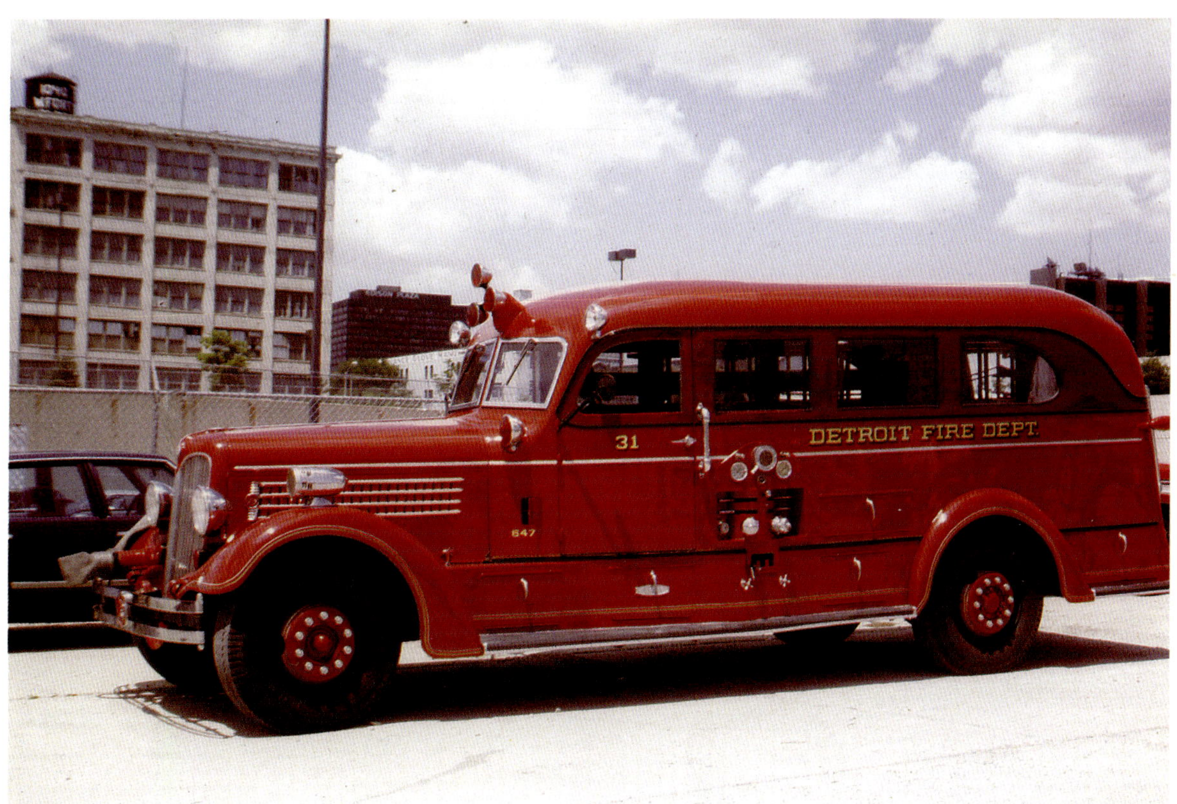

Detroit Engine 31, 1937 Seagrave, Safety Sedan. Less than one hundred were manufactured and Detroit purchased 67.

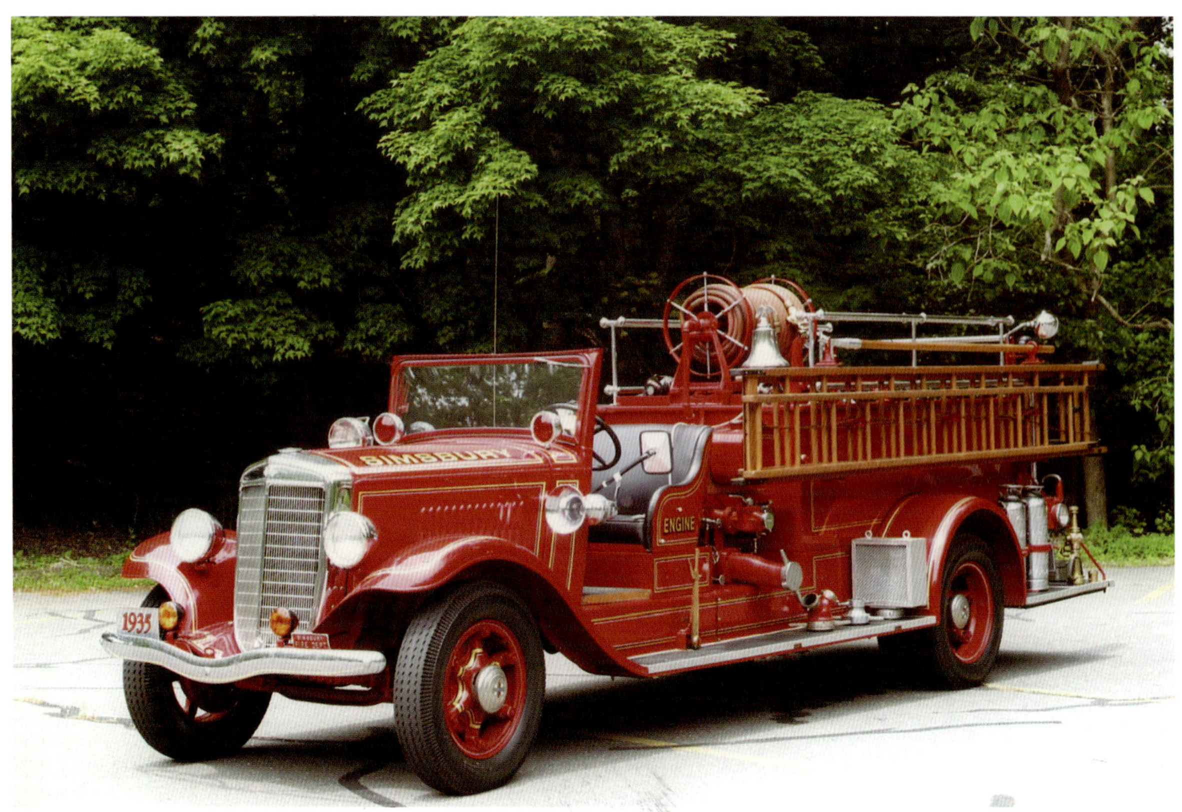

Simsbury, CT Engine 1, 1935 International/American LaFrance, 500 GPM.

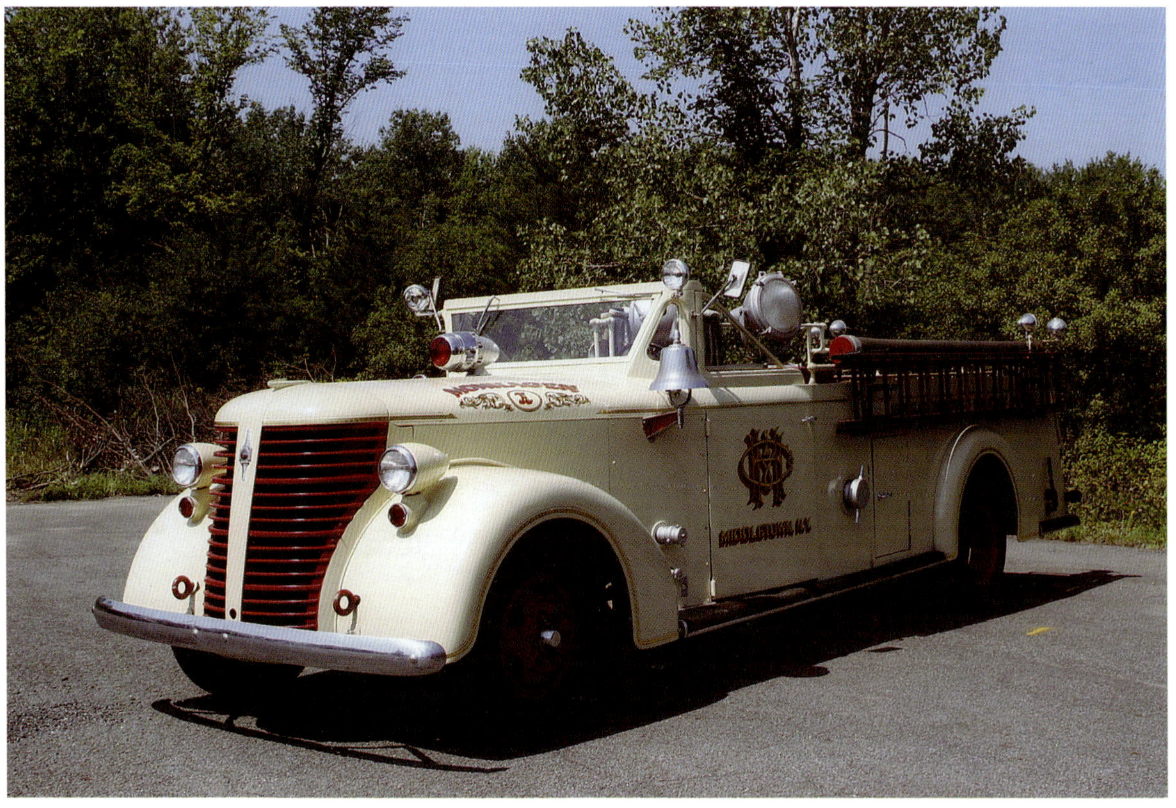

Middletown, NY, Monhagen Hose and Salvage Co. No. 1, 1943 American LaFrance.

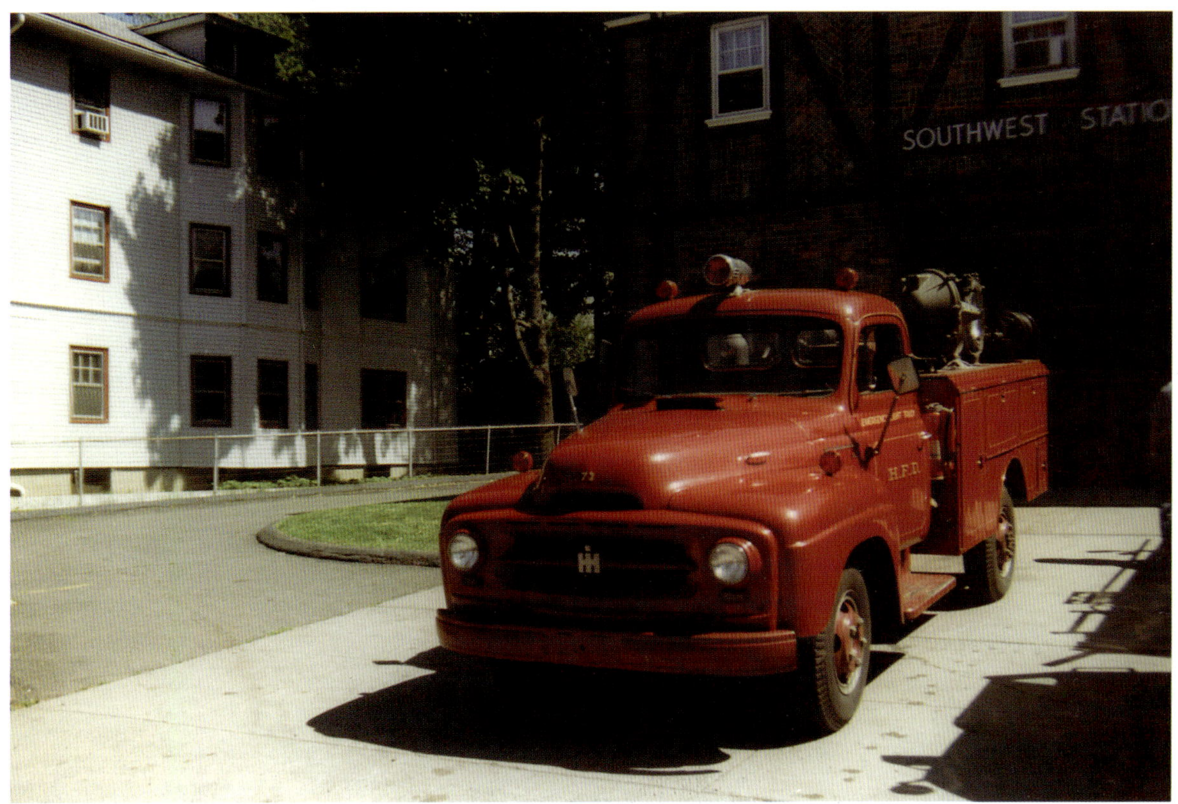

Hartford, CT Lighting Truck, 1955 International.

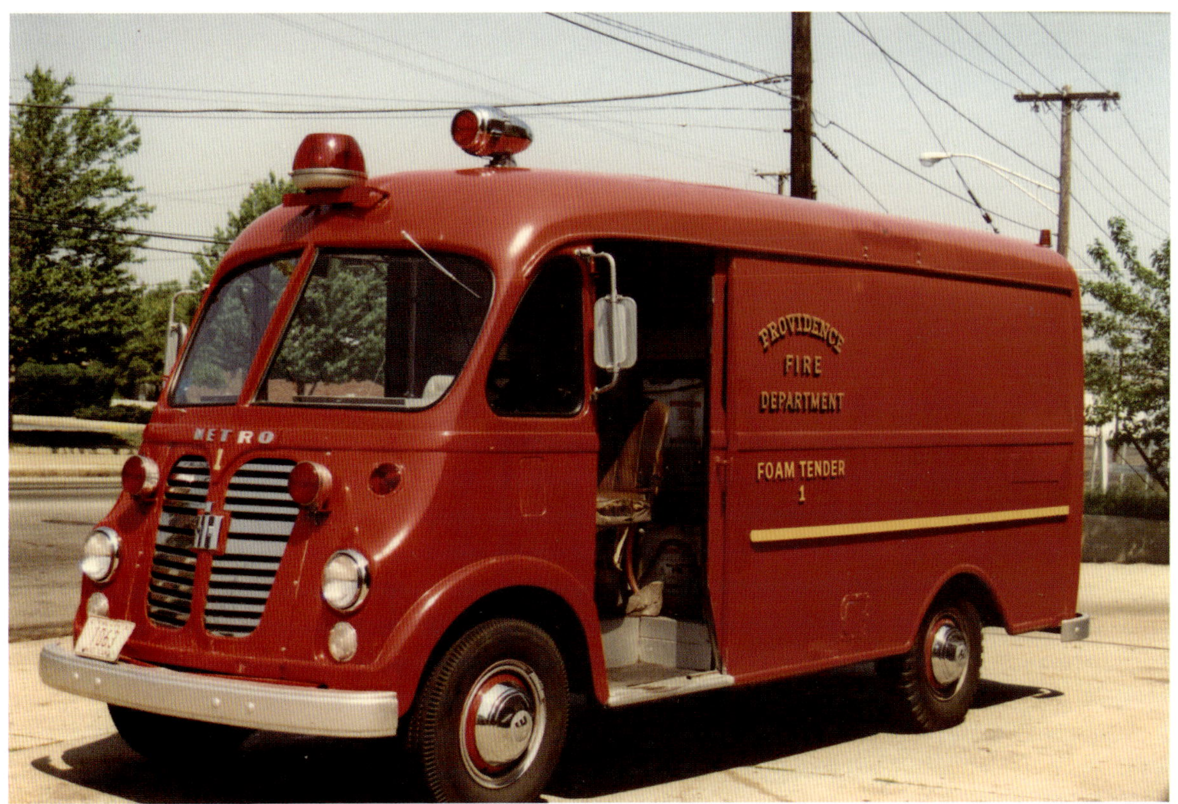

Providence, RI Foam Tender 1, 1961 International Metro Van.

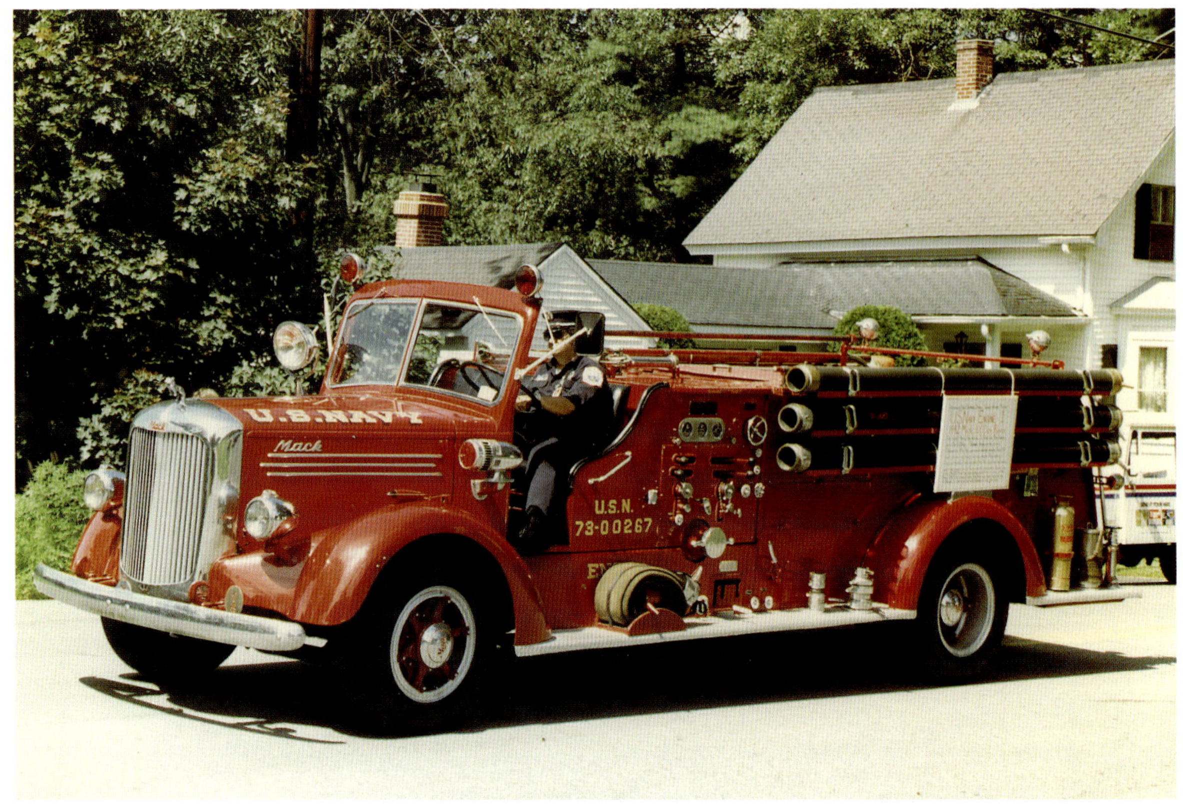

Portsmouth Naval Shipyard, Kittery, ME, 1942 Mack which was built for Manchester, NH, but redirected to the Shipyard by The Federal Government to support the war effort.

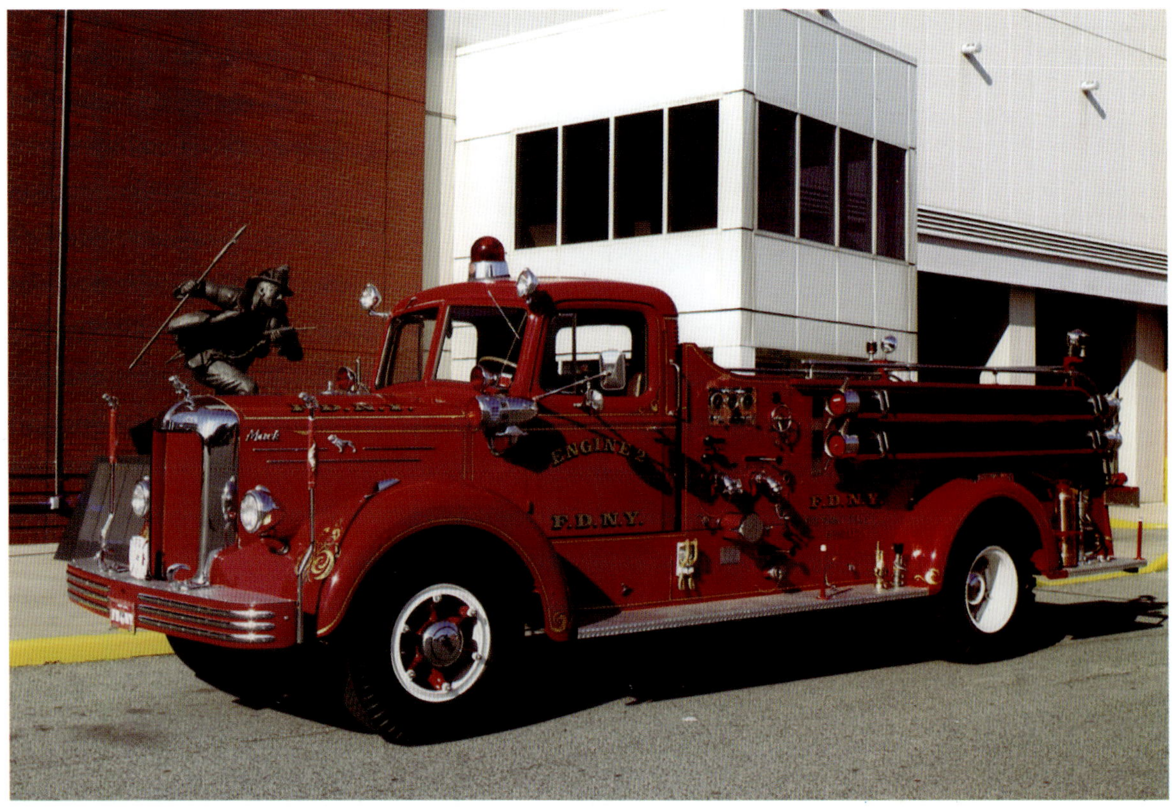

1954 Mack L Model, owned by The FDNY Fire Family Transport Foundation, acquired from Aberdeen, MD.

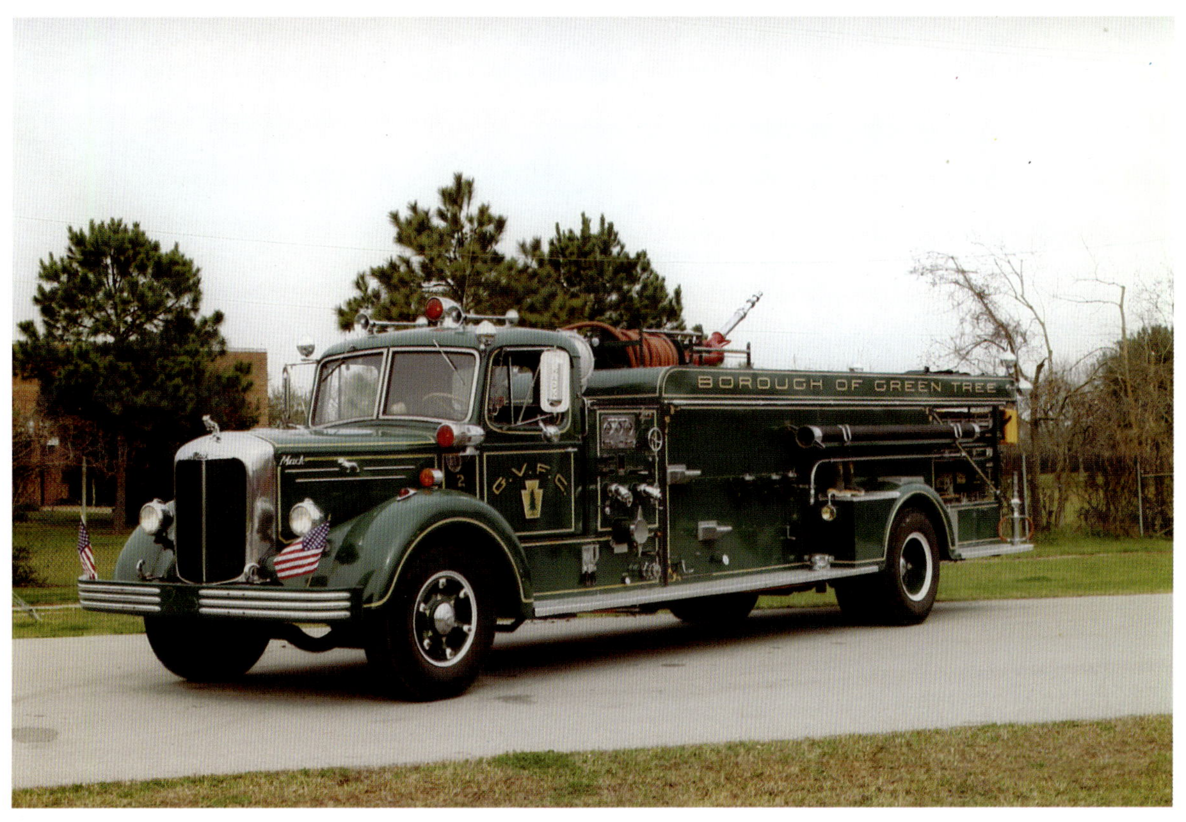

Green Tree Volunteer Fire Company, Pittsburgh, PA,1950 Mack L Model now privately owned in Texas.

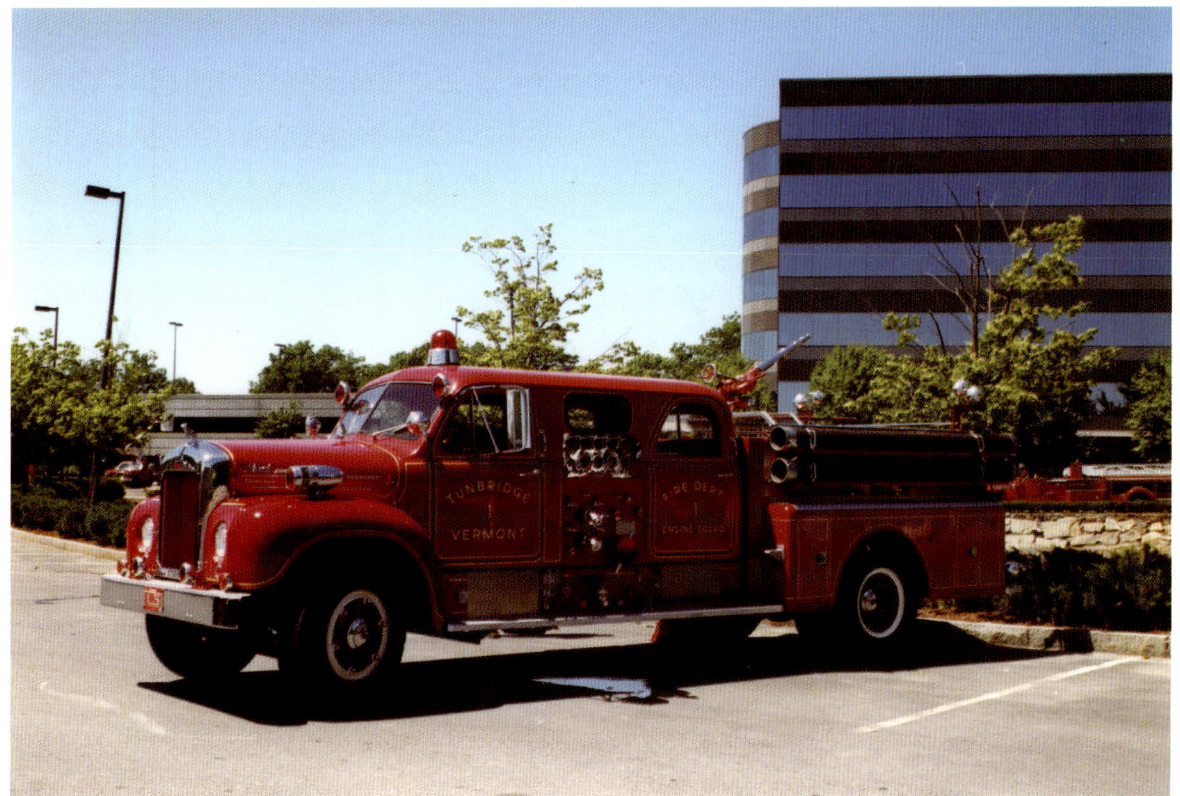

Turnbridge, VT 1961 B Model Mack 1,000 GPM, with crew cab, acquired from Bryan, Ohio.

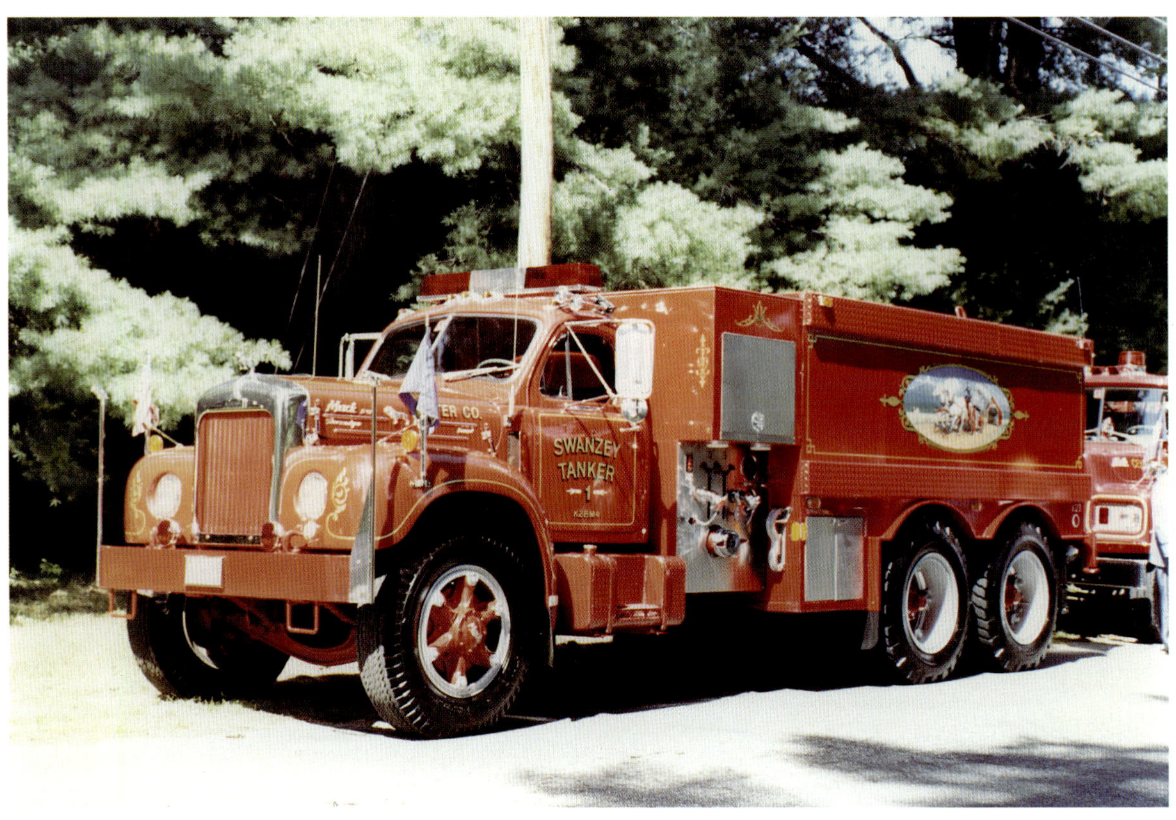

Swanzey Center, NH, Tanker 1, 1961 B Model Mack 750/3000, a former cement mixer and built in house.

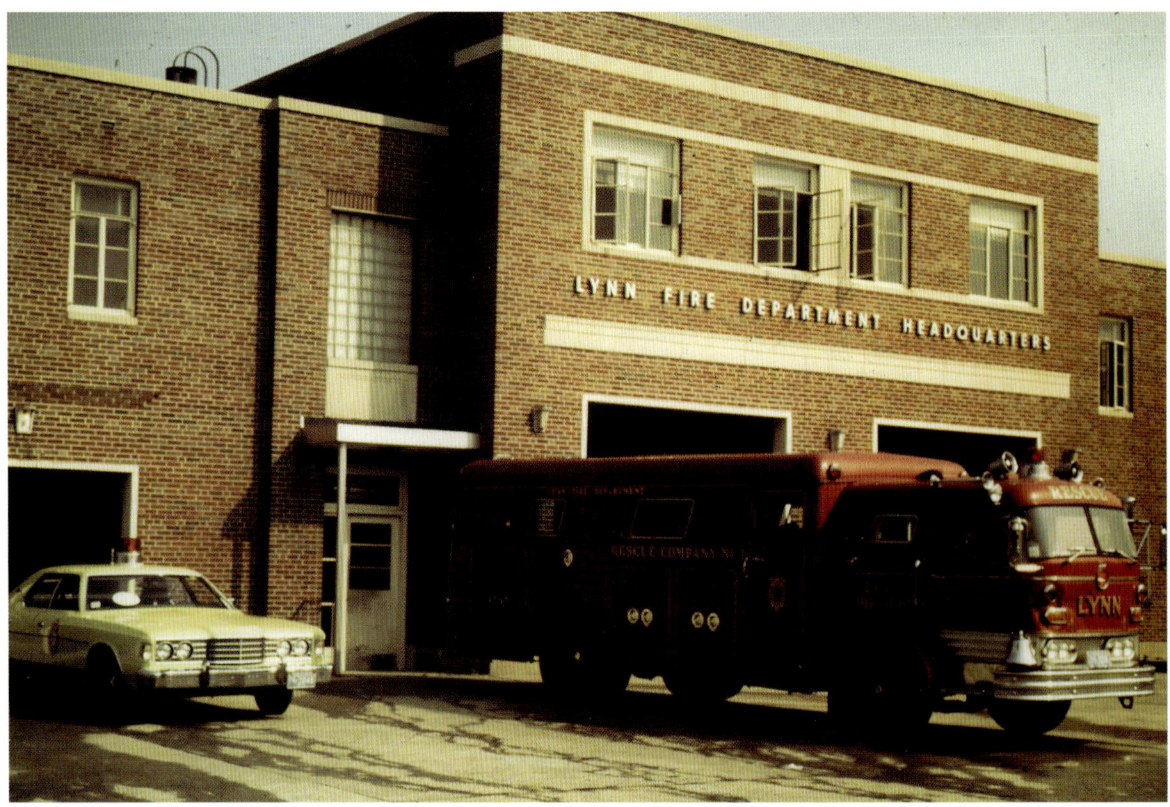

Lynn, MA 1967 Mack C Model/Gerstenslager Rescue, shortly before being refurbished and painted the color of the chief's car.

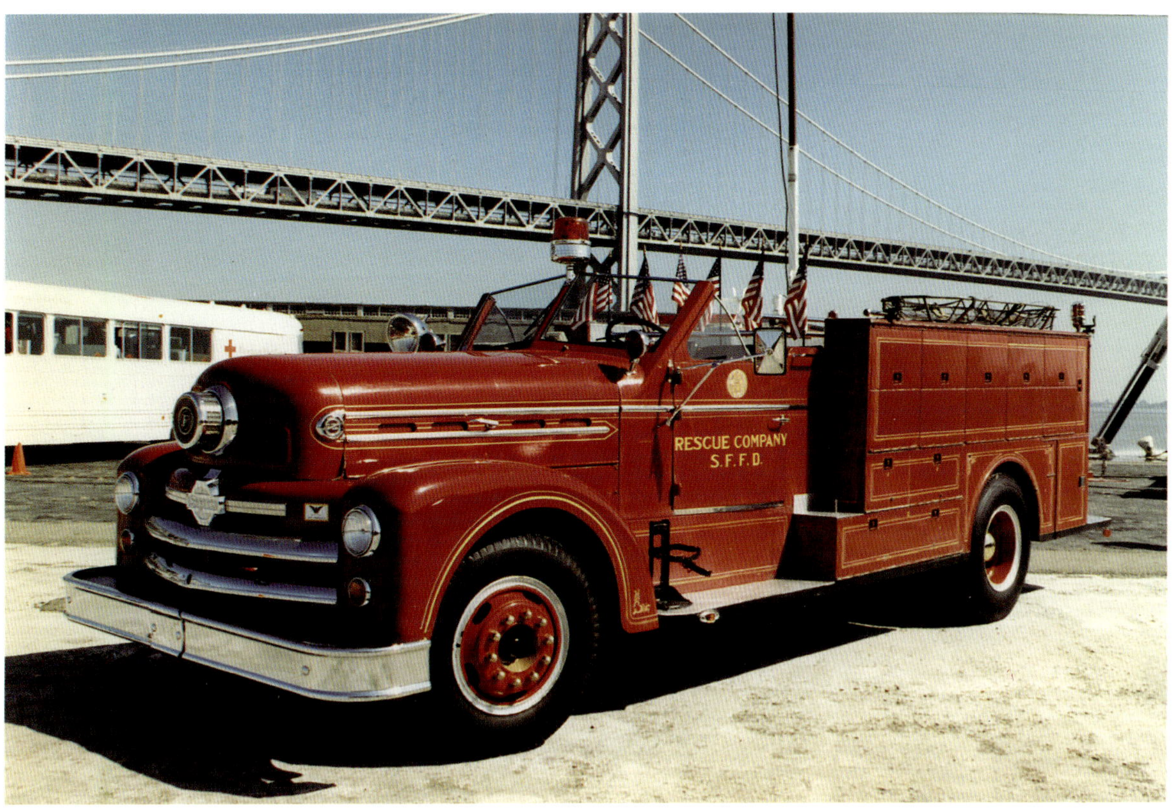

San Francisco Rescue 2, 1956 Seagrave with a V-12 engine. Originally a tank wagon and in service until the late 80's.

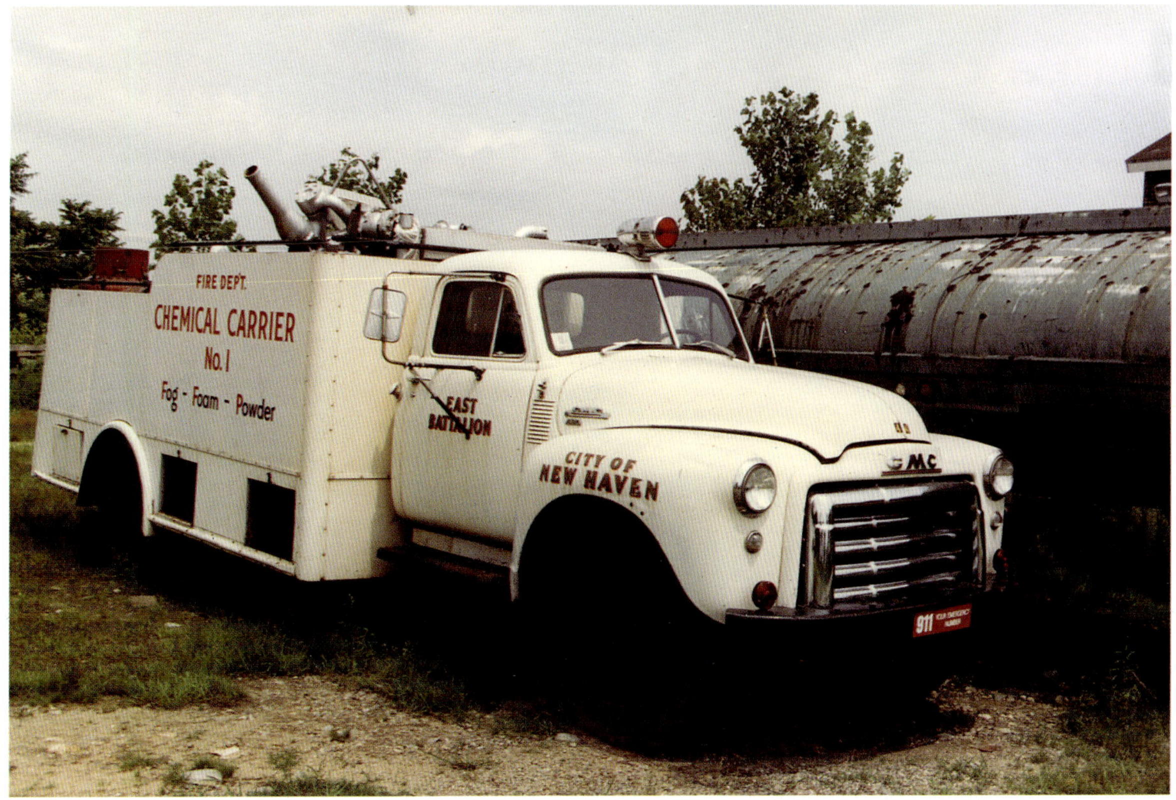

New Haven, CT Chemical Carrier No. 1, 1950 GMC.

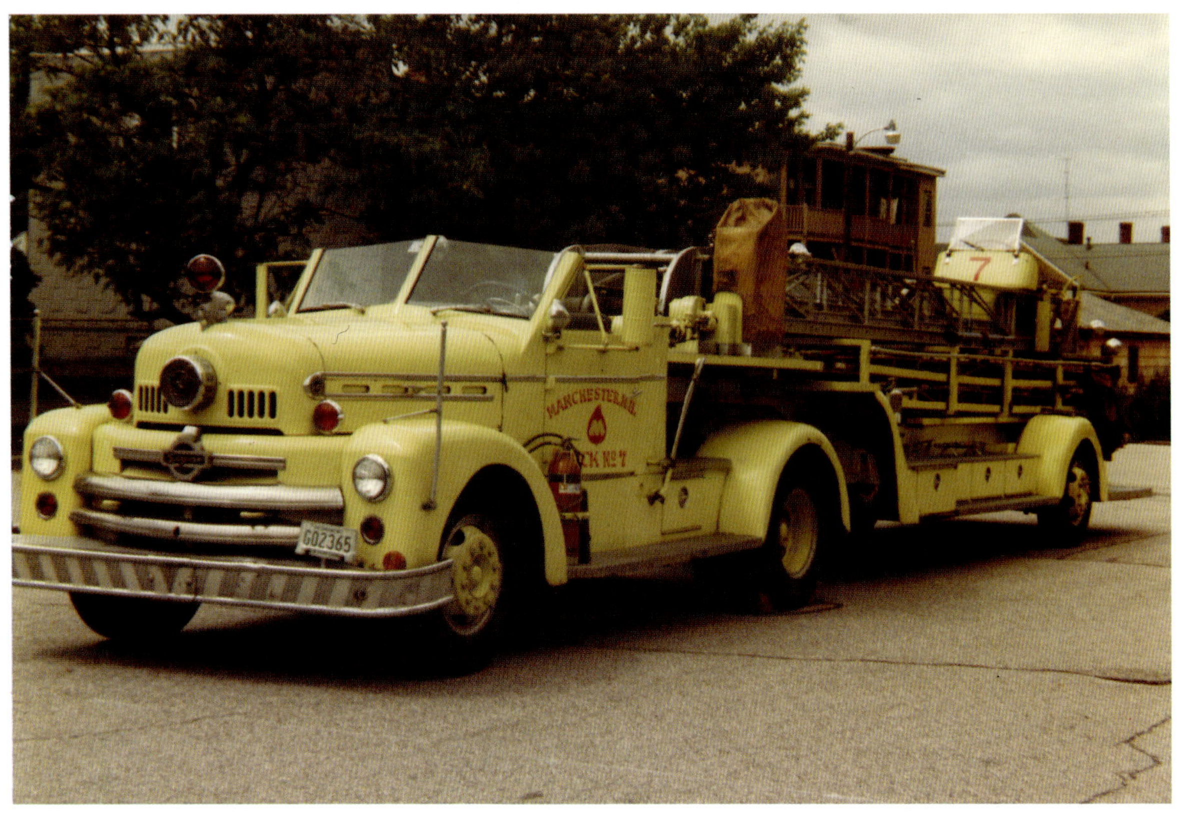

Manchester, NH Ladder 7, 1956 Seagrave 75 foot aerial.

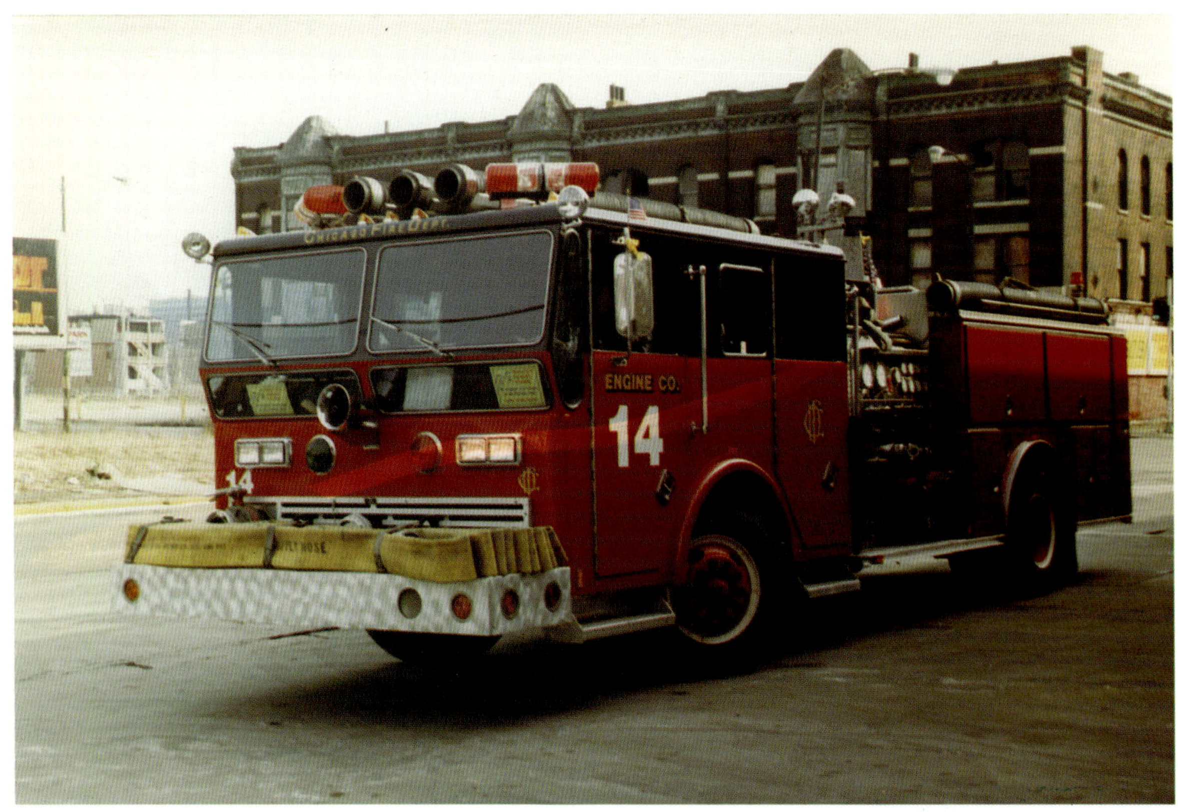

Chicago Engine 14, 1970 Ward LaFrance, rebuilt in 1990 using Ranger and Emergency- One parts. Previously served Engines 113, 34, 19, 109 and 72.

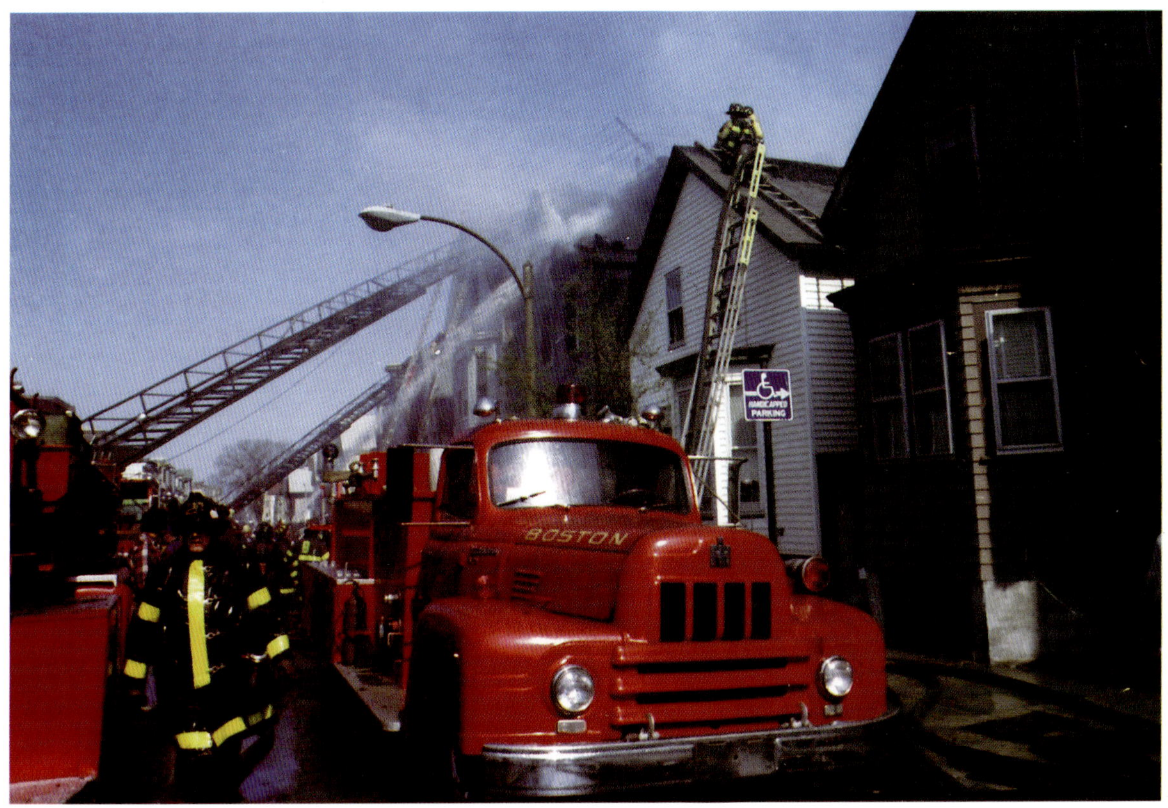

Boston Engine 5 Hose Wagon, 1964 International acquired from The Charlestown Navy Yard on January 22, 1976. It also served as Engine 54 on Long Island.

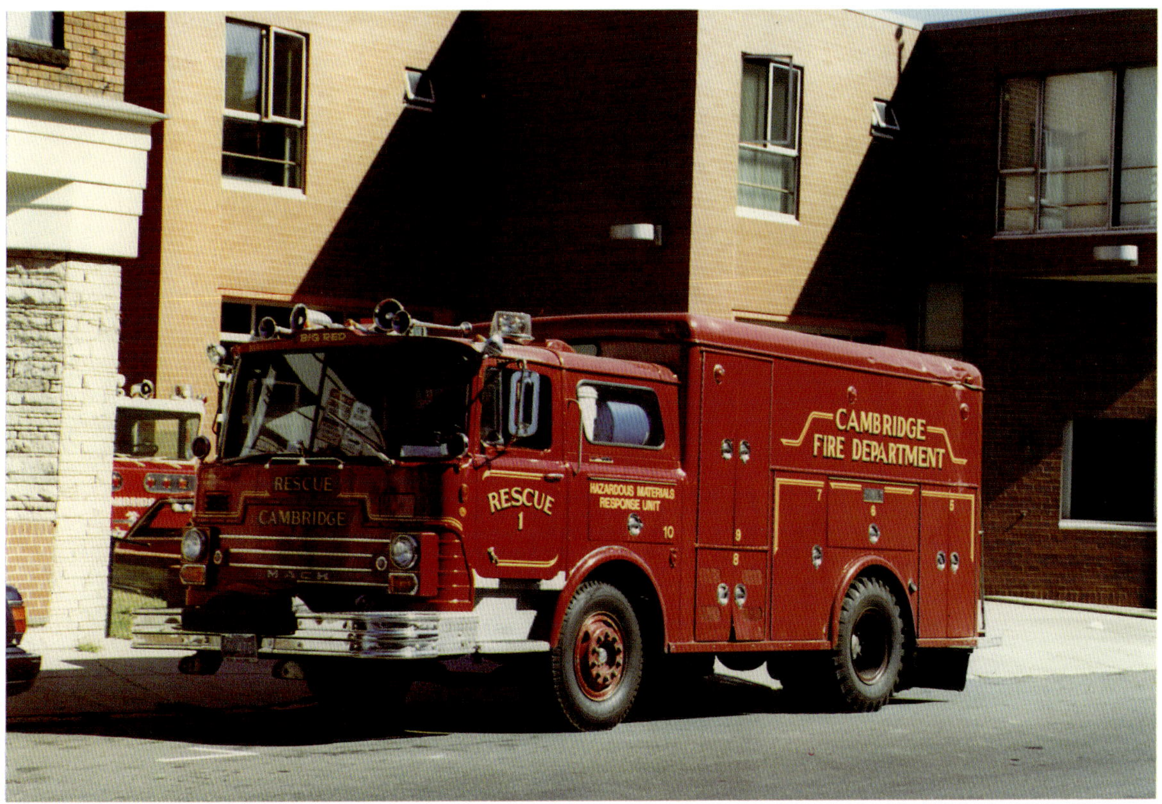

Cambridge, MA Former Rescue 1 and Haz-Mat Truck, 1969 Mack CF600/Gerstenslager.

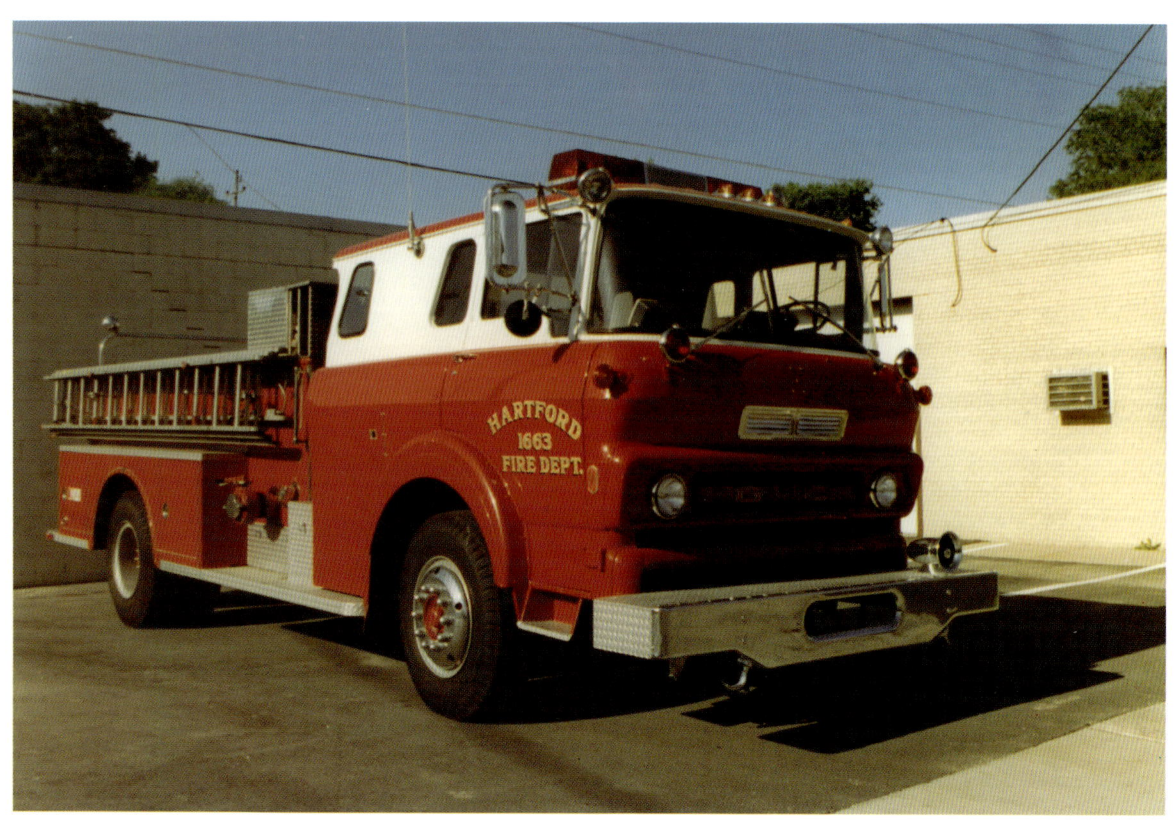

Hartford, WI Reserve Engine, 1969 GMC/Central Fire Apparatus, 1000 GPM.

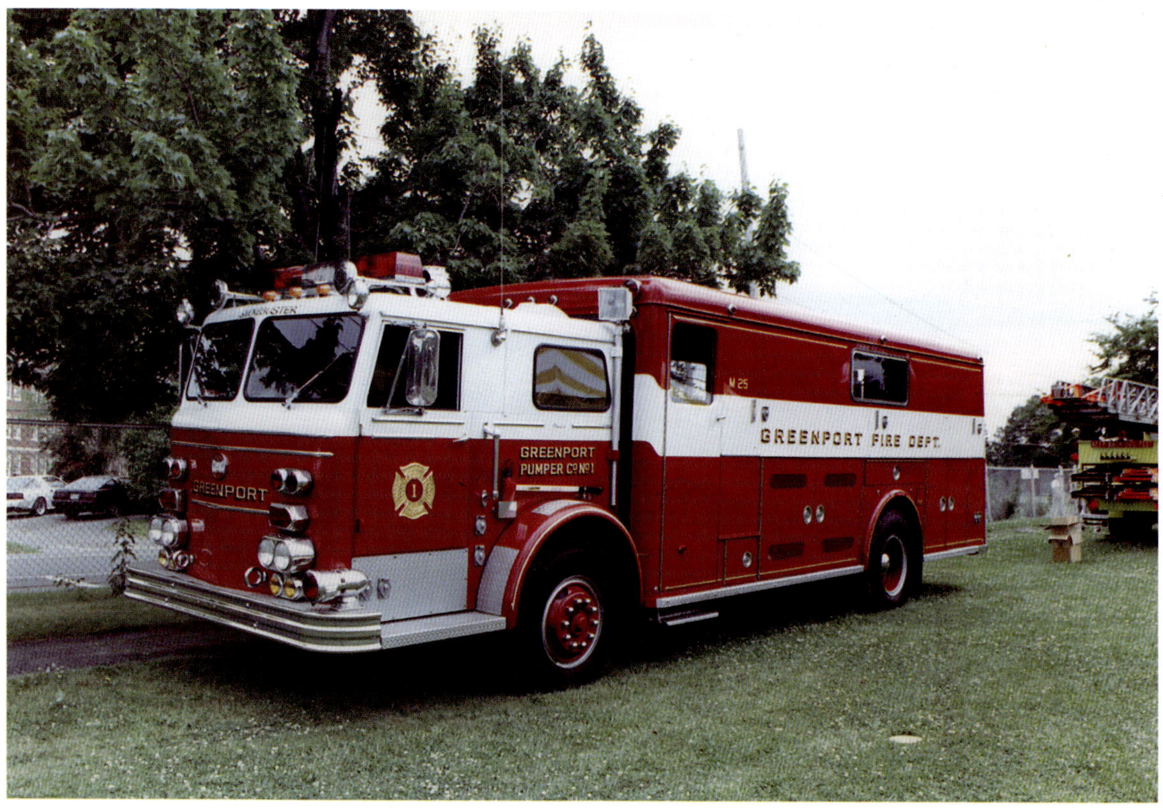

Greenport, NY 1967 Maxim/Gerstenslager, which formerly served Central Islip, NY.

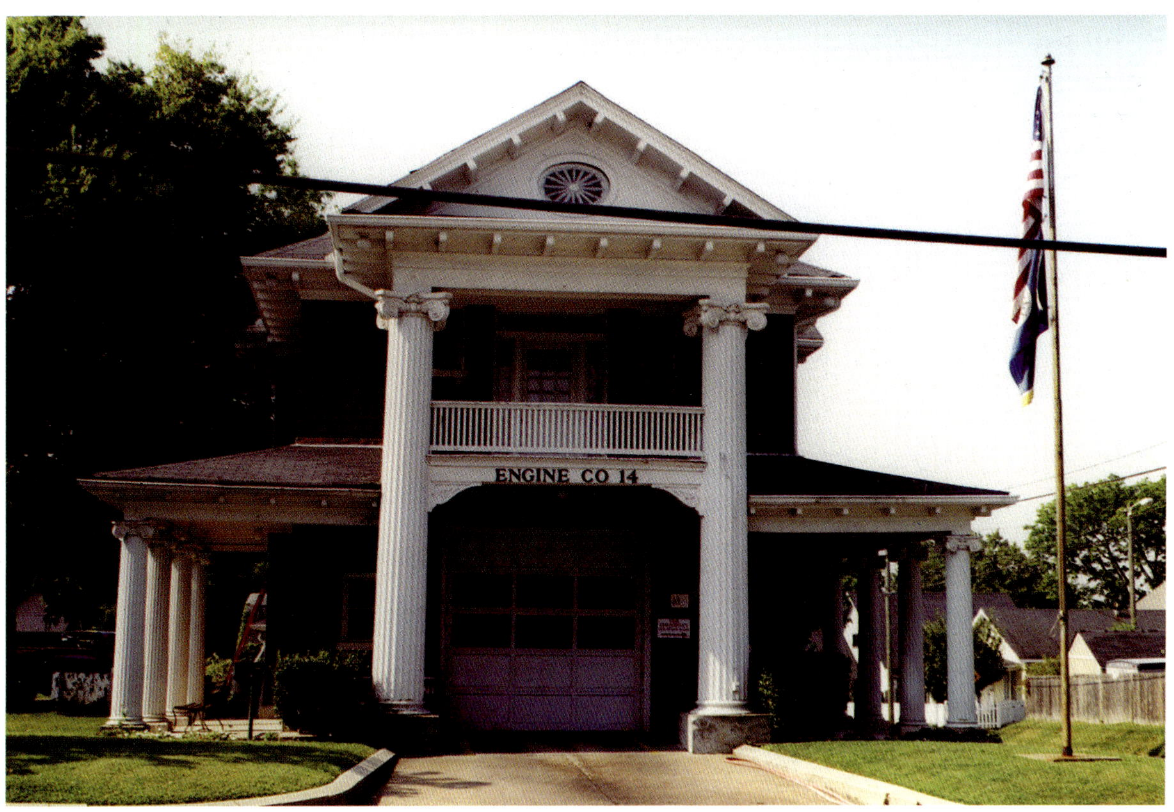

The Holly Street Fire Hall, the oldest, active fire hall in Nashville. It was dedicated on October 1, 1914 and has been the quarters of Engine 14 ever since.

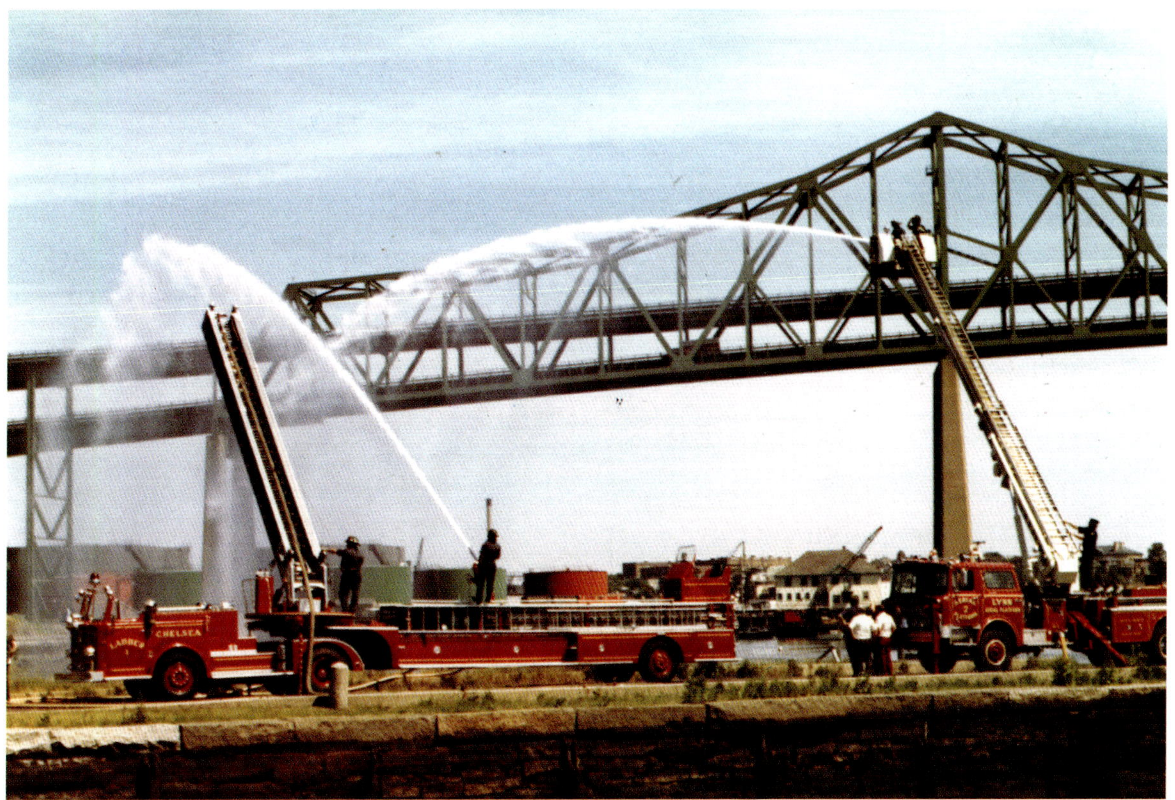

Chelsea Ladder 1 and Lynn Aerial Platform 2 drill on the Mystic River, Chelsea, in 1974. During their long careers, they worked at hundreds of extra alarm fires, including conflagrations in their respective cities. The Lynn Tower also worked at Chelsea's 1973 conflagration.

APPARATUS ACROSS AMERICA

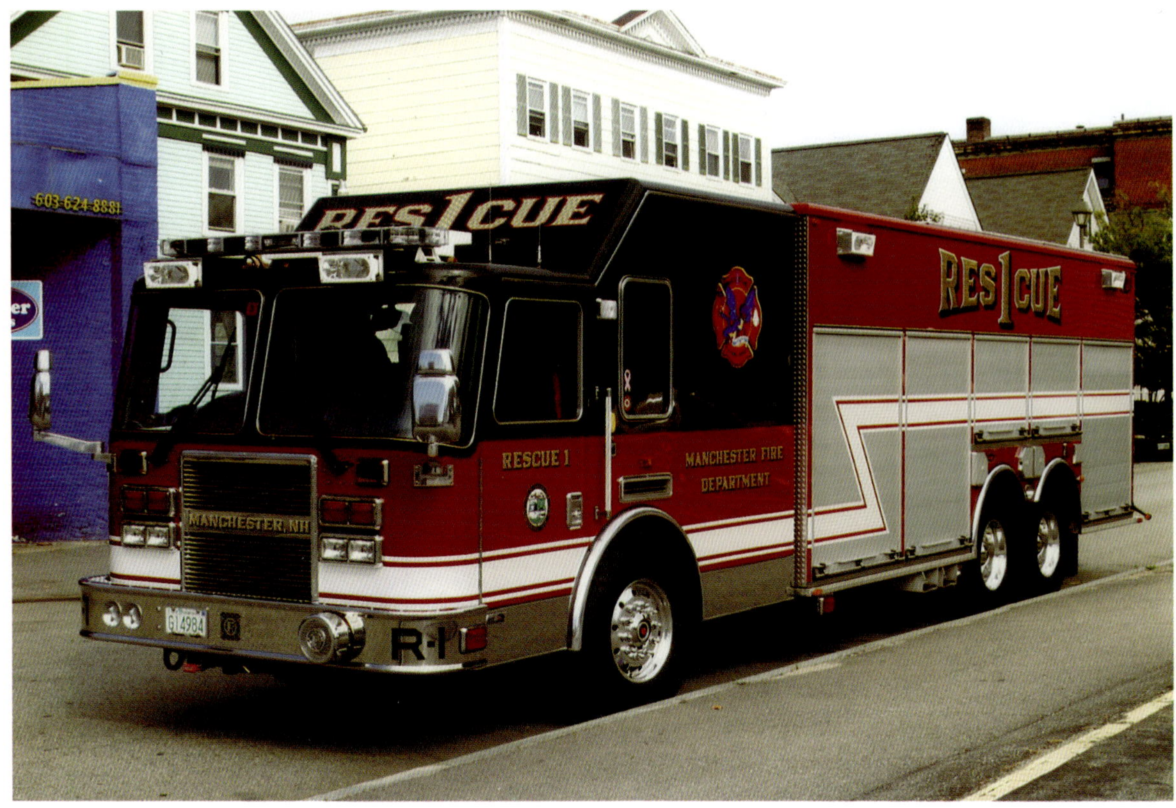

Manchester, NH Rescue 1, 2010 KME.

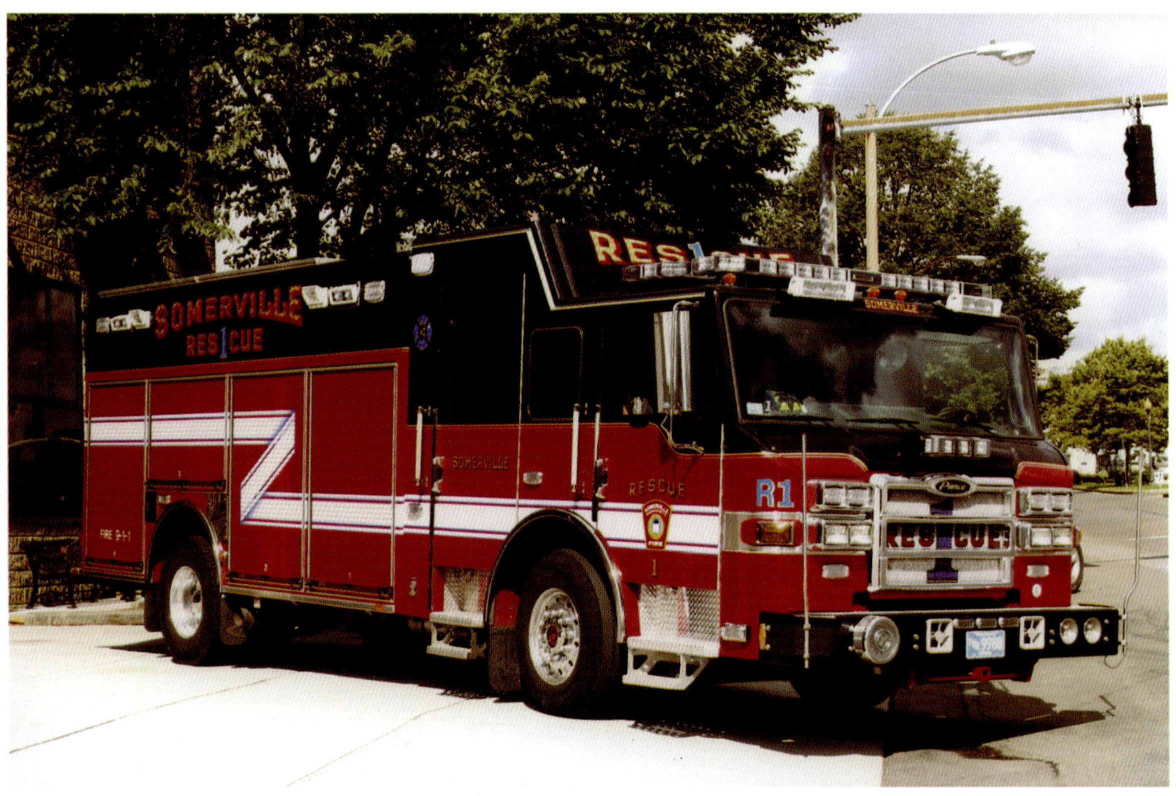

Somerville, MA Rescue 1, 2010 Pierce/Impel.

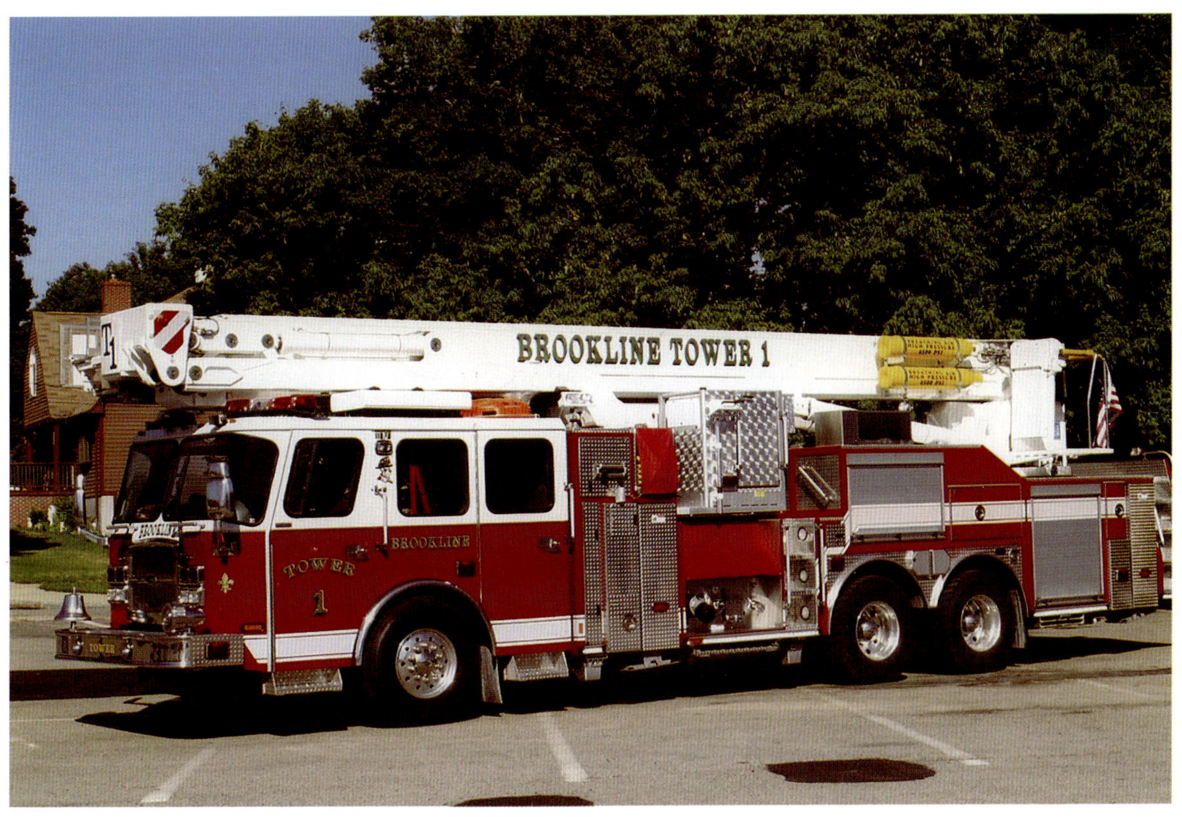

Brookline, MA Tower 1, 2007 Emergency-One/Bronto Skylift, 100 foot 2000/750.

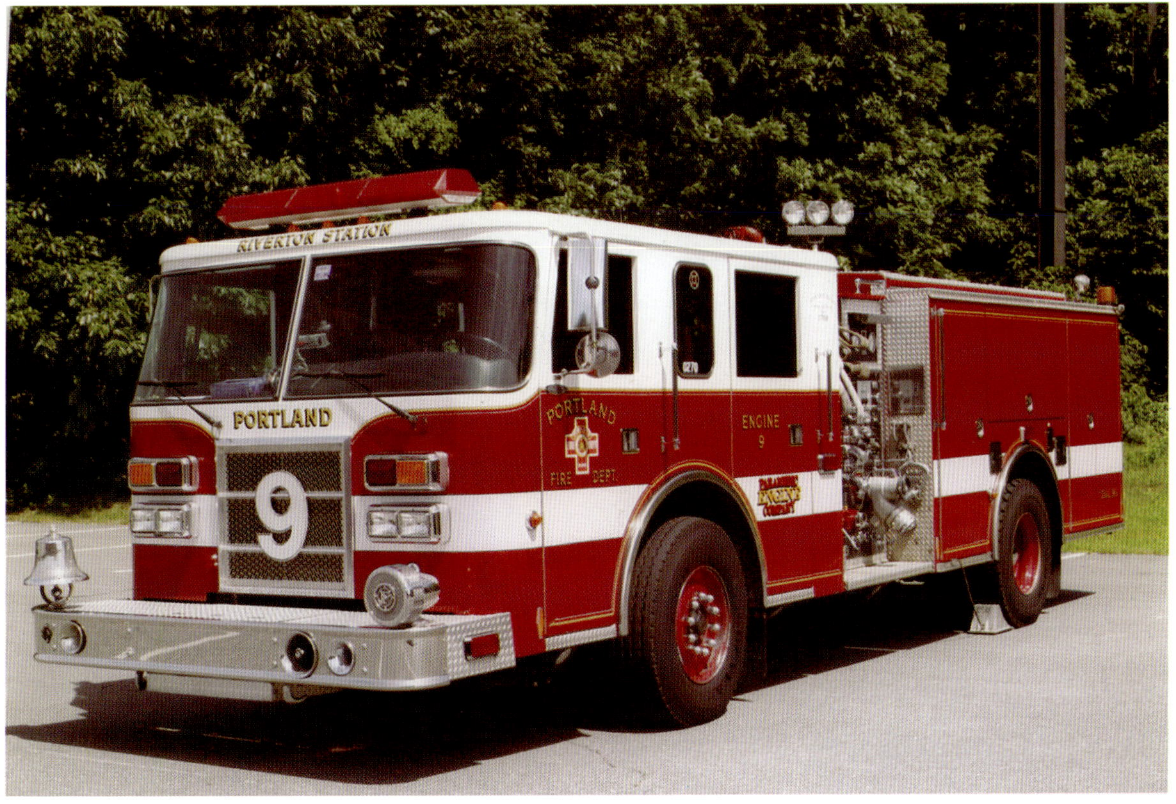

Portland, ME Engine 9, 1998 Pierce, Lance 1500/750 (Paramedic Engine Company).

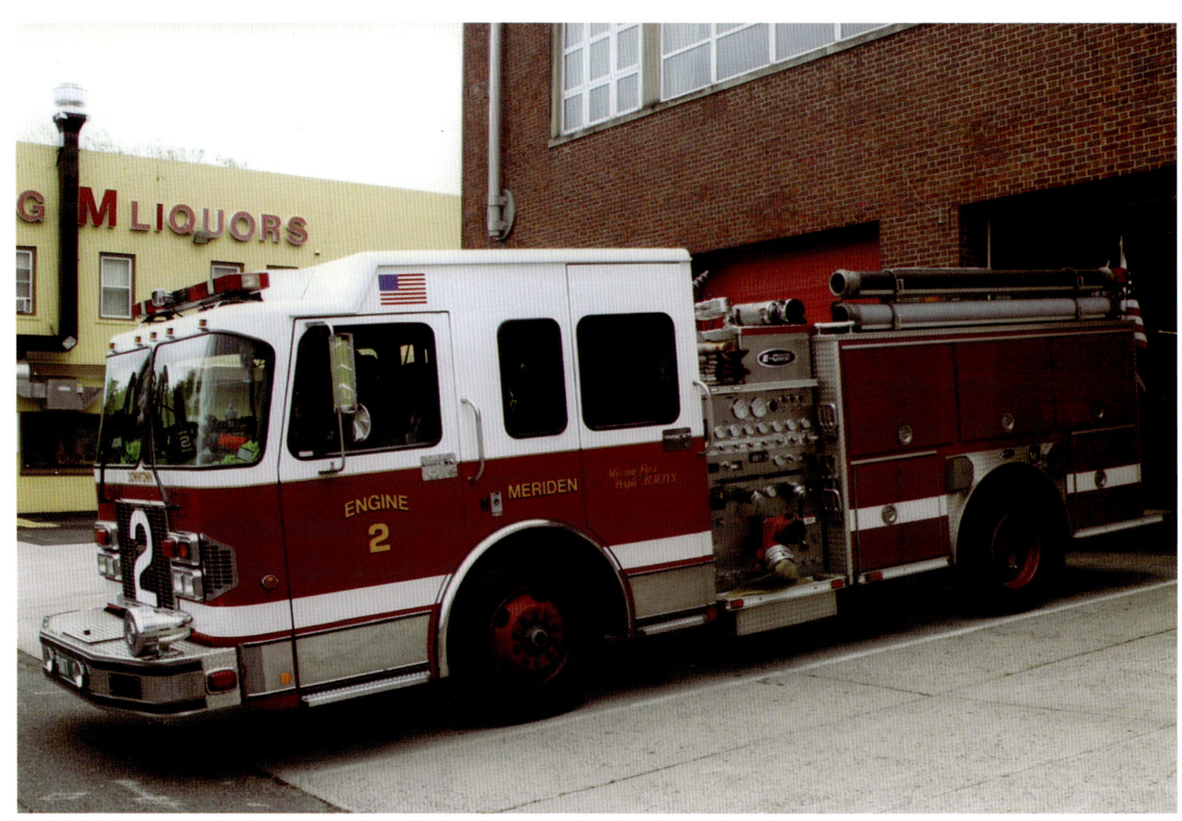

Meriden, CT Engine 2, 2001 Spartan/Emergency-One, originally built for Ocala, FL

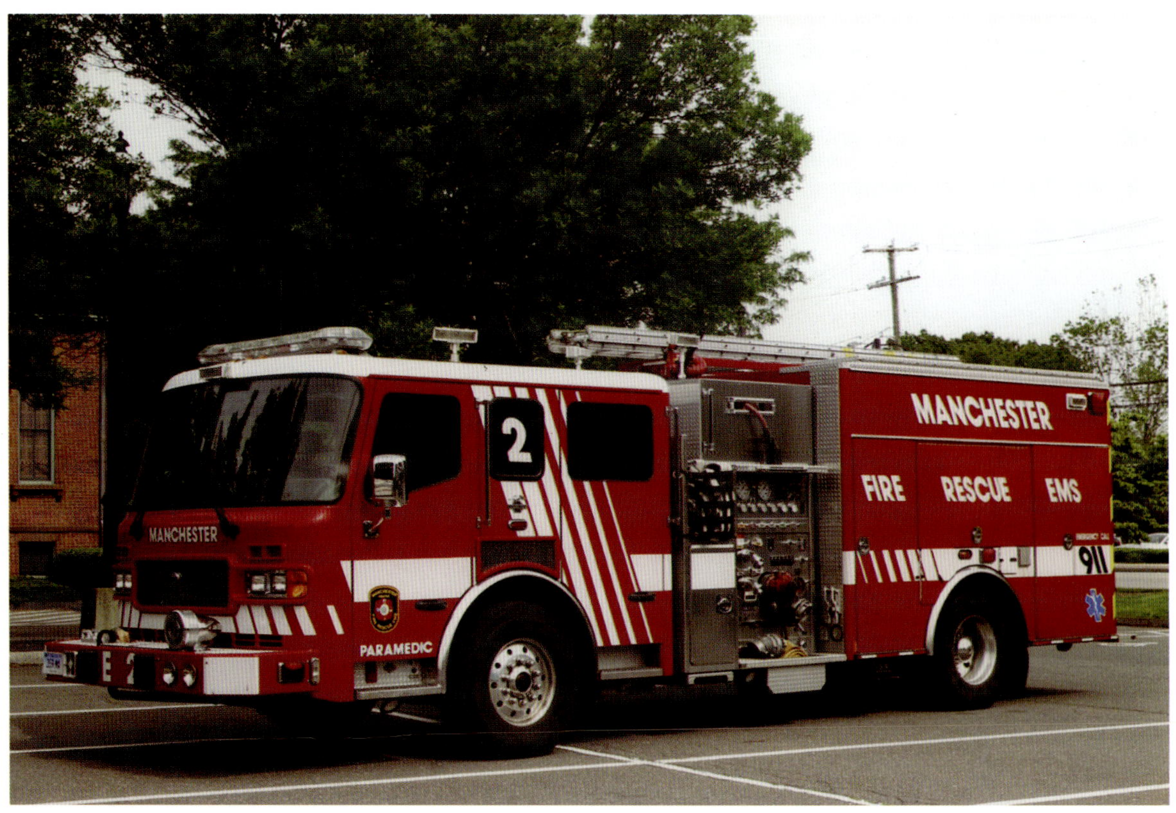

Manchester, CT Engine 2, 2006 American LaFrance 1500/750/20.

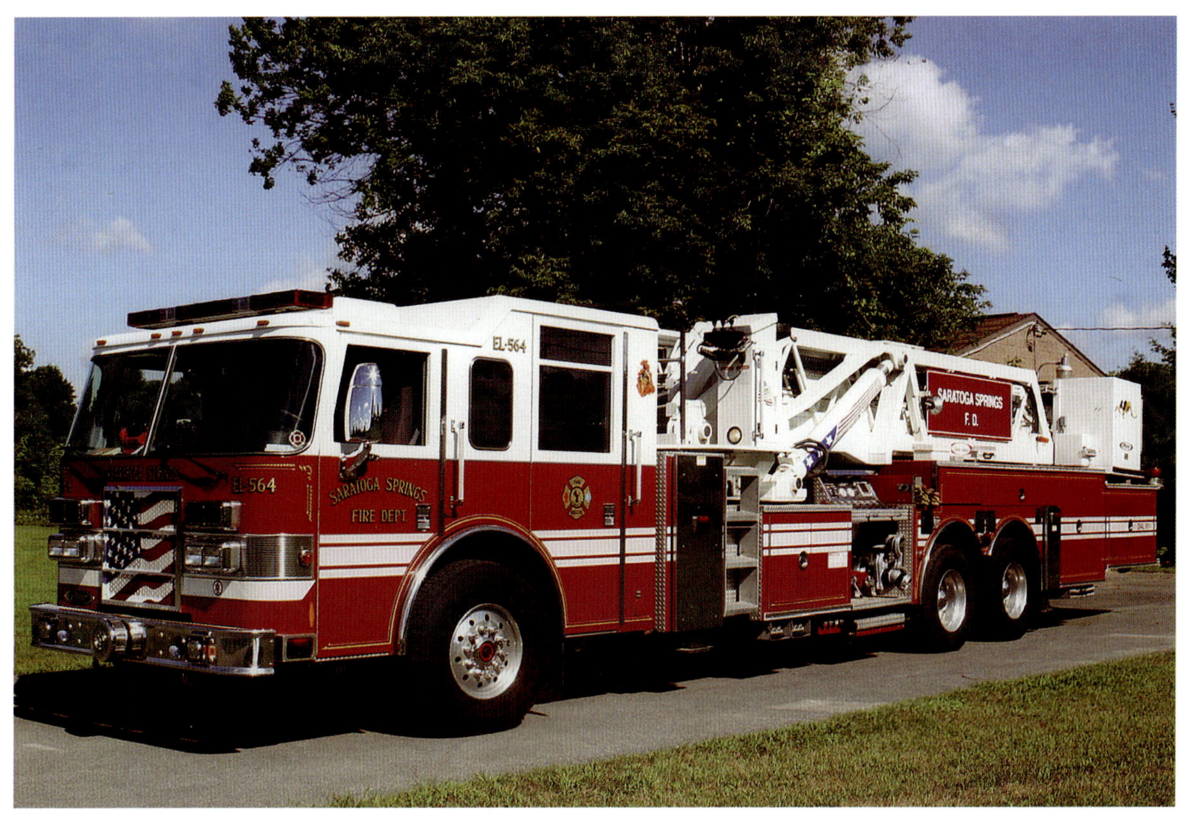

Saratoga Springs, NY 1996 Pierce 95 foot Aerial Tower, one of the first mid-mounts manufactured by Pierce.

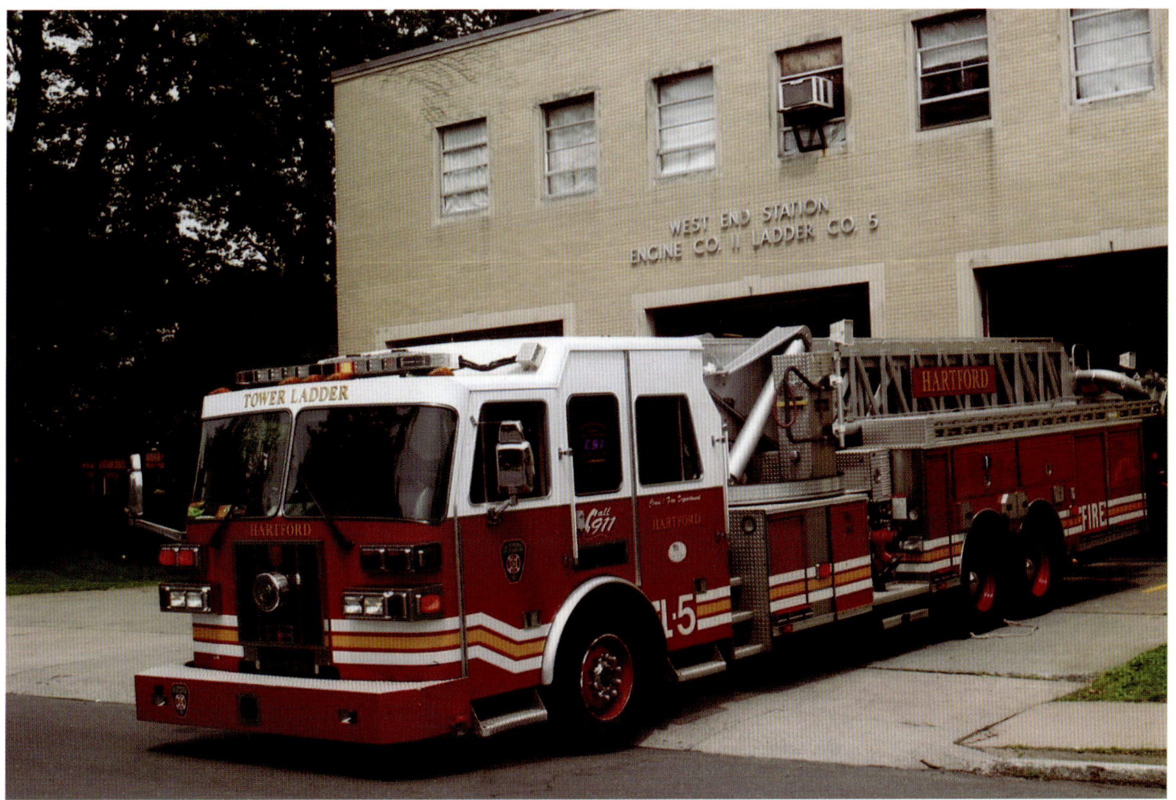

Hartford, CT TL-5, 2004 Sutphen 95 foot 1500/300. All of Hartford's five truck companies are Sutphen Aerial Towers.

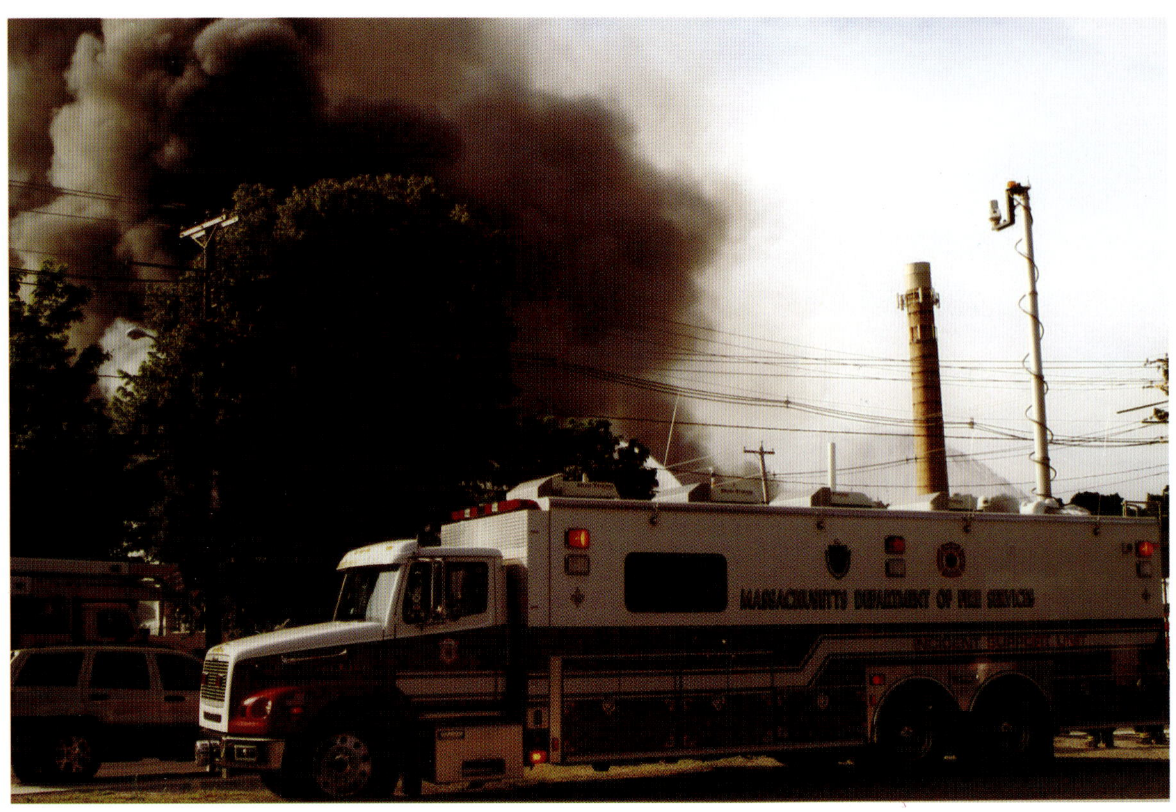

Massachusetts Department of Fire Services Command Post, 2000 Freightliner/Saulsbury.

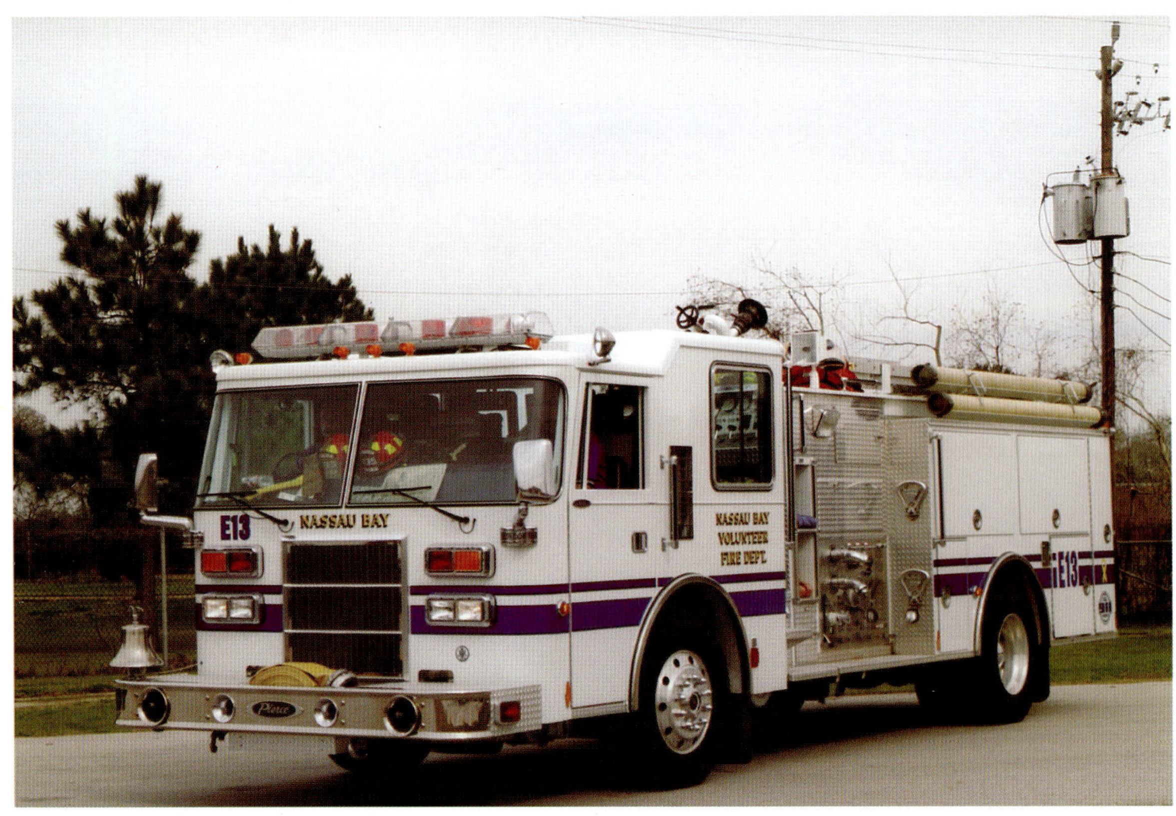

Nassau Bay, TX 1993 Pierce, Dash.

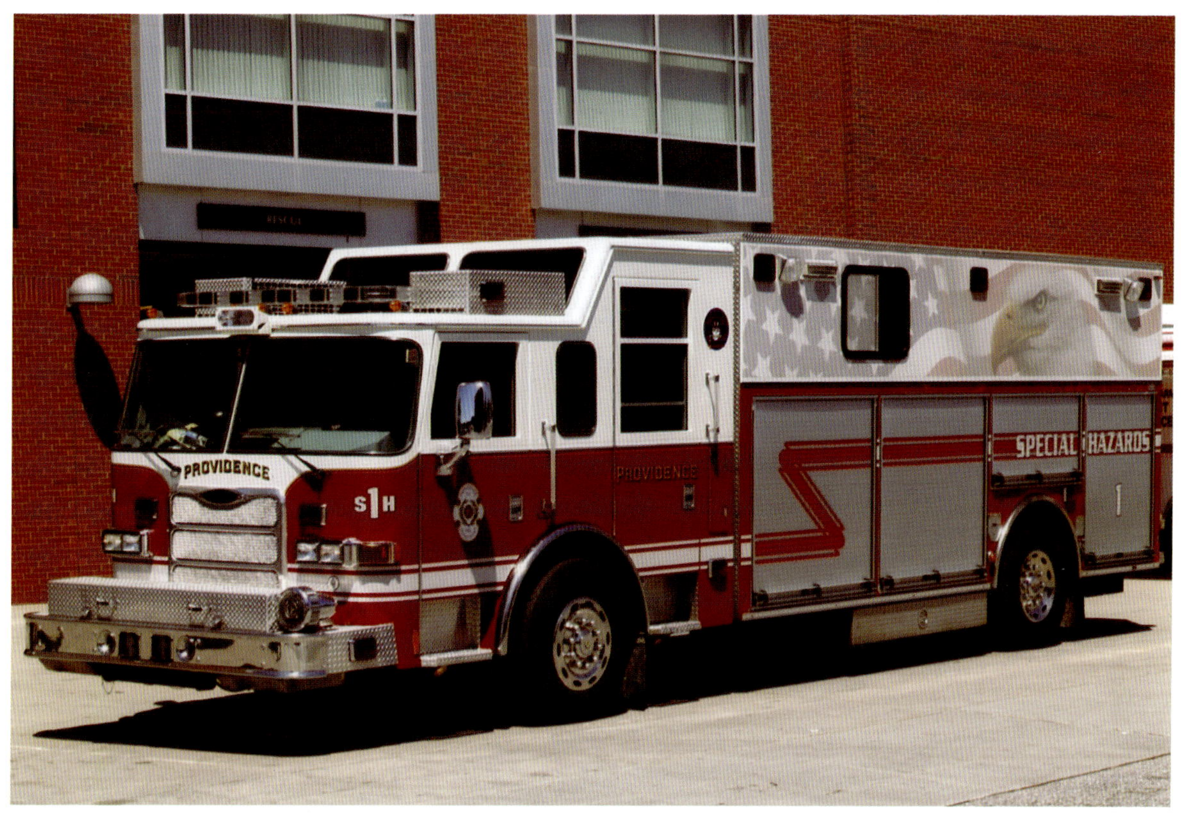

Providence, RI Special Hazards 1, 2004 Pierce, Enforcer.

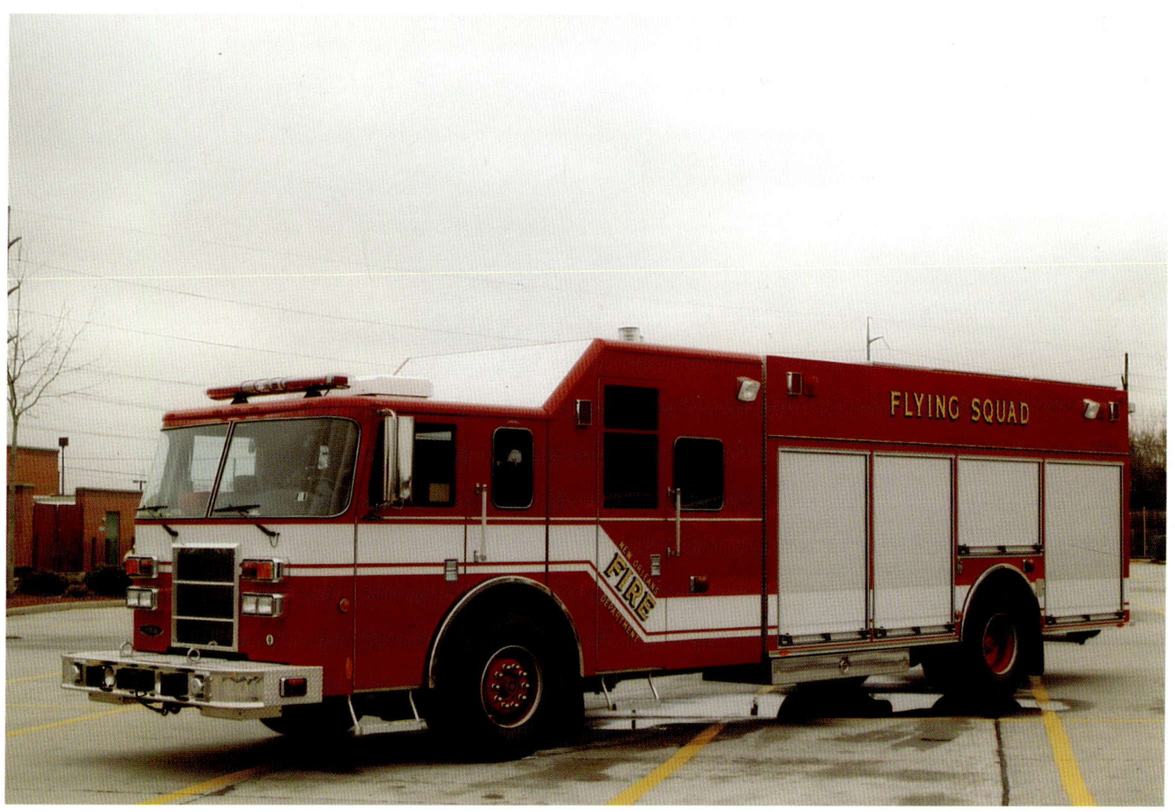

New Orleans Flying Squad, 1995 Pierce, Lance.

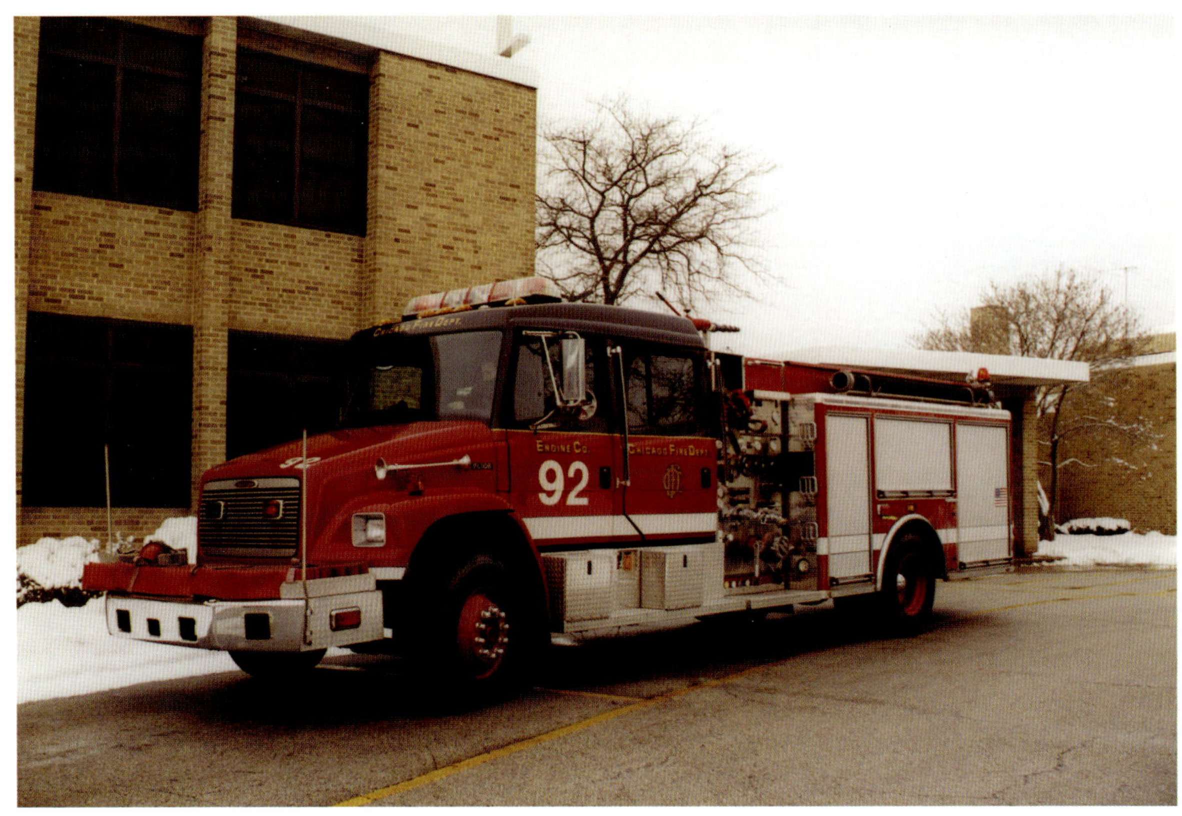

Chicago Engine 92, 2000 Freightliner/3D/American LaFrance, 1500/500. One of a kind for Chicago, a demonstrator purchased on an emergency basis.

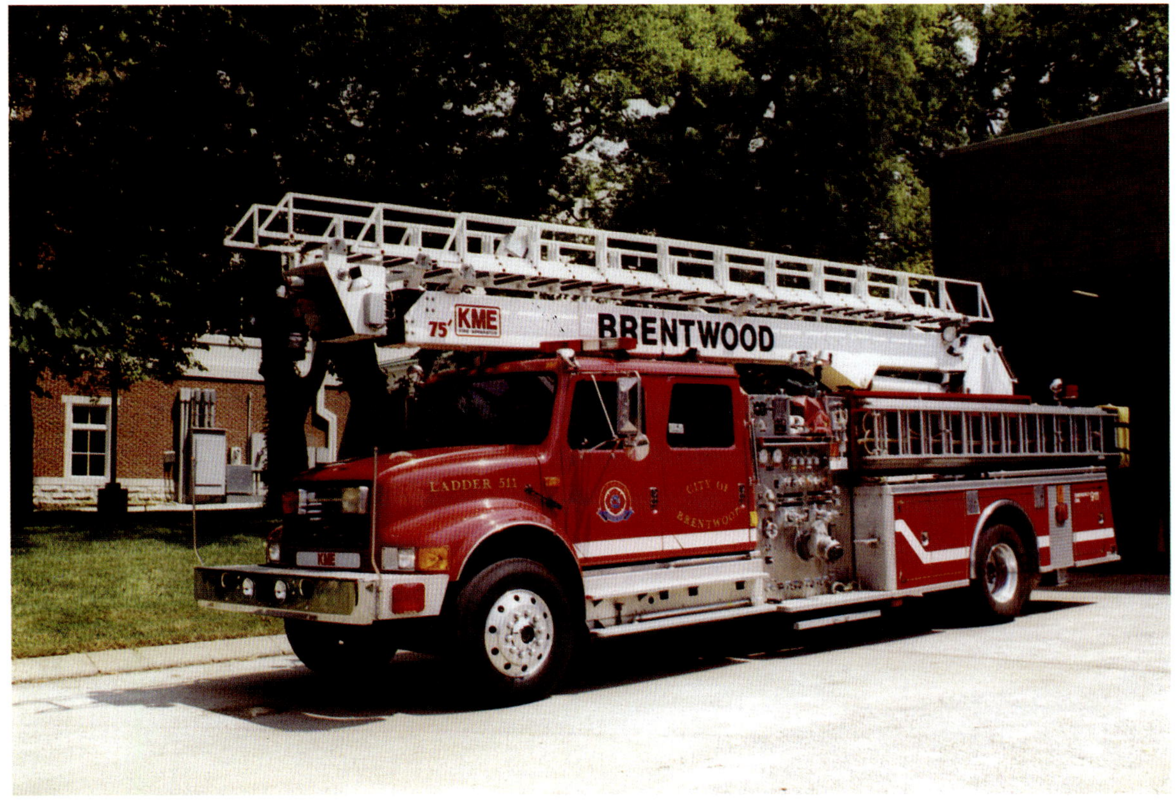

Brentwood, TN Ladder 511 International/KME 75 foot.

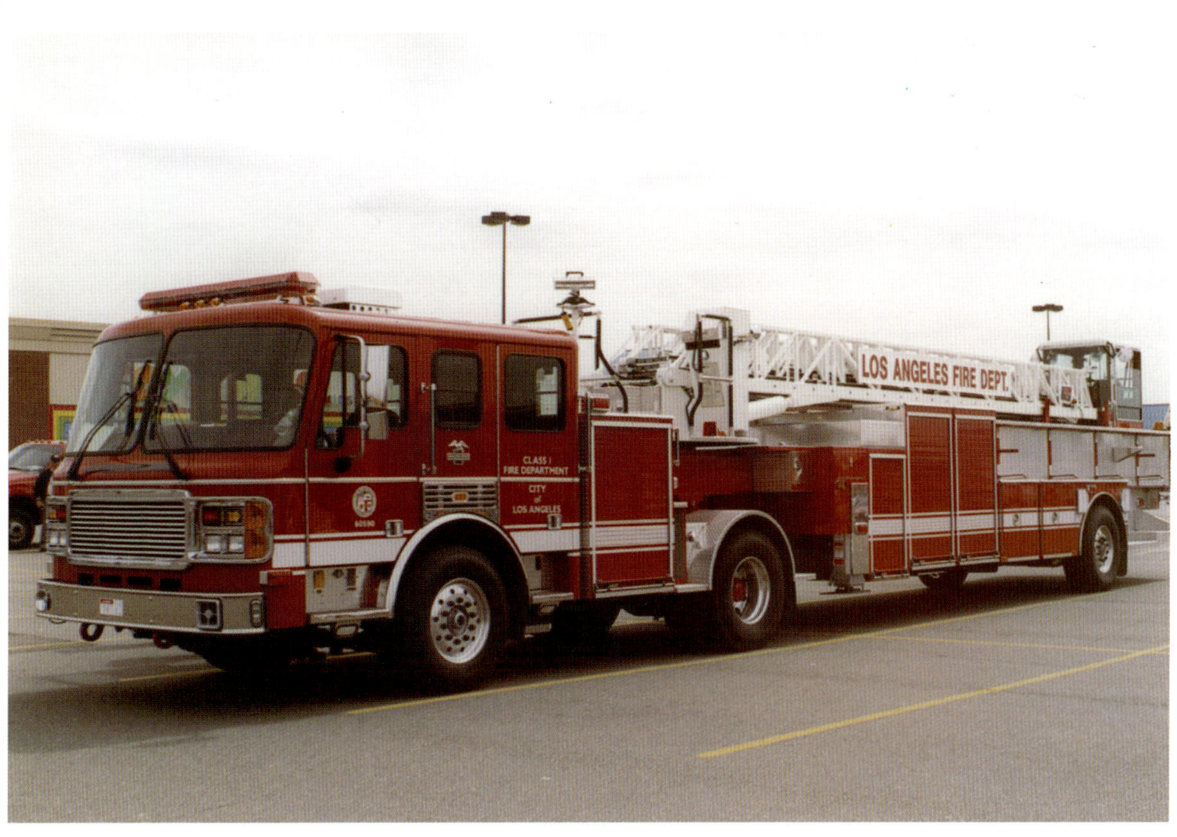

Los Angeles City Truck 60, 2003 American LaFrance 100 foot Tiller.

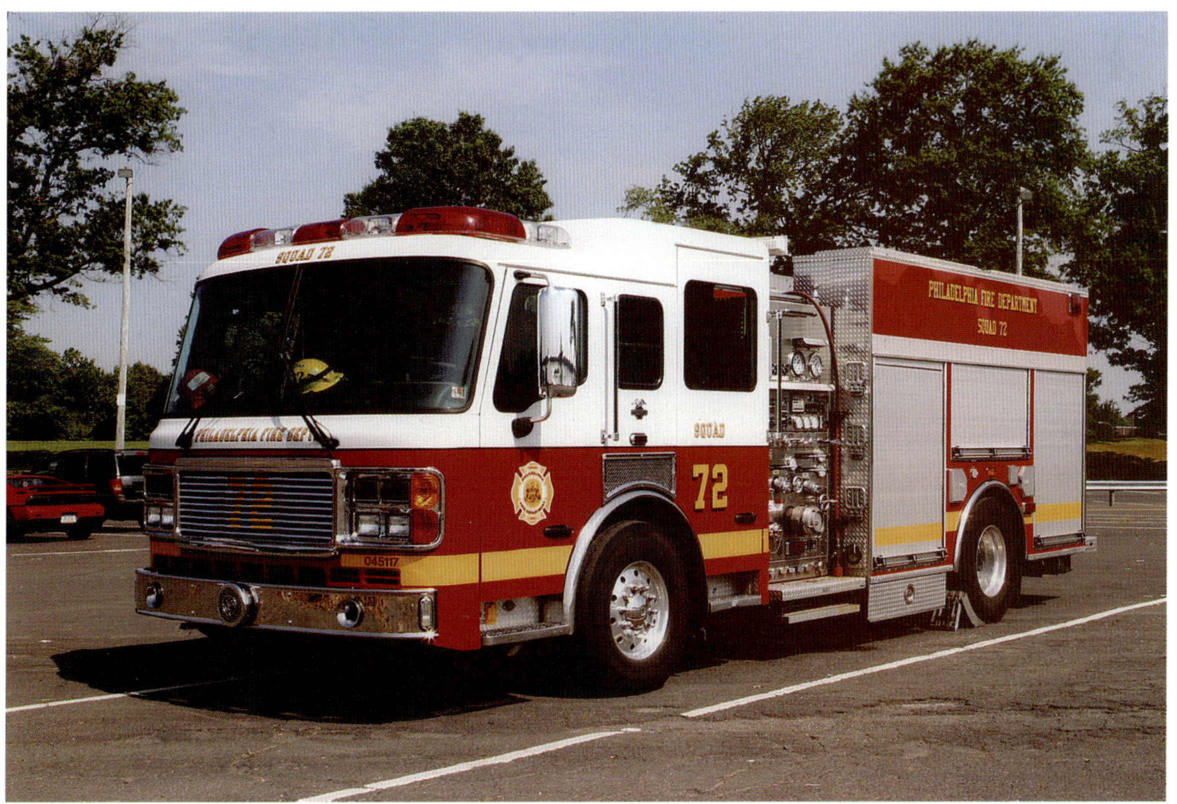

Philadelphia Squad 72, 2004 American LaFrance, Eagle, Rescue Pumper. Shortly after this photo was taken, it was wrecked in a traffic accident.

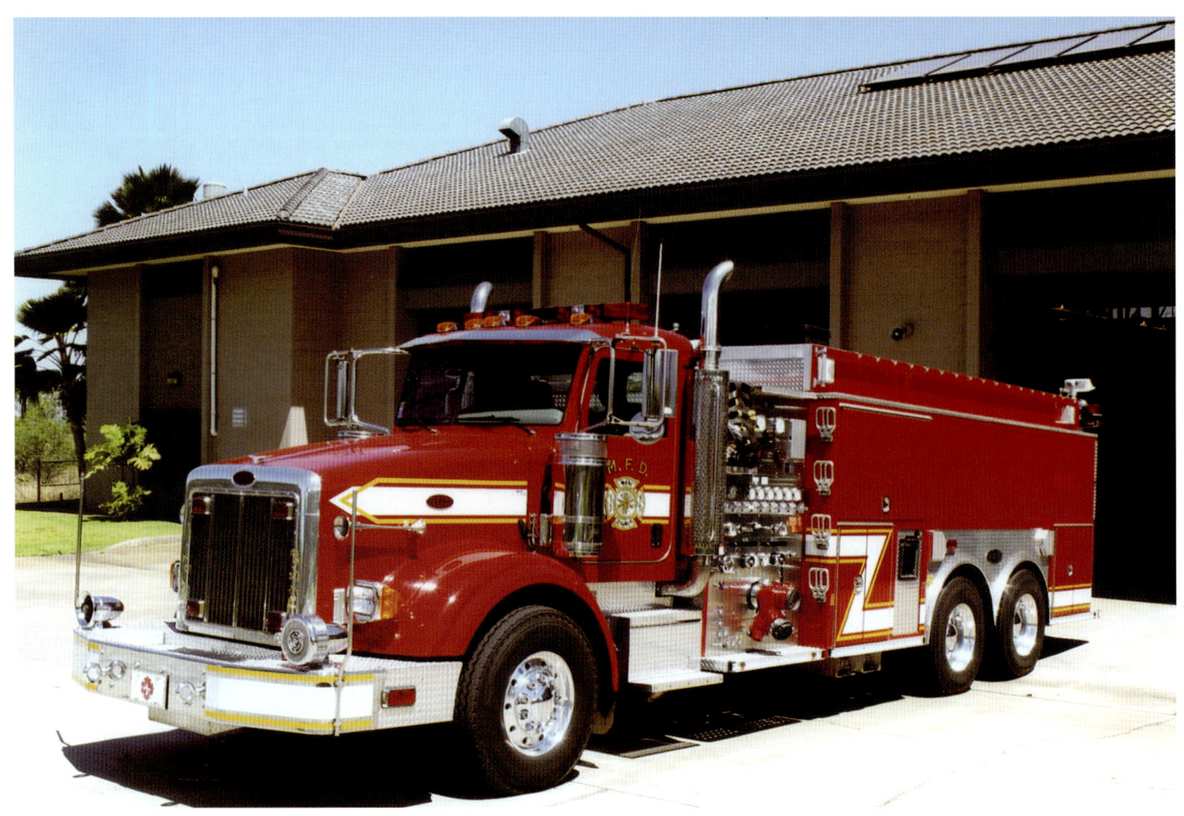

Maui, Hawaii (Wailea Station) Tanker 14, 1999 Emergency-One on a 2006 Peterbilt Chassis, 1500/2500. One of only two red apparatus on the Island.

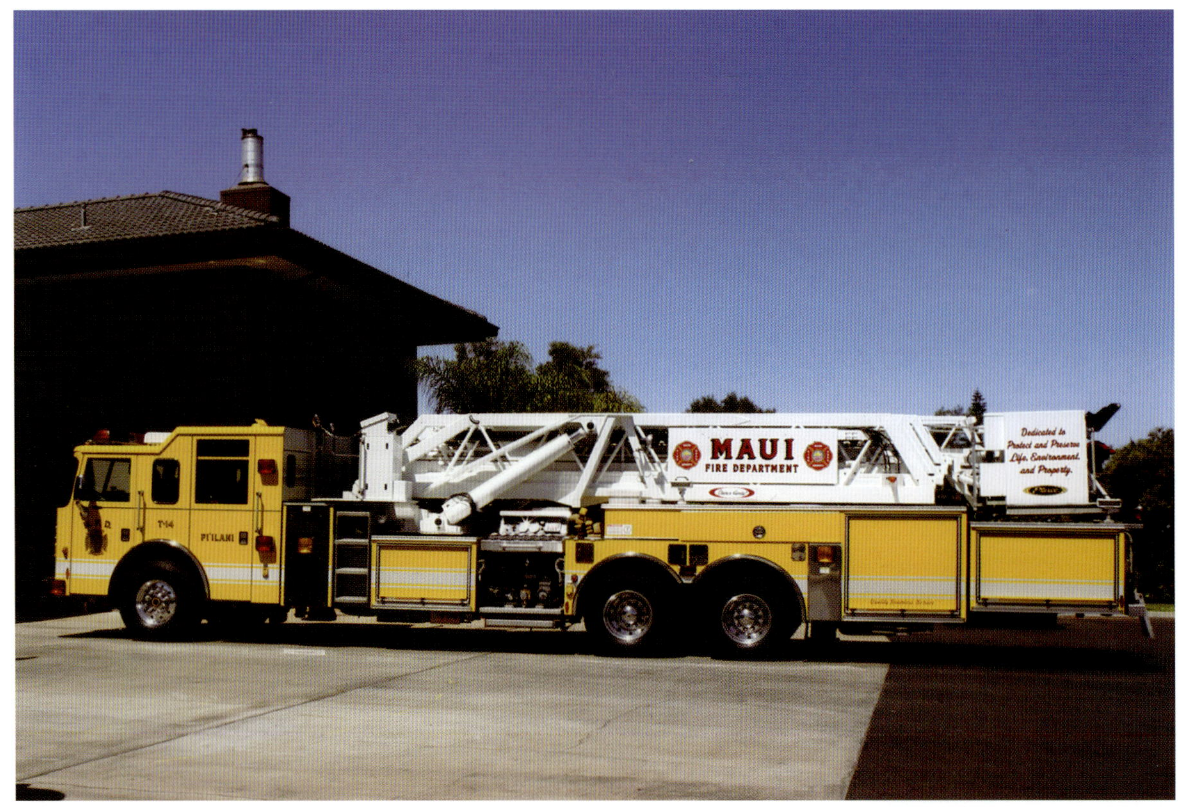

Maui, Hawaii Tower 14, 2002 Pierce, Dash, 95 foot 2000/300.

TILLERS

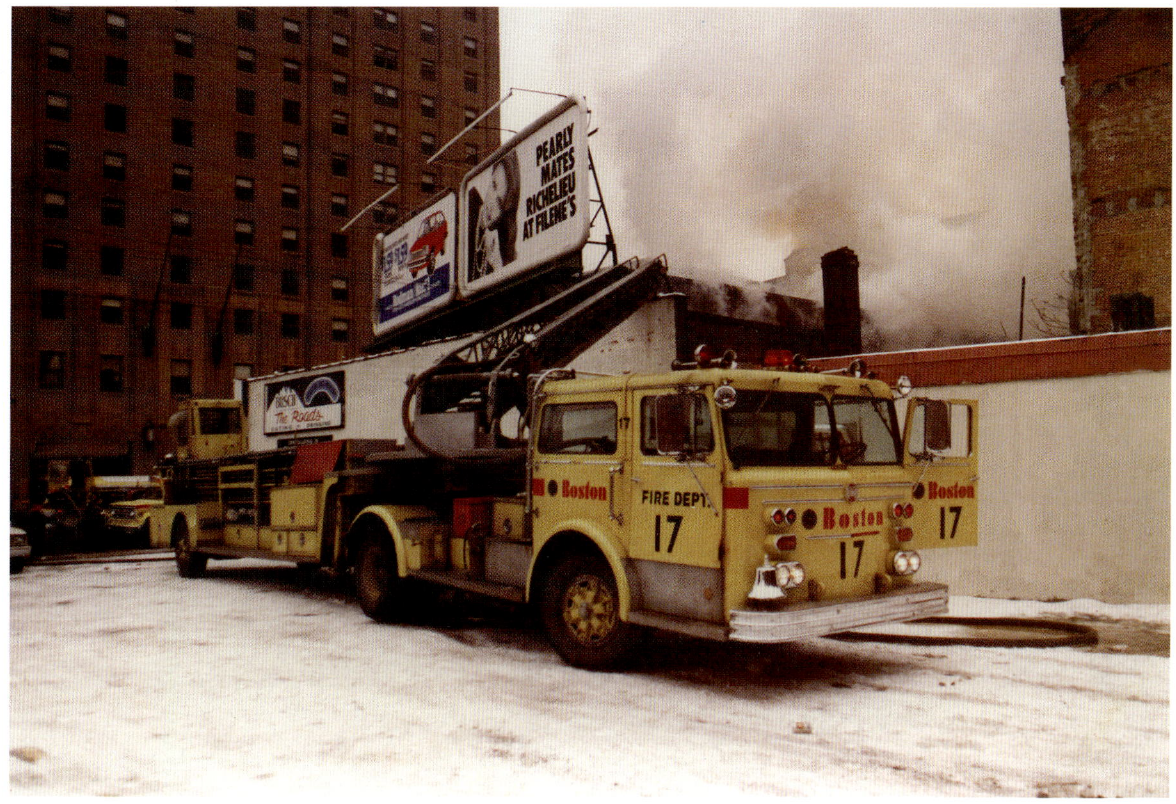

Boston Ladder 17, 1971 Maxim "F" Model (delivered red).

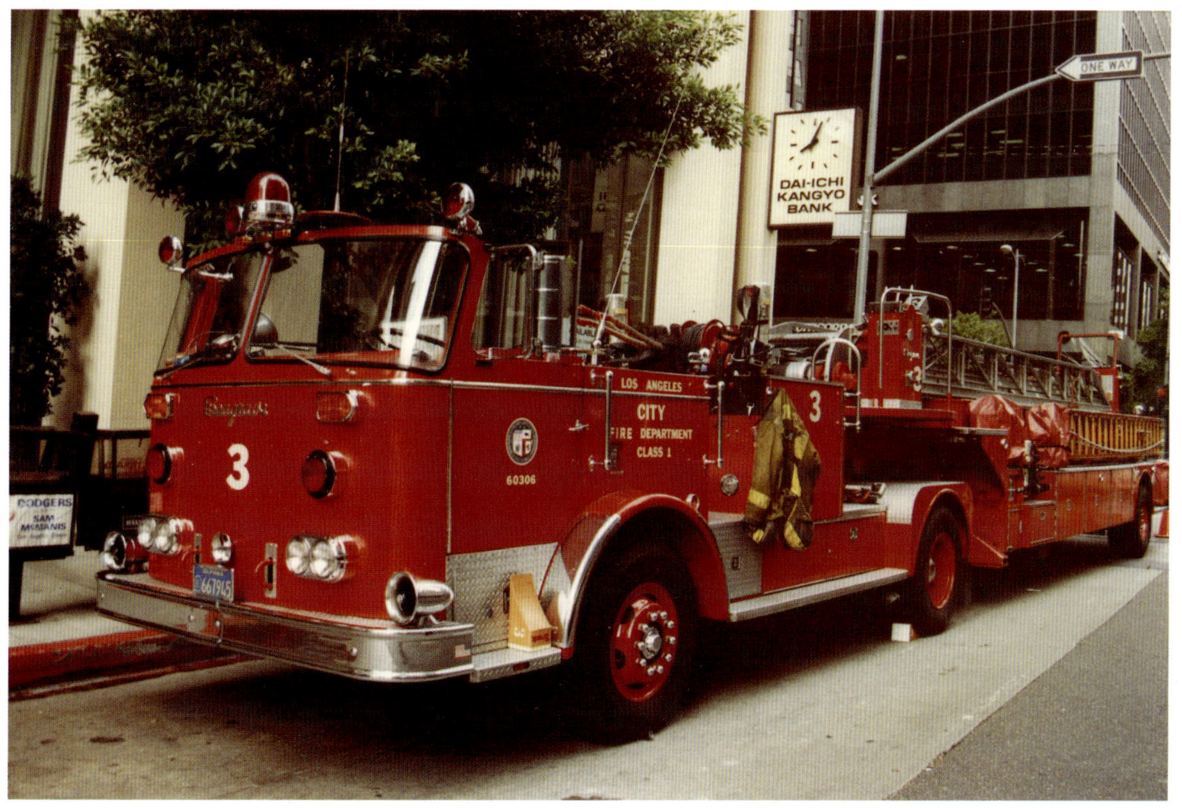

Los Angeles City Ladder 3, 1975 Seagrave.

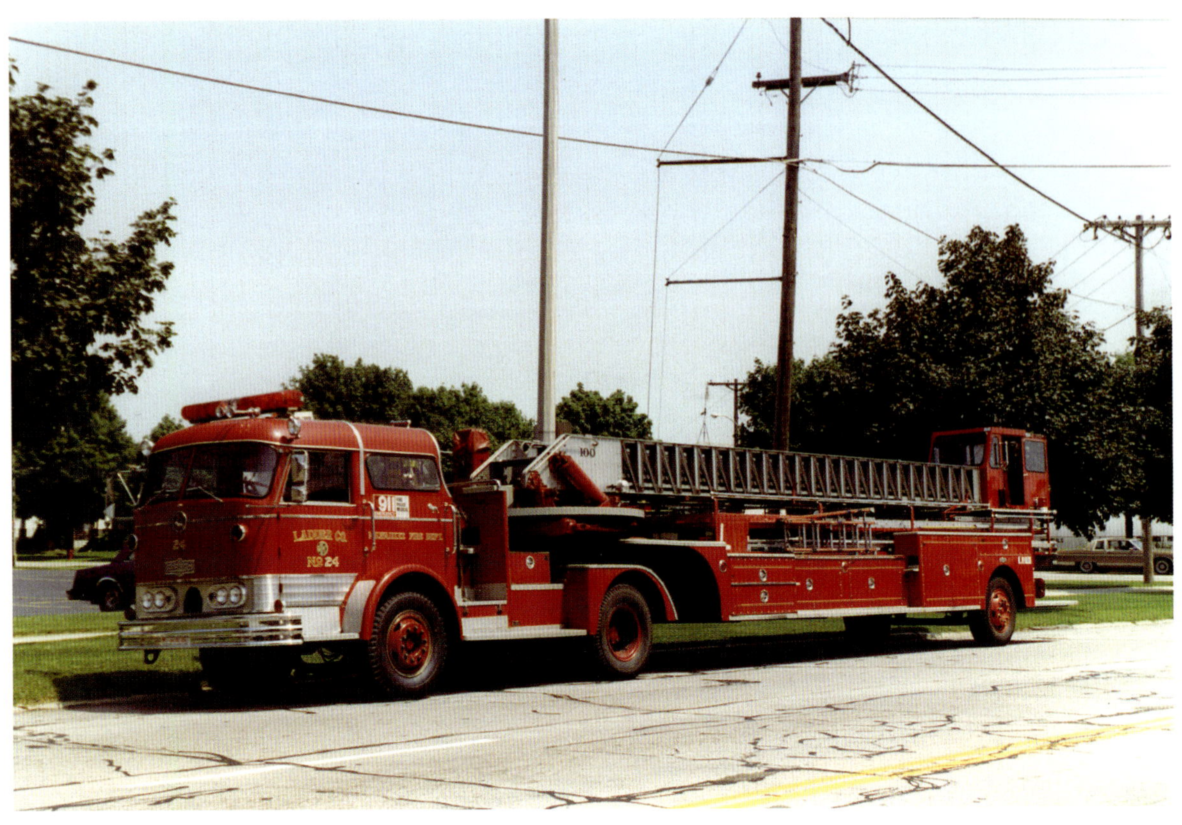

Milwaukee Reserve Ladder 24, 1965 Mack/Pirsch.

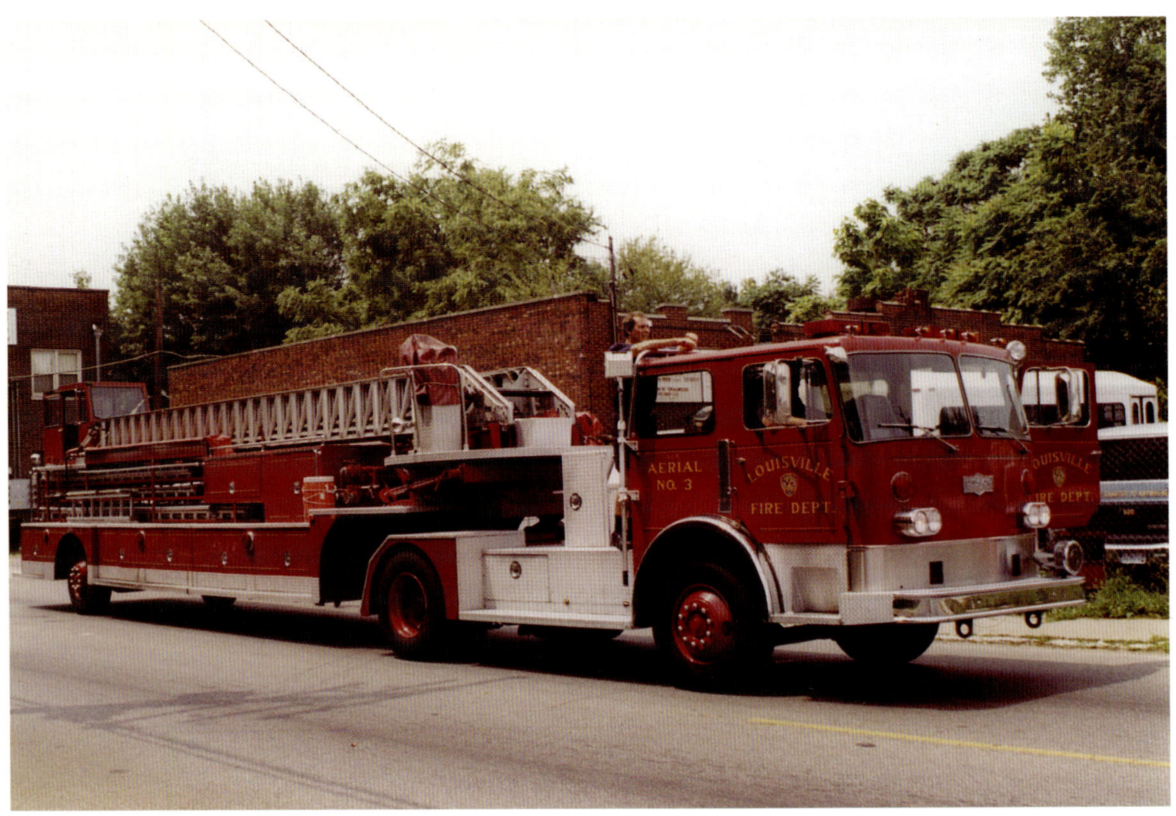

Louisville, KY Aerial 3, 1983 Pirsch.

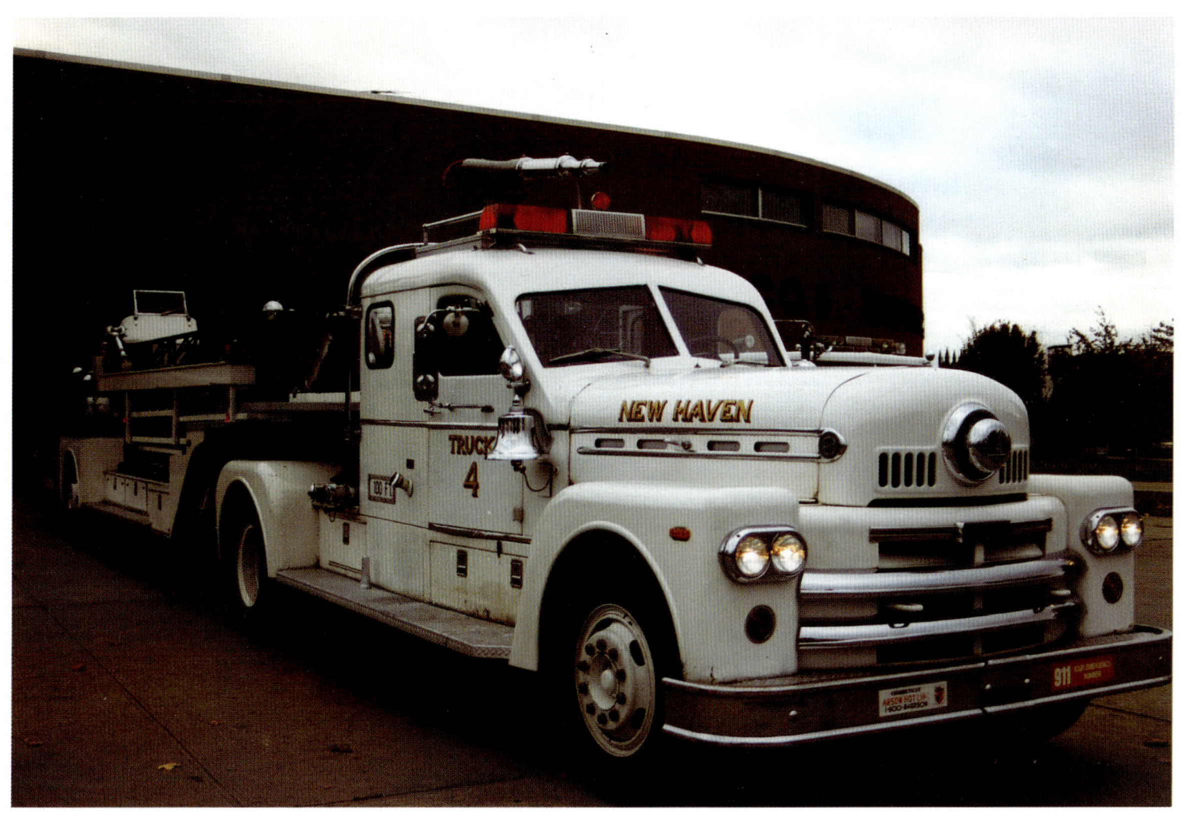

New Haven, CT Truck 4, 1961 Seagrave, with roof gun.

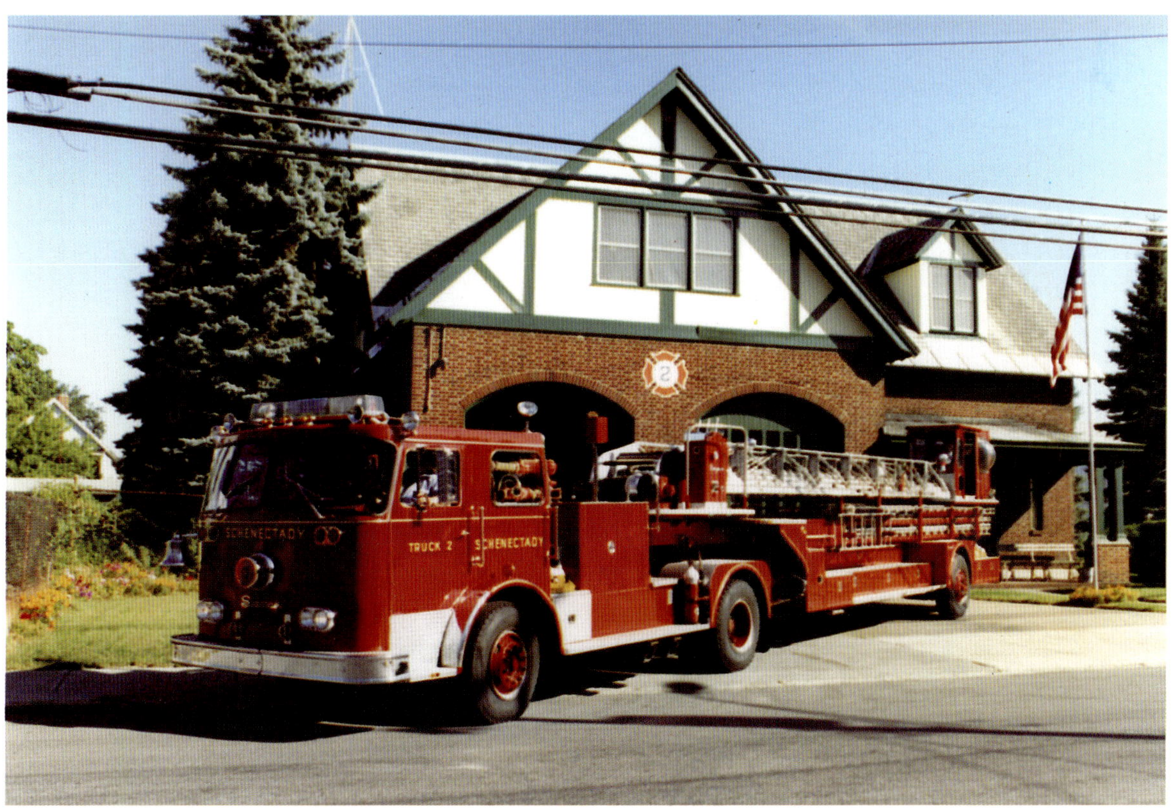

Schenectady, NY Truck 2, 1979 Seagrave.

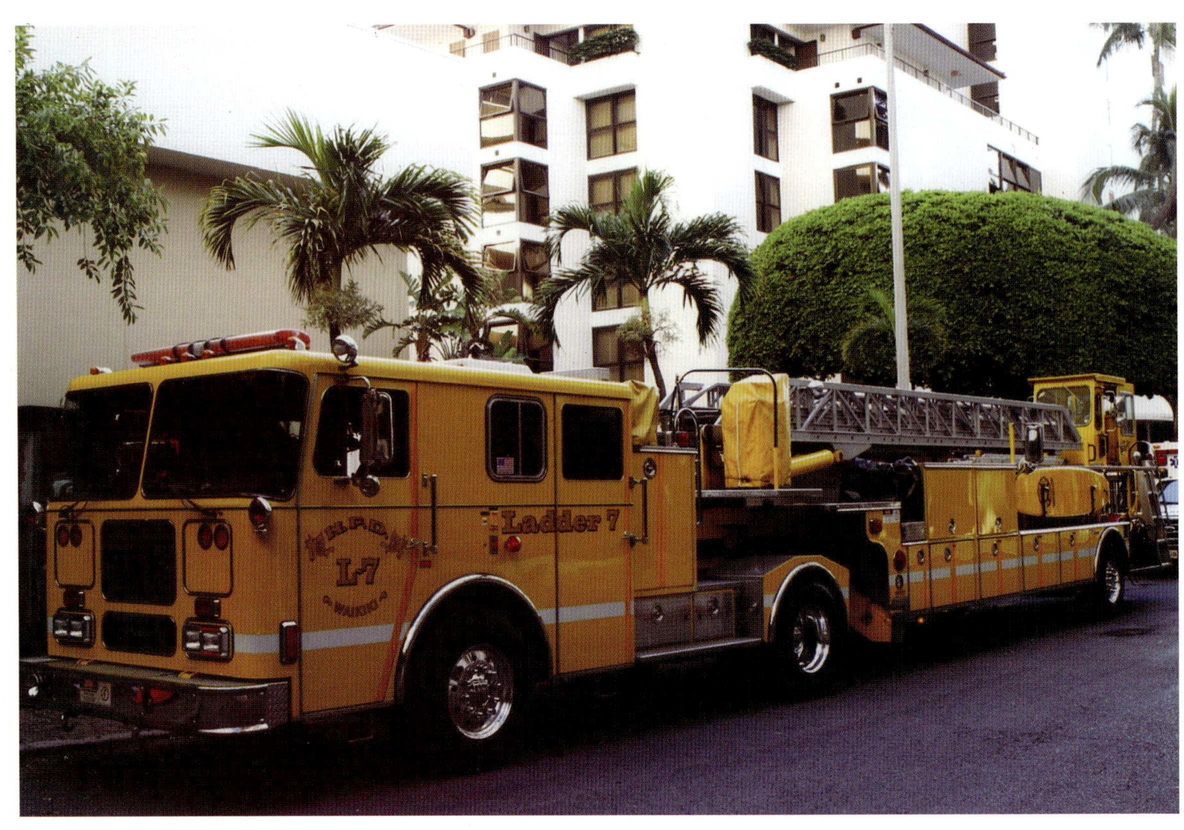

Honolulu Ladder 7, 2004 Seagrave, with surf board.

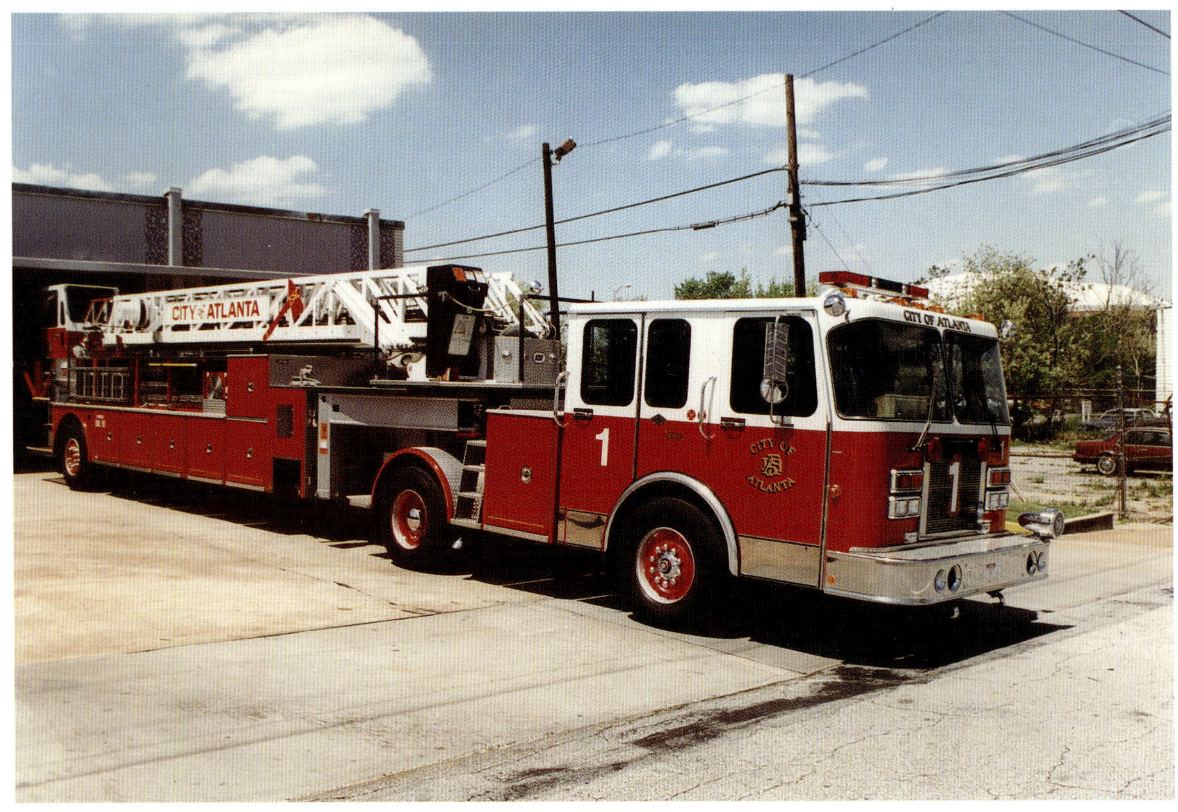

Atlanta Truck 1, 1990 Spartan/LTI . Now Truck 6 in Hilton Head, SC.

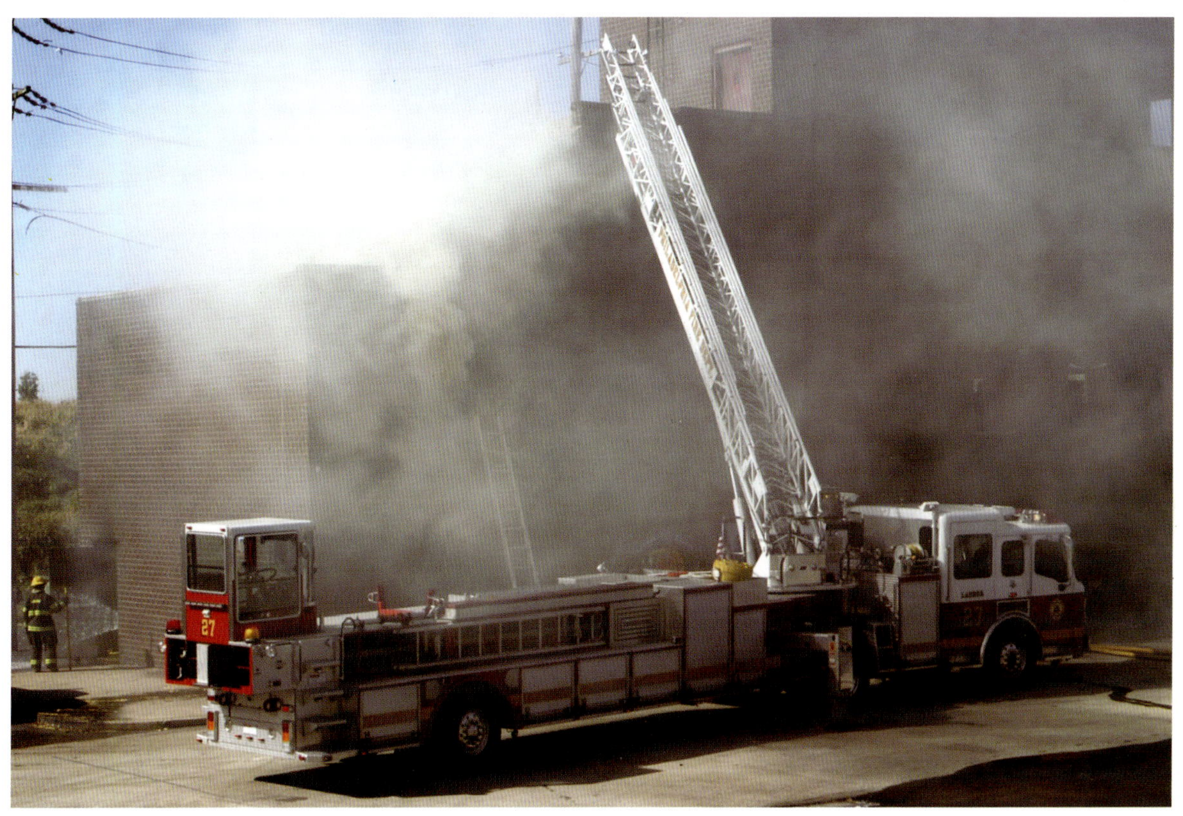

Philadelphia Ladder 27, 2005 American La France.

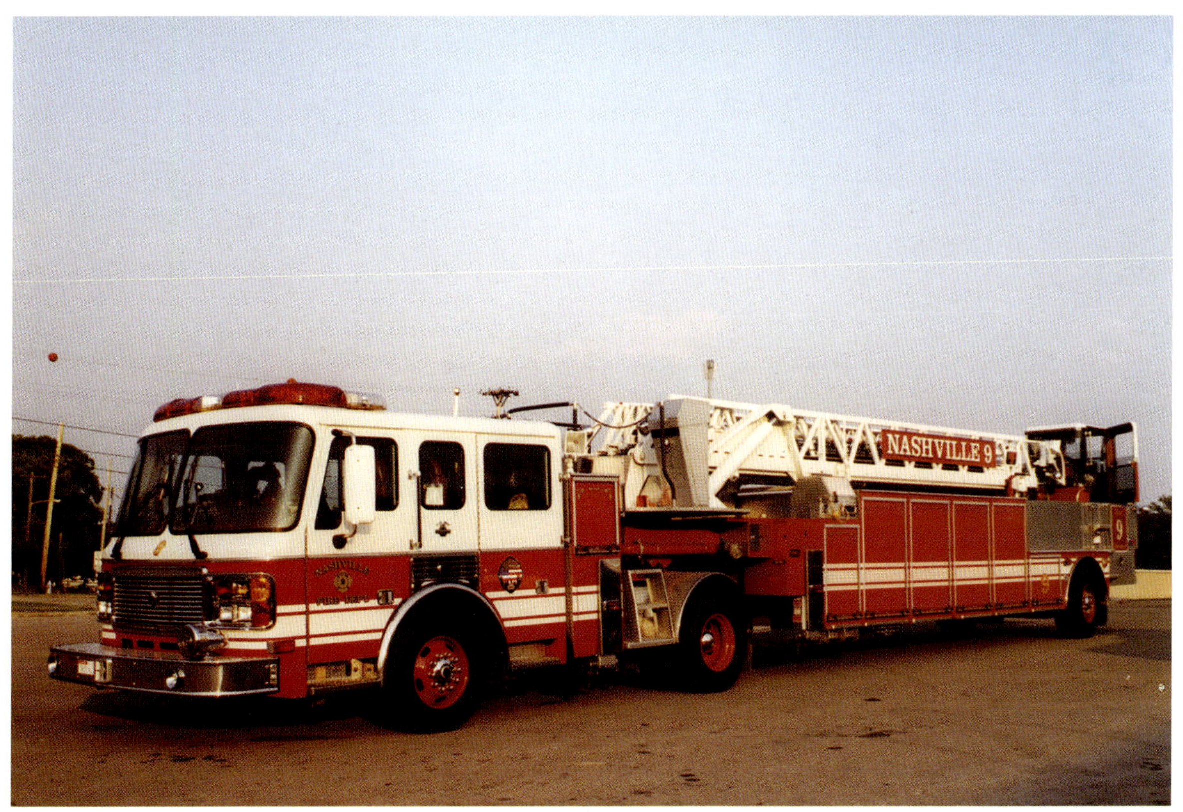

Nashville Ladder 9, 2002 American LaFrance

SECOND CAREER APPARATUS

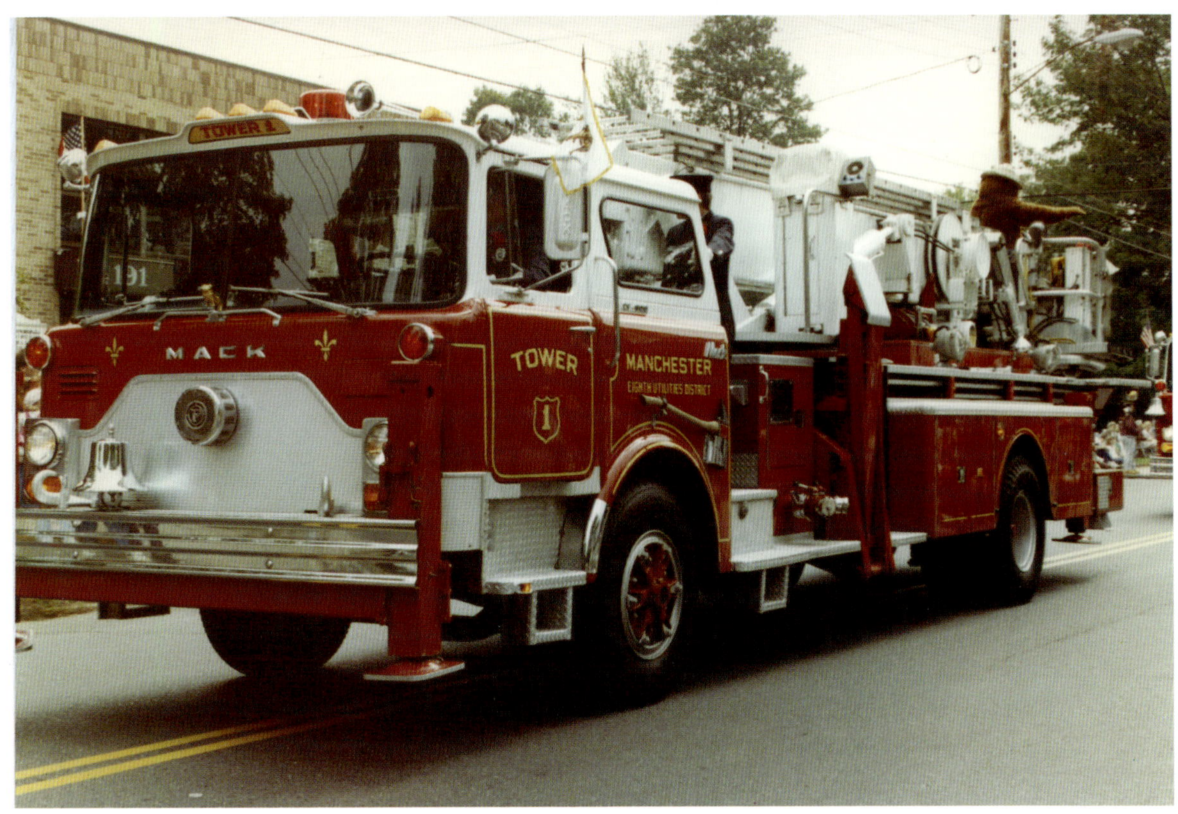

Manchester, CT, Tower 1, 1978 Mack/Baker, 75 foot Tower.

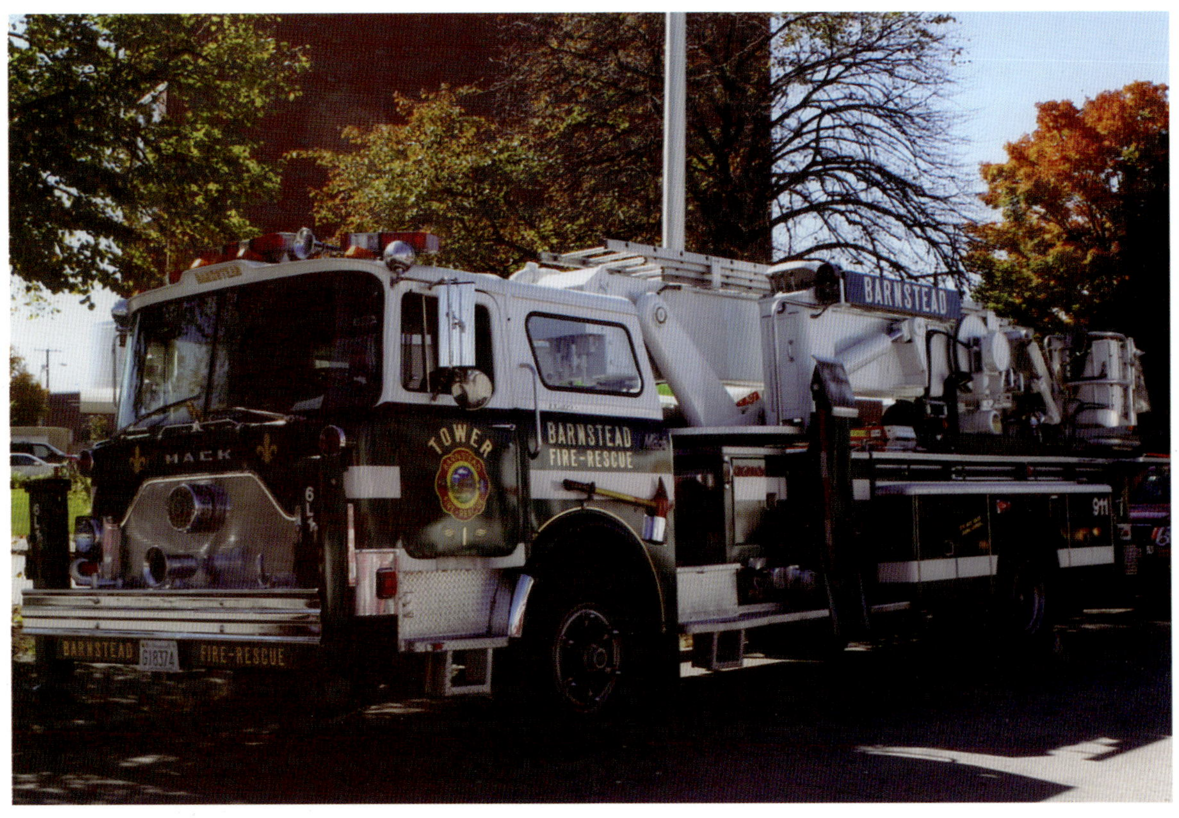

Refurbished and purchased in 2007 by Barnstead, NH.

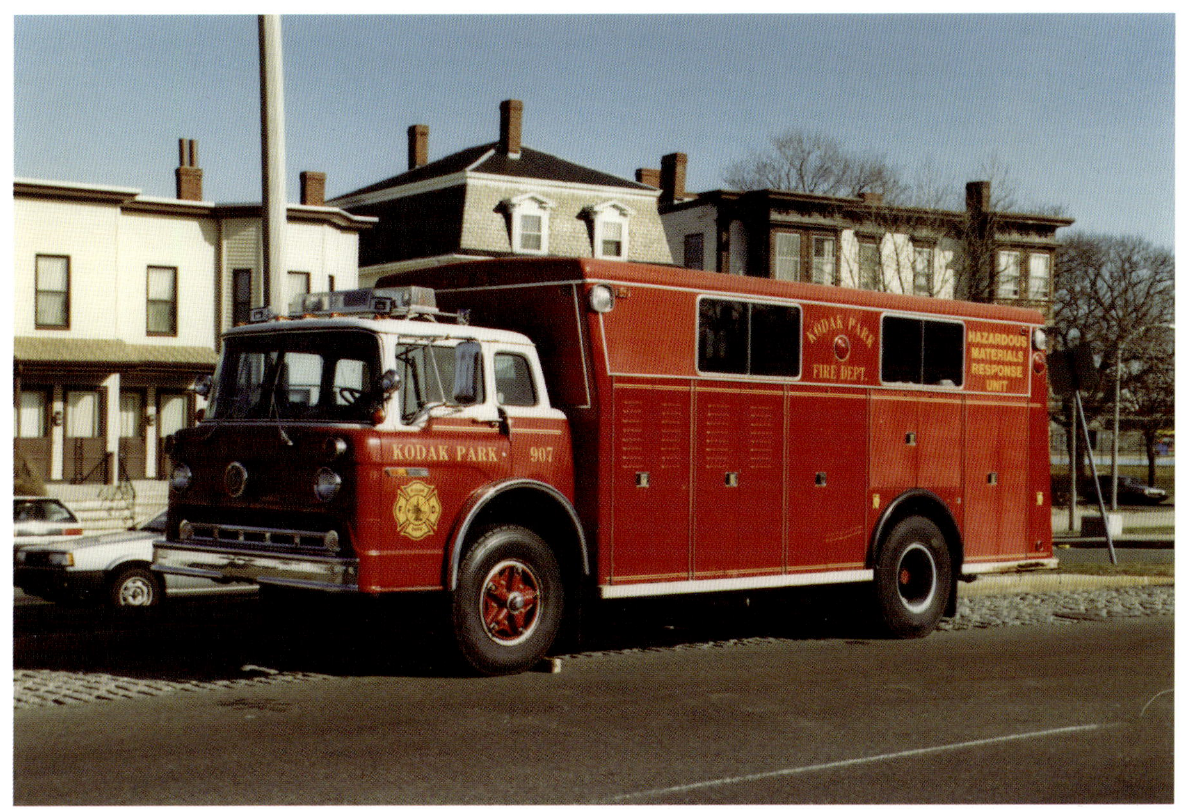

Kodak Park, (Rochester), NY, Hazmat, 1974 Ford C-75/Welch fire equipment.

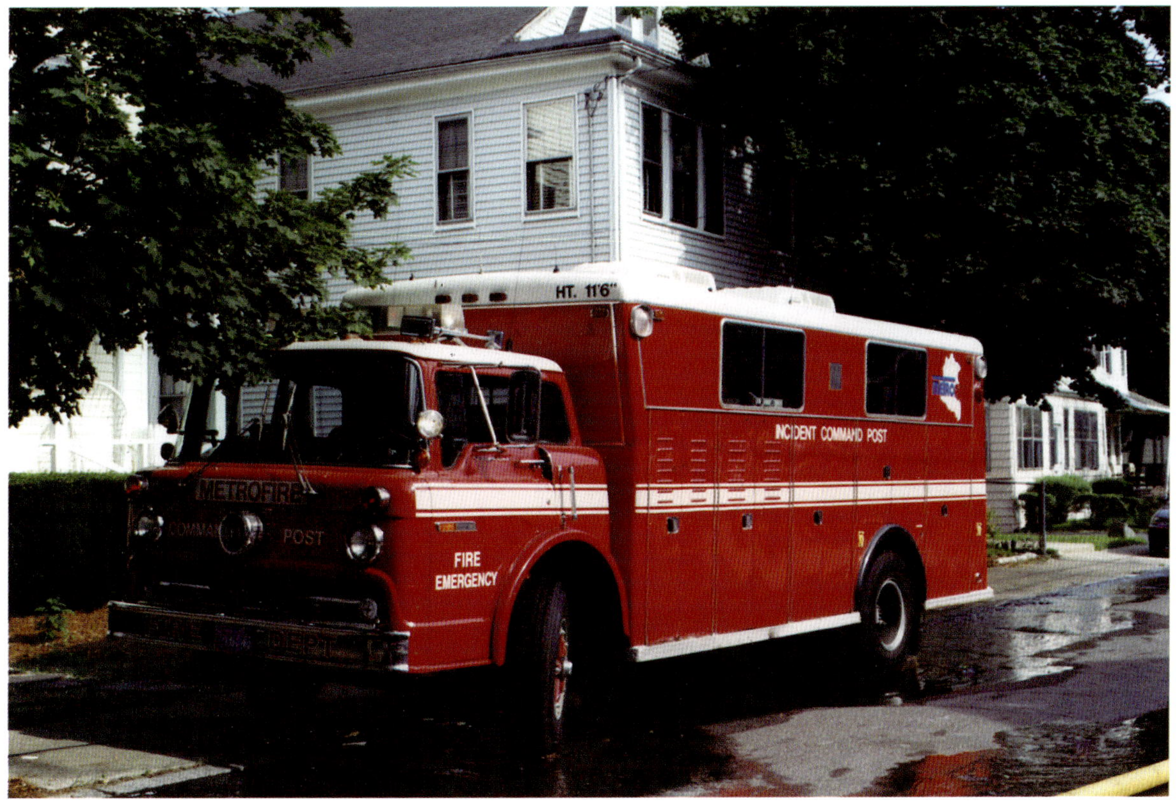

Massachusetts Metro-Fire Command Post, was it's second career.

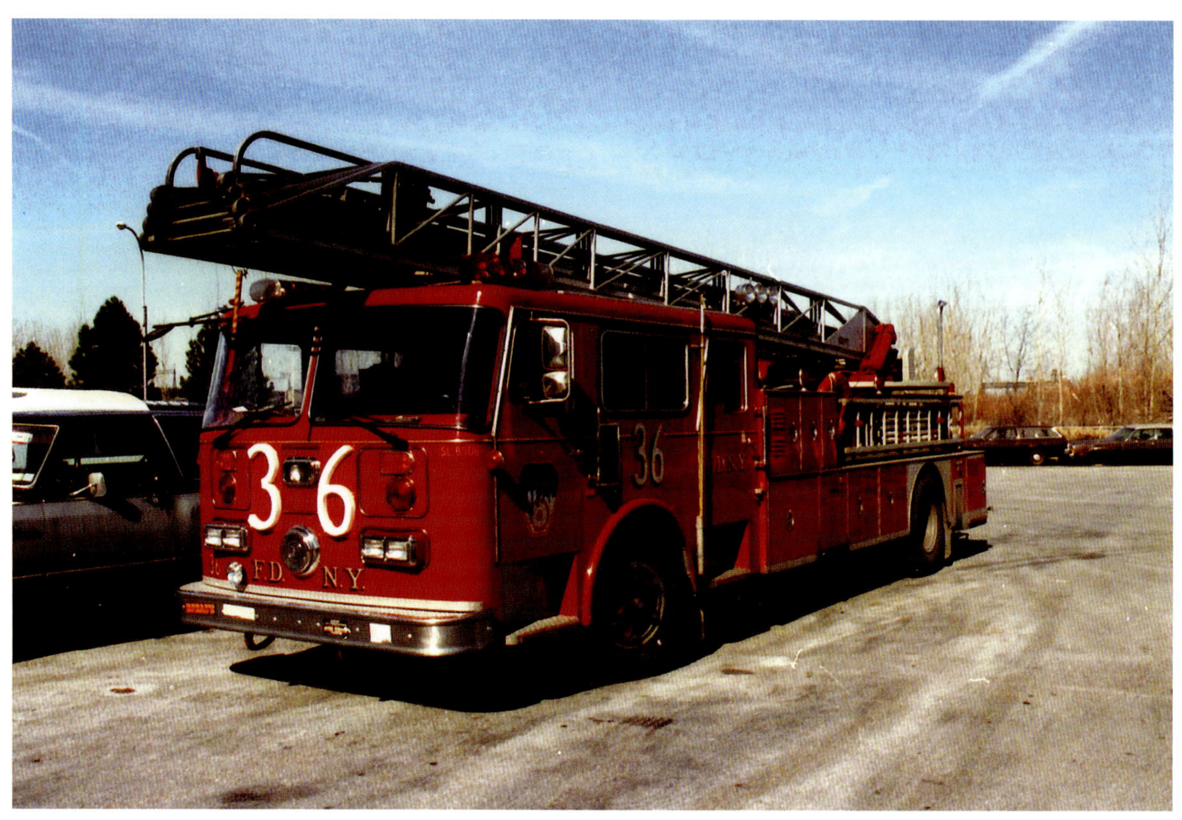

FDNY Ladder 36, 1985 Seagrave.

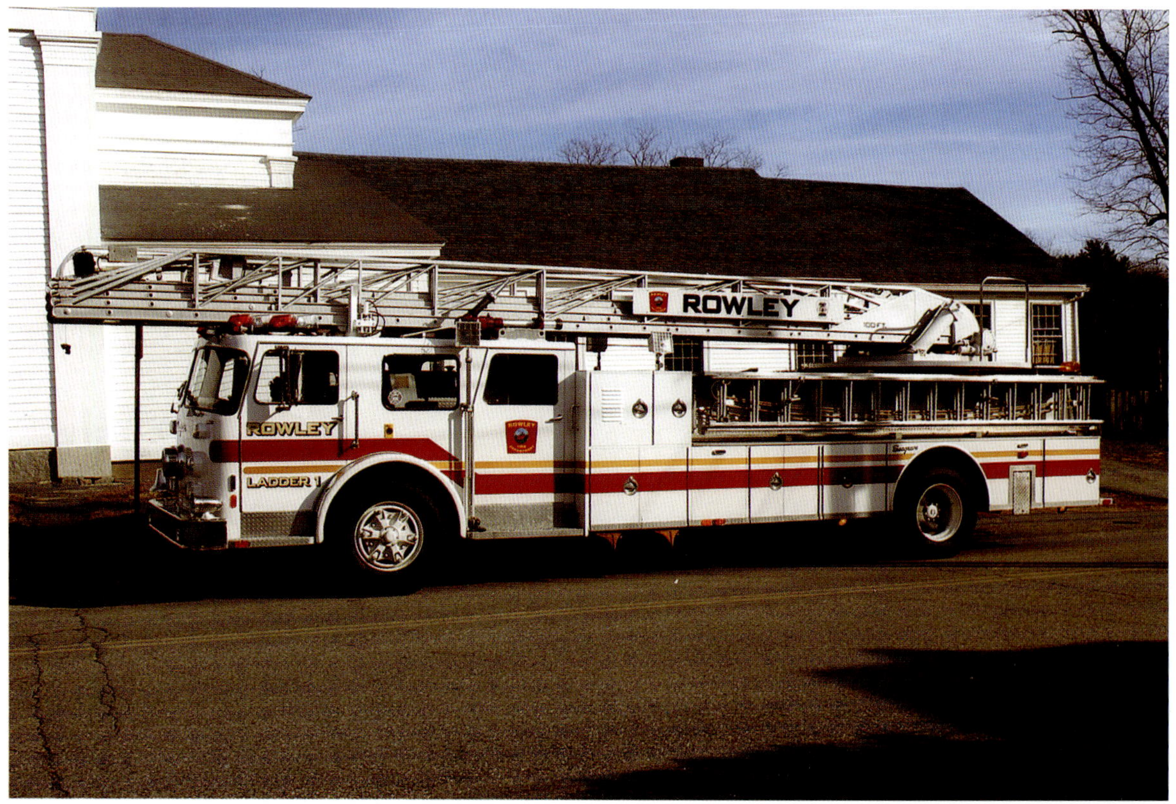

Completely rebuilt and sold to Rowley, MA.

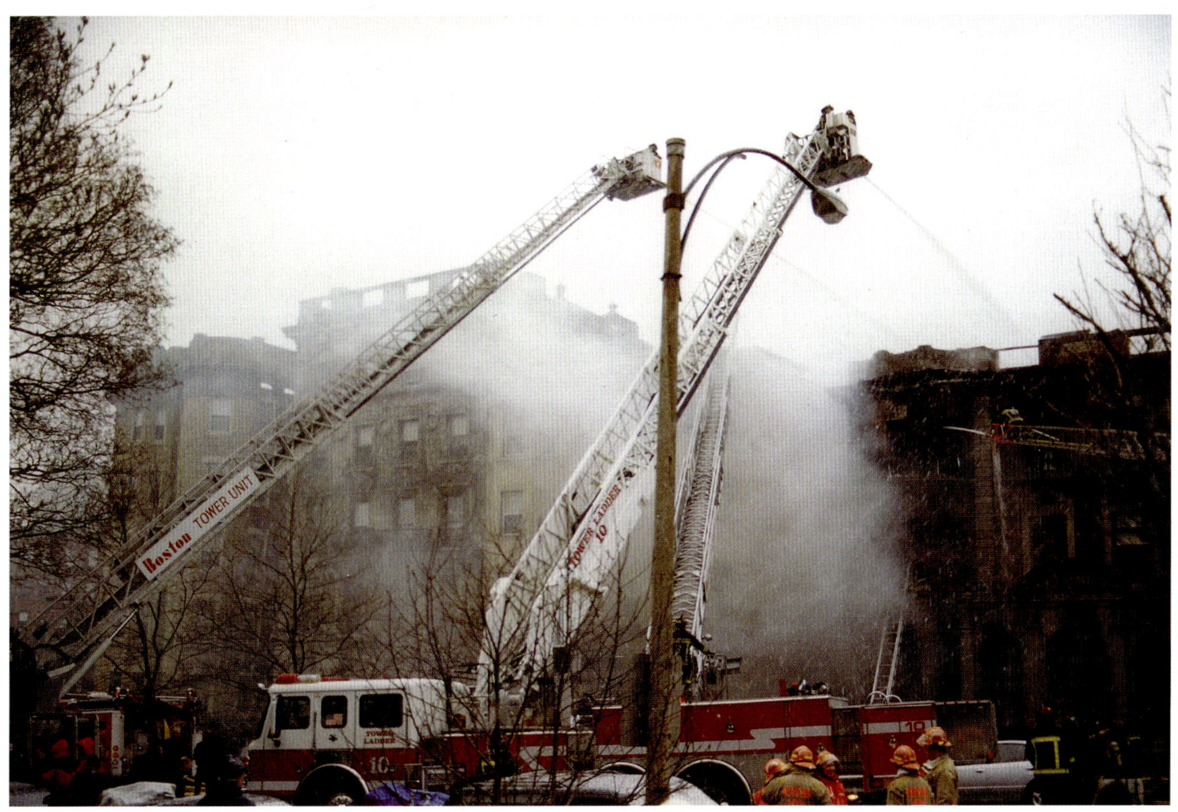

Boston Tower Ladder 10, 2001 American LaFrance, 75 foot Tower, in service for only six months for evaluation.

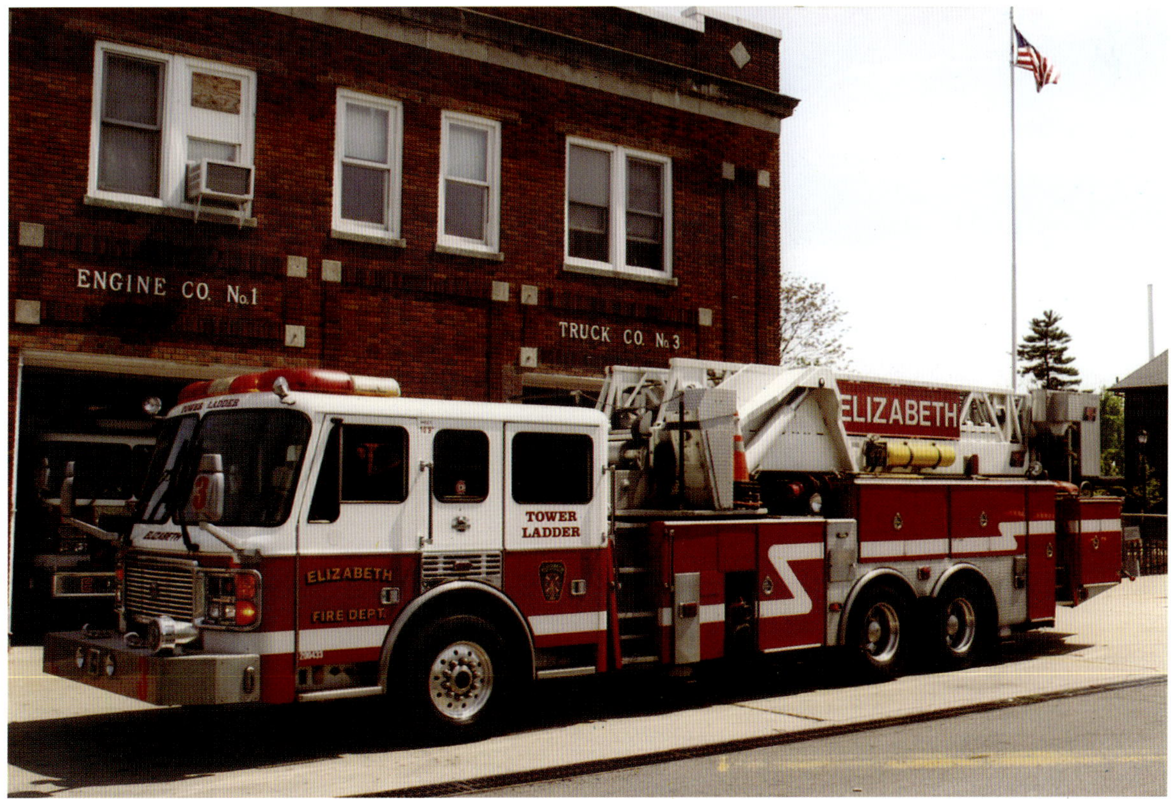

Now Tower Ladder 3, Elizabeth, NJ.

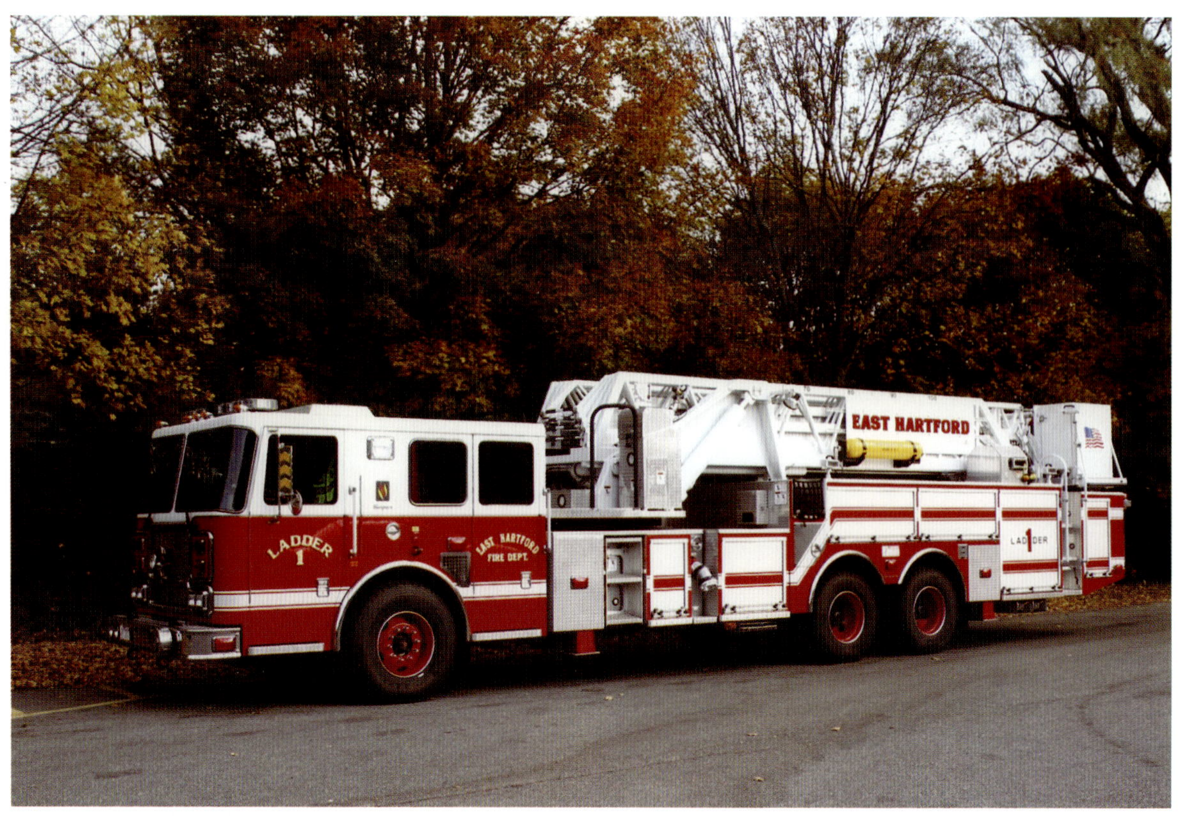

East Hartford, CT, 2007 Seagrave, 95 foot Aerialscope, but never placed in service.

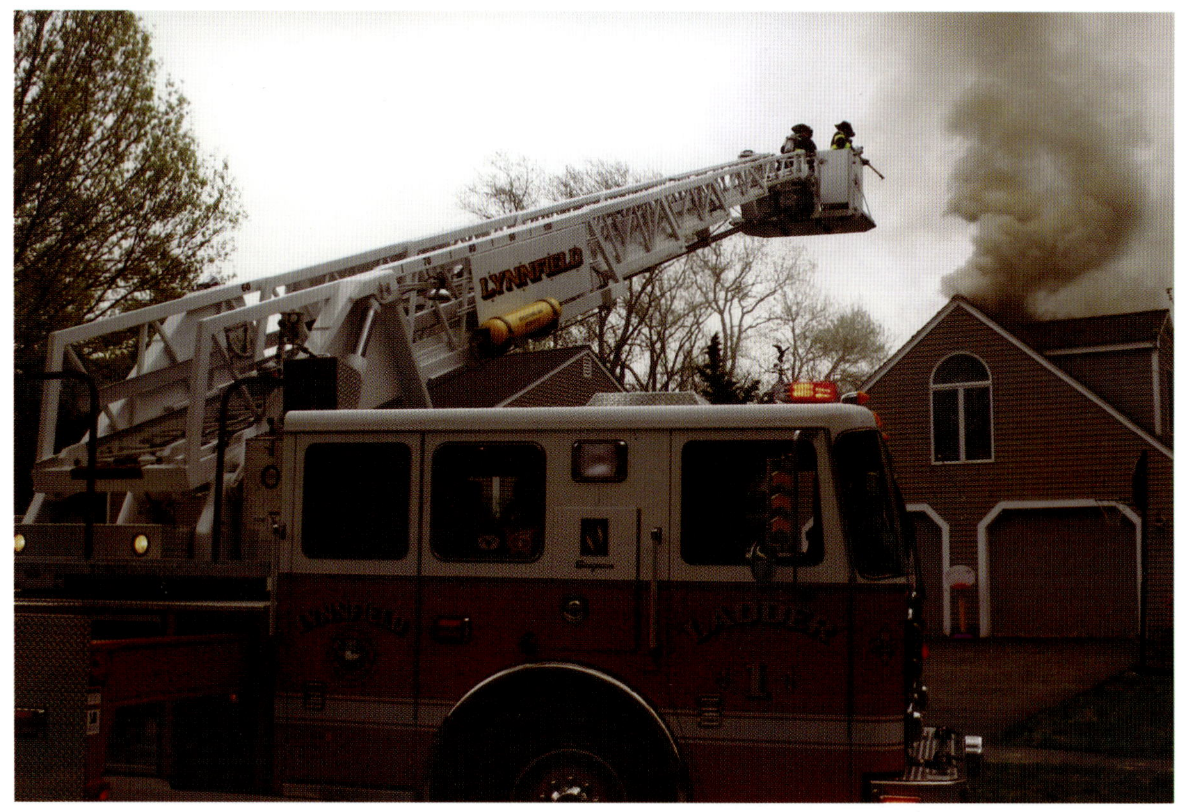

Acquired by Lynnfield, MA in 2008.

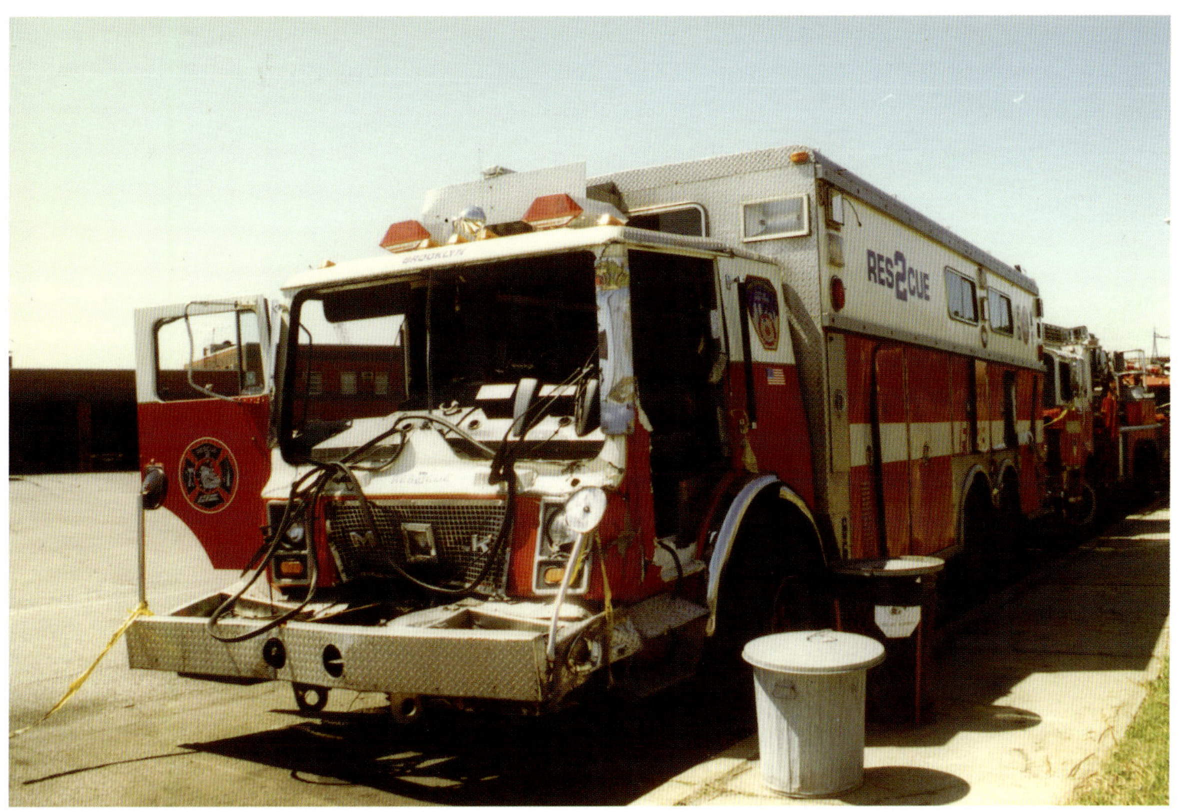

FDNY Rescue 2, 1990 Mack/Saulsbury, after a major traffic accident in Brooklyn.

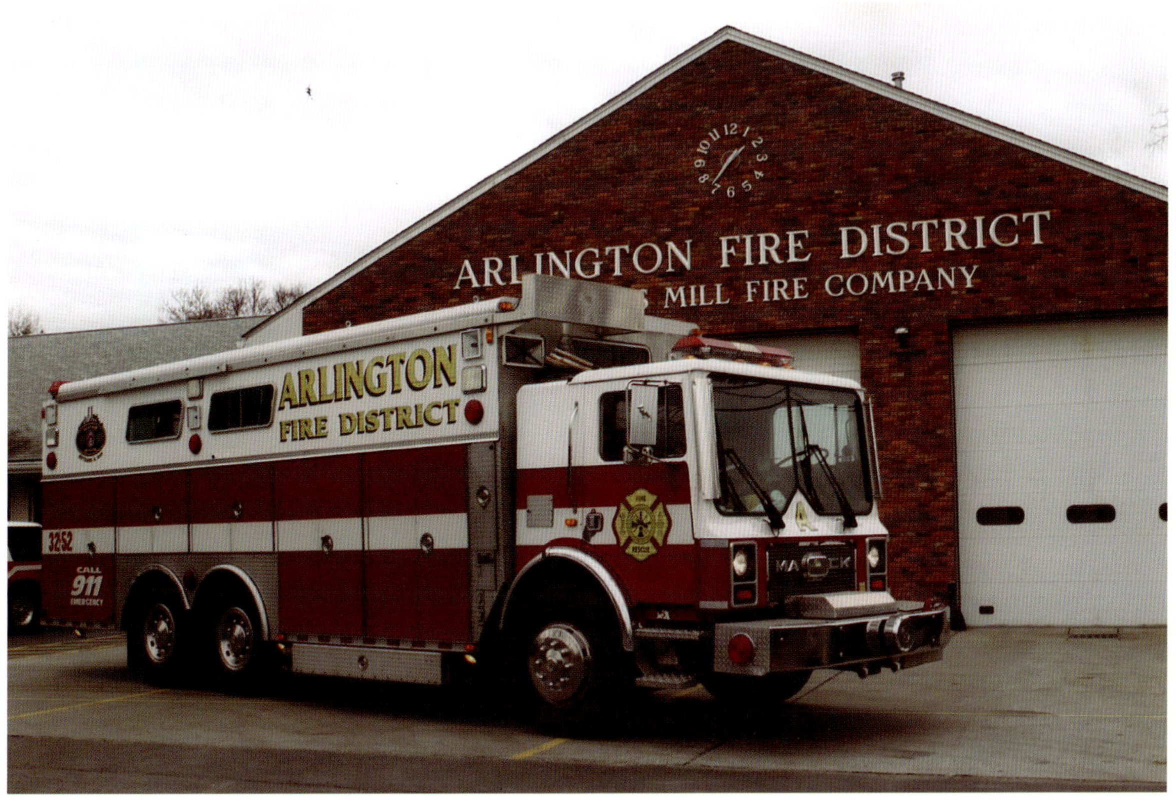

Rebuilt in 1995 by the Arlington Fire District, Poughkeepsie, NY. Now in service in South America.

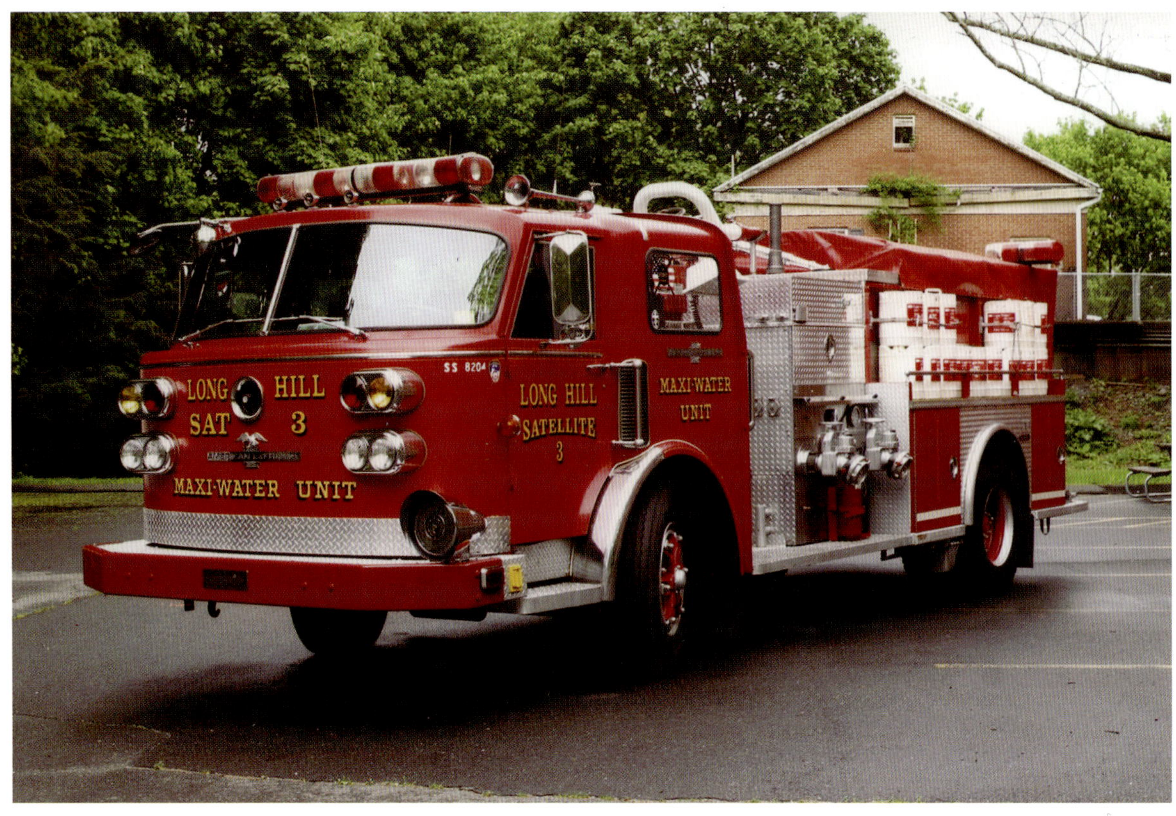

Long Hill FD, Trumbull, CT, Satellite 3, 1982 American LaFrance/Saulsbury, former FDNY Maxi-Water Unit.

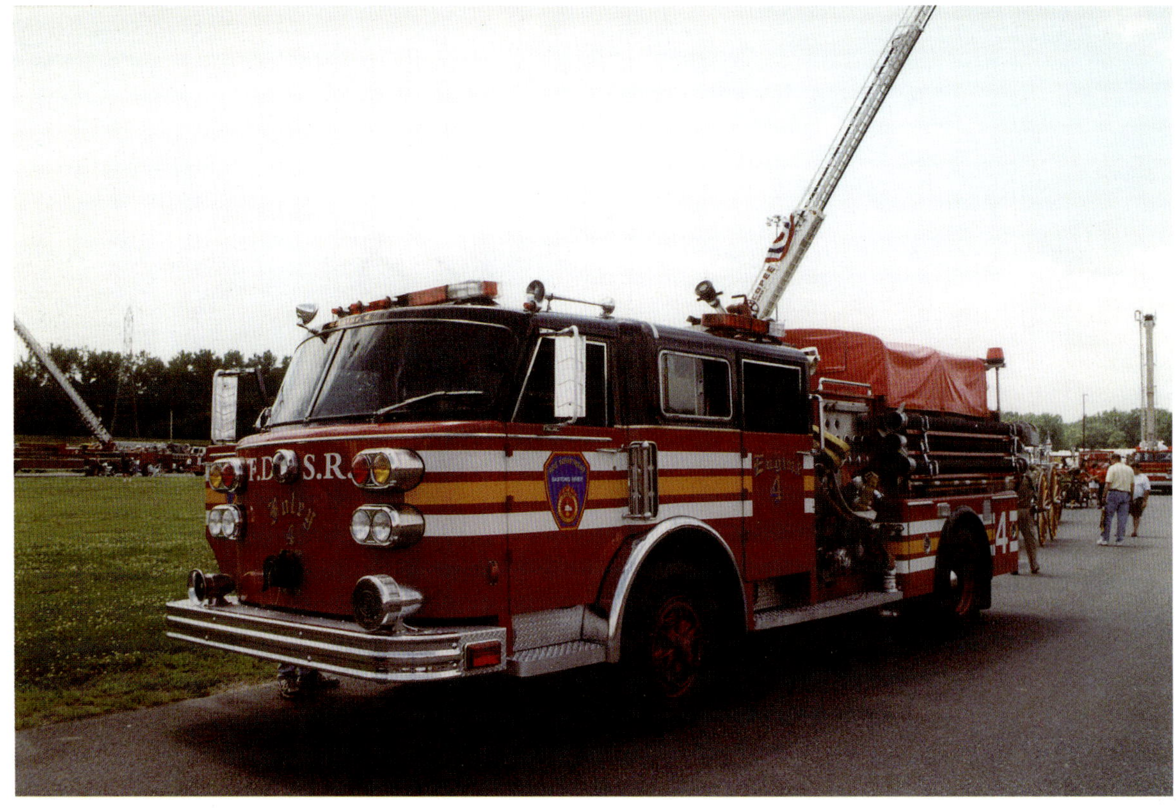

Saxton River, VT Engine 4, 1980 American LaFrance, former FDNY Engine 259.

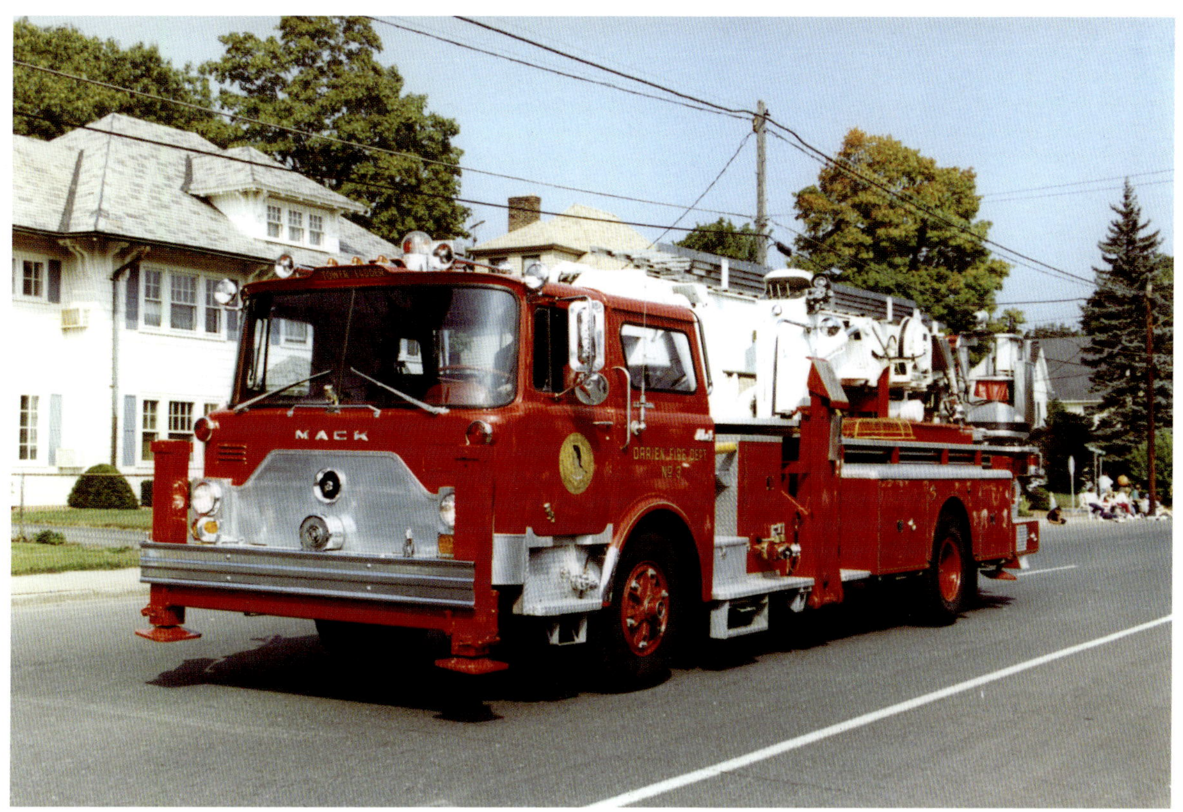

Darien, CT, 1971 Mack/Baker, 75 foot Tower Ladder, the first to be delivered in Connecticut. It has since been refitted with a 2011 Seagrave Marauder II chassis.

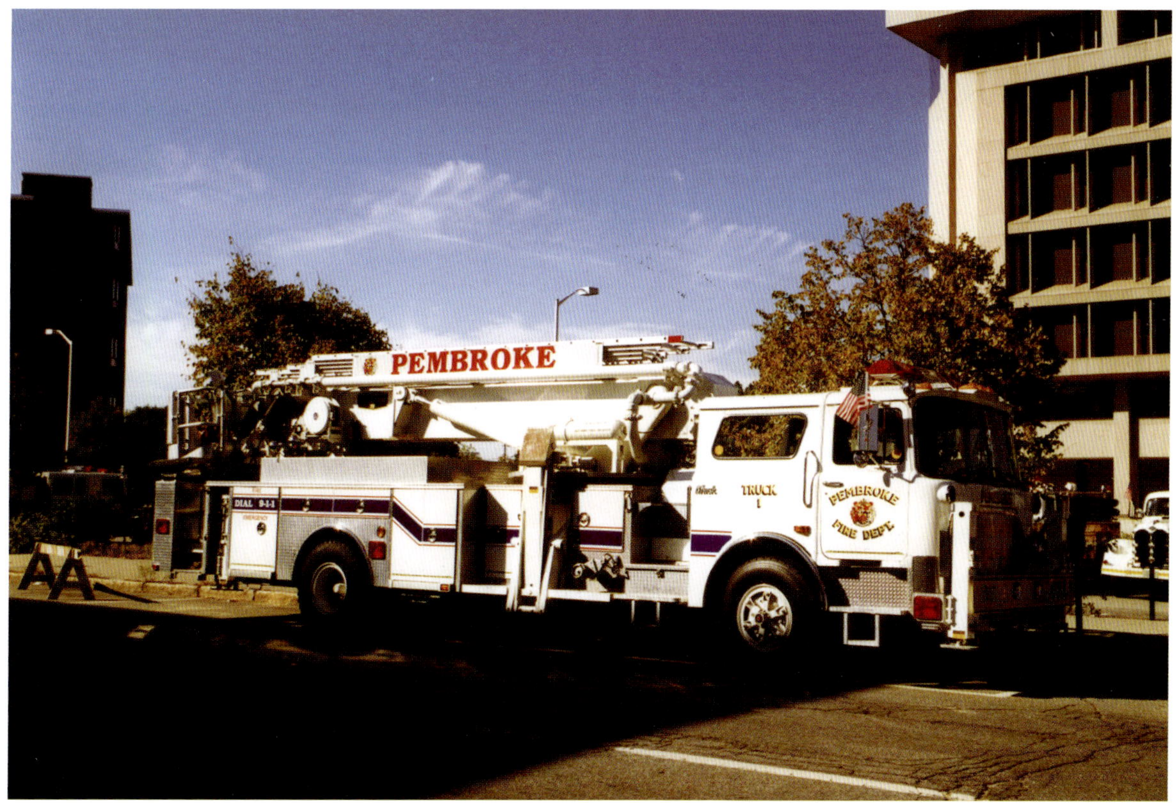

Pembroke, NH Truck 1, 1979 Mack/Baker, former FDNY Tower Ladder 114.

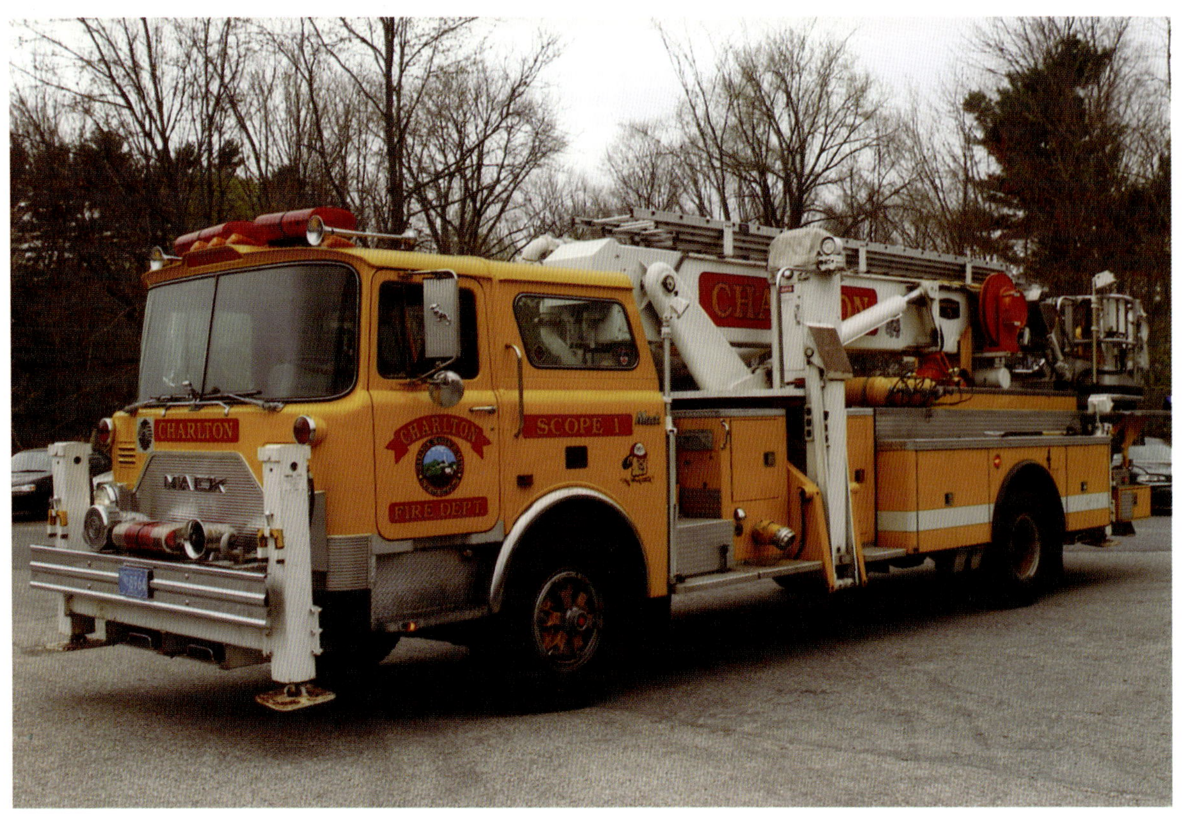

Charlton, MA Scope 1, 1974 Mack/Baker, former FDNY TL 158, refurbished and painted yellow in 1988 by Taylor, PA, and acquired by Charlton in 2005.

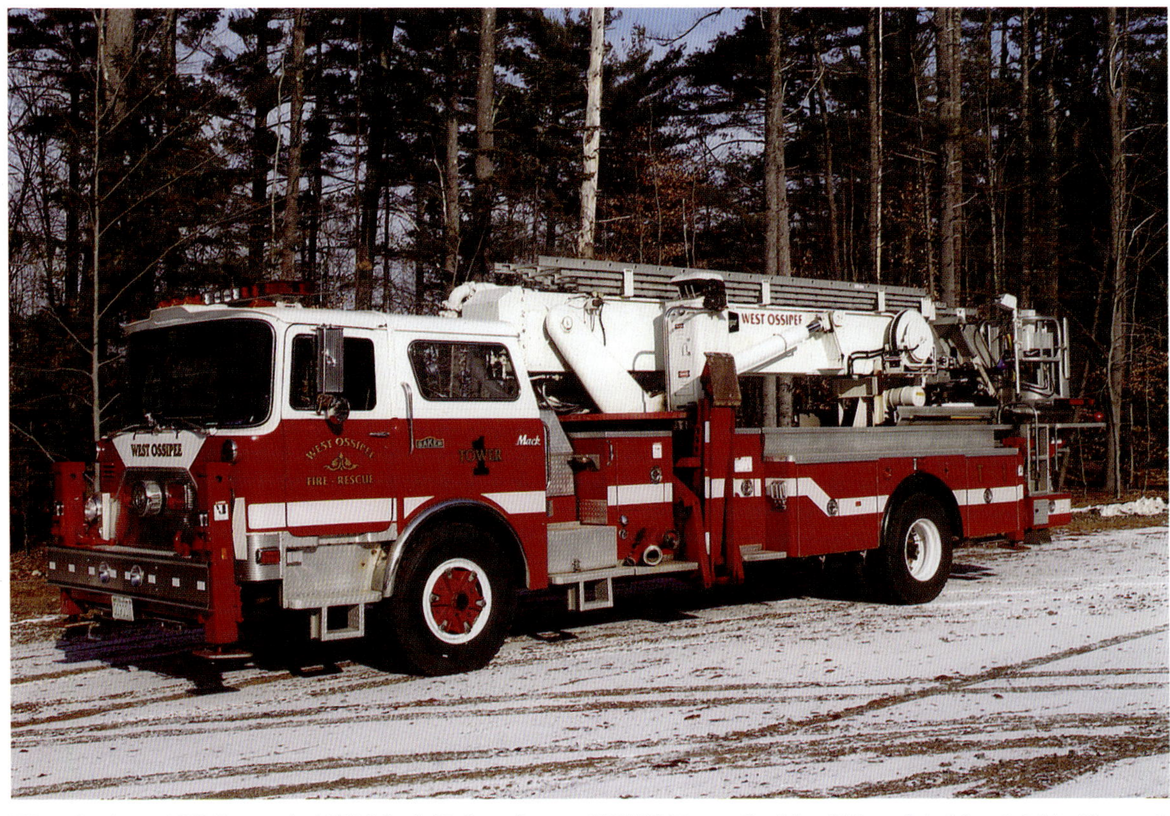

West Ossipee, NH Tower 1, 1979 Mack/Baker, former FDNY Tower Ladder 120 and Ashland, MA, Tower 1.

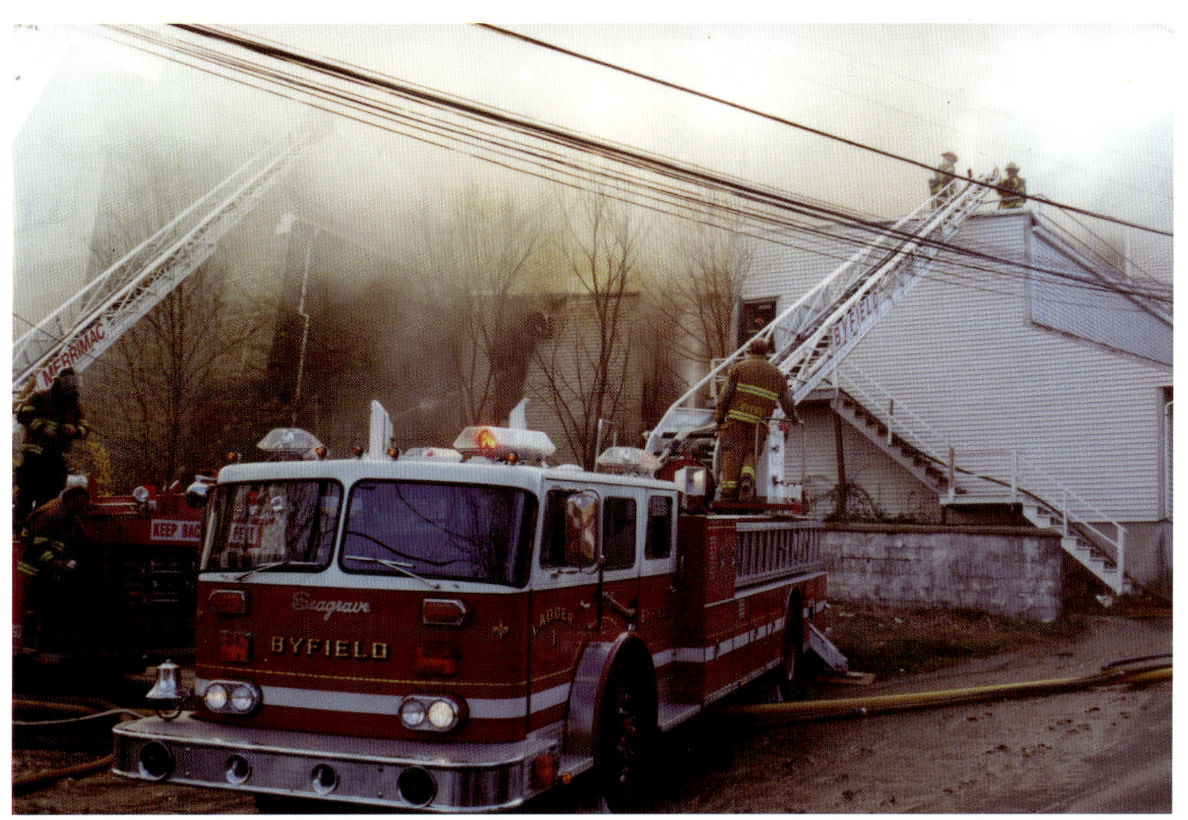

Byfield, MA Ladder 1, 1982 Seagrave, 100 foot, former FDNY Ladder 48.

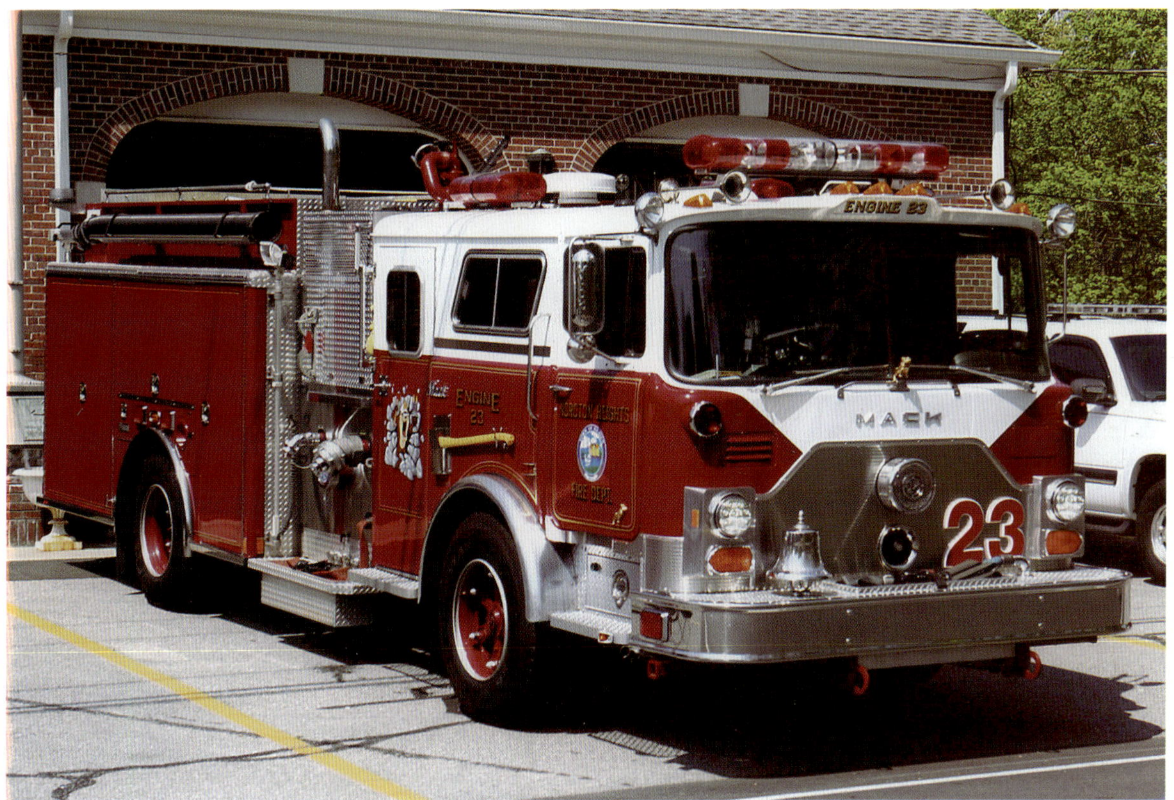

Noroton Heights FD, Darien, CT., Engine 23, 1989 Mack CF/Ward, former FDNY assigned to the Training Division.

MASSACHUSETTS FIRES

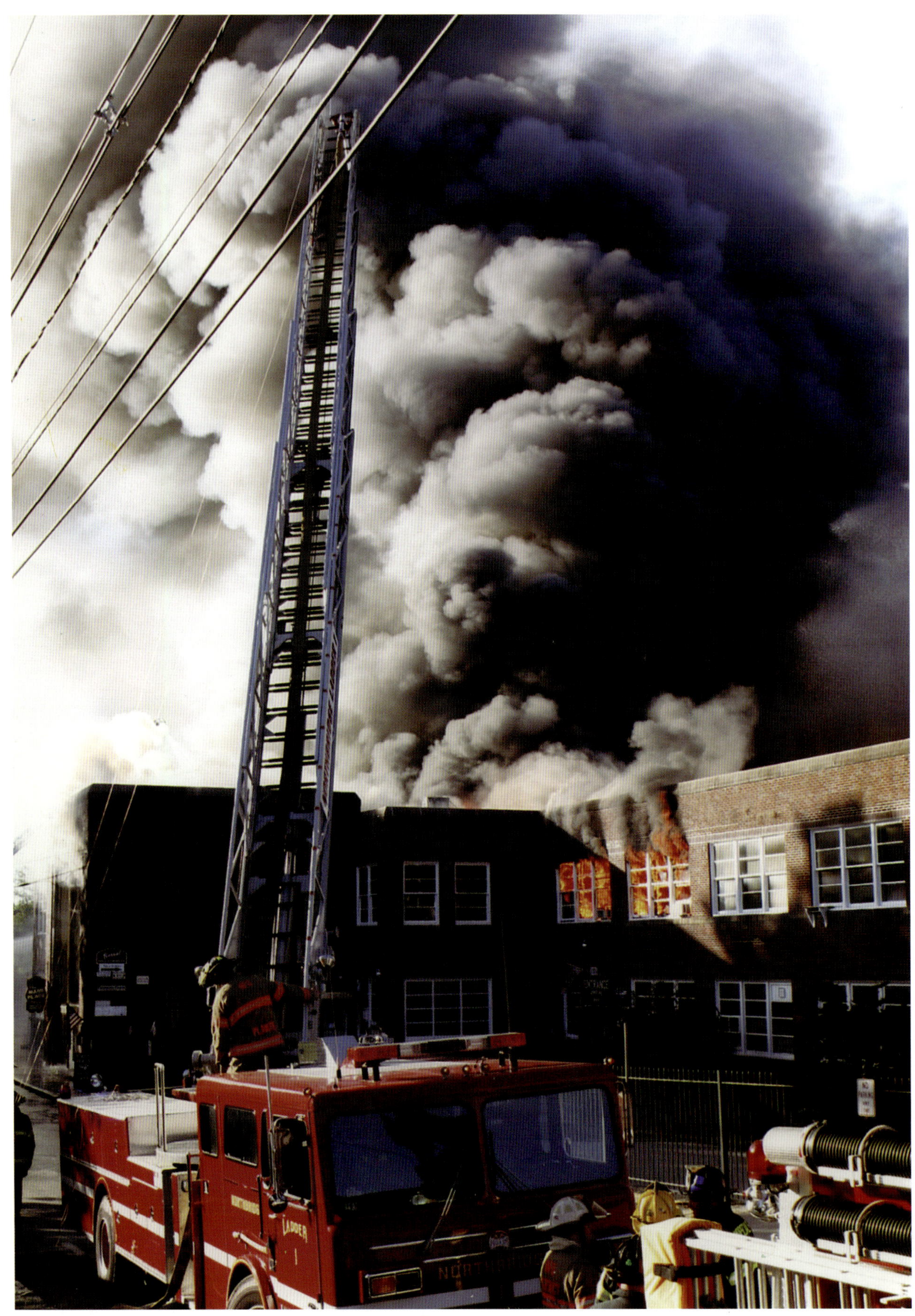

The Bernat Mill Complex at 19 Depot Street, Uxbridge, is destroyed in an 8 alarm fire on July 21, 2007. 400 firefighters from 36 communities in MA and RI fought the fire.

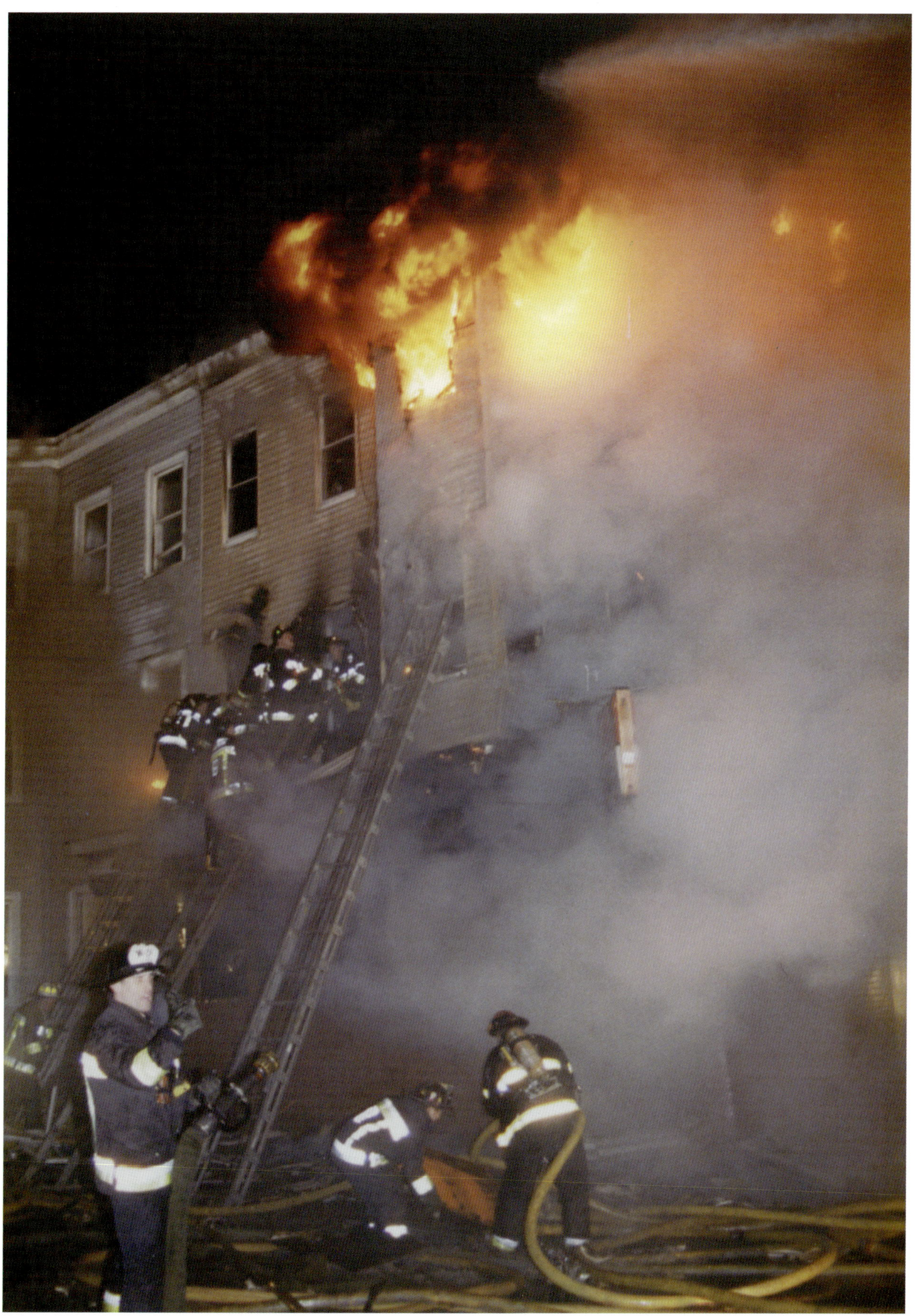

4 alarms, on February 8, 2003, at East 3rd and O Streets, South Boston.

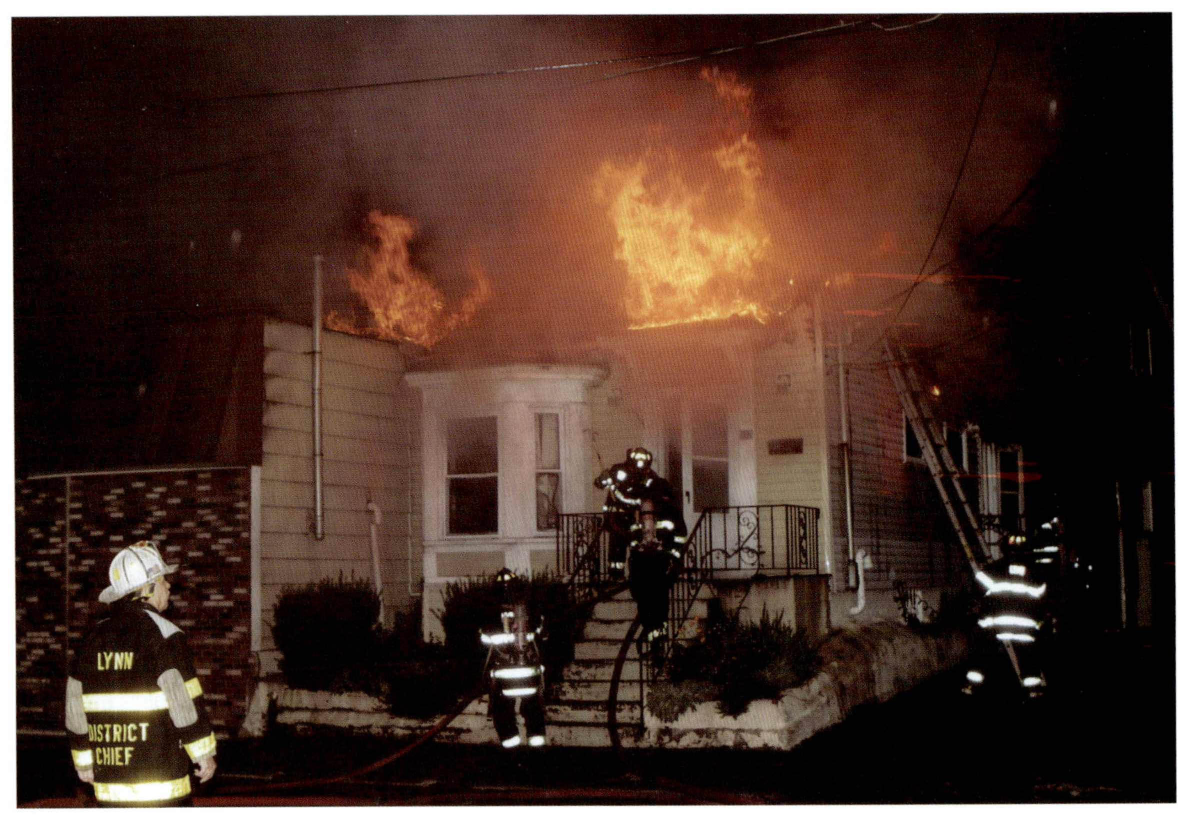

Two buildings at 512 Chatham Street and 113-115 Western Avenue, Lynn, burn in a 3 alarm fire on July 6, 2006.

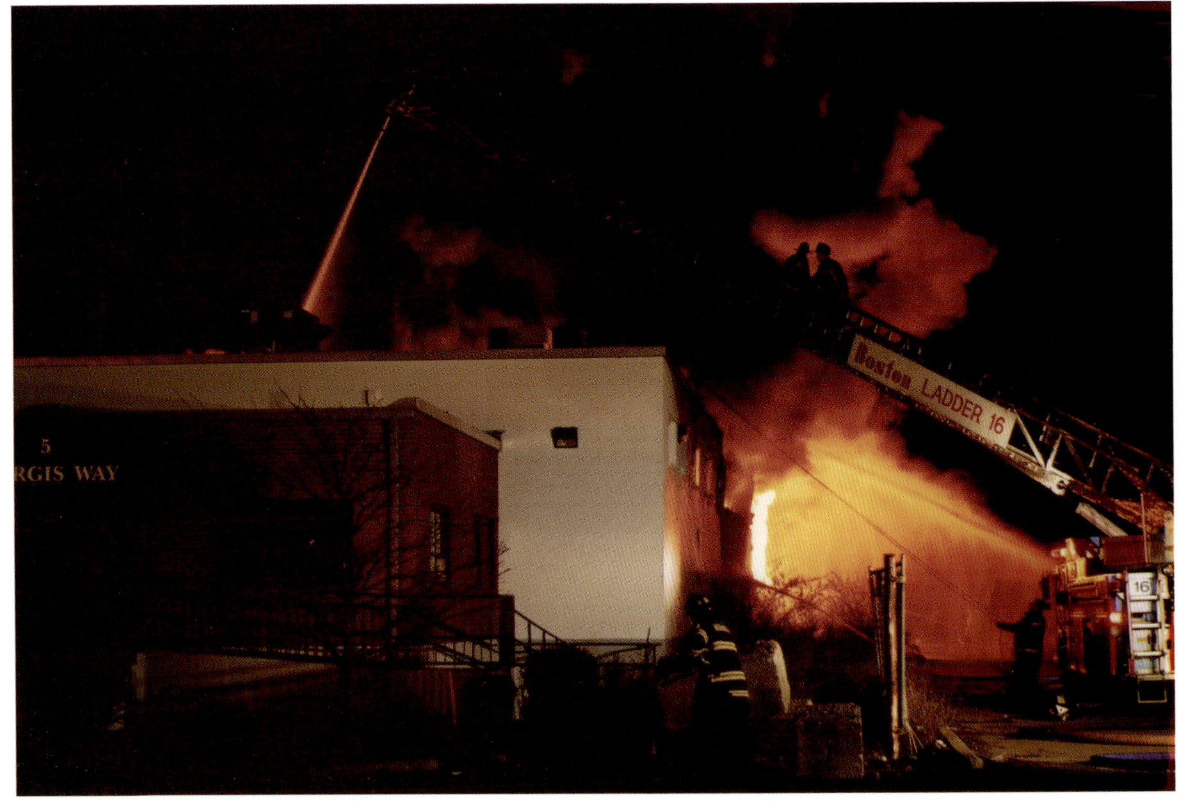

Mutual aid from Boston responded to a 3 alarm fire at 5 Stergis Way, Dedham, on December 2, 2005.

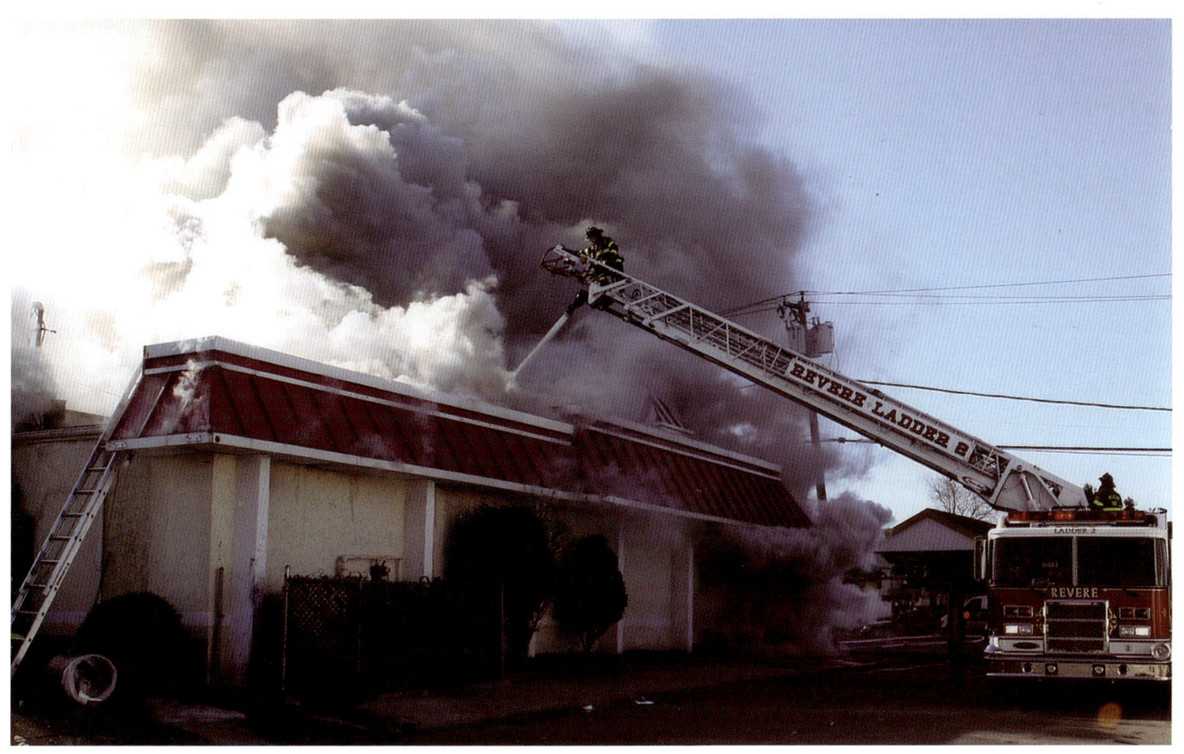

The KFC at 169 Squire Road, Revere, was destroyed in a 2 alarm fire on February 16, 2009.

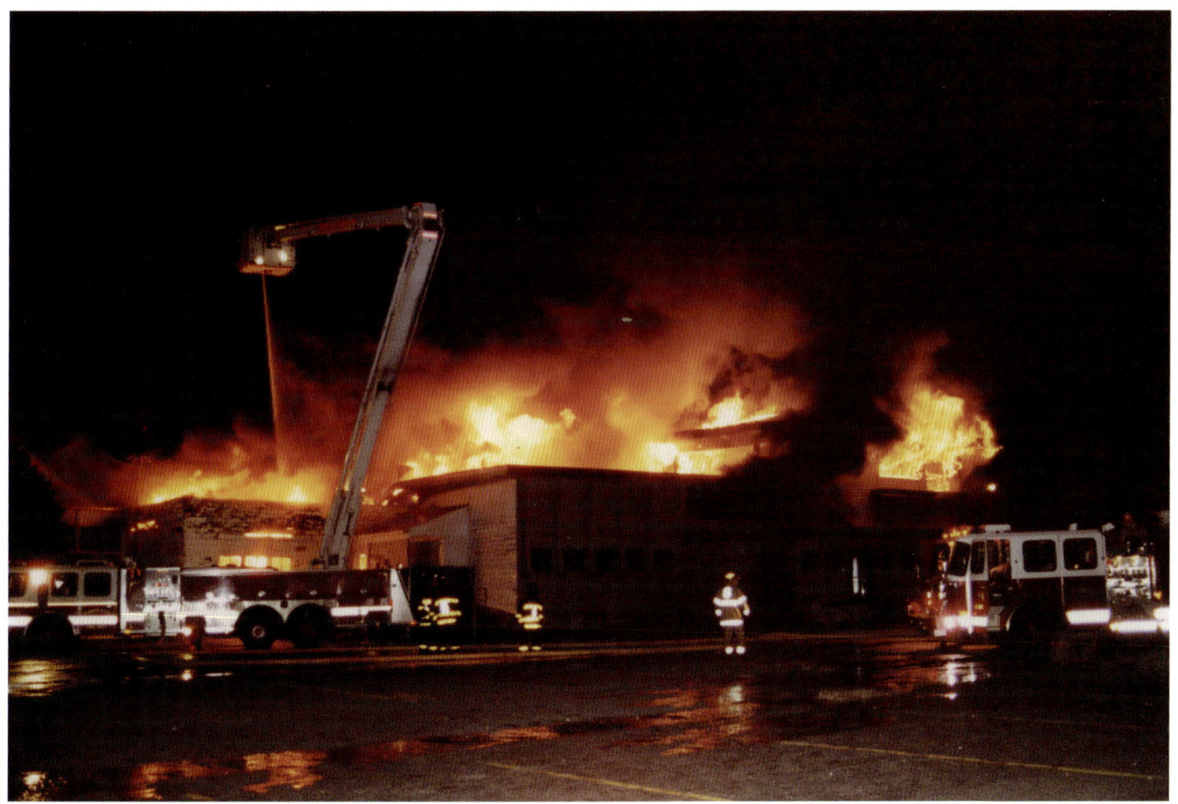

The Lawrence Snorkel works, at a vacant night club at 280 Merrimack Street, Methuen, on November 9, 2001. Three alarms were sounded.

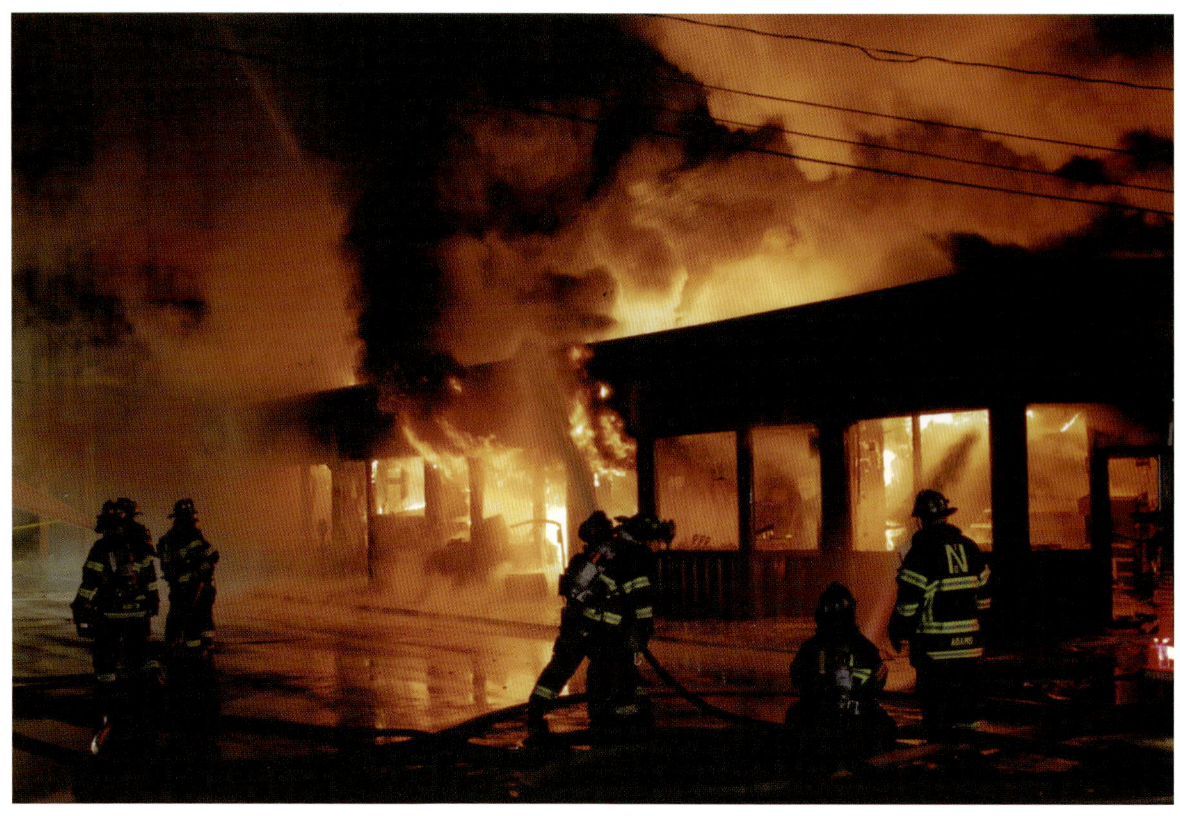

A taxpayer is fully involved in a 4 alarm fire at 12-18 Pond Street, Natick, on June 19, 2008.

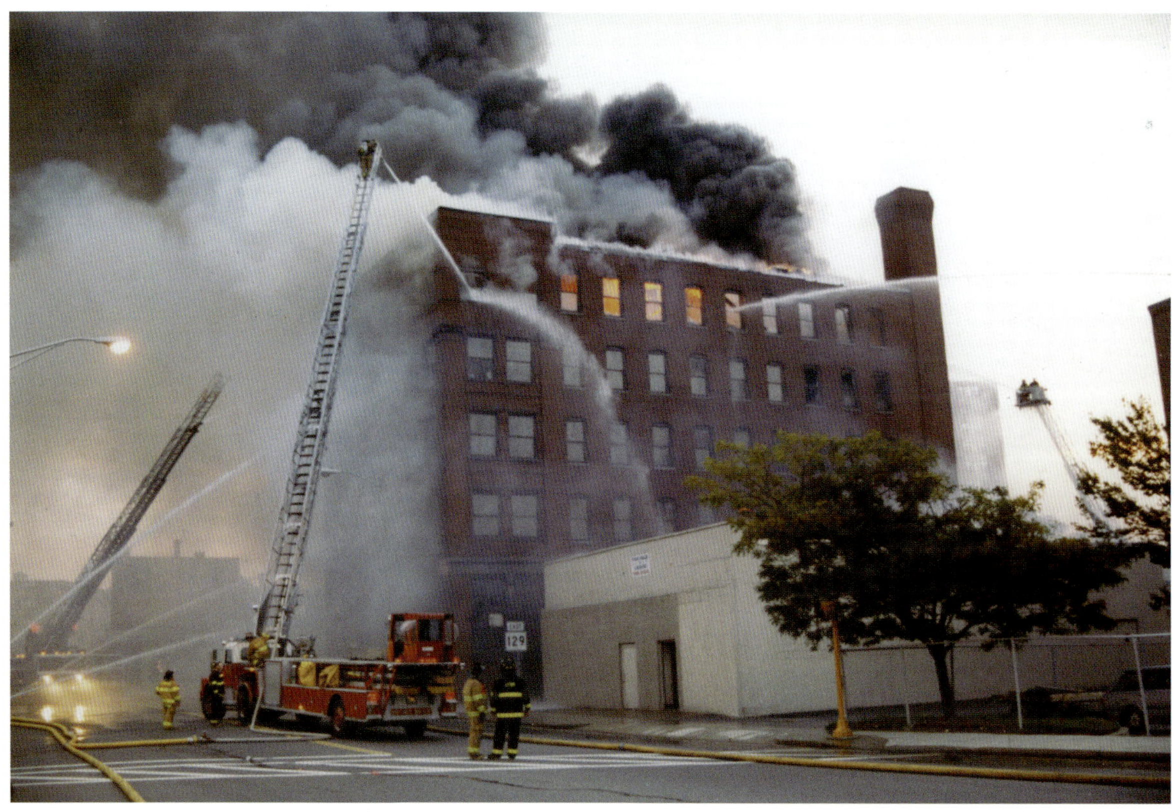

Four alarms in a vacant factory at 202 Broad Street, Lynn, on September 28, 1999.

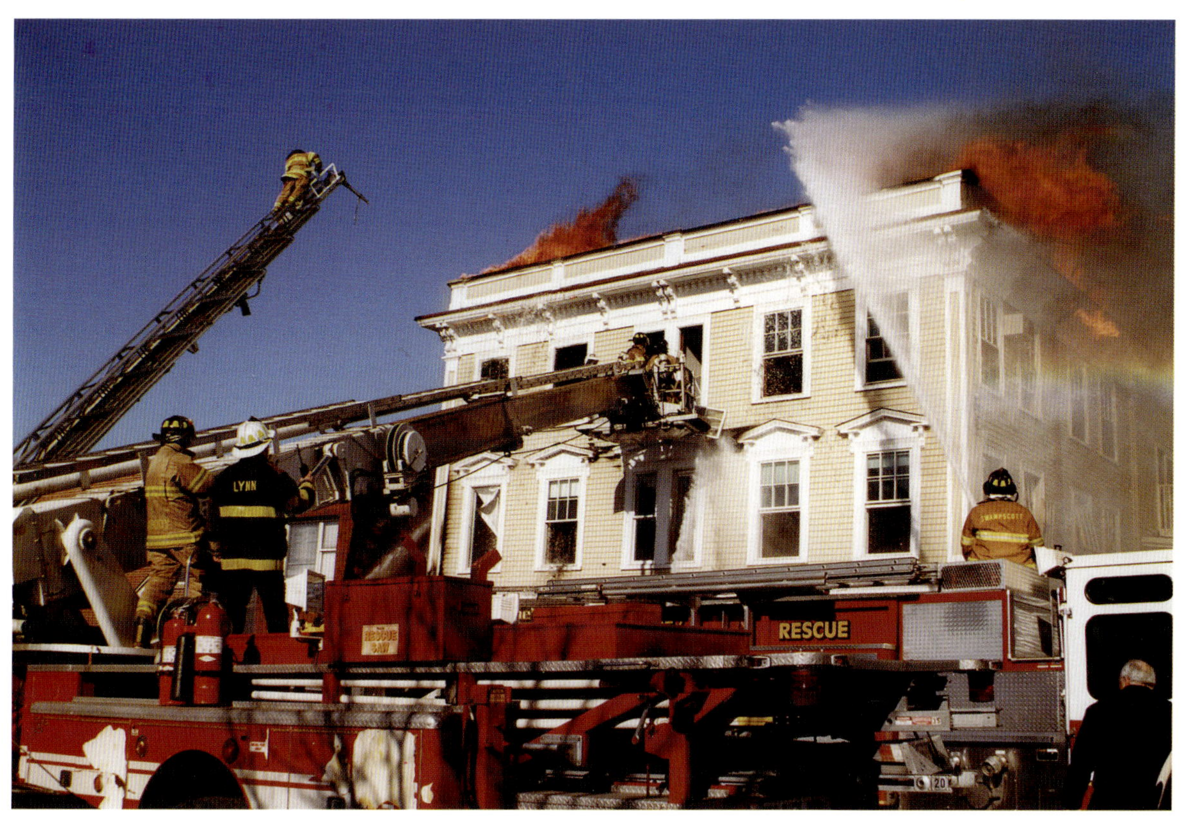

Four alarms at 168 Humphrey Street, Swampscott, on January 23, 2002.

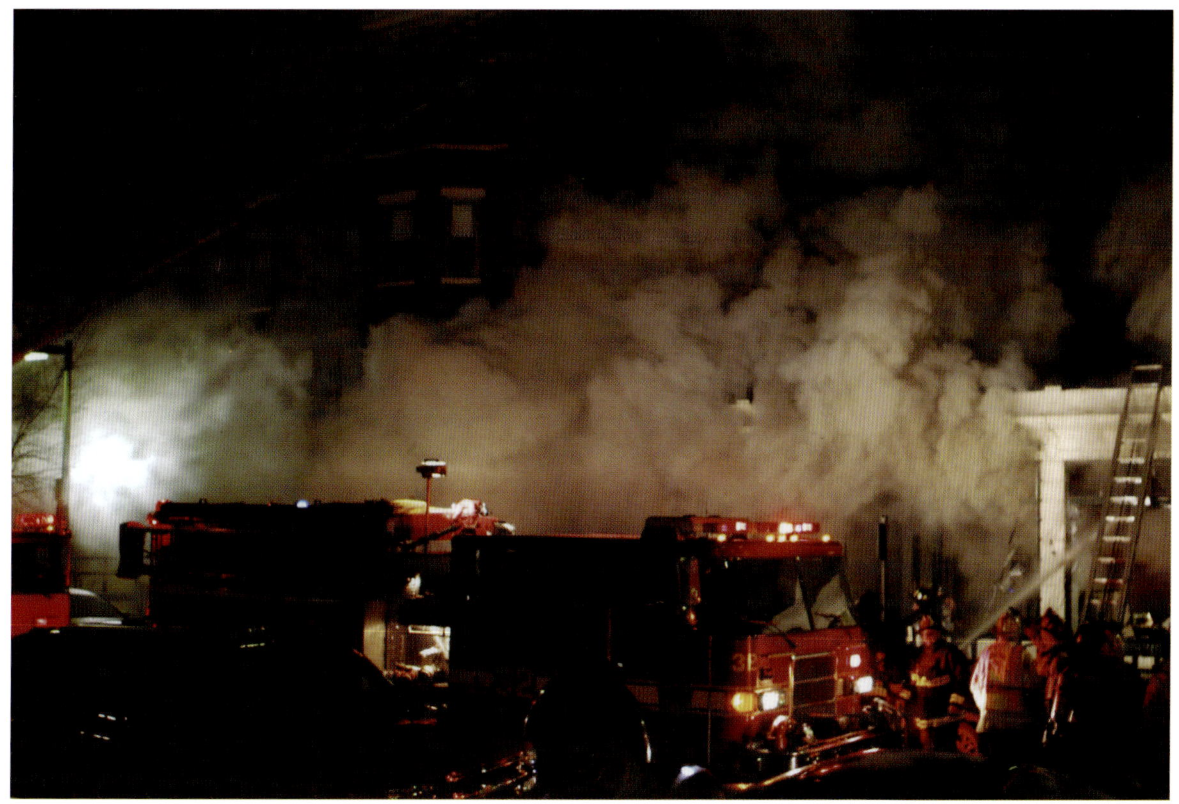

A taxpayer across from Fenway Park, burns all night in a 4 alarm fire at 84-100 Peterborough Street, on January 6, 2009.

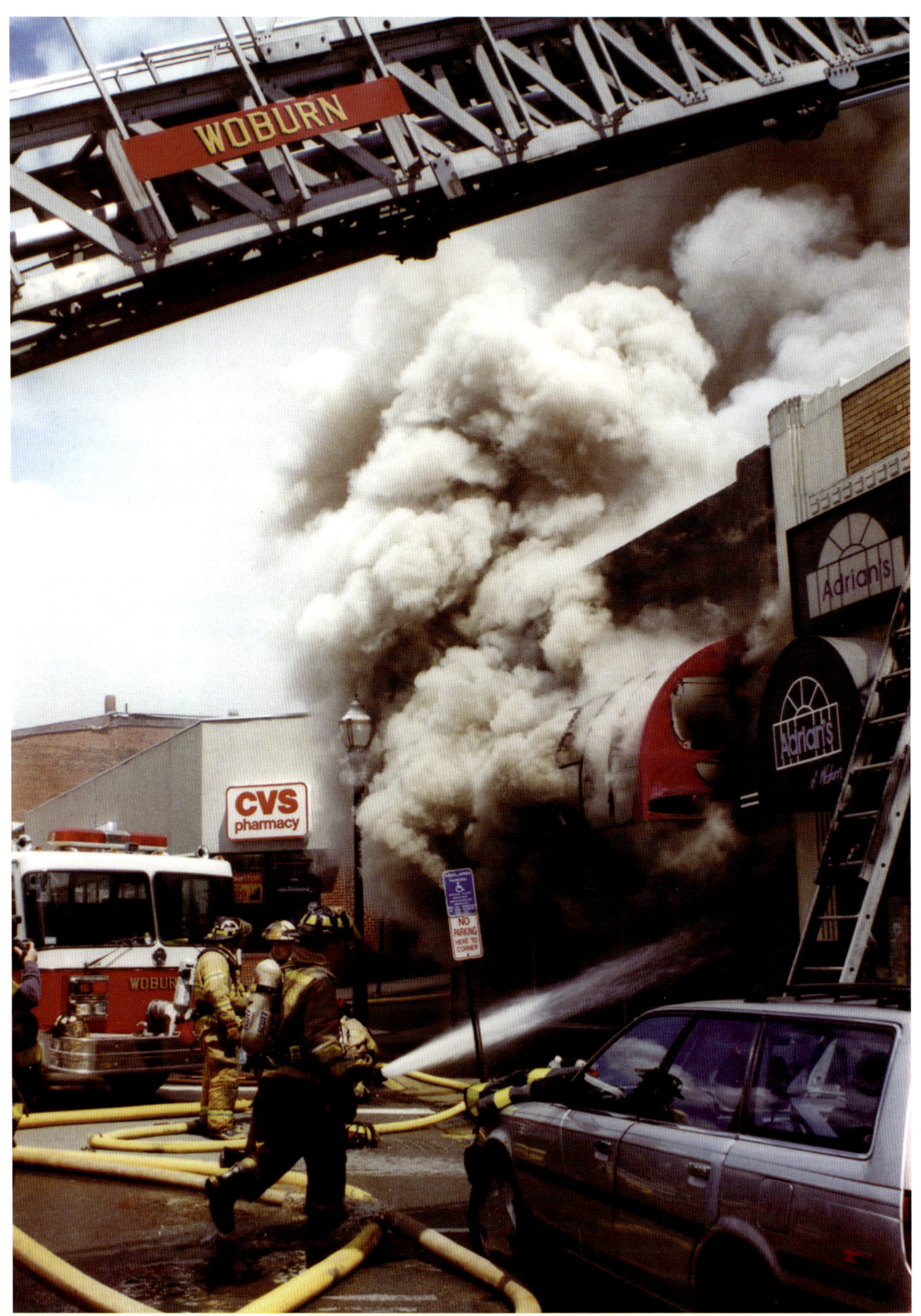

Four alarms at 409 Main Street, Woburn, on May 20, 2002.

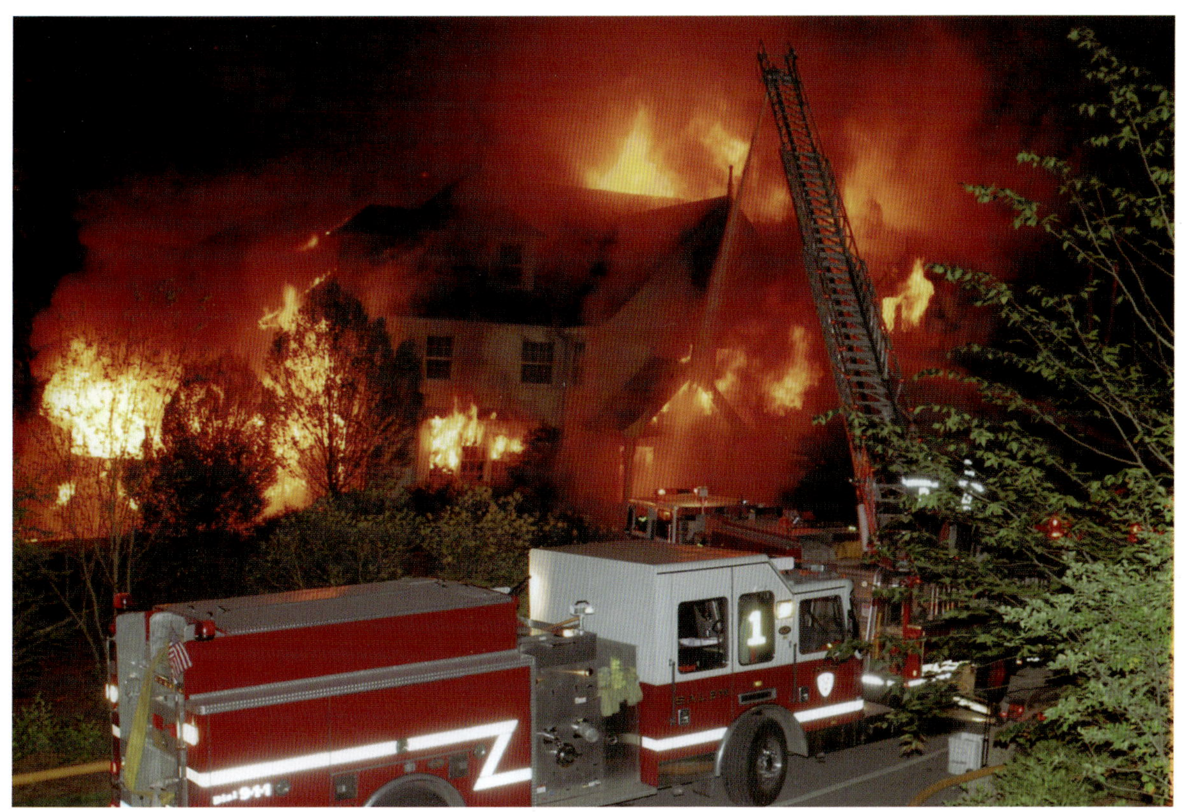

A 3 alarm fire ripped through a mansion at 890 Hale Street, Beverly Farms, on August 21, 2008.

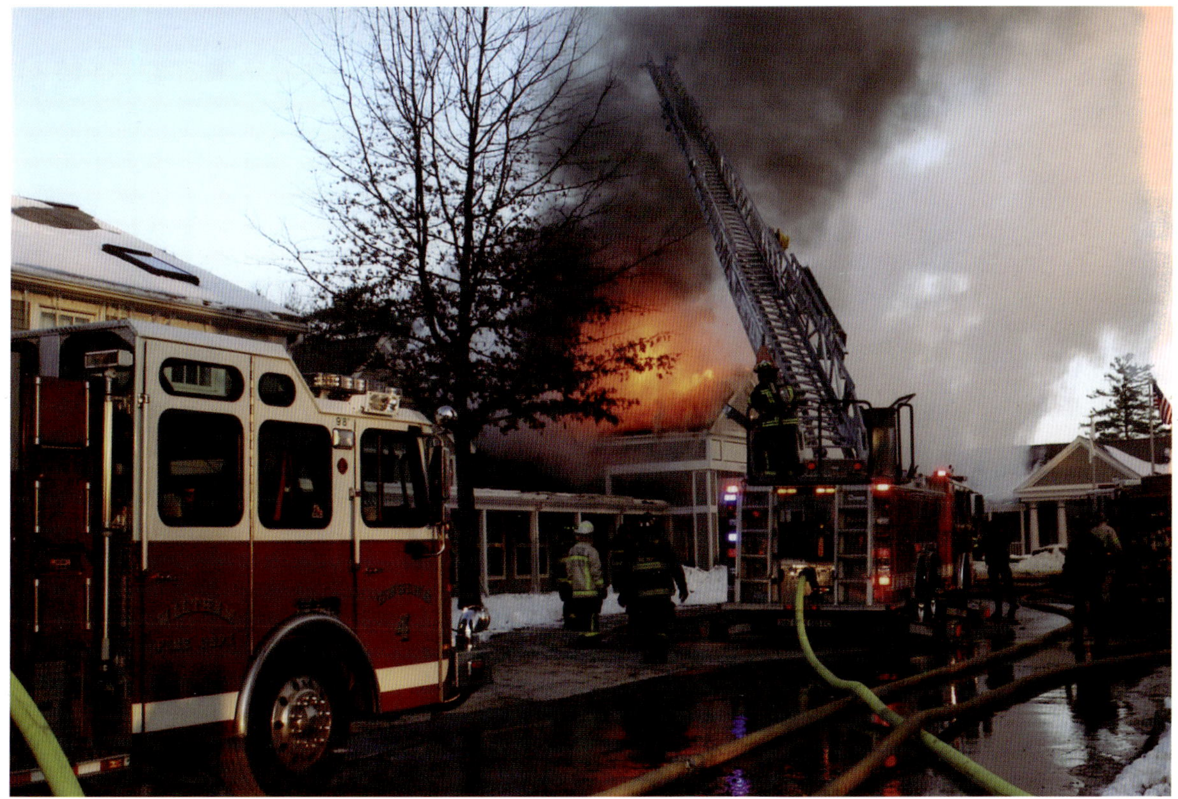

The Gifford School, at 177 Boston Post Road, Weston, is heavily damaged in a 4 alarm fire on December 23, 2009.

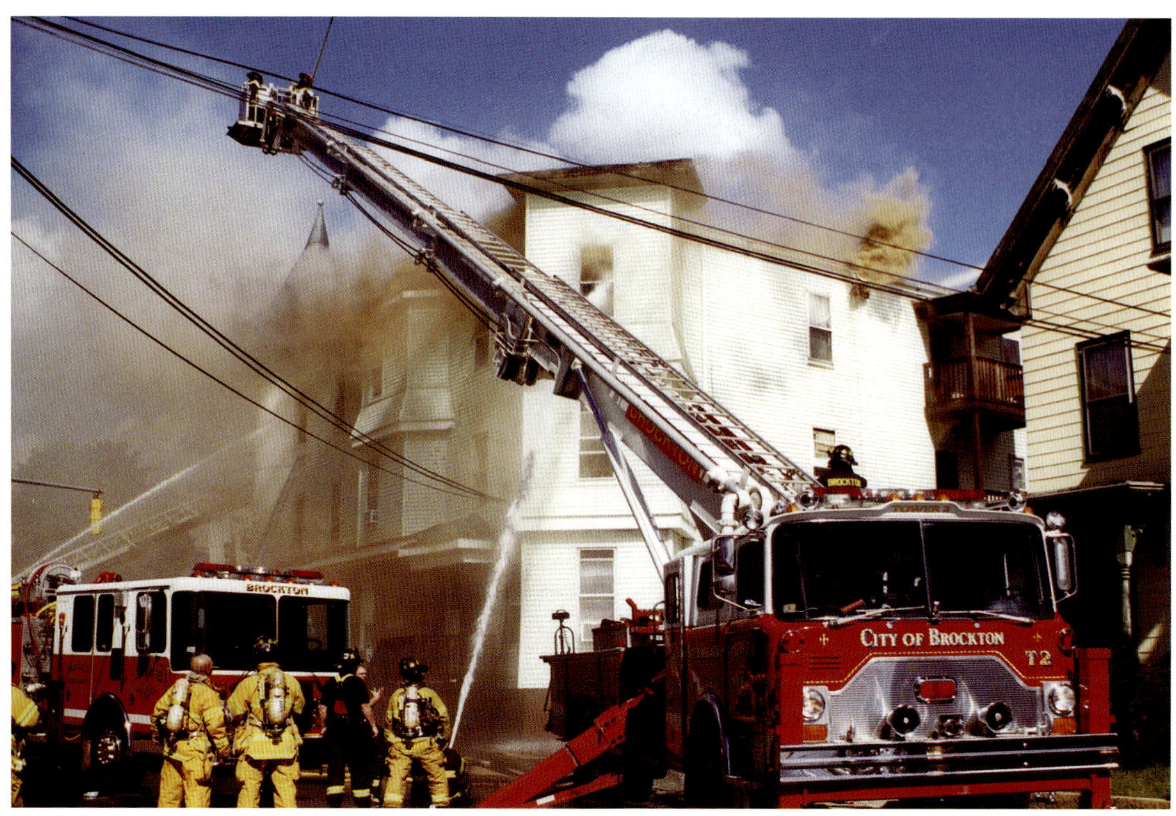

Three alarms in a rooming house at 96 West Elm Street, Brockton, on September 27, 2003.

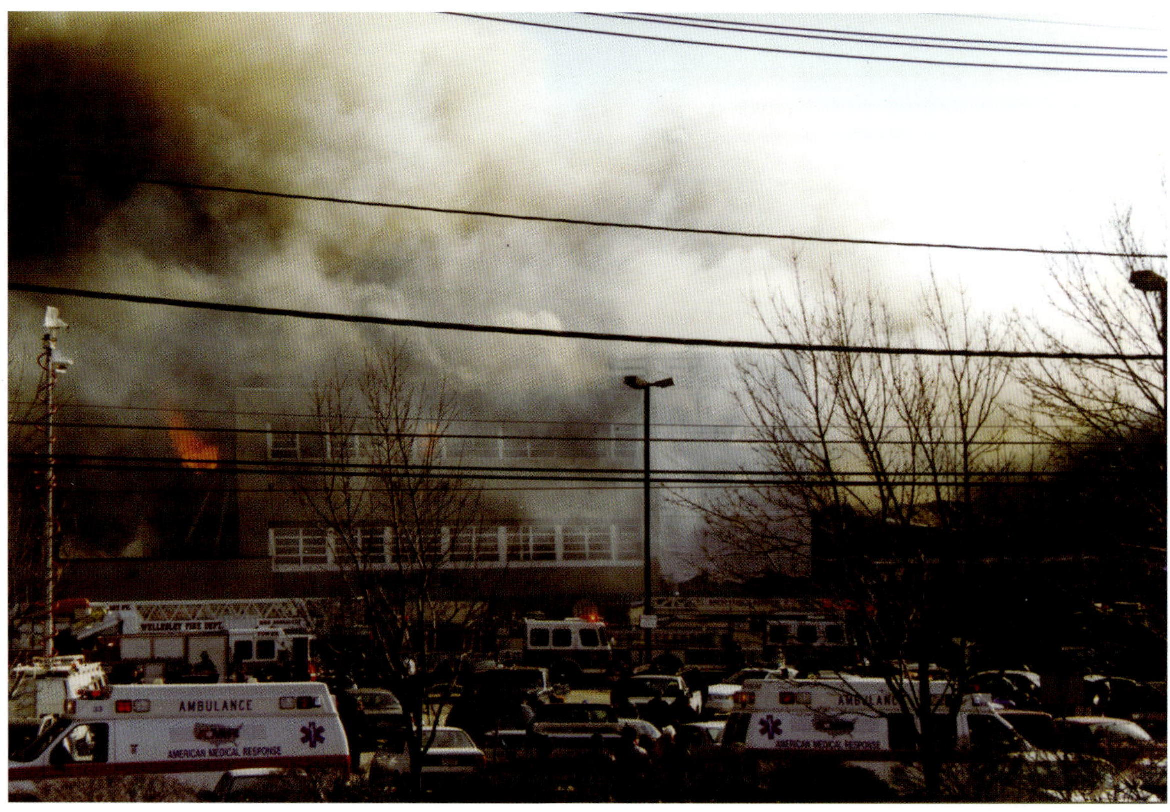

Five office workers died in a noon-time, 5 alarm fire at 200 Worcester Street, Newton, on February 9, 2000. Many ladder rescues were made.

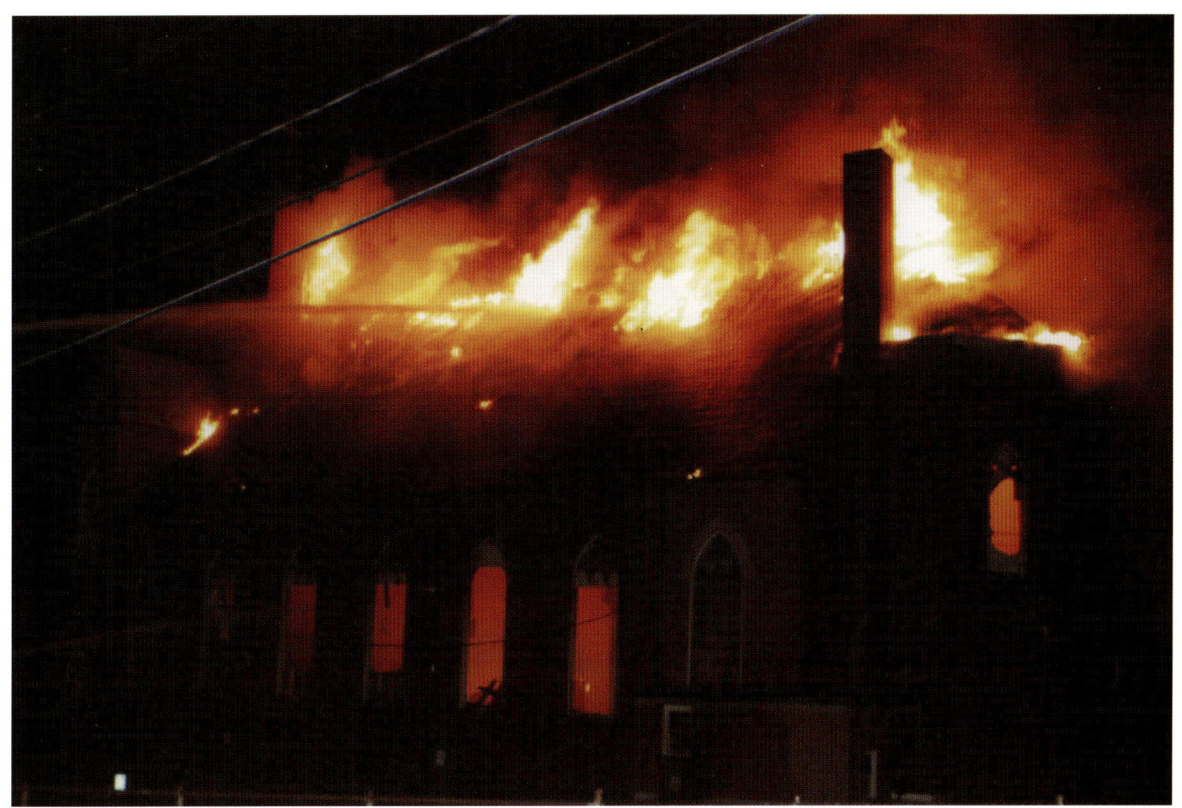

The Sacred Heart Church is destroyed in a 7 alarm fire at 70 Washington Street, Weymouth, on June 9, 2005.

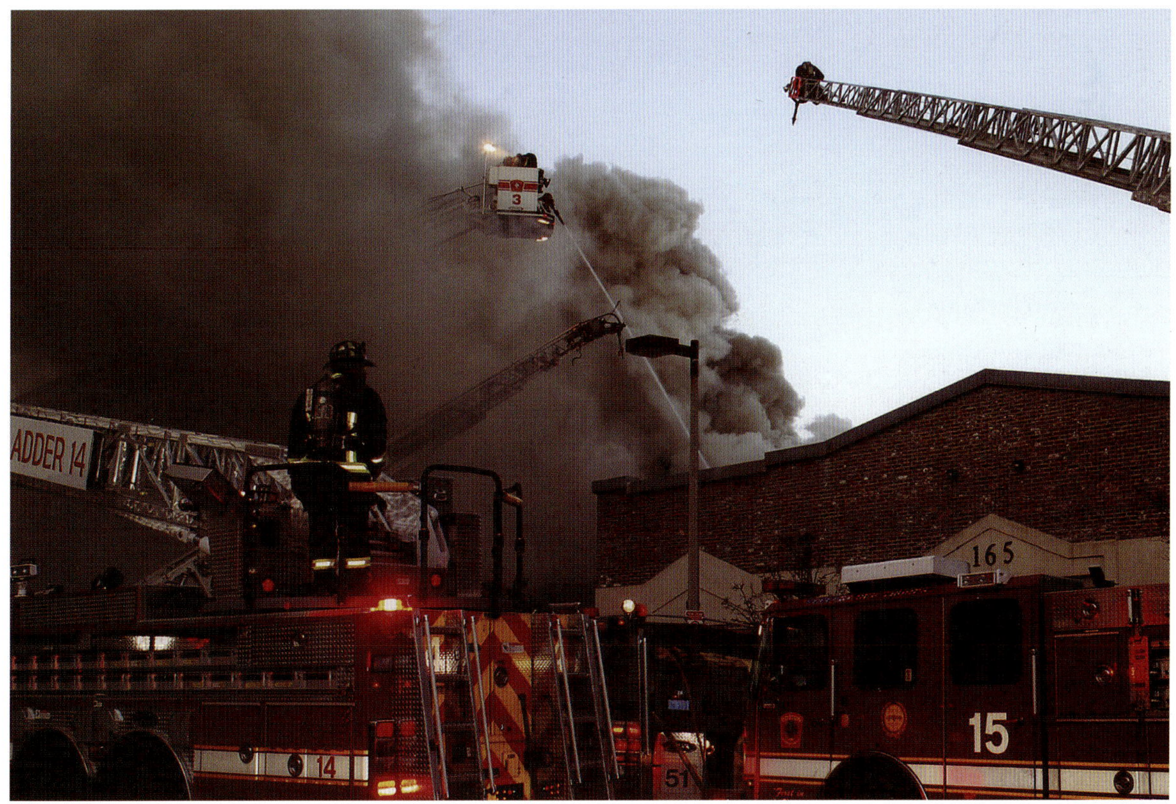

A taxpayer is gutted in a 4 alarm fire at 169-183 Chestnut Hill Avenue, in the Brighton section of Boston, on February 12, 2012.

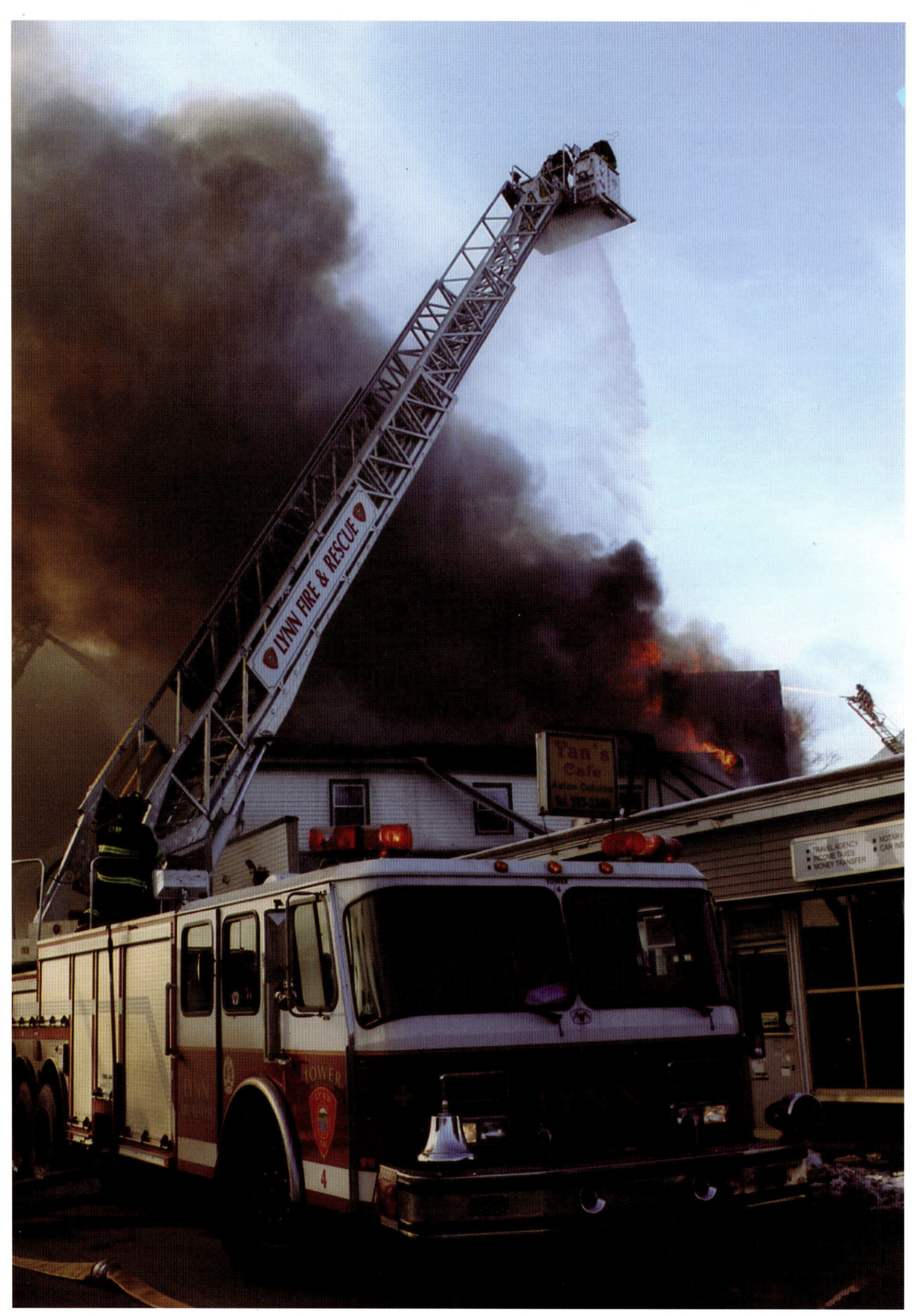

Two buildings at 219 Lewis Street and 3 Chestnut Street, Lynn are destroyed in a 4 alarm fire on January 14, 2009.

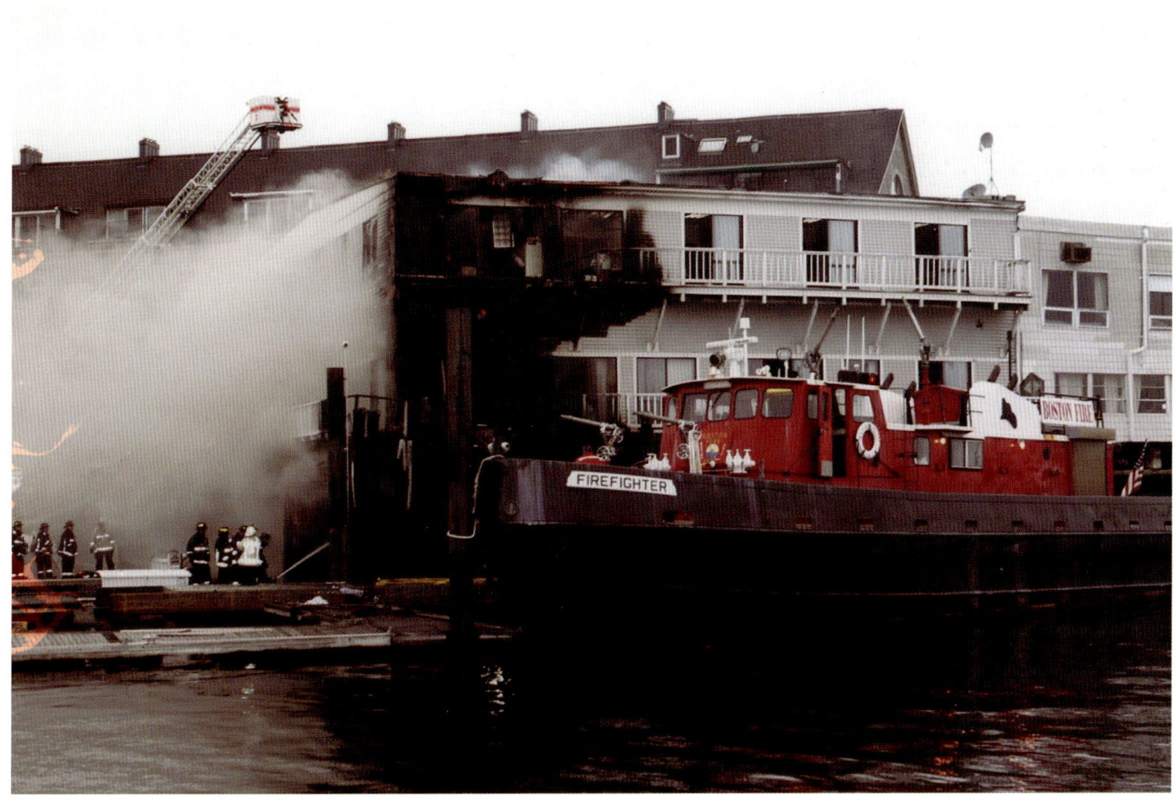

Careless disposal of smoking material caused a 3 alarm fire at 95 Commercial Wharf in the North End section of Boston, on May 4, 2011.

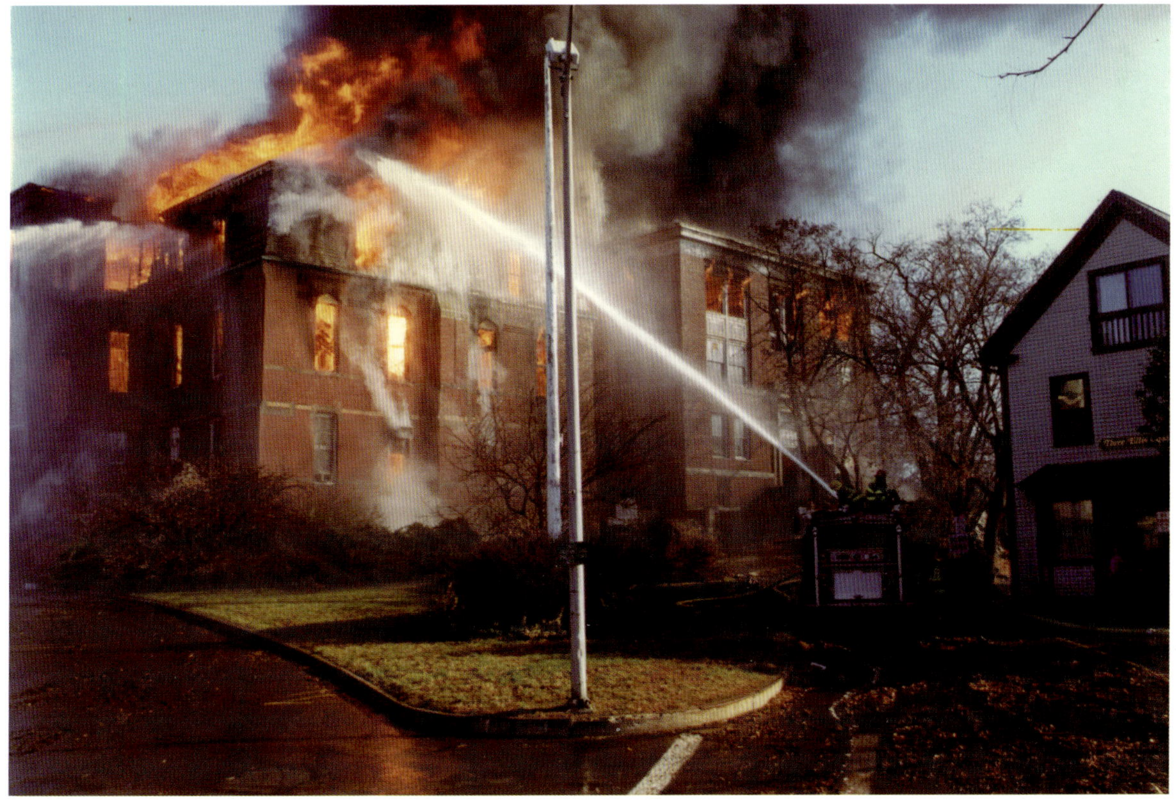

3 alarms at 3 Essex Street, Beverly, on November 24, 1996.

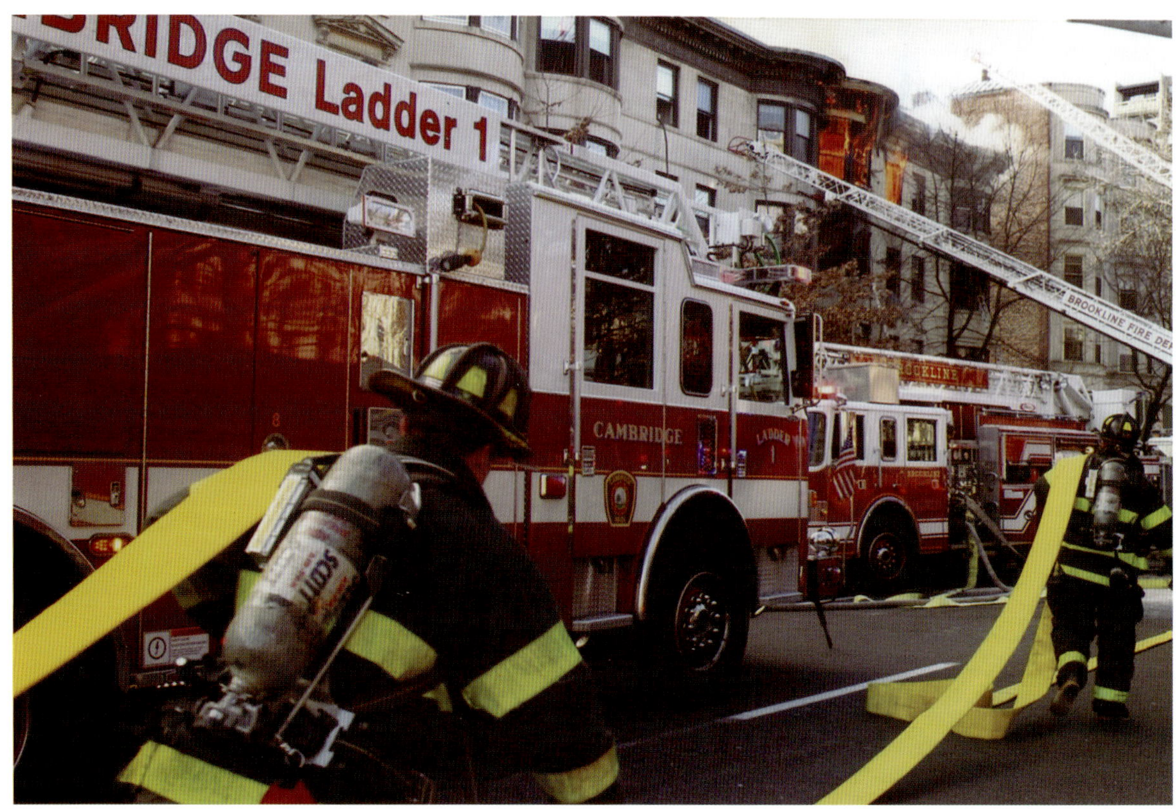

Mutual aid from Boston, Cambridge and Newton were required to control a 4 alarm fire at 1471 Beacon Street, Brookline, on January 16, 2012.

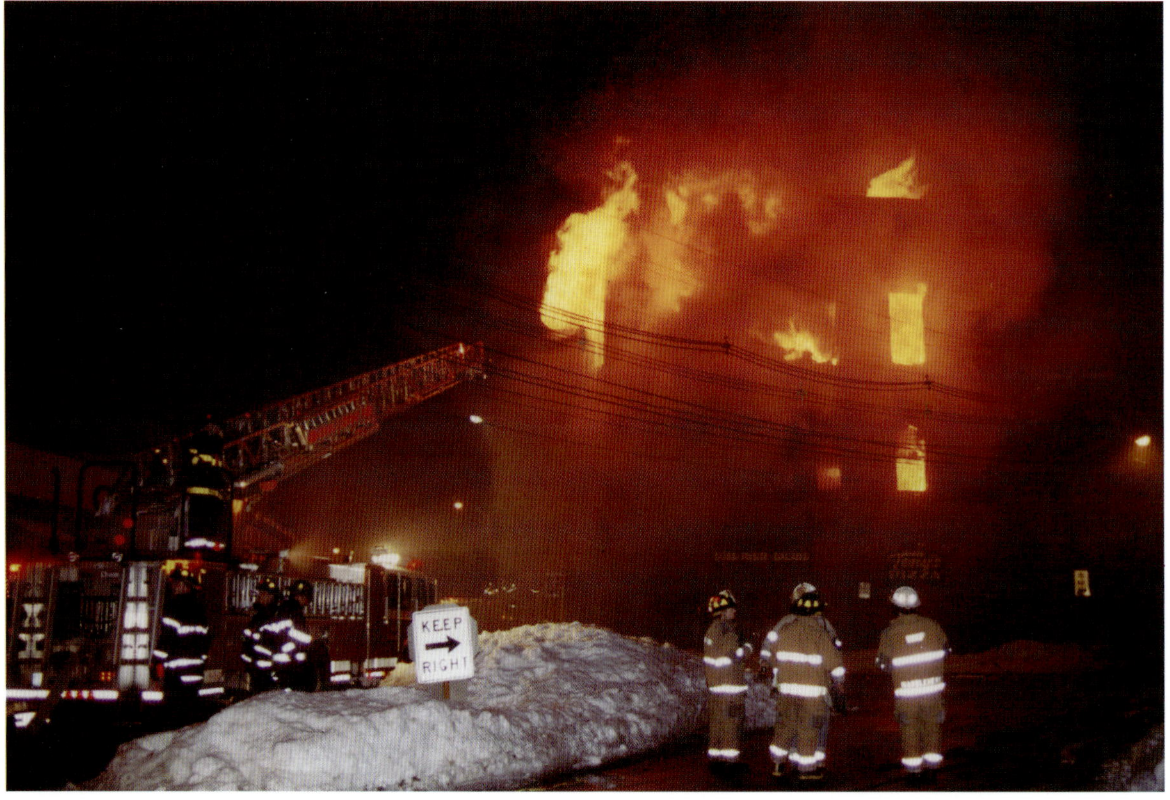

This 4 alarm fire started in a pizza shop at 1 School Street, Marblehead, a 114 year old building, on February 19, 2003.

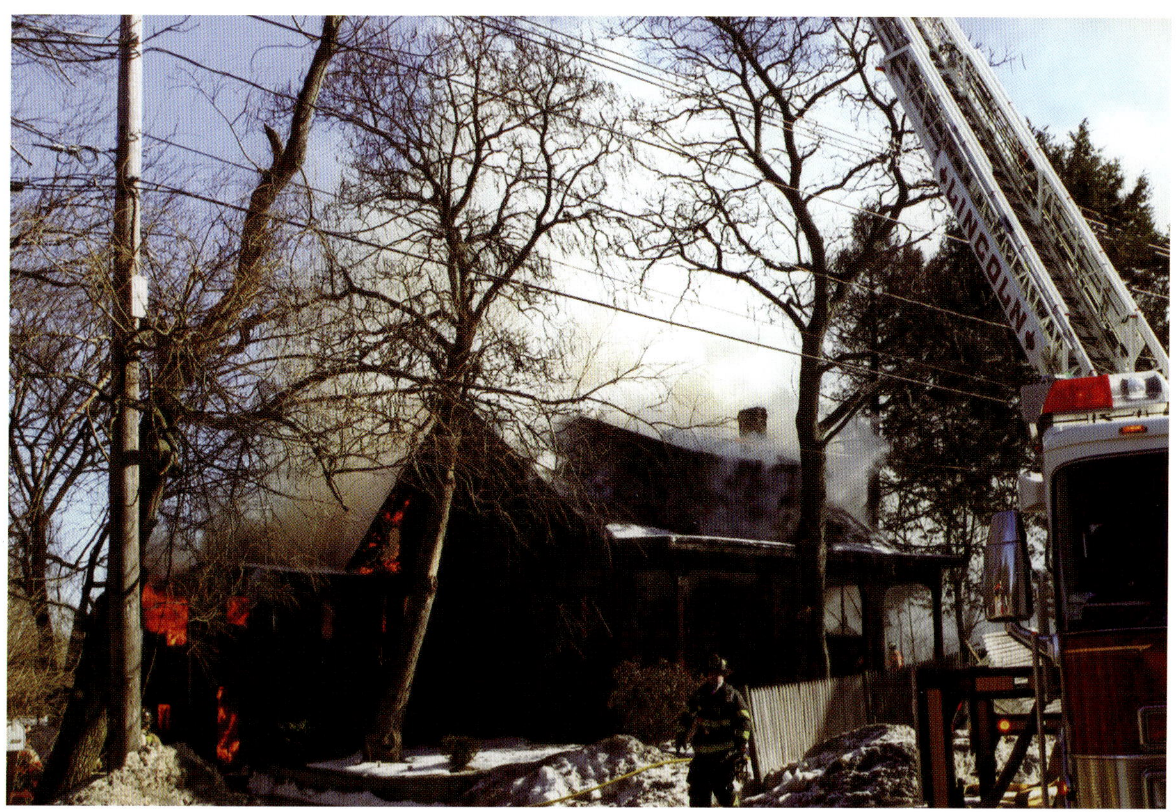

Two alarms at 320 Concord Turnpike, Lincoln, on February 24, 2007.

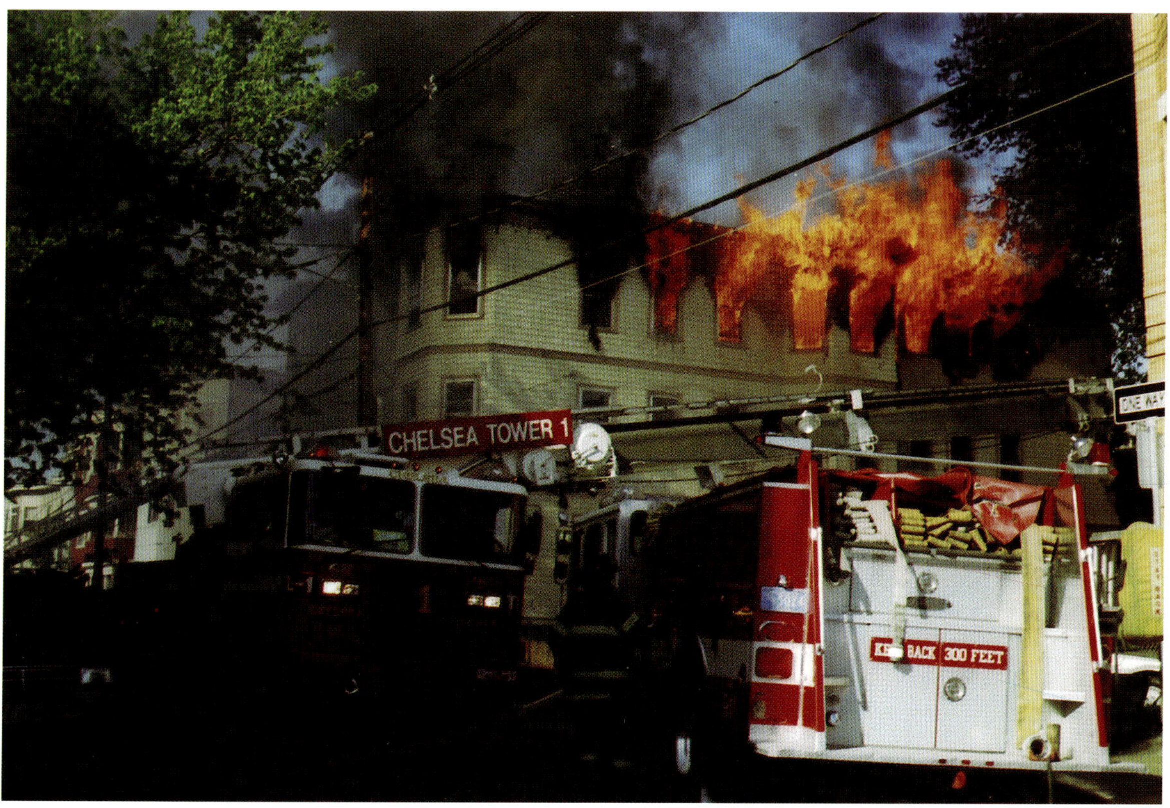

Four alarms were sounded for a multi-family apartment house at 61 Shurtleff Street, Chelsea, on June 19, 1999.

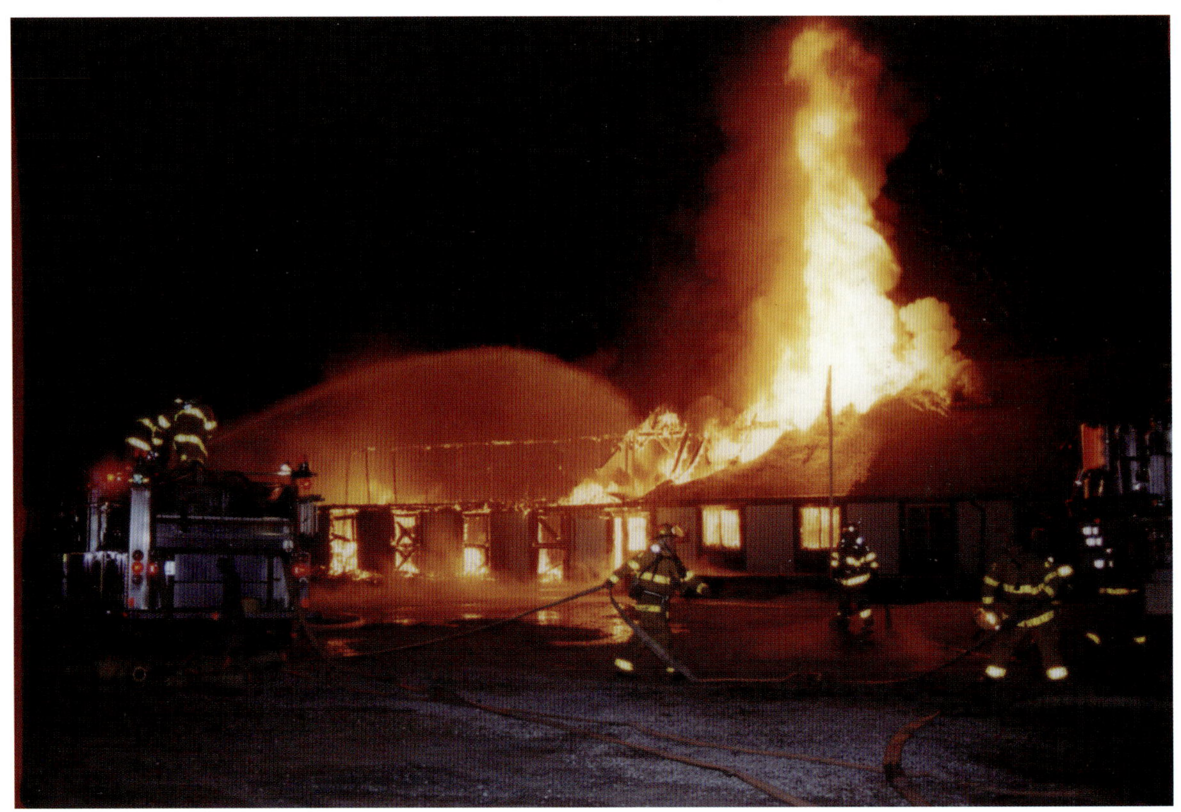

A former horse stable on Kimball Lane, Lynnfield is fully involved, on November 4, 2000.

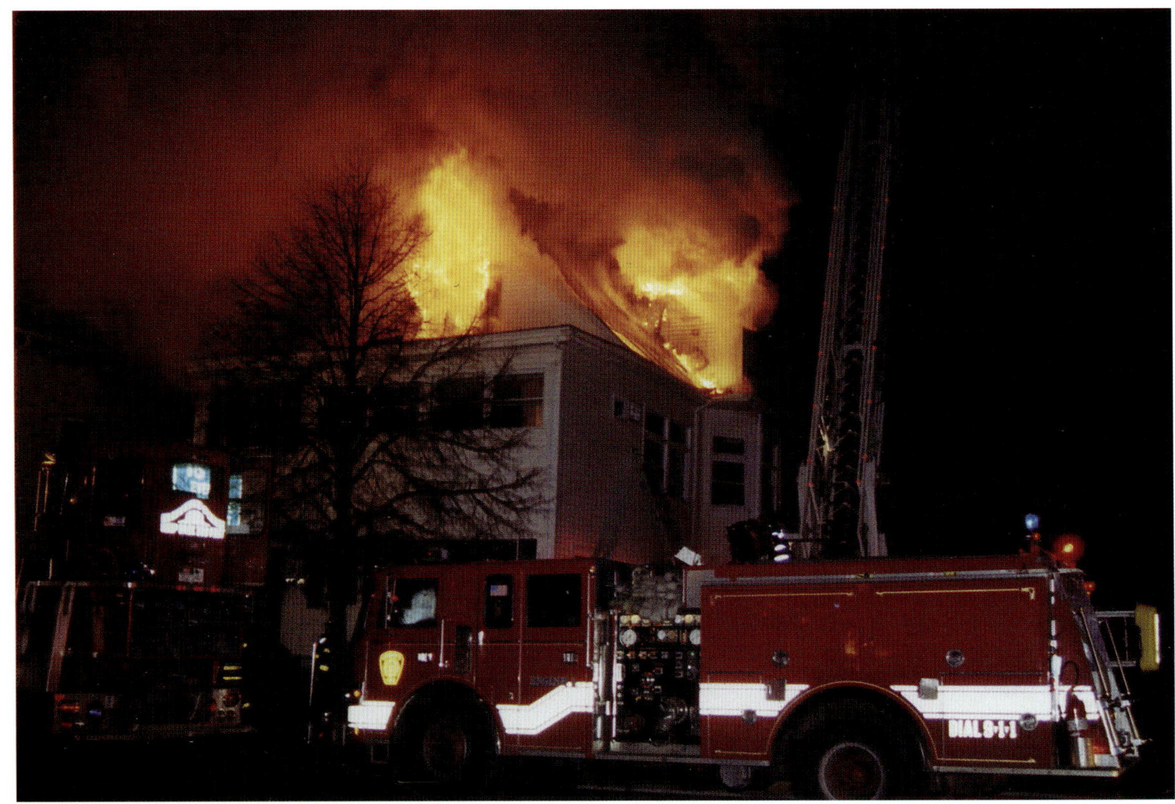

4 alarms at 118 Broadway, Revere, on January 11, 2004.

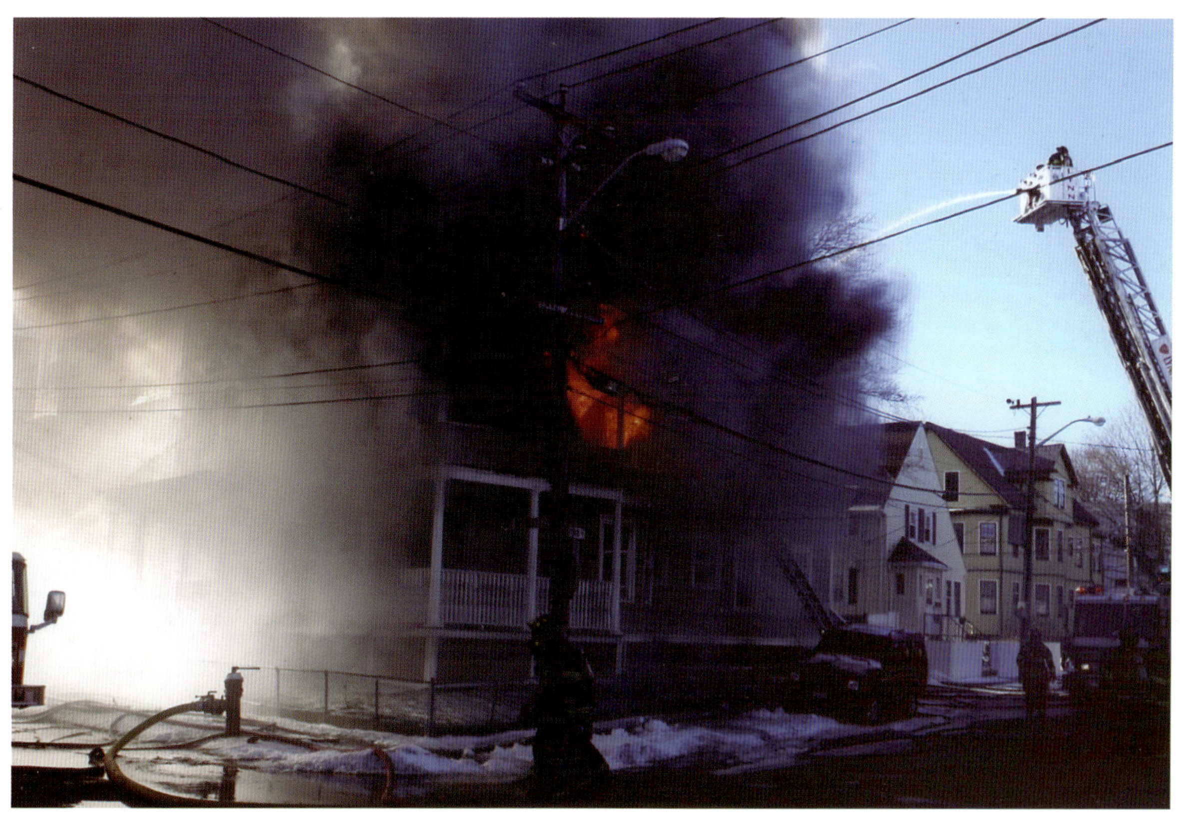

3 alarms at 62 Burrill Street, Lynn, on January 9, 2009.

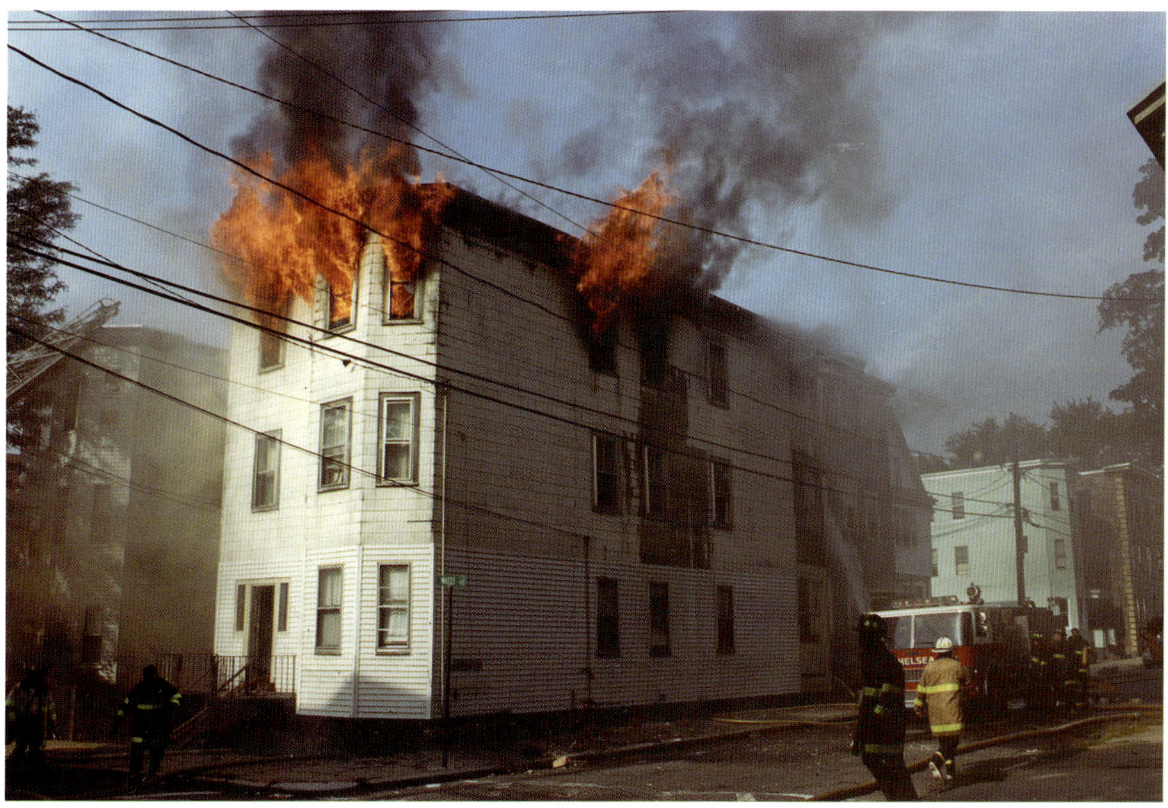

First arriving companies encounter heavy fire at 94 Watts Street, Chelsea, on September 9, 1994.

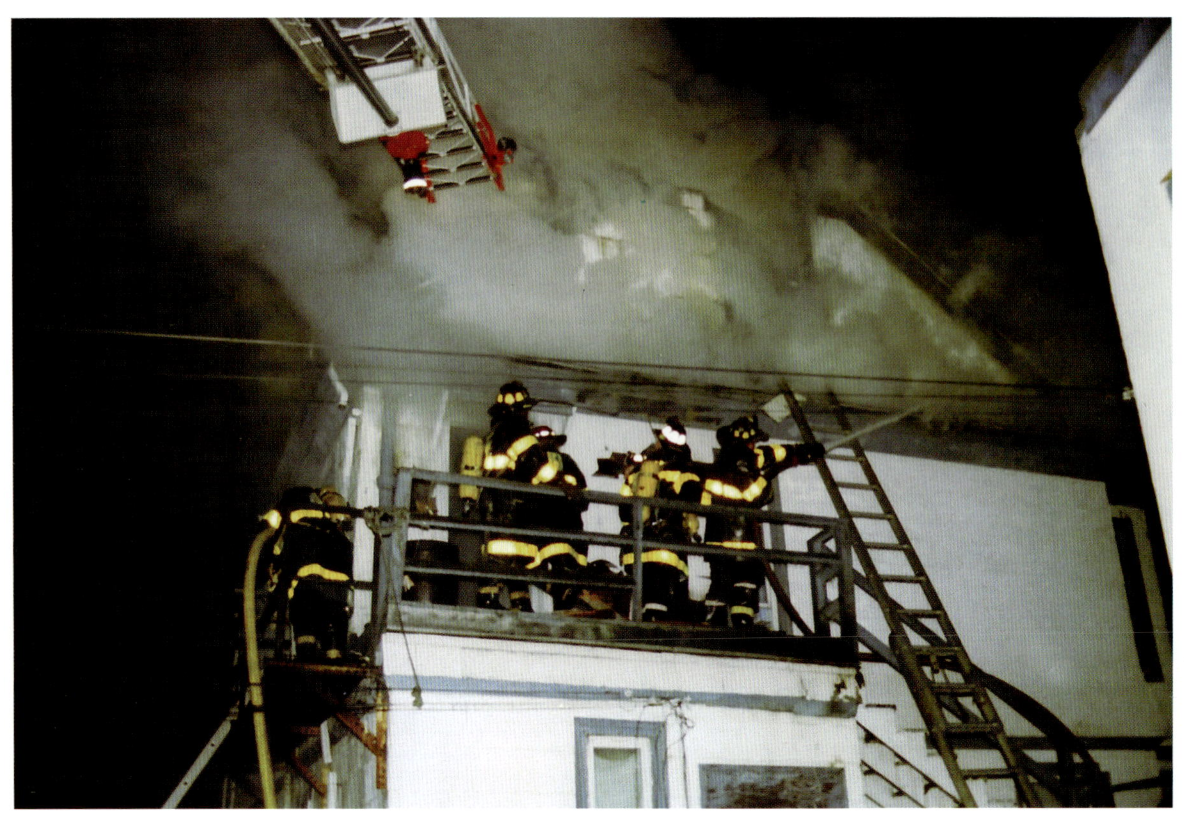

Two alarms at 3 Stearns Terrace, Revere, on February 7, 1995.

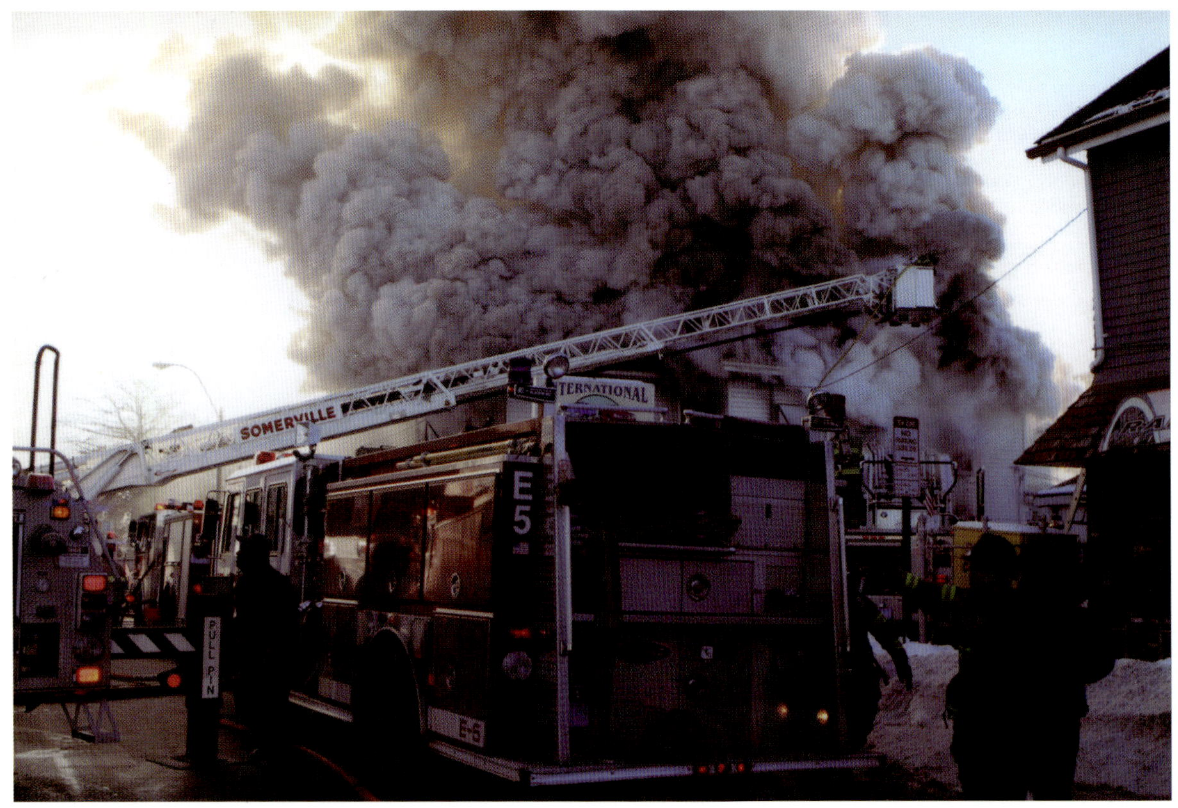

502-504 Somerville Avenue, Somerville, 6 alarms on January 29, 2005.

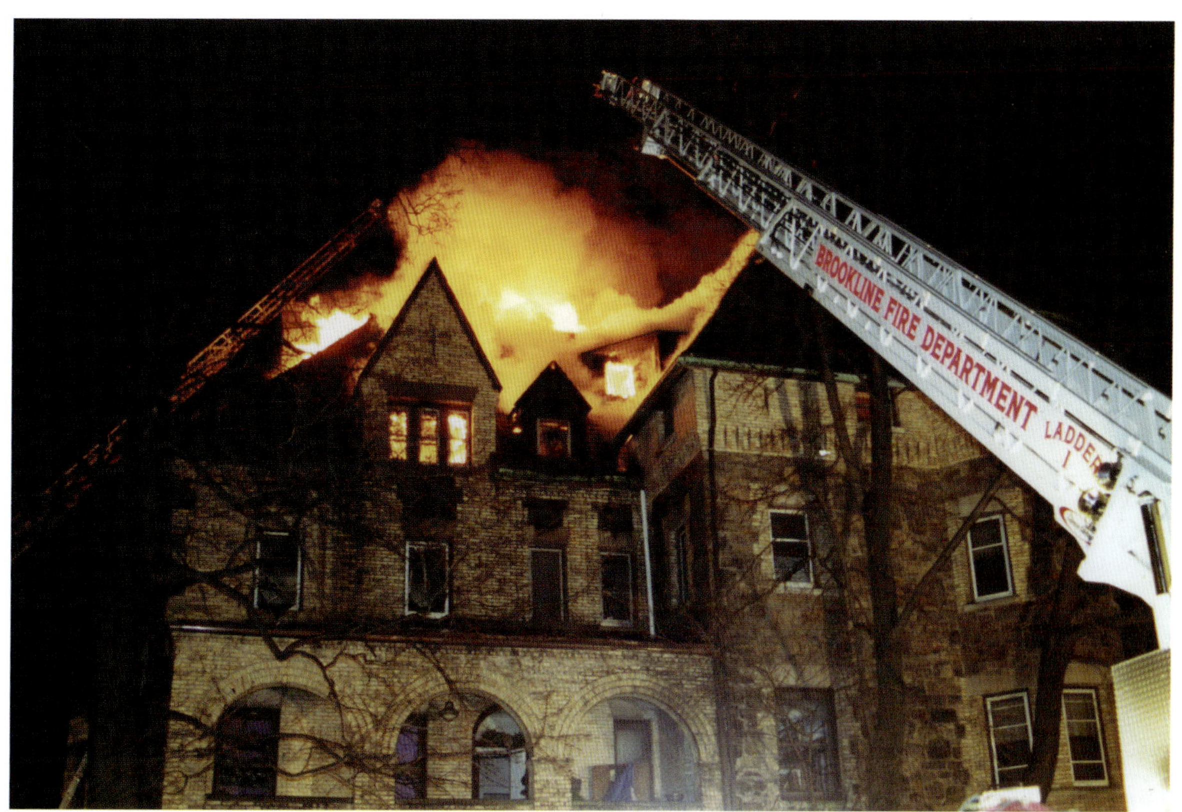

4 alarms on New Year's Day, 2001, at 366 Tappen Street, Brookline.

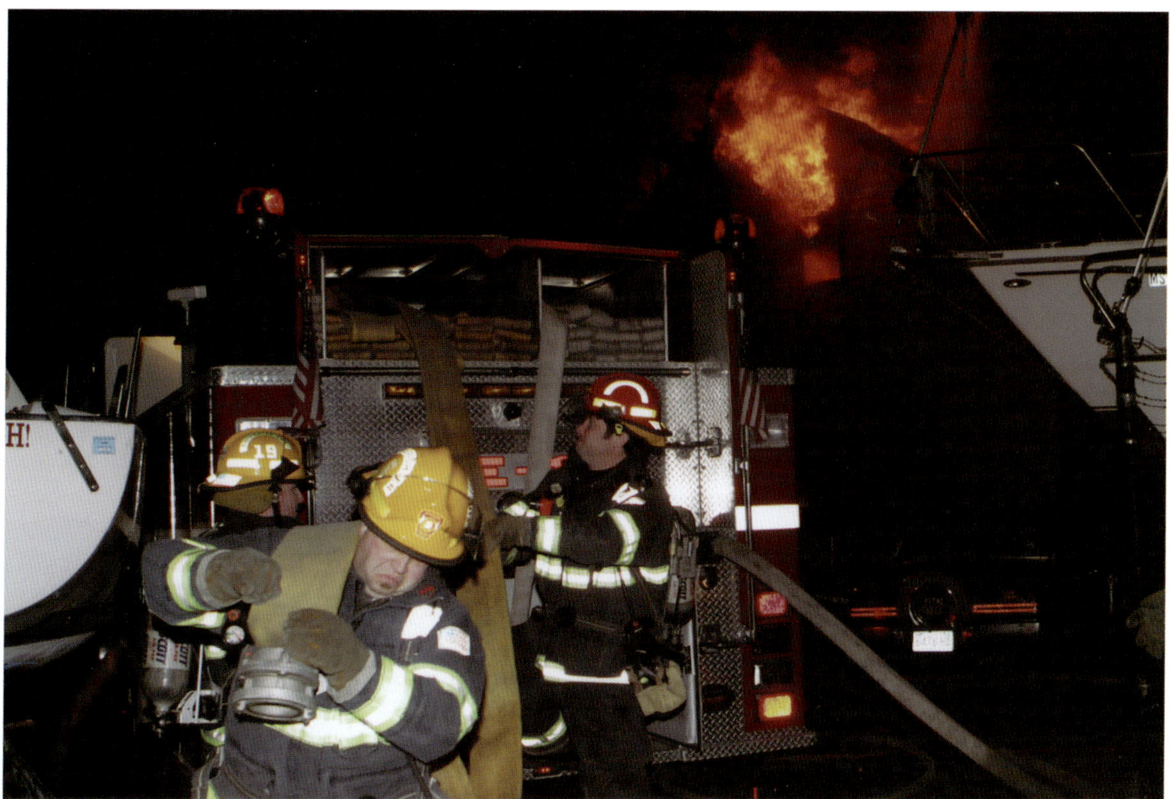

Danvers Firefighters assist the Salem Fire Department at a marina fire at 10 White Street, on January 30, 2007.

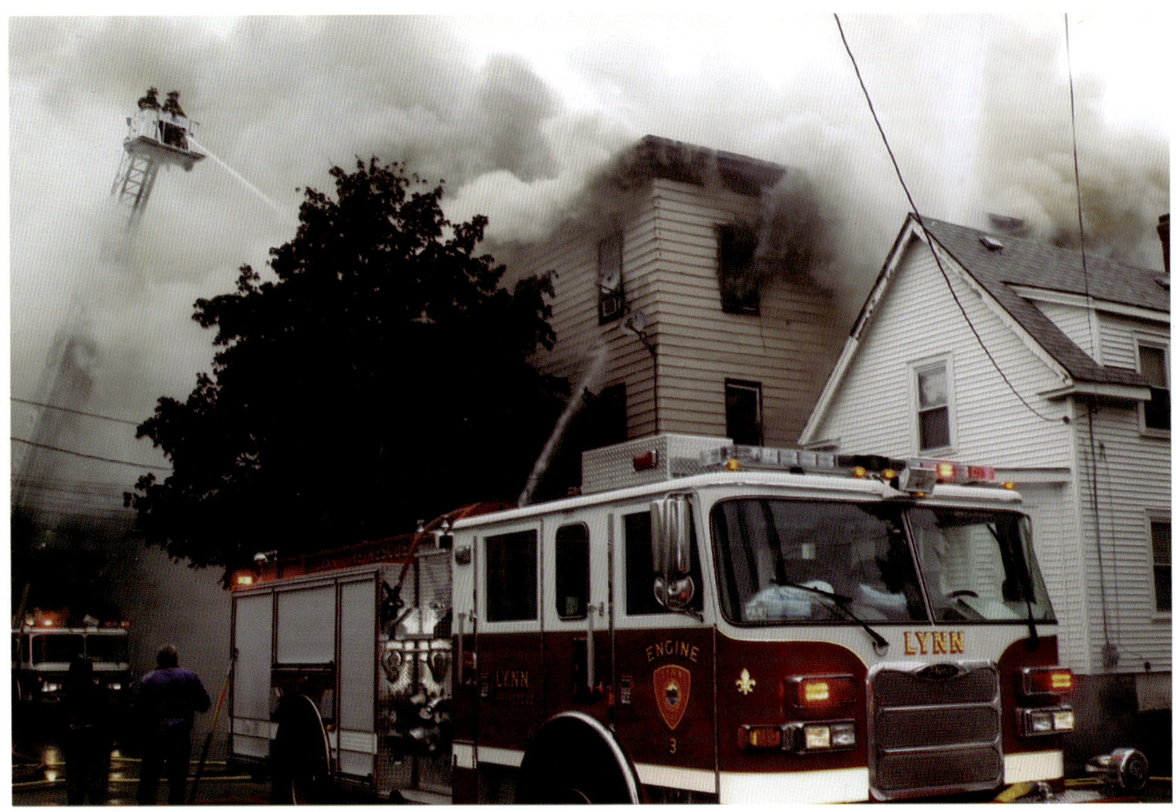

3 alarms at 143 South Street, Lynn, on October 3, 2009.

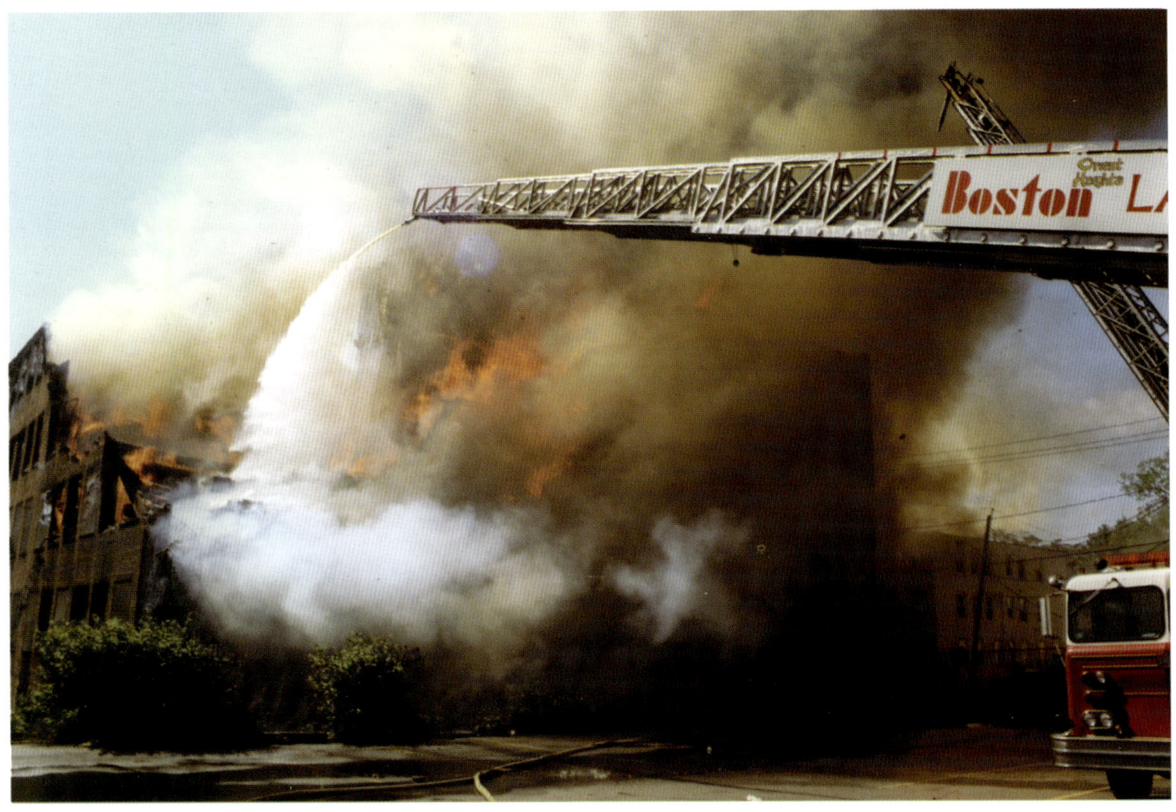

A box factory burns to the ground at 28 Gerrish Avenue, Chelsea, on June 6, 1997. 8 alarms were sounded.

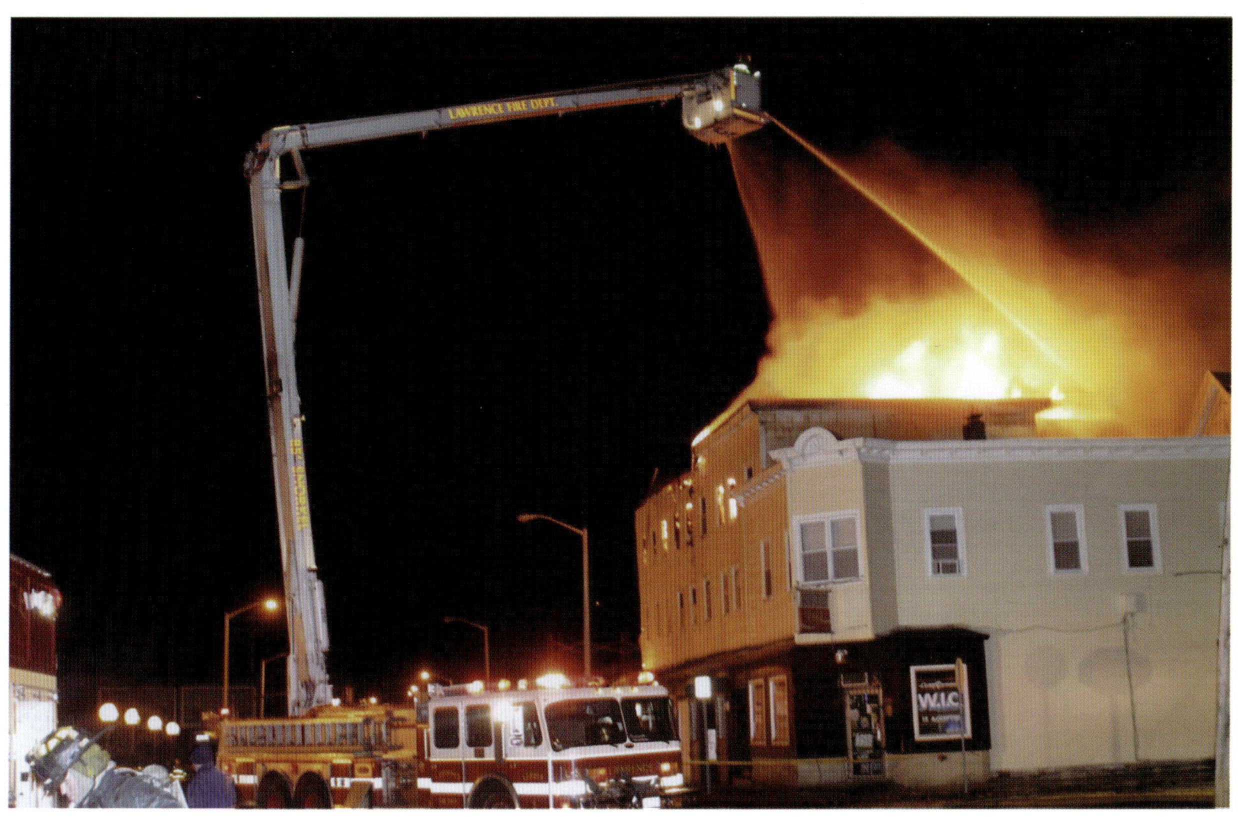

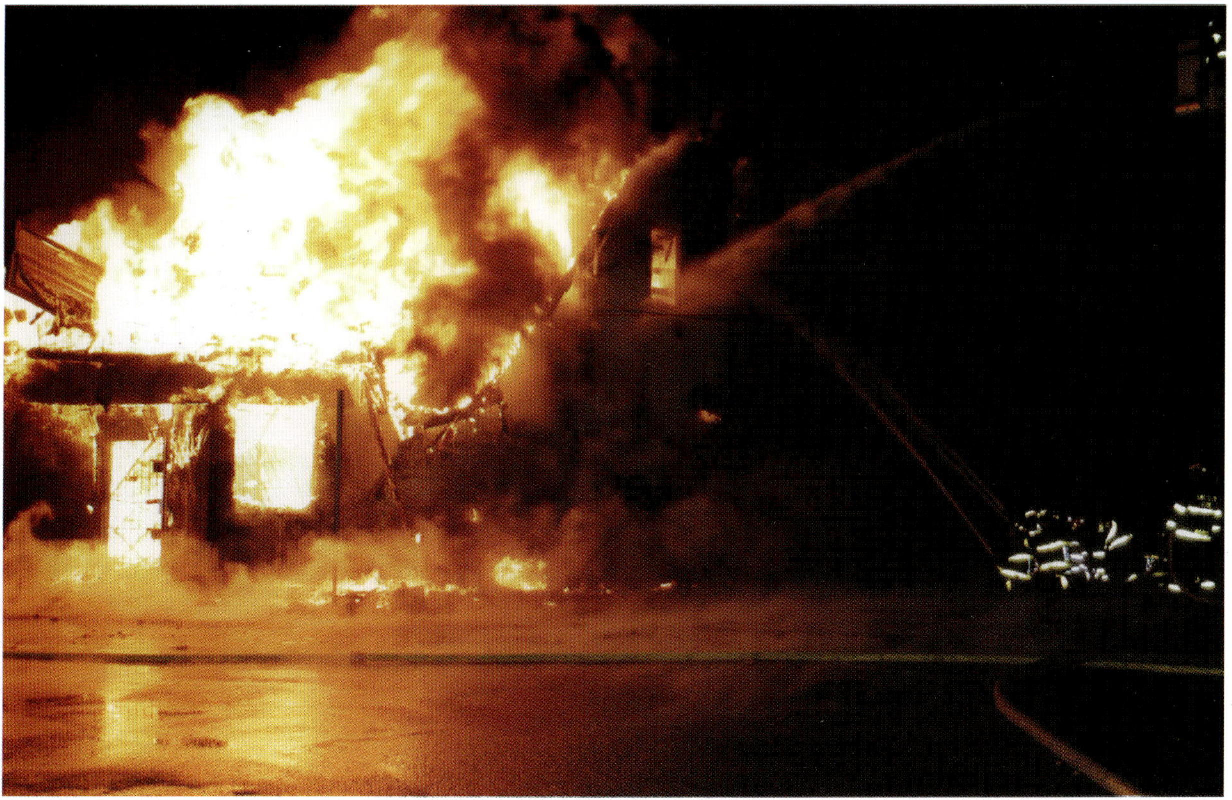

Fifteen buildings on Market, Parker and Springfield Streets, Lawrence, are destroyed in a 5 alarm fire.

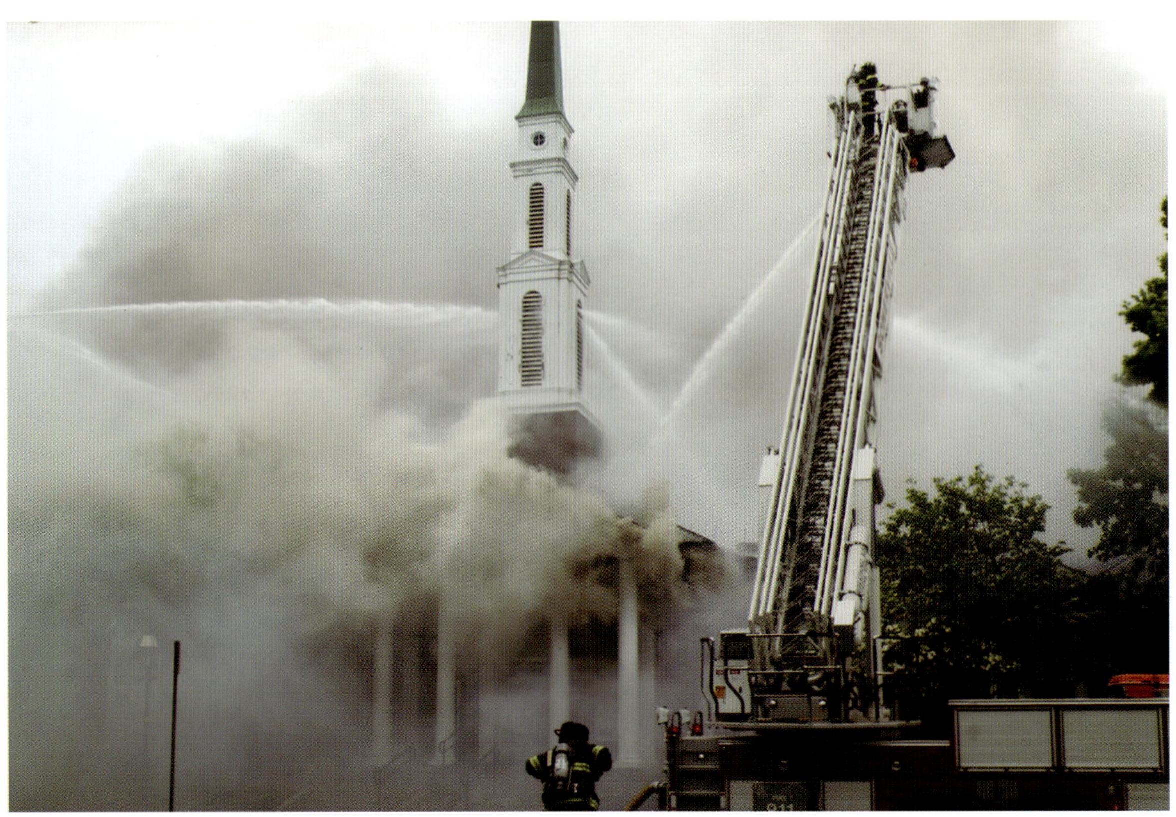

The Church of Latter Day Saints, at 4 Longfellow Place, Cambridge, is gutted in a 4 alarm fire, on May 17, 2009.

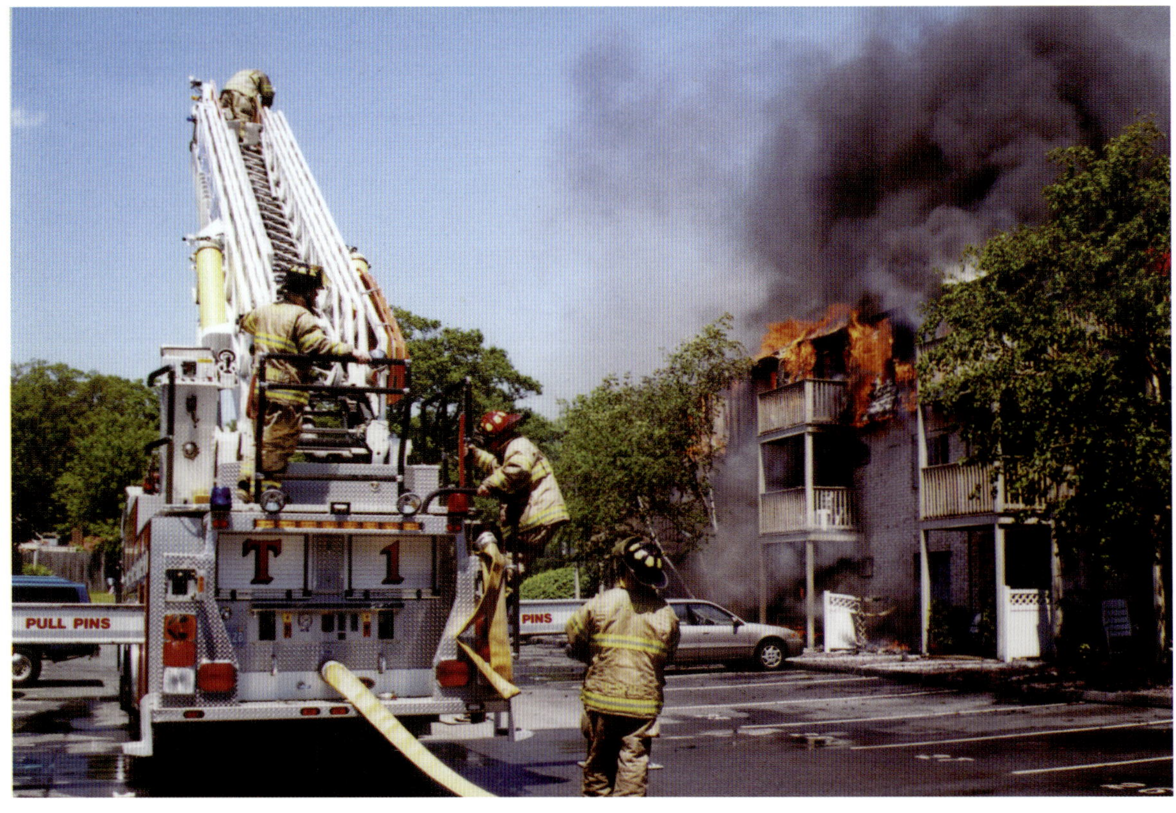

A large apartment complex is heavily damaged in a 5 alarm fire, at 20 Ocean Avenue, Gloucester, on June 1, 2002.

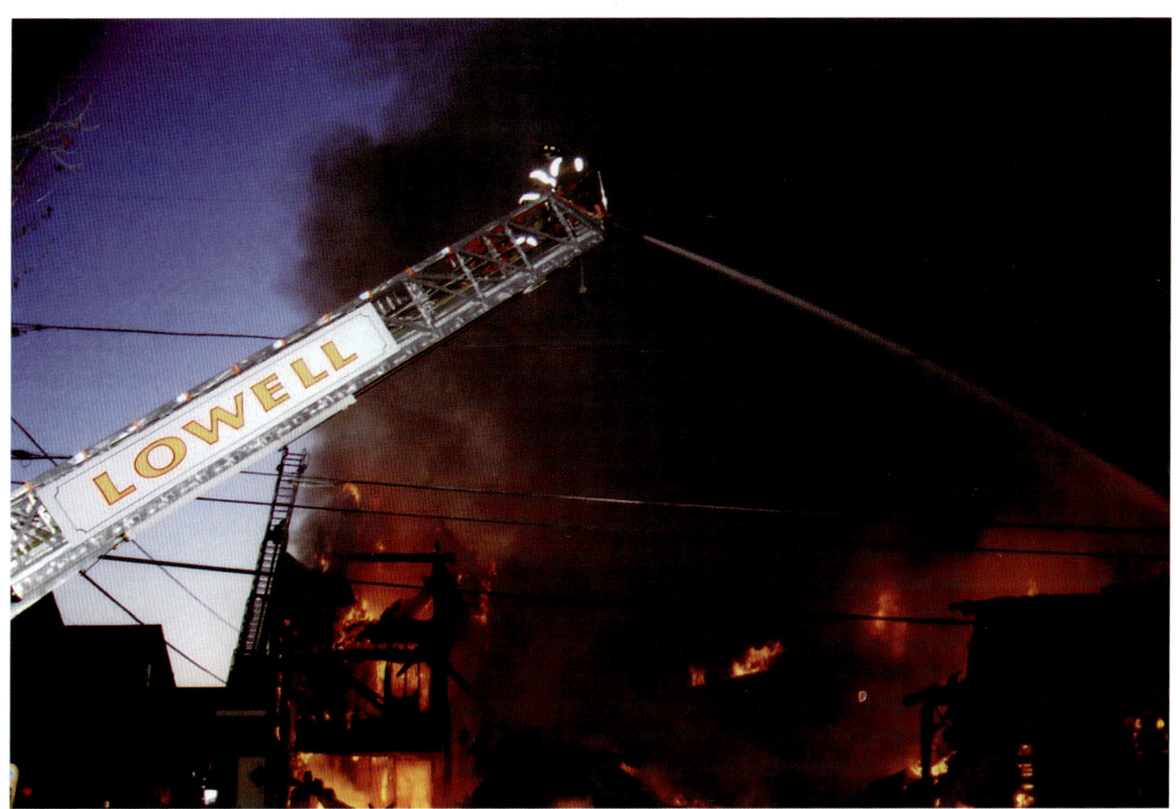

The Assumption of the Virgin Mary Church, at Mt. Vernon and Butterfield Streets is destroyed in a 5 alarm fire, on April 25, 1999.

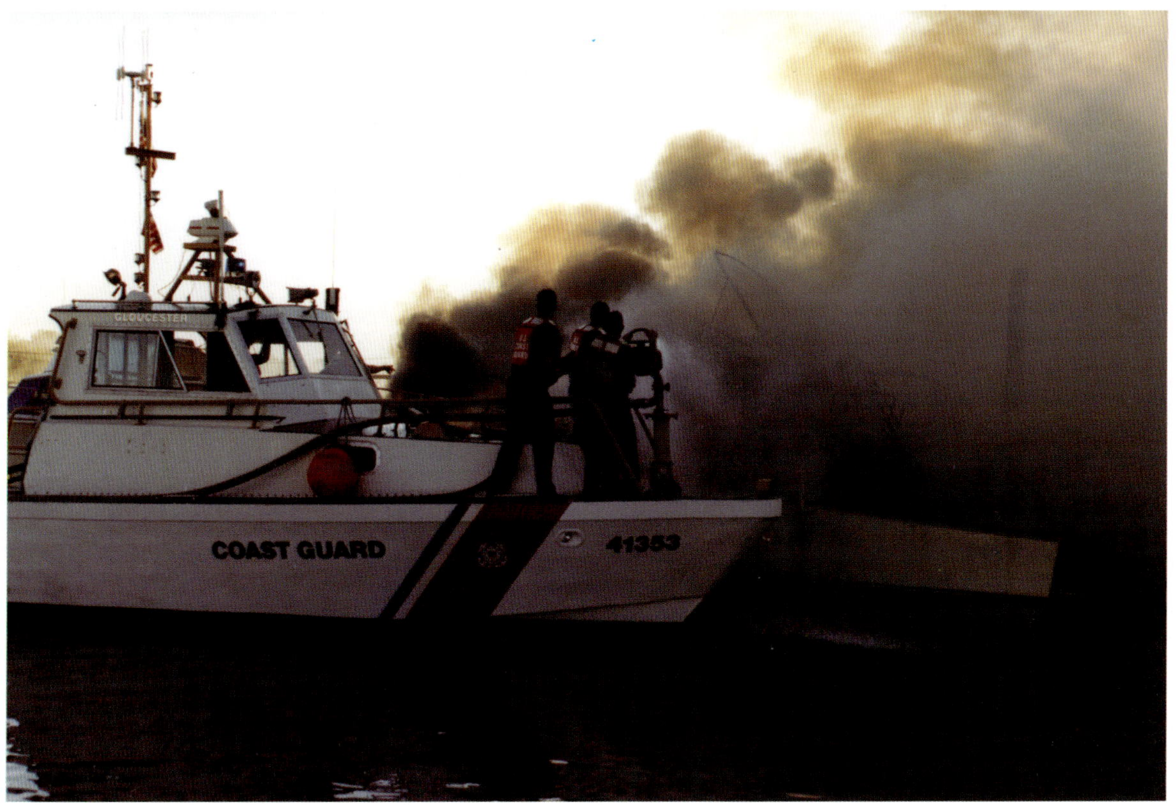

Six boats burn at a 2 alarm fire outside the Danversport Yacht Club, Danvers.

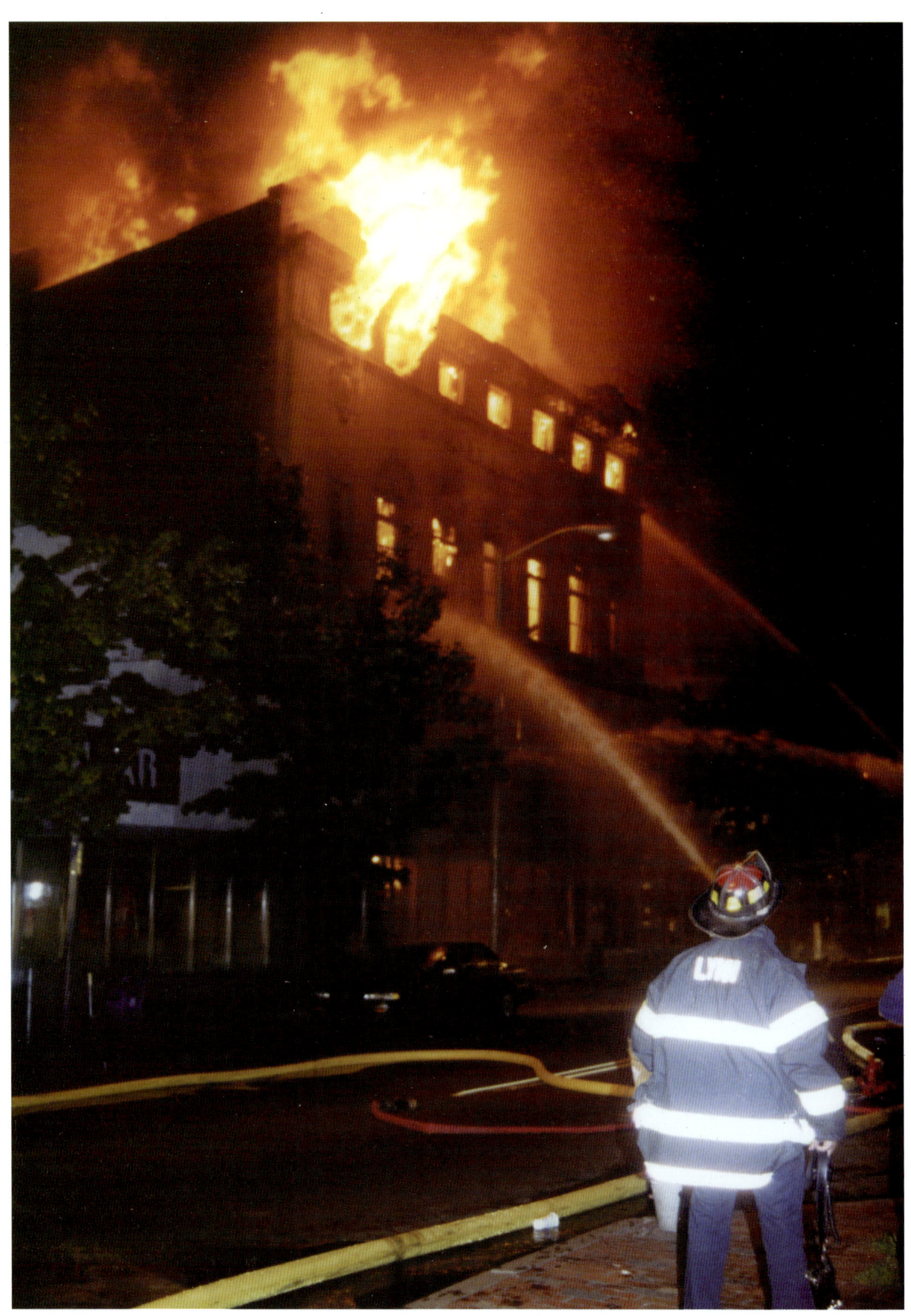

A city block, on Union Street, in downtown Lynn is gutted, on August 29, 2001 in a 3 alarm fire.

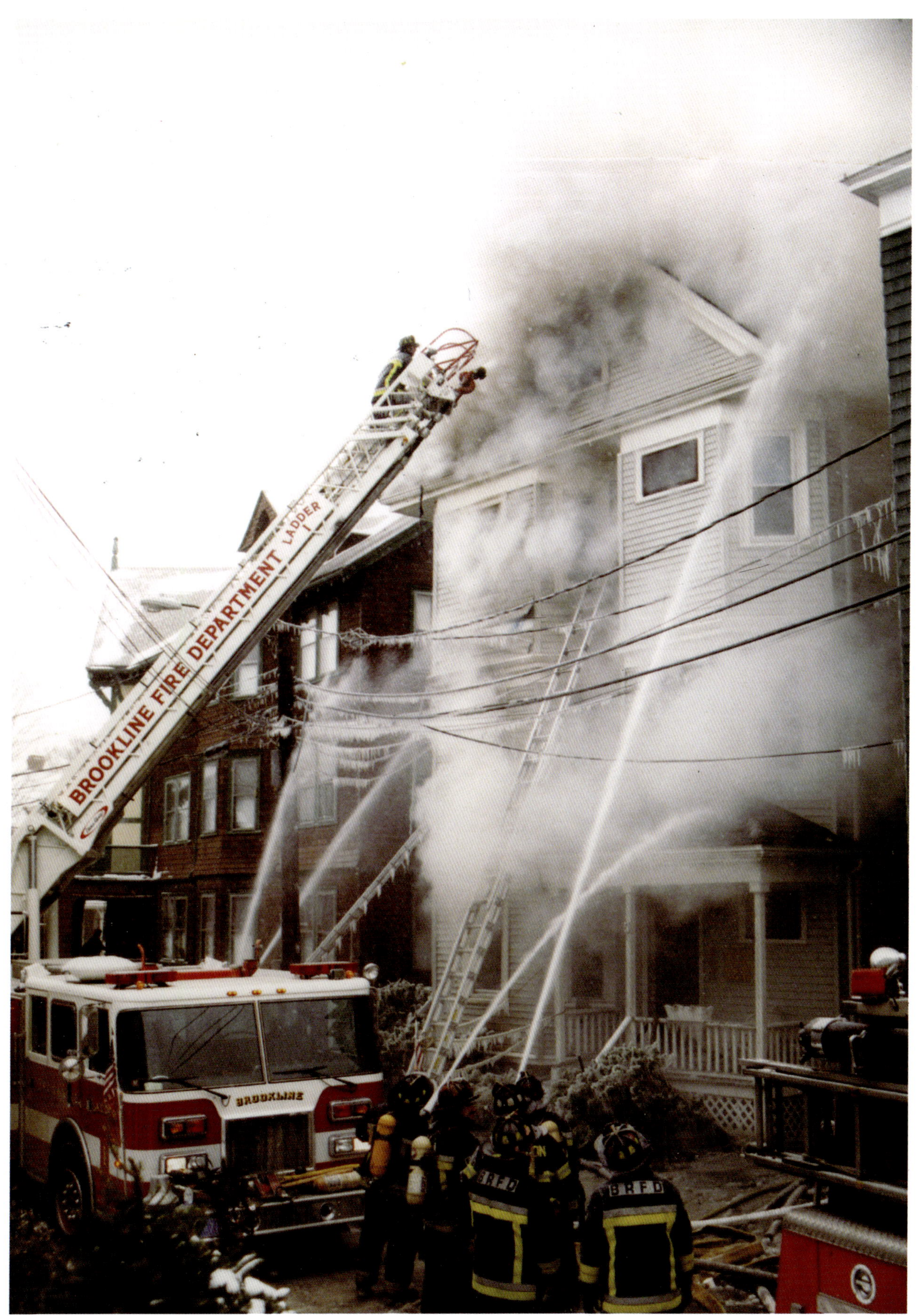

Below freezing temperatures hampered the Brookline Fire Department in a 4 alarm fire at 7 Elm Street, on January 14, 1999.

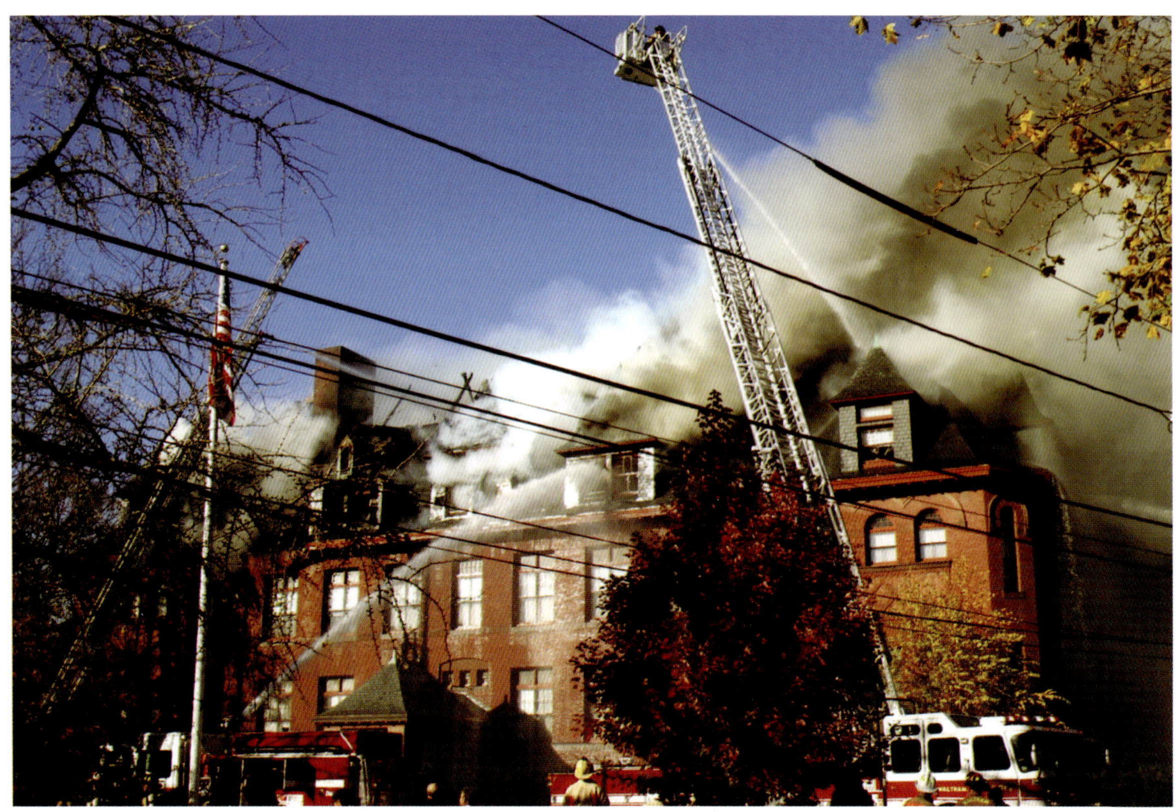

A 19 unit condominium, (former school) at 33 Forest Street, Lexington, is heavily damaged in a 4 alarm fire, on October 31, 2008.

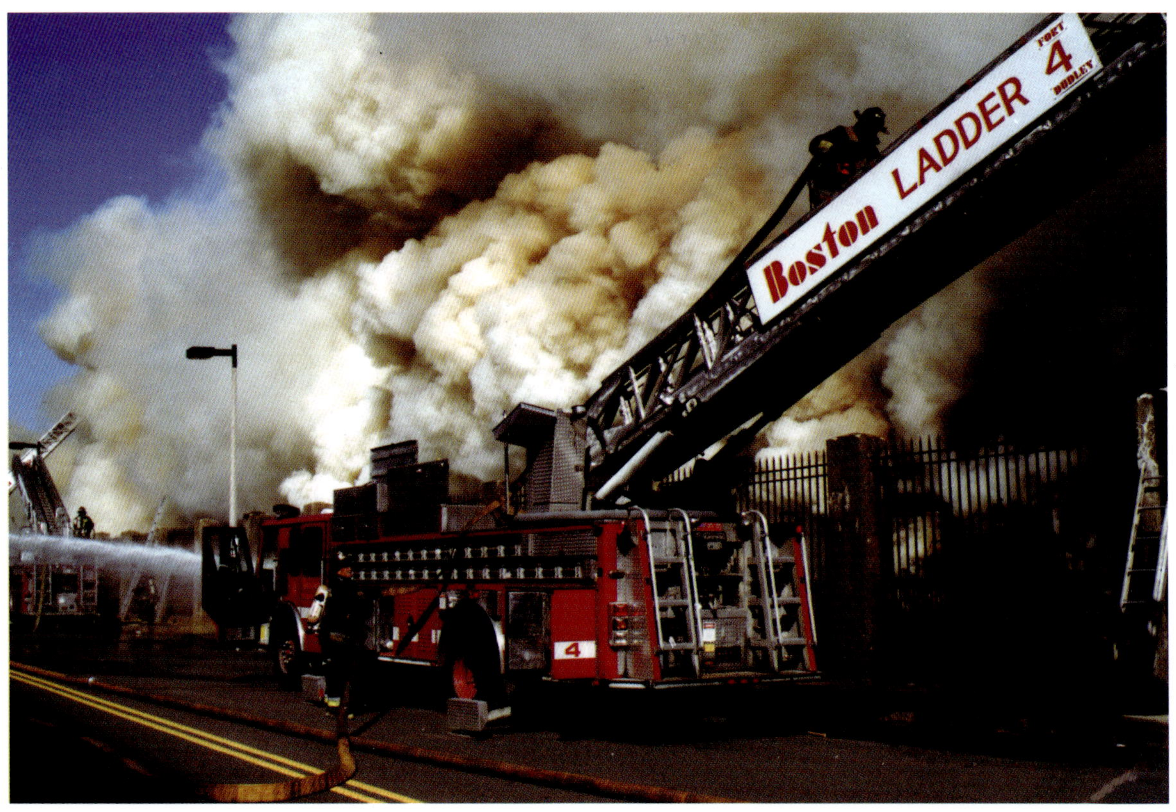

A vacant factory burns in a 9 alarm fire at 58 3rd Avenue, Charlestown, on May 4, 2002.

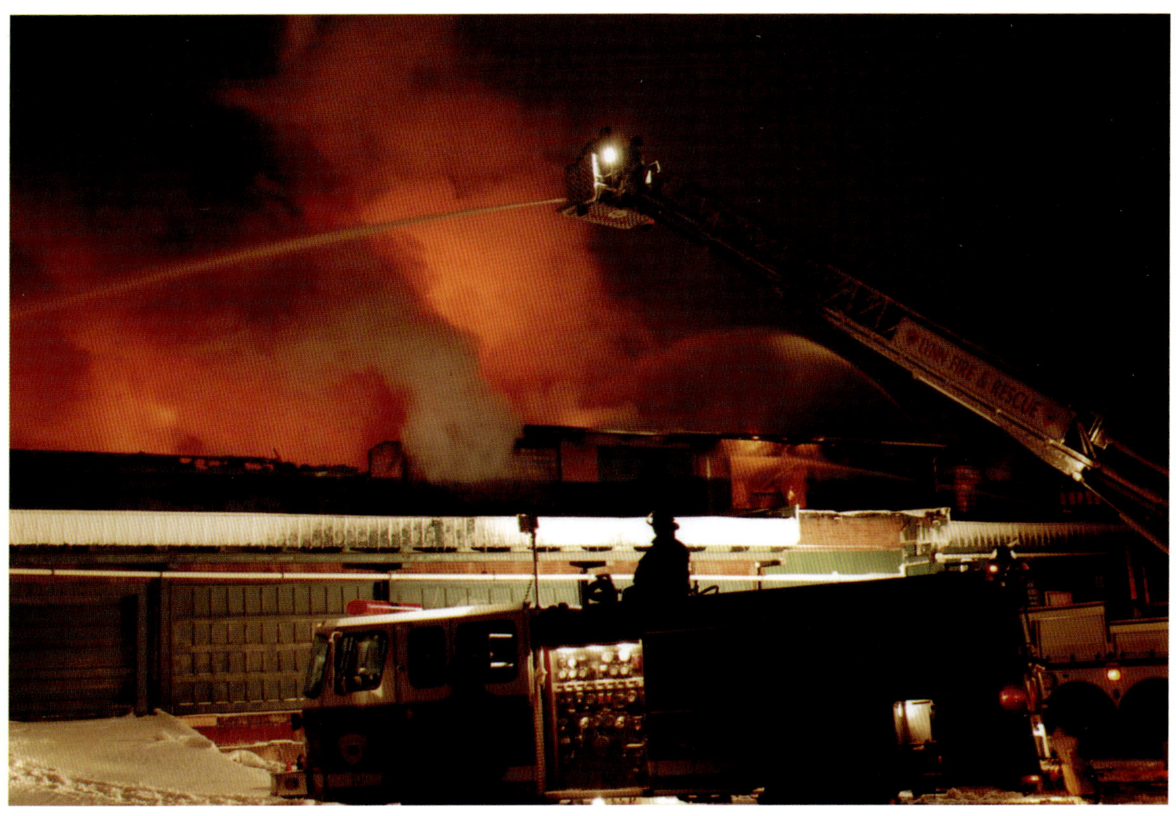

A vacant bakery at 114 Brookline Street, Lynn, on November 14, 2008.

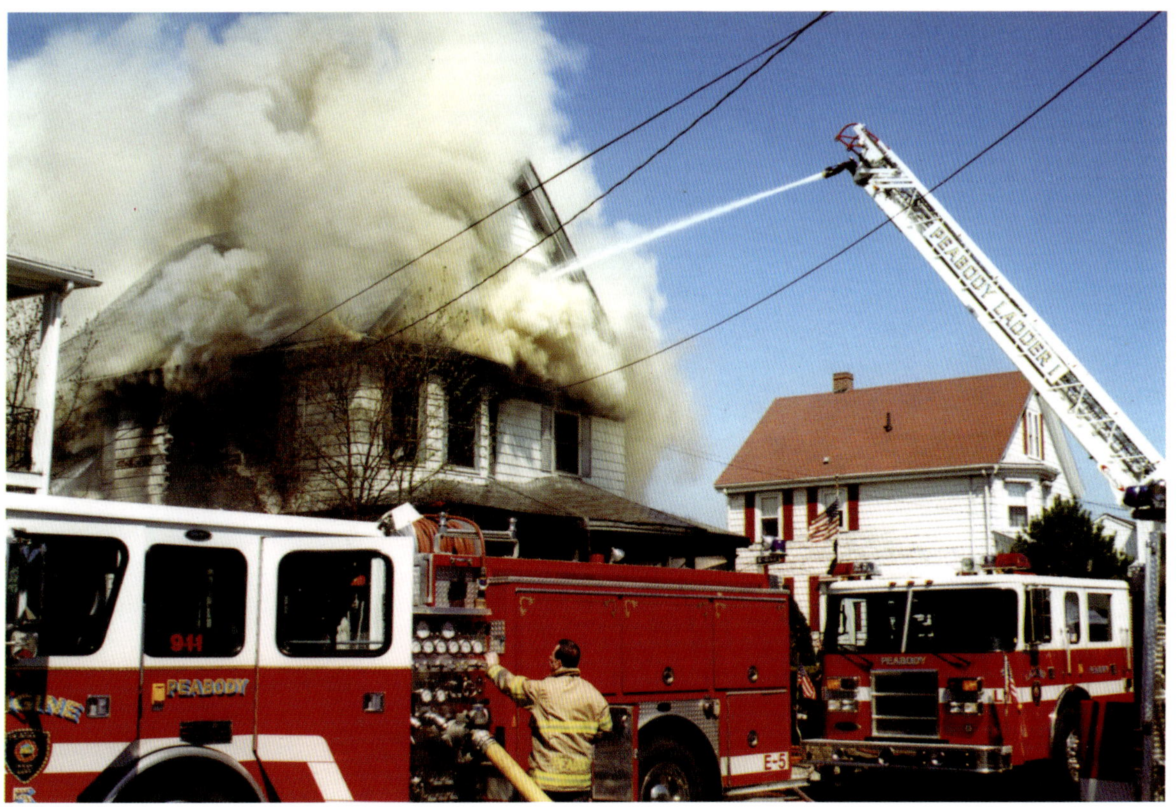

Two alarms at 129 Lynnfield Street, Peabody, on April 28, 2003.

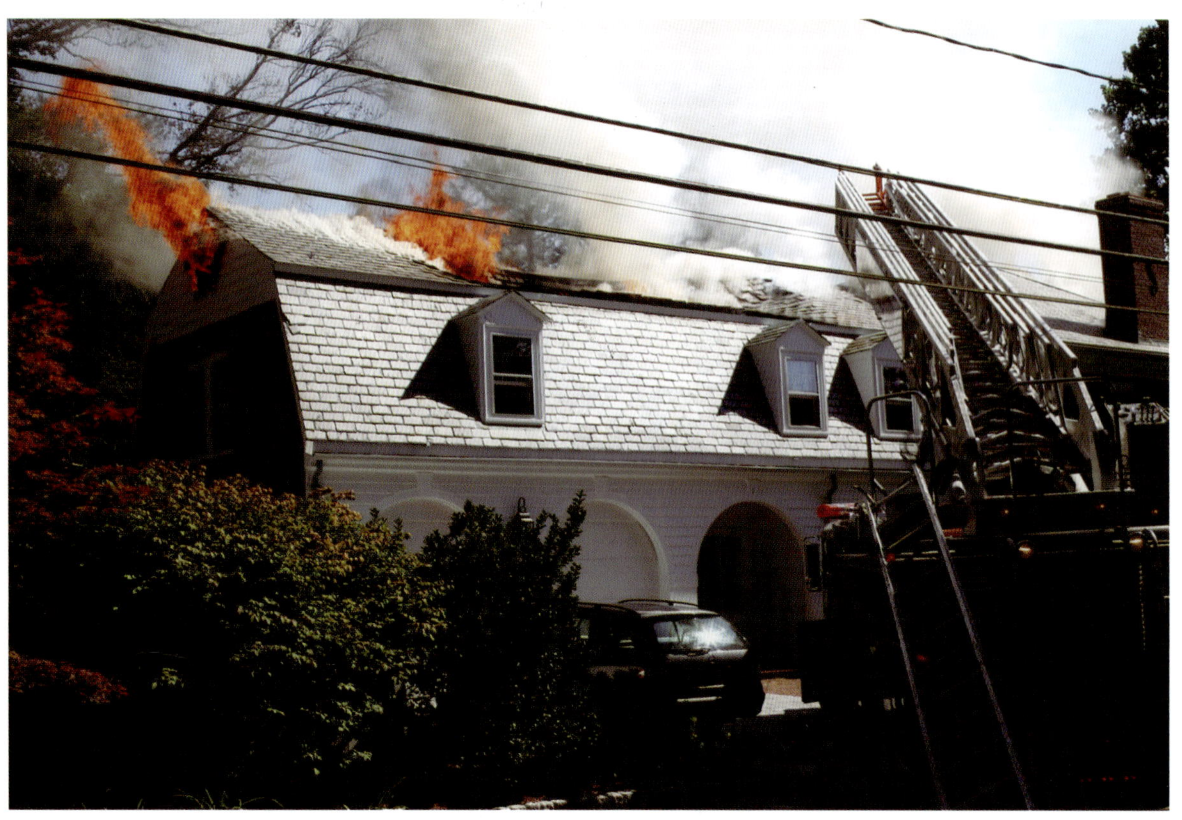

Two alarms at 1 Central Green, Winchester, on September 4, 2008.

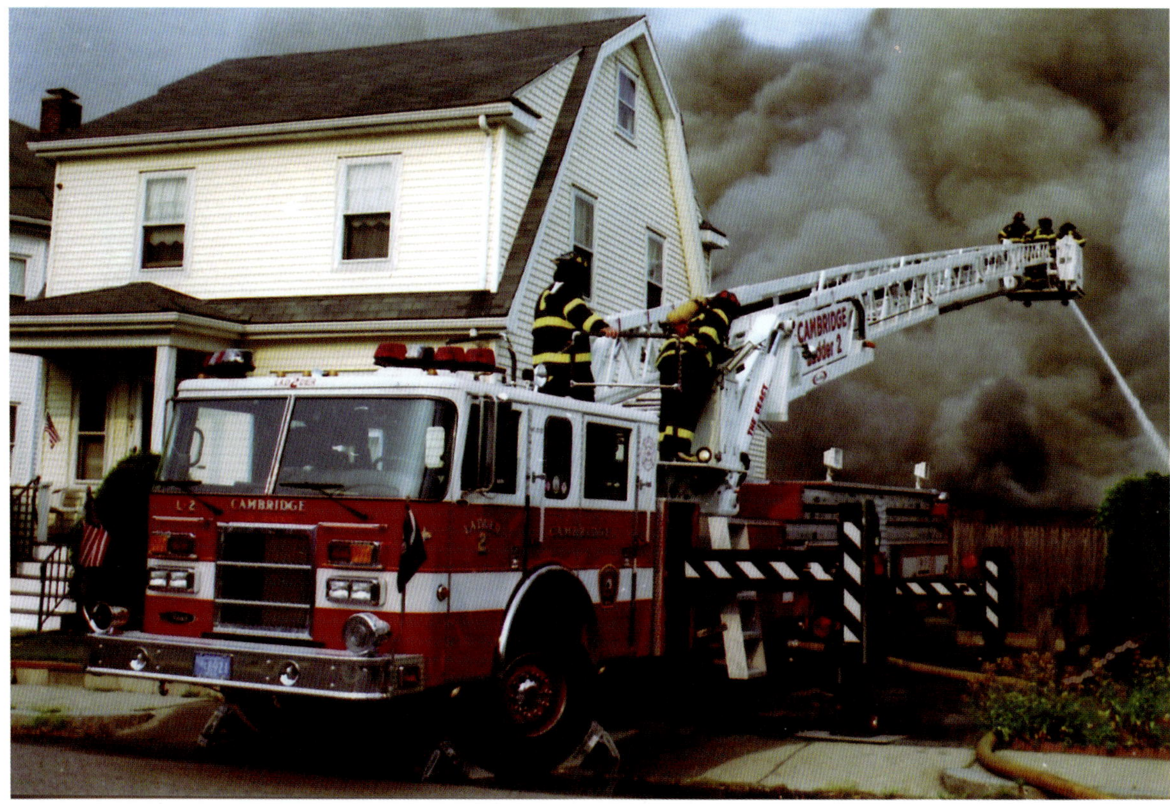

Mutual aid from Cambridge, Boston, Newton and Waltham battle a 4 alarm fire in a commercial building at 19 Calvin Road, Watertown, on August 14, 2002.

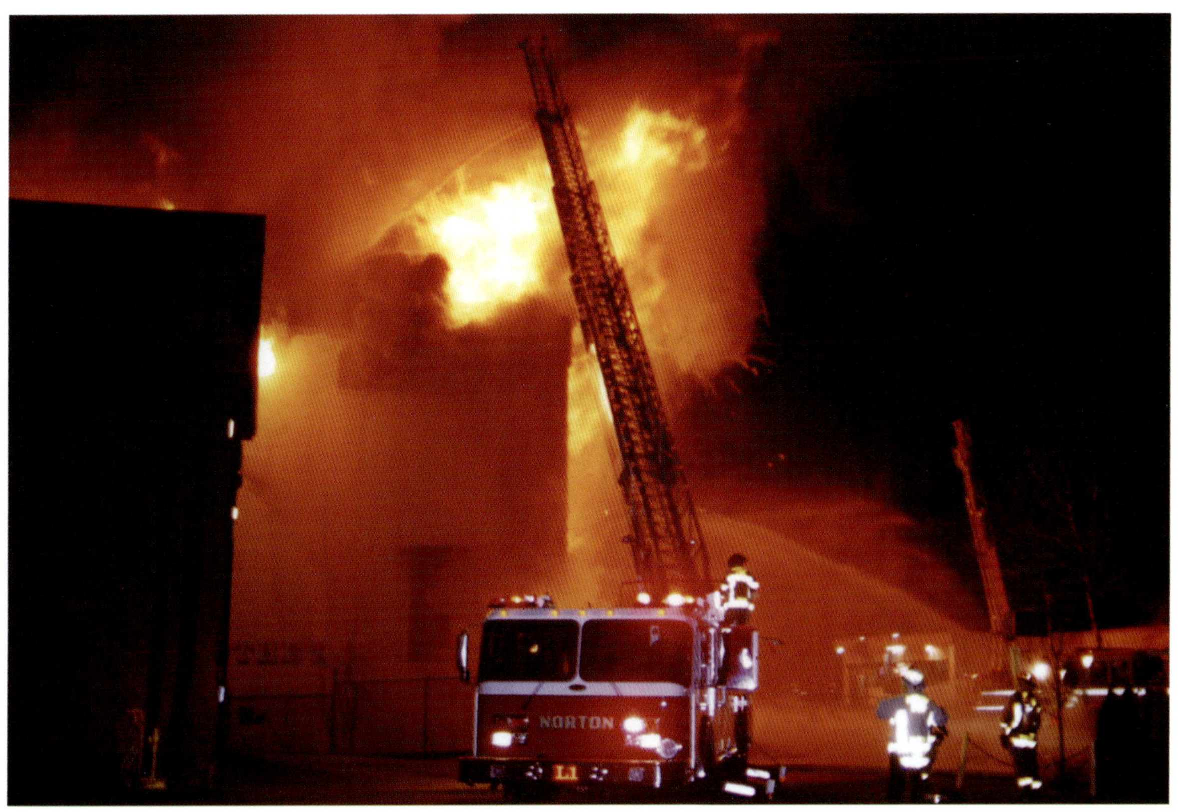

General alarm in a furniture store at 24 Winthrop Street, Taunton, on February 28, 2004.

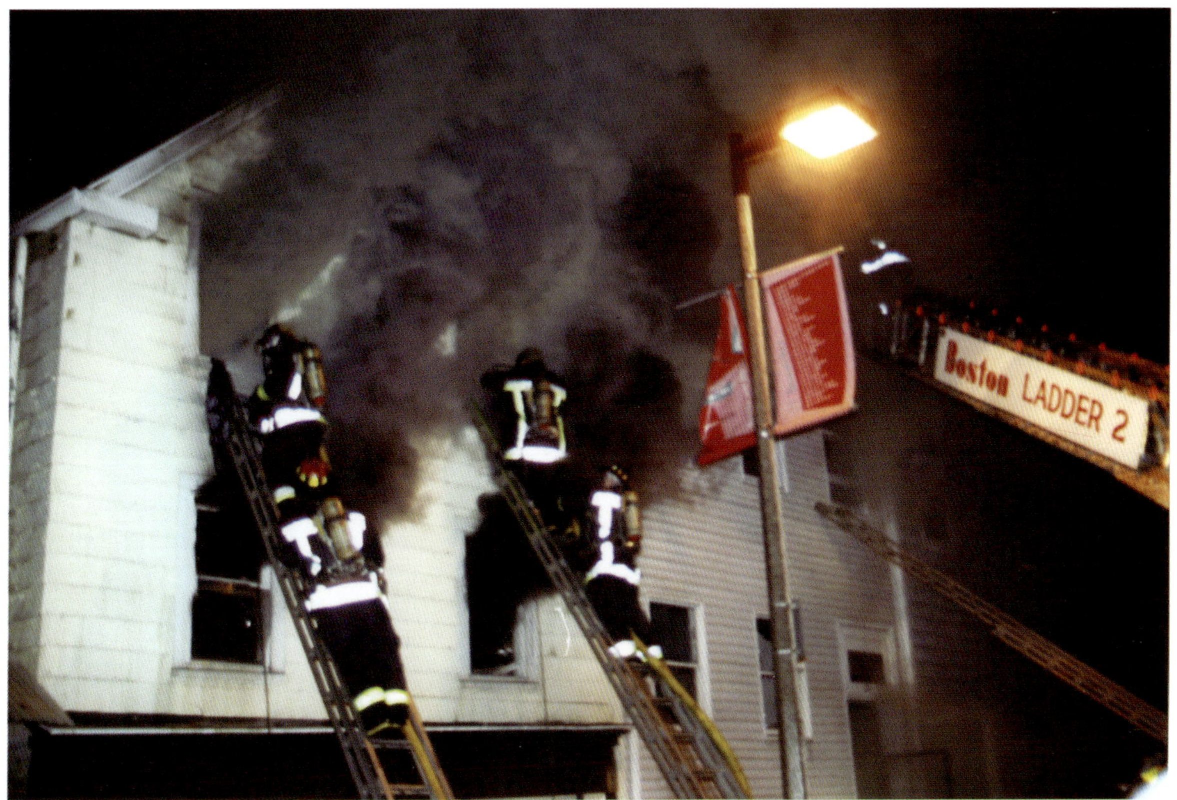

Three alarms at 292-294 Meridian Street, East Boston, on February 13, 2004.

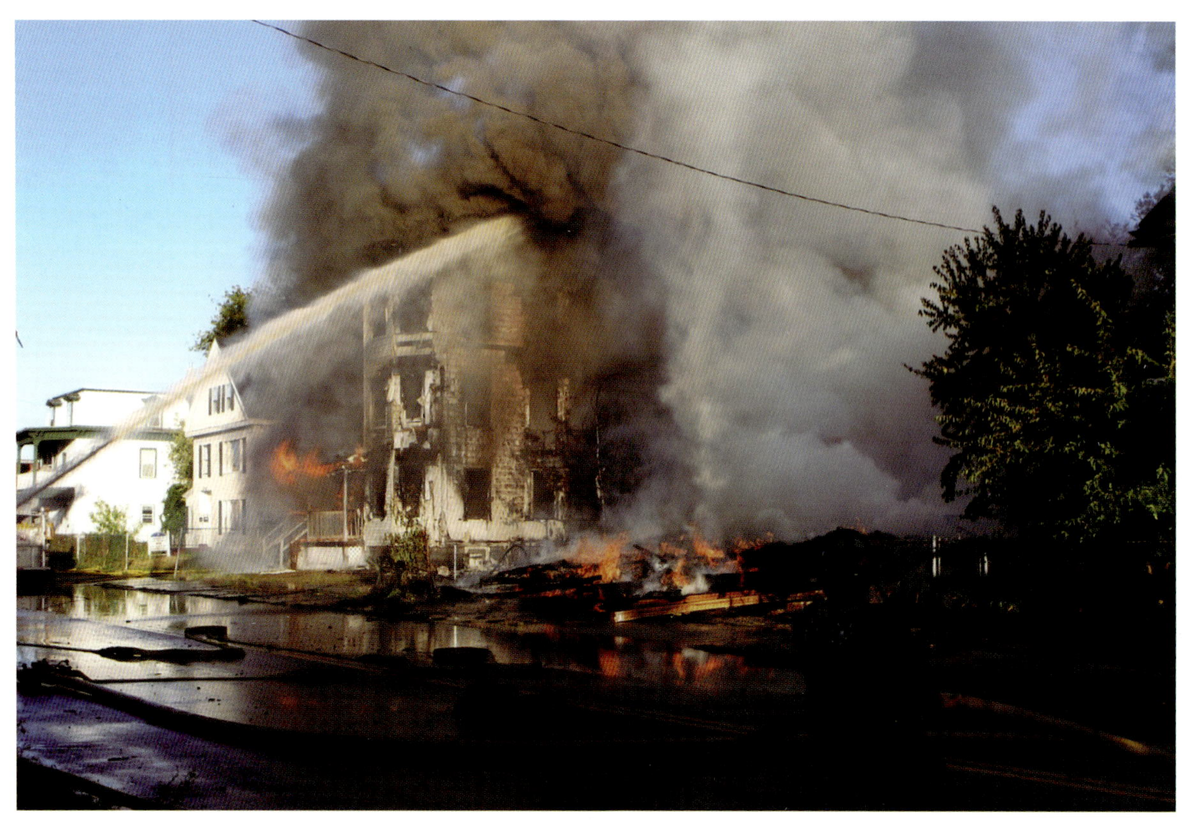

Three buildings burn on Parker Street, Lawrence in a 4 alarm fire, on September 2, 2007.

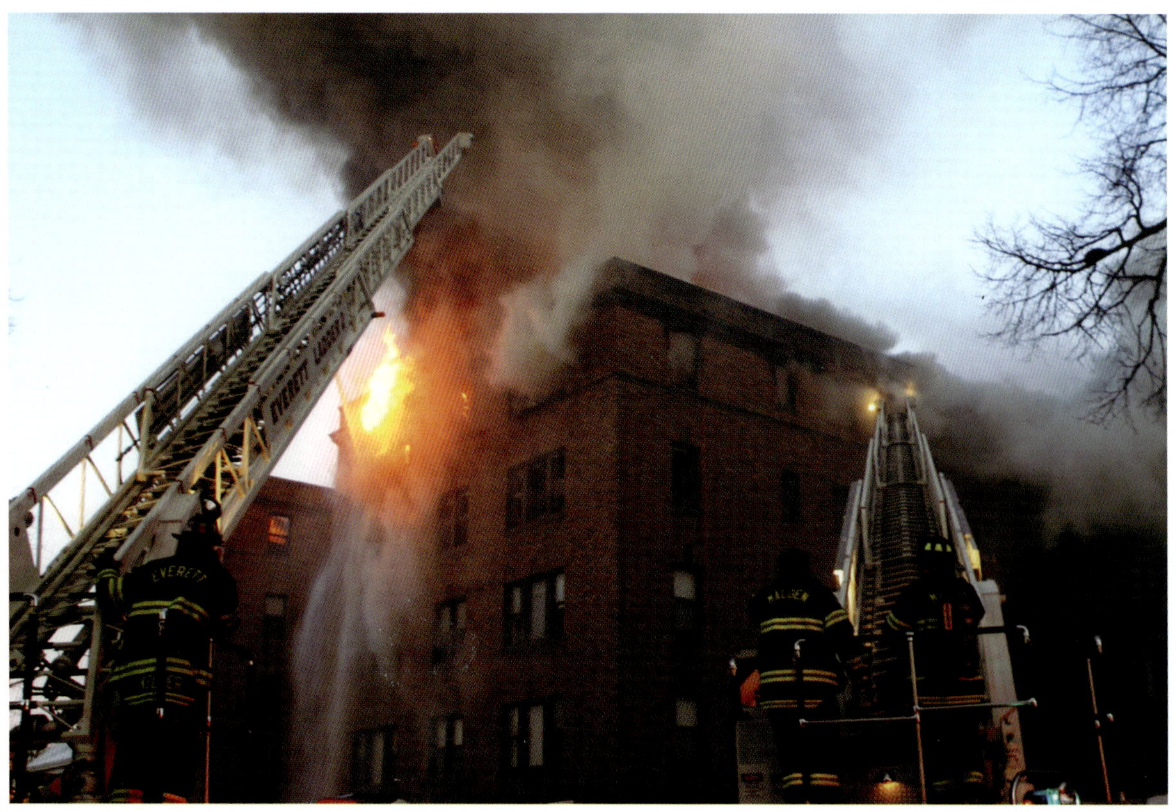

A large apartment building at 505 Pleasant Street, Malden, is heavily damaged in a 6 alarm fire, on January 9, 2010.

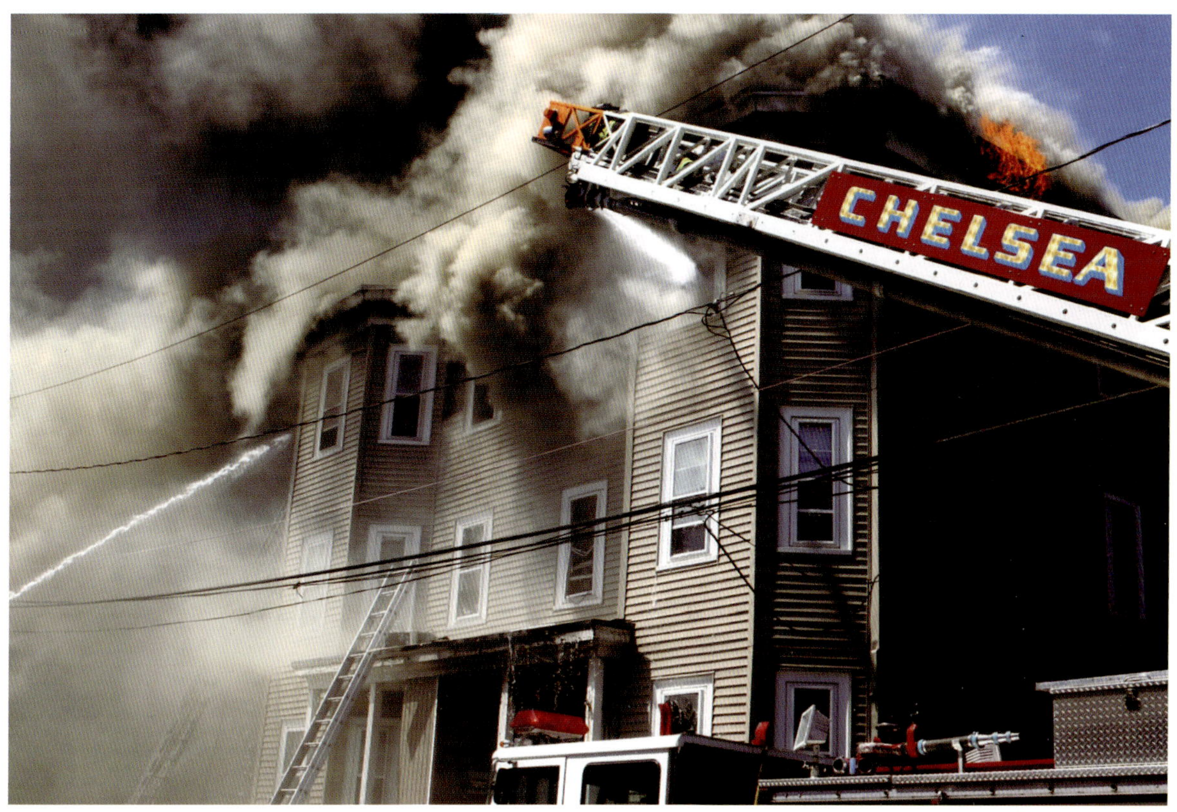

3 alarms at 130 Essex Street, Chelsea, on July 16, 2008.

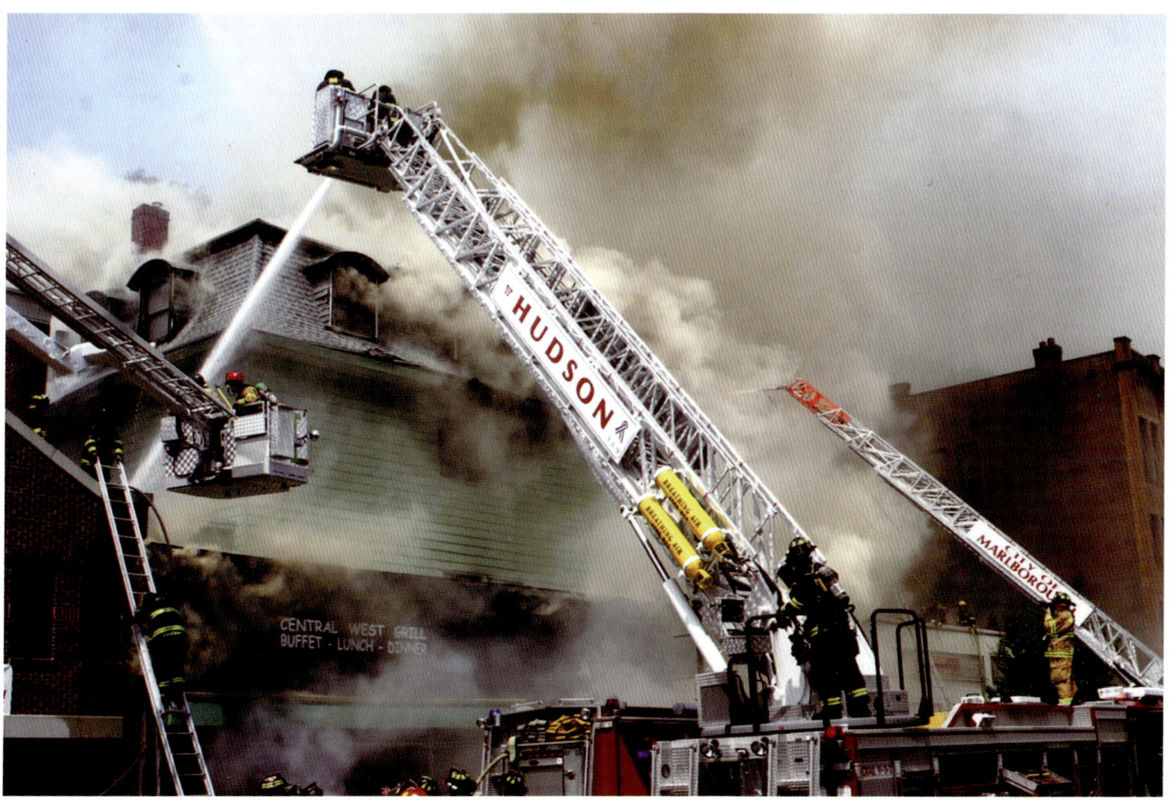

A commercial building in downtown Marlborough burns to the ground in an 8 alarm fire, on June 26, 2010.

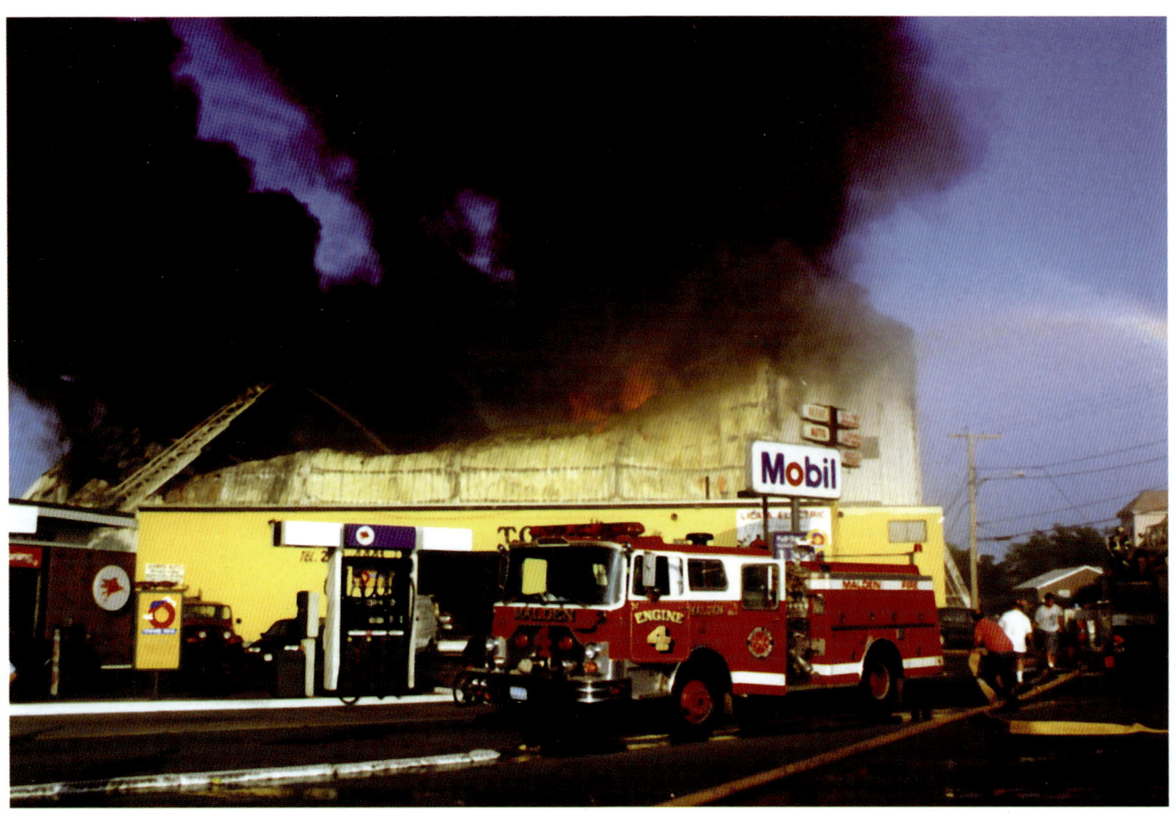

A 4 alarm fire rips through a commercial building at 22 Naples Road, Revere, on July 9, 1996.

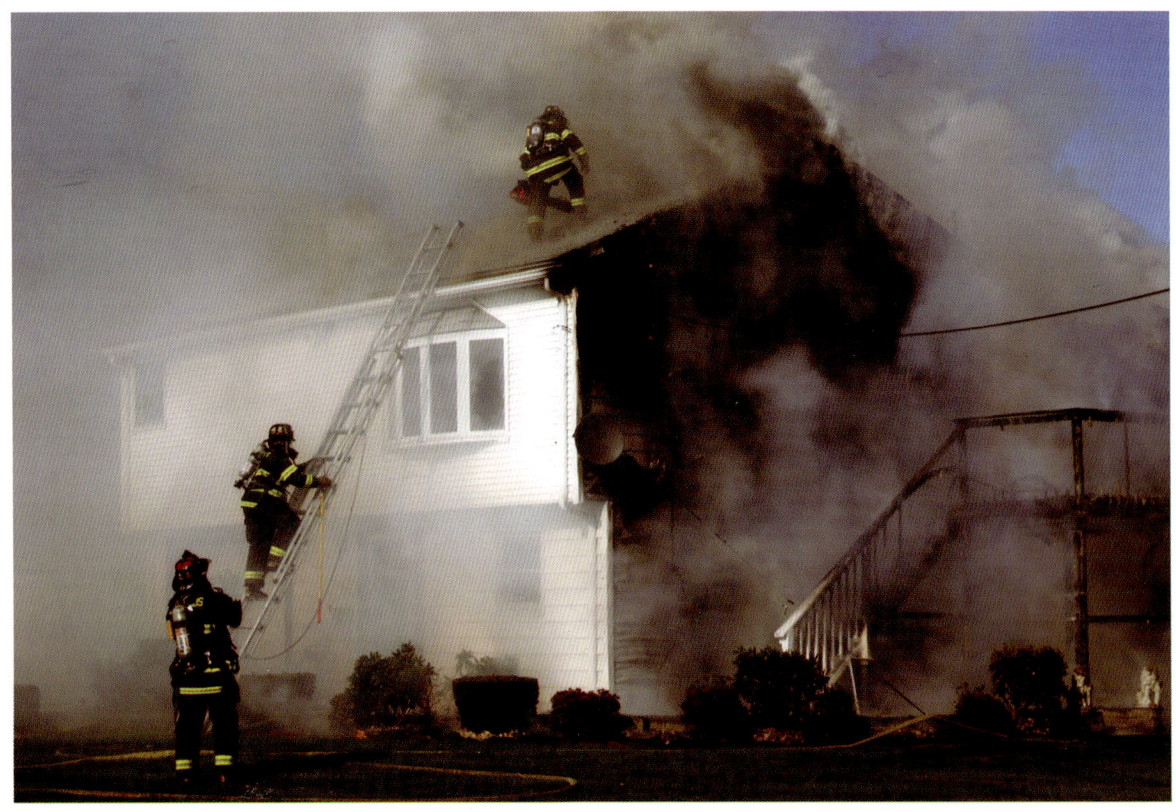

Saugus Firefighters make a great stop in a 2 alarm fire at 54 Spencer Avenue, on May 6, 2007.

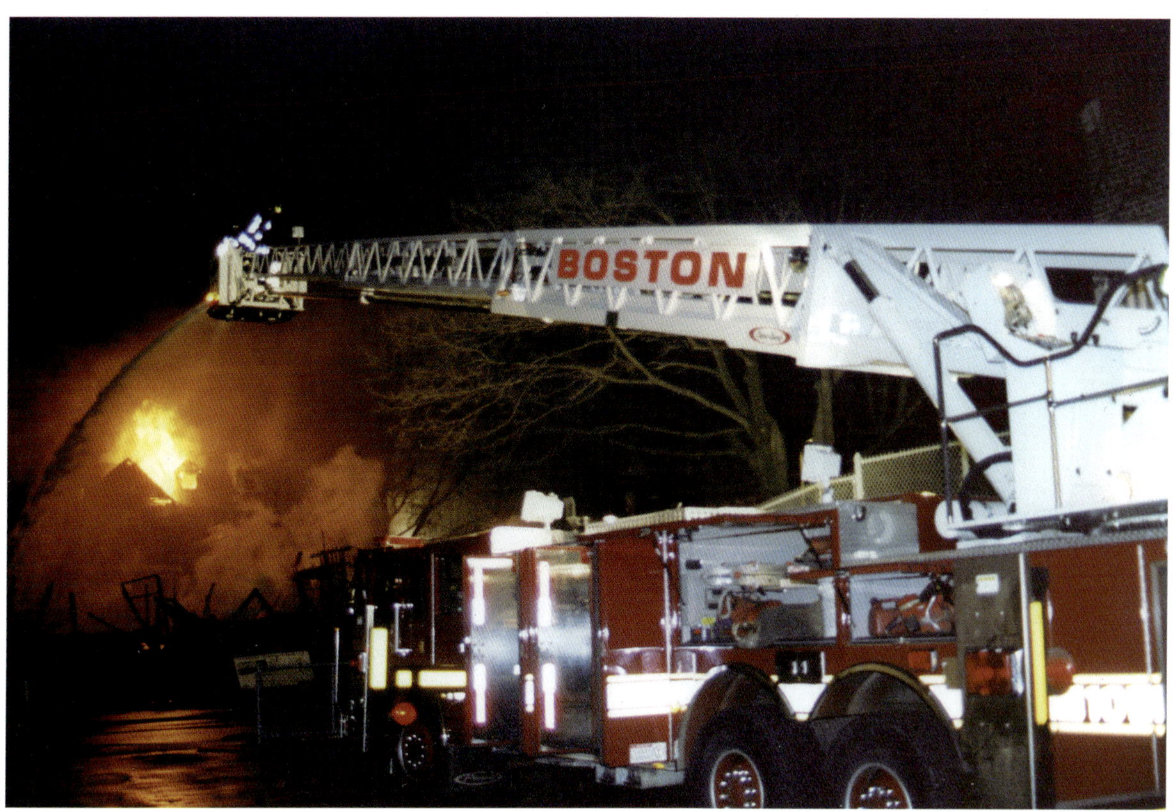

An unfinished condo complex burns in a 9 alarm fire at 125 Ruthven Street, Roxbury, on November 3, 2002.

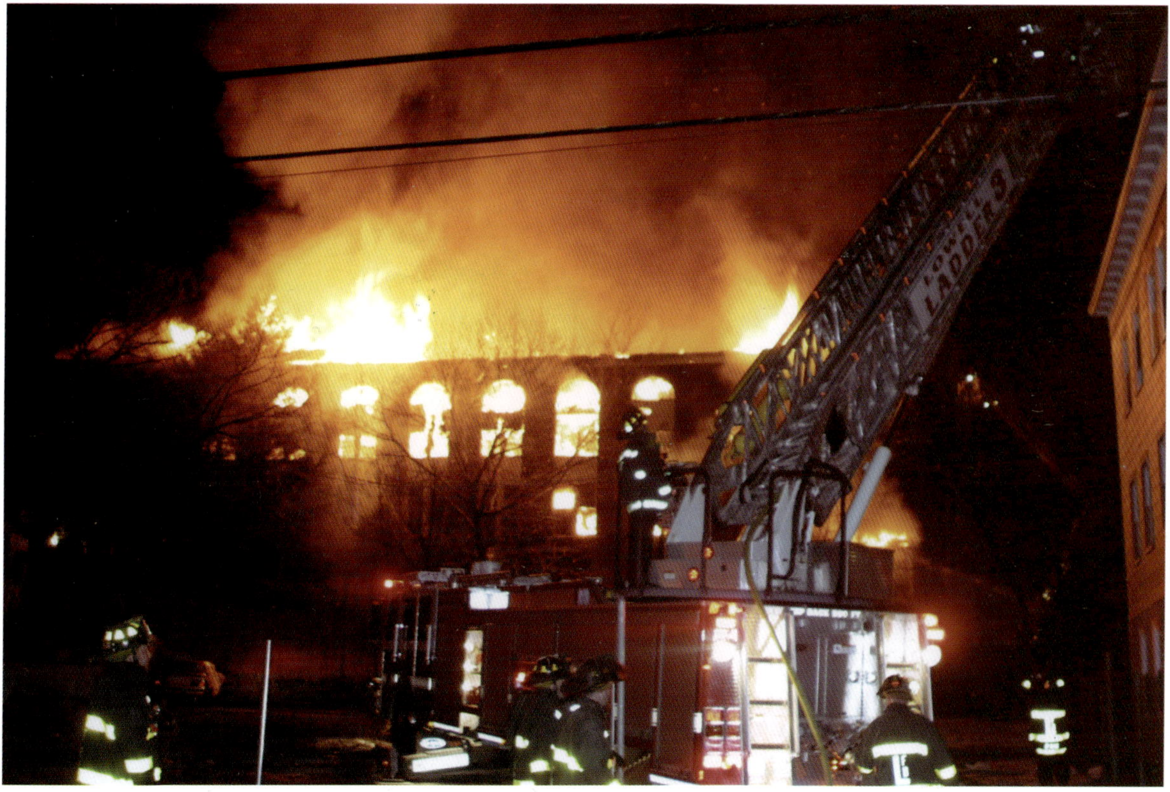

A former religious school is destroyed in a 4 alarm fire at 44 Park Street, Lawrence, on November 13, 2008.

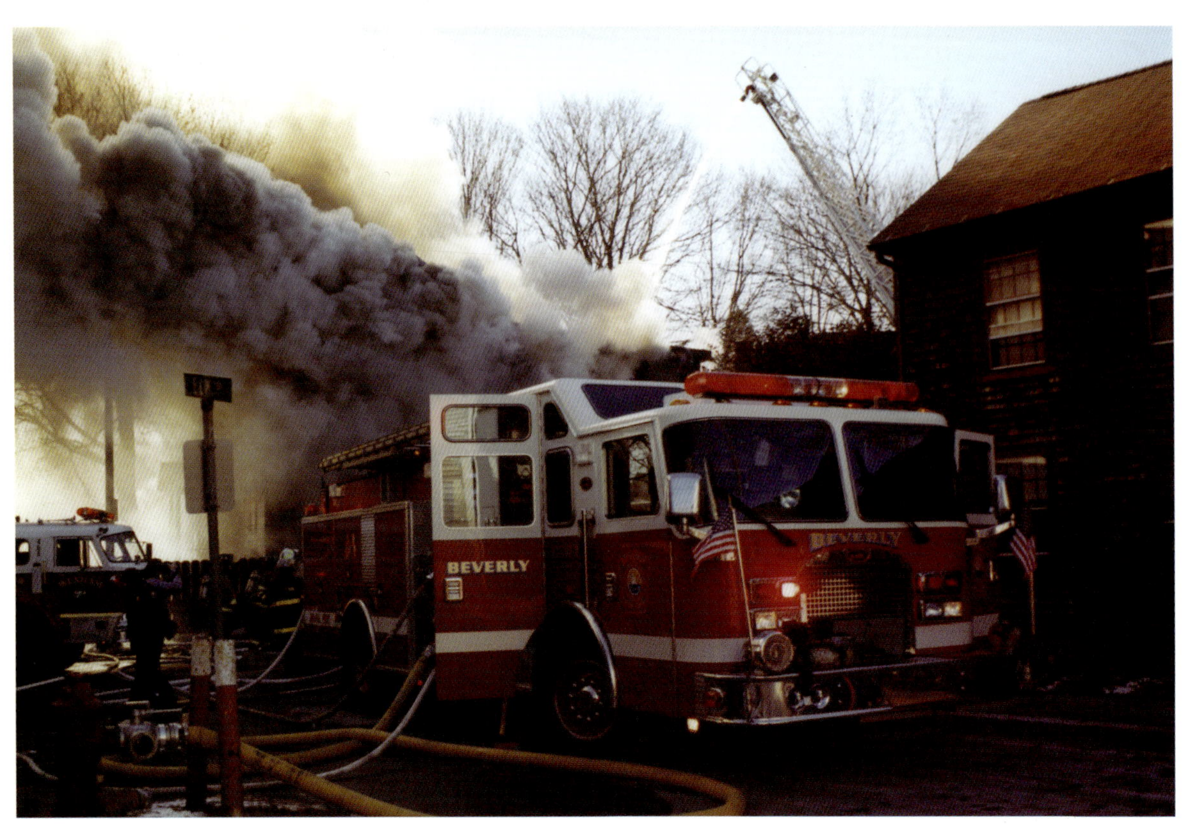

3 alarms at 22 Railroad Avenue, Beverly, on December 4, 2002.

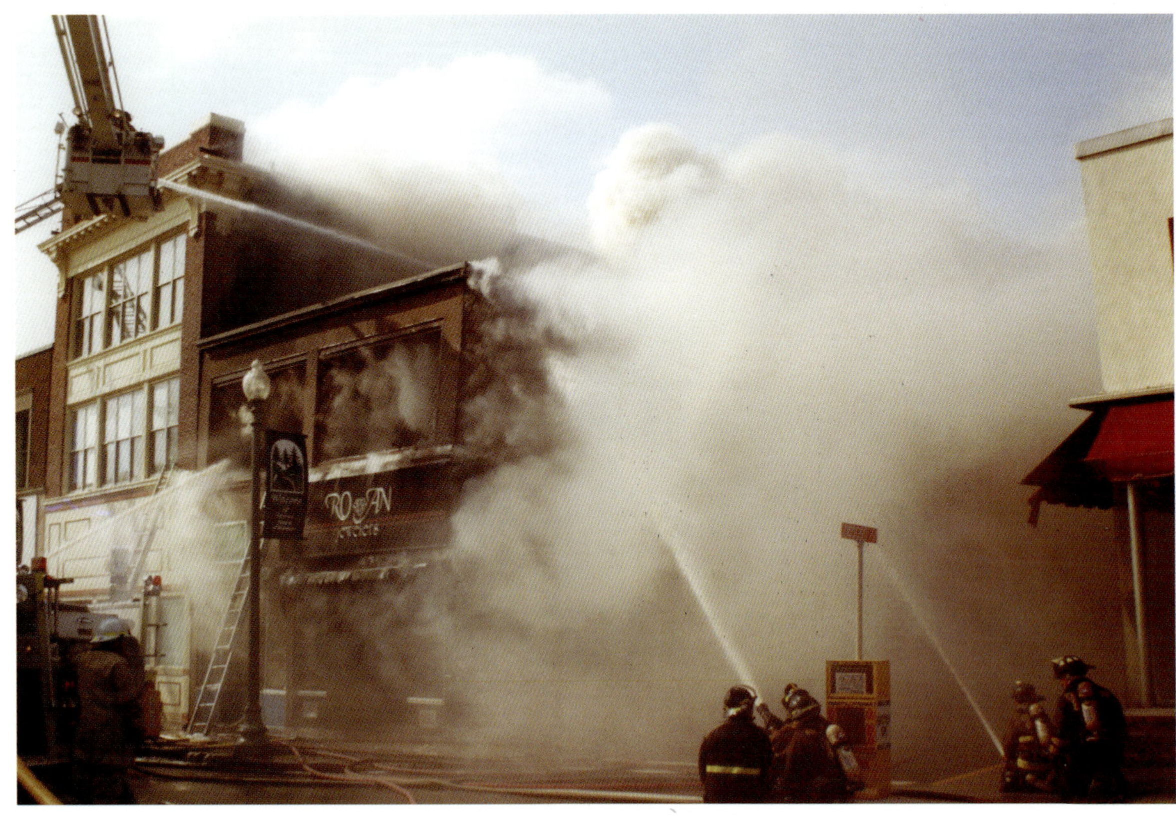

General alarm at 36 Main Street in downtown Taunton, on April 21, 2001.

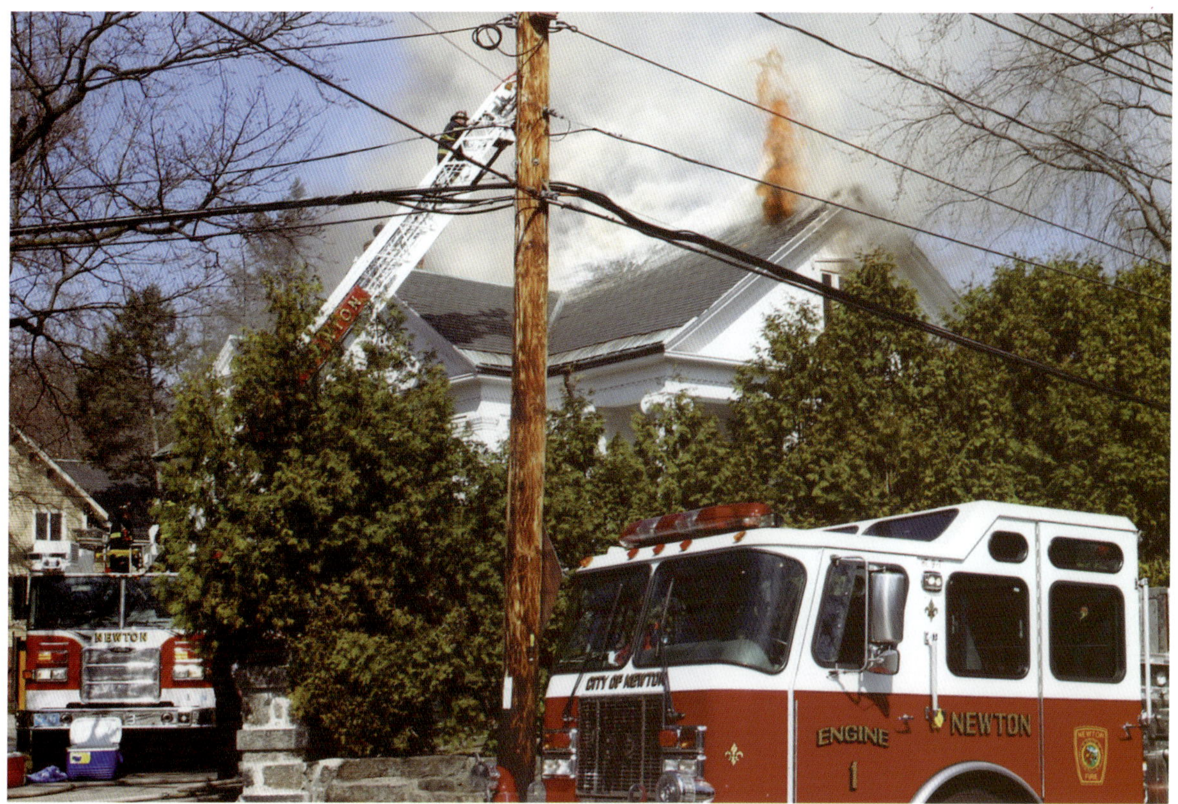

The Bracket House, a 19th Century historic mansion is heavily damaged in a 3 alarm fire at 621 Centre Street, Newton, on March 20, 2010.

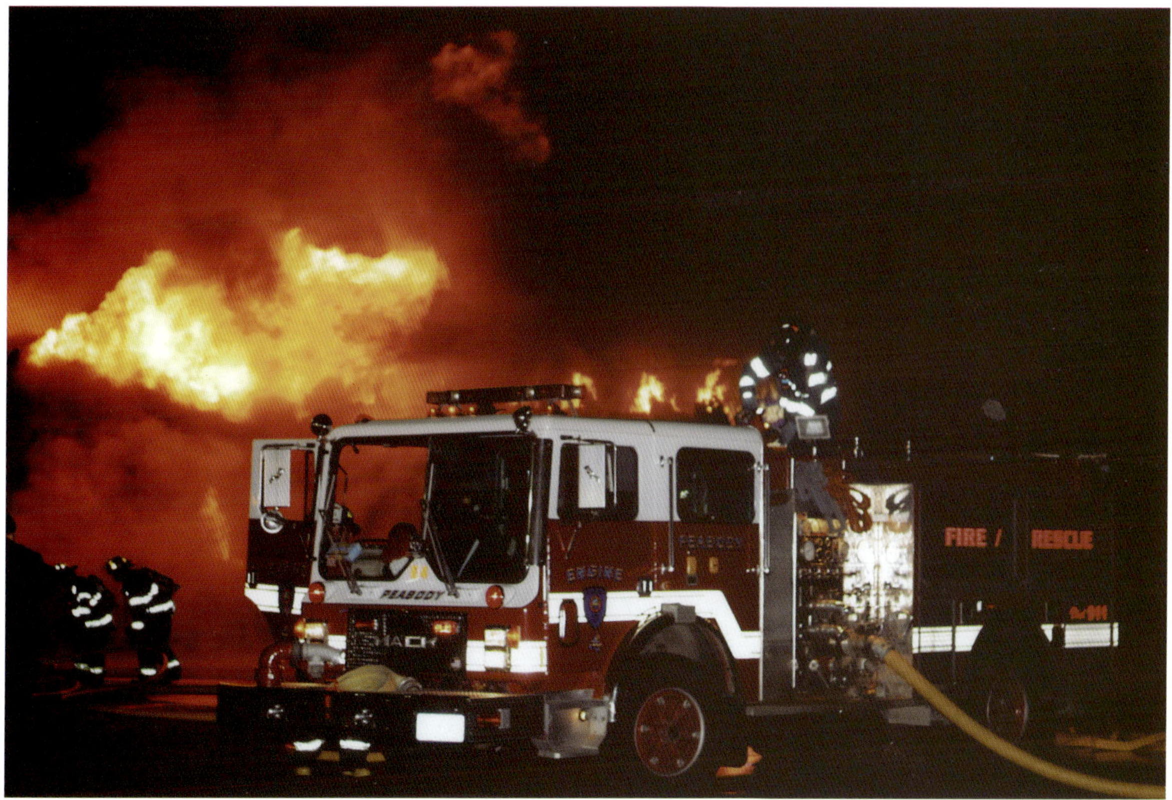

3 alarms at a video store on Route 1, Peabody, on January 22, 2006.

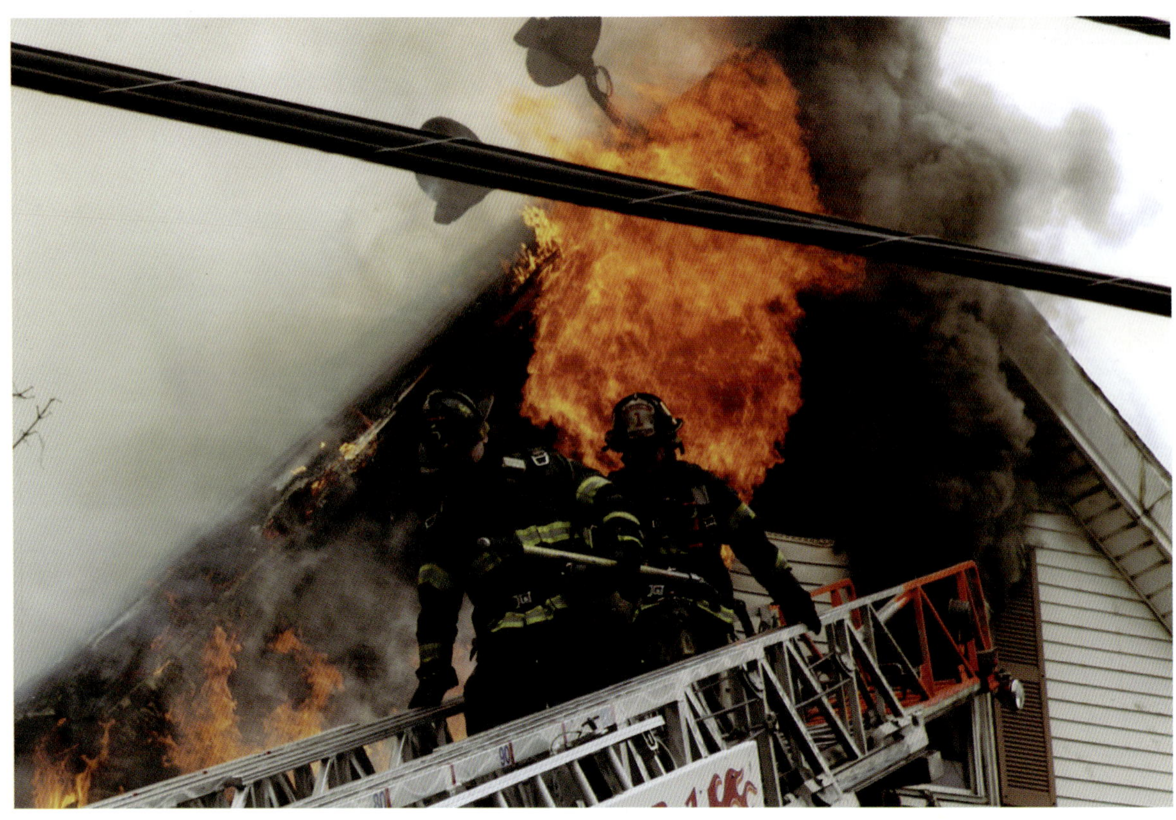

2 alarms at 37 Williams Avenue, Lynn, on March 16, 2012.

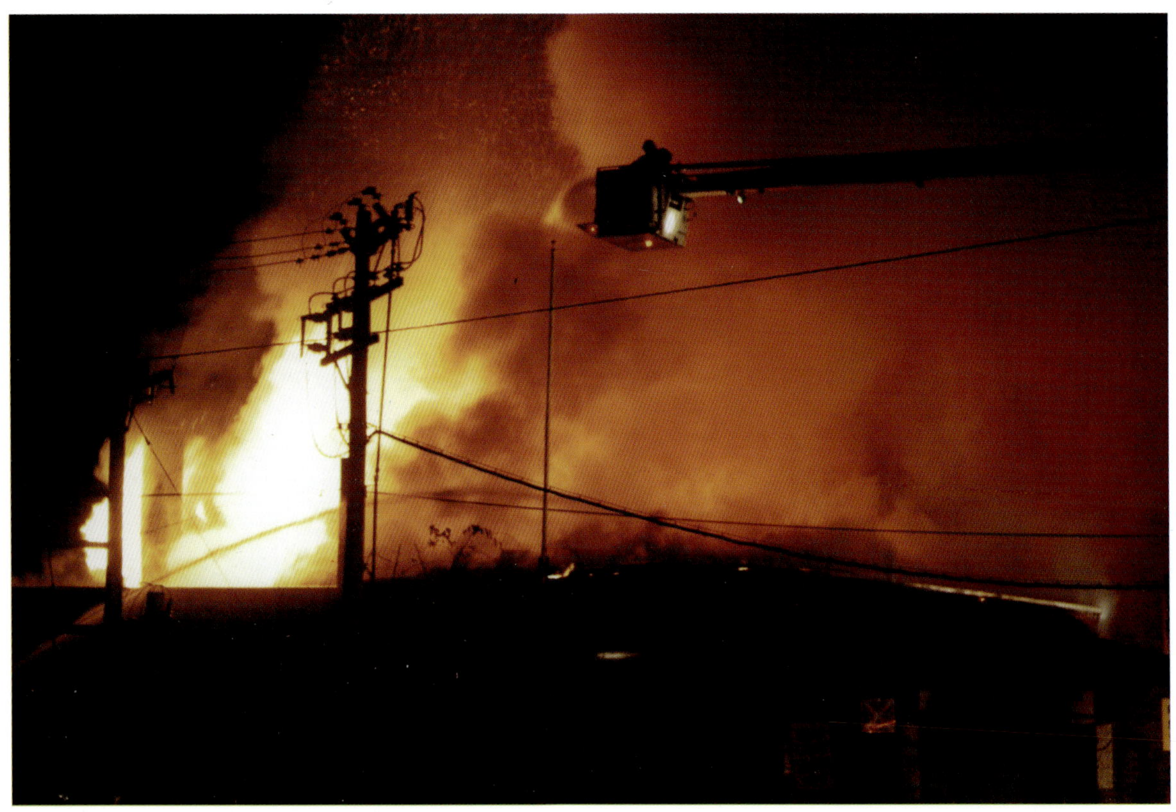

A vacant paper mill at 9 South Canal Street, Lawrence, gutted in a 3 alarm fire, on November 6, 2009.

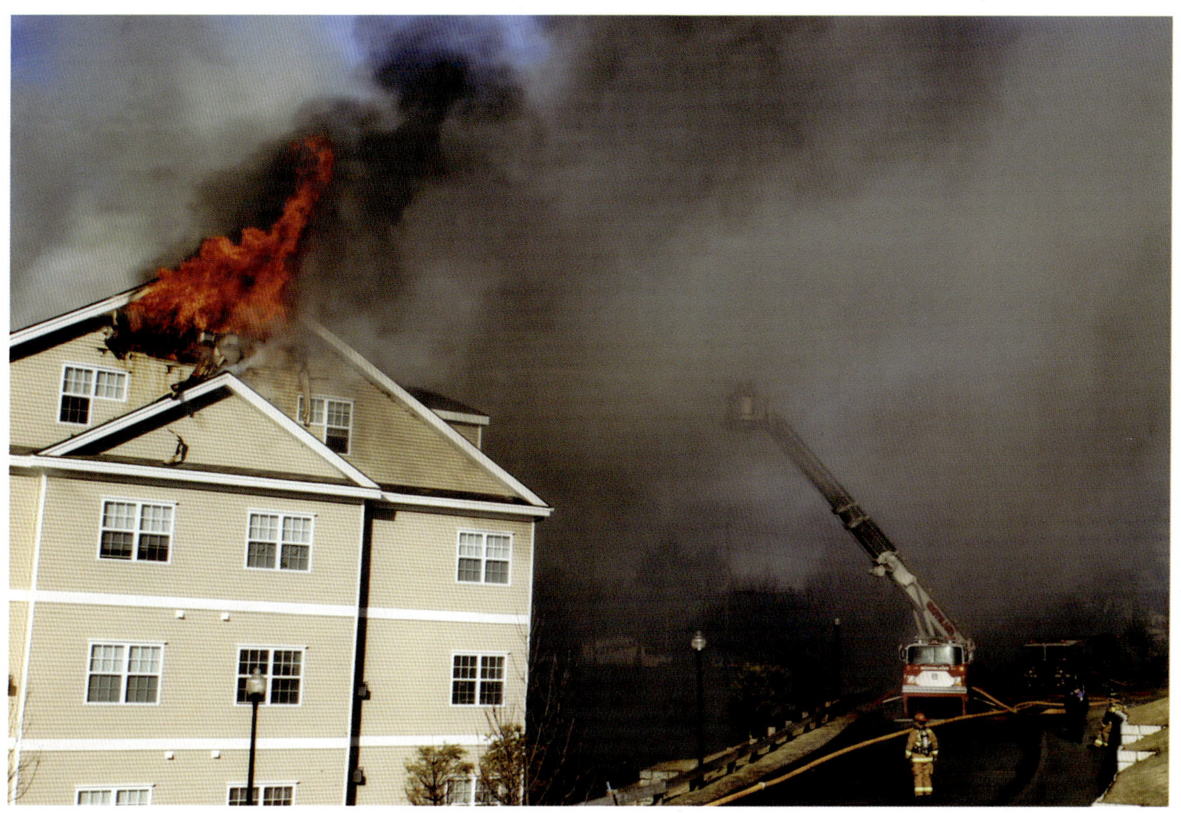

4 alarms at 7 Patriot Lane, Georgetown, on January 3, 2007.

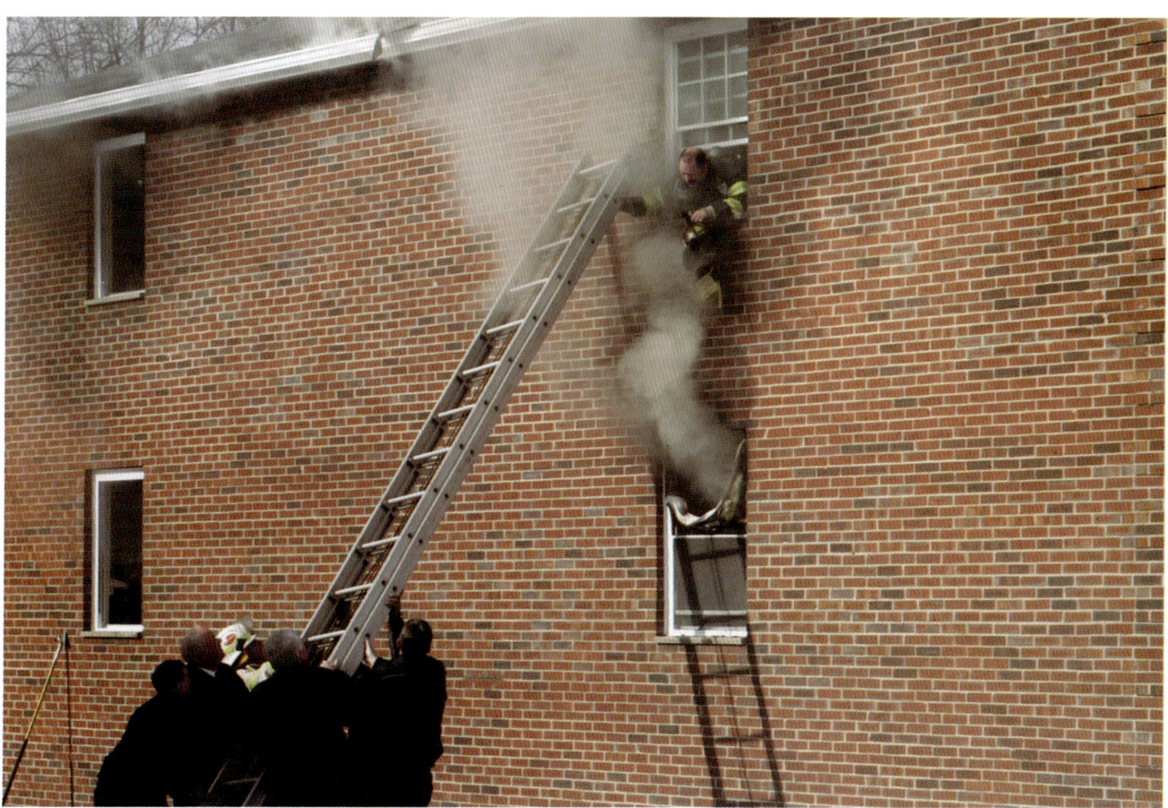

A Peabody Firefighter in need of assistance due to a malfunctioning face mask at 36 Essex Place. Three alarms were sounded.

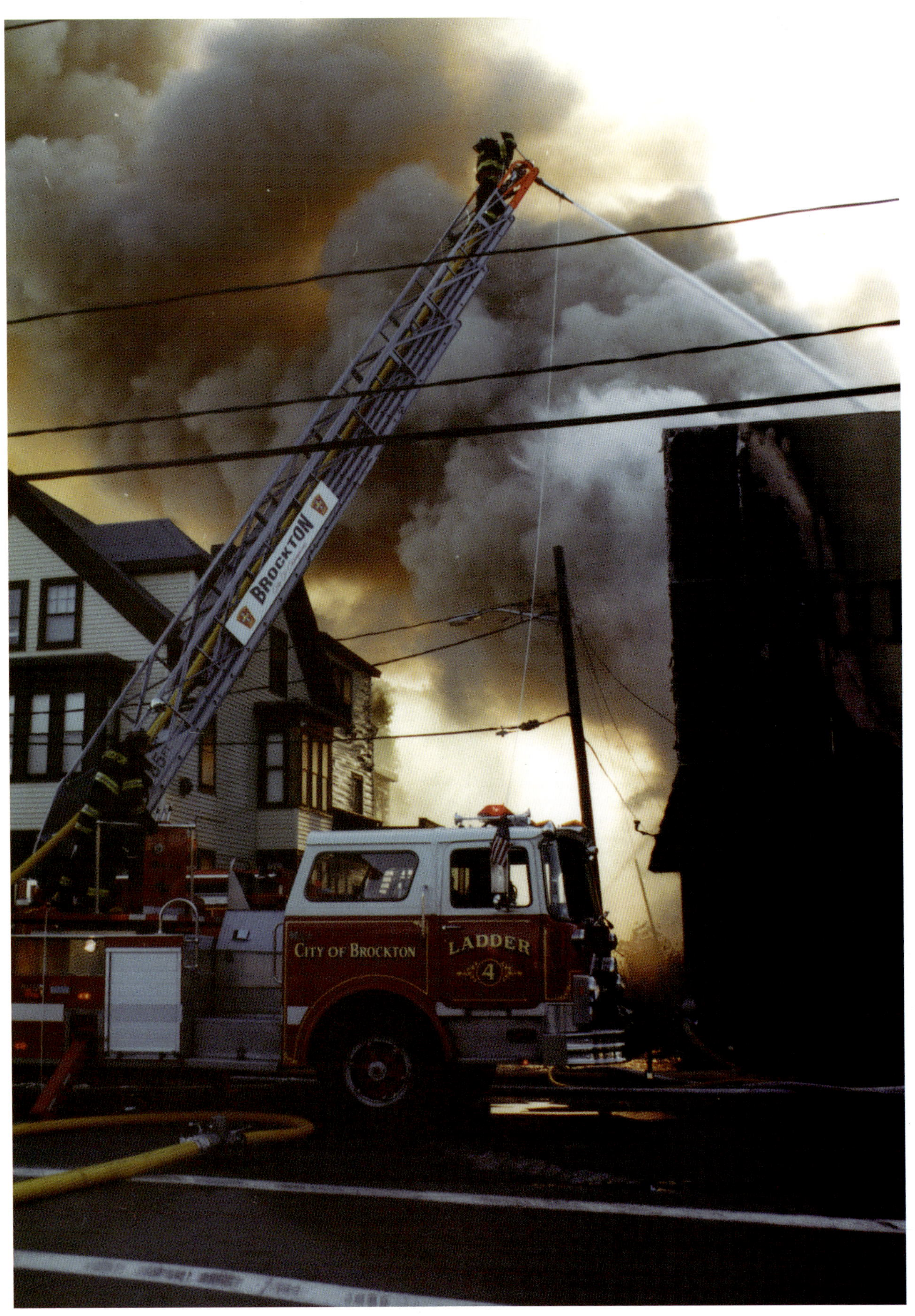

4 alarms at 660 Main Street, Brockton, on May 29, 1999.

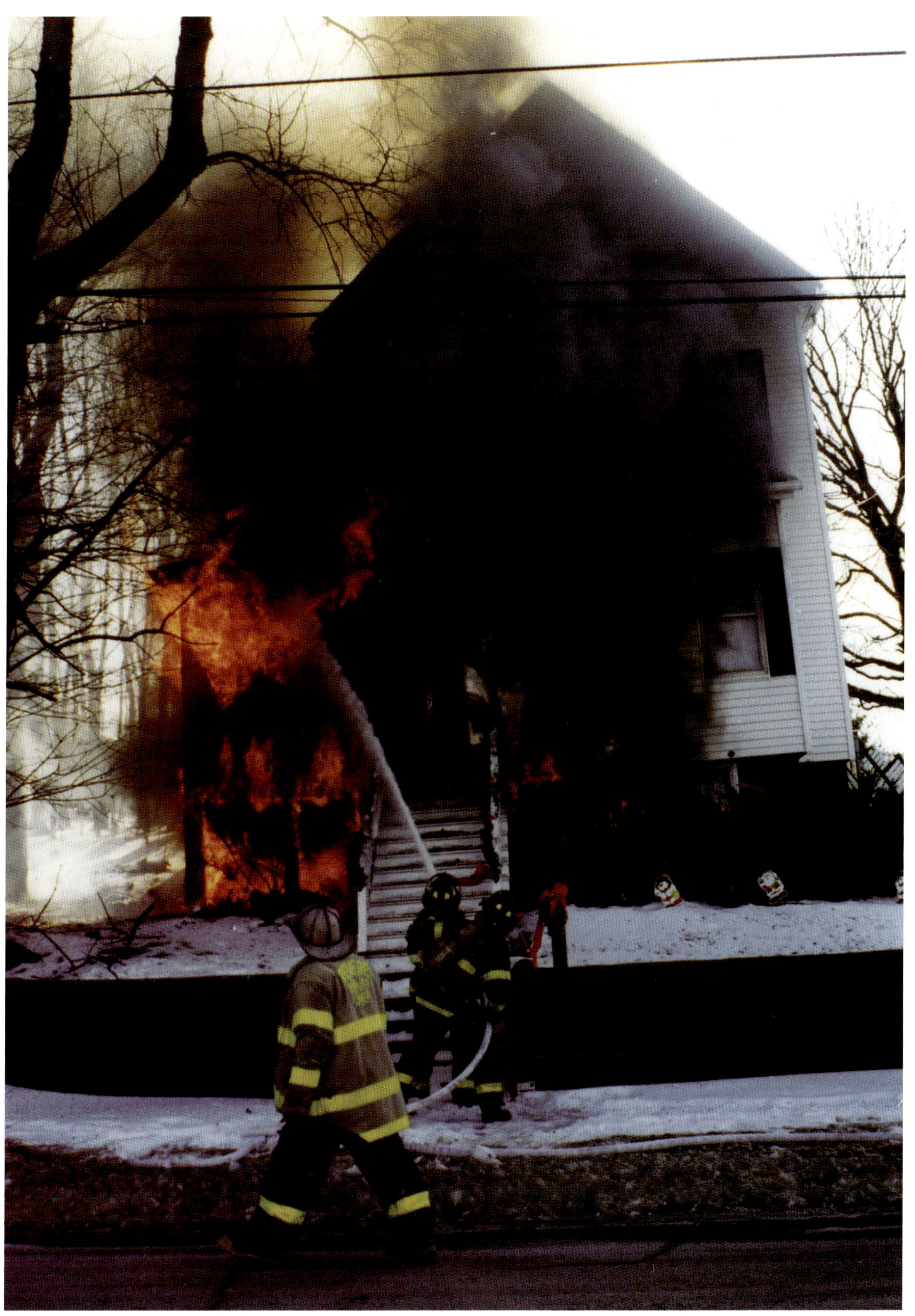

First arriving Revere Firefighters quickly knock down this fire at 574 Proctor Avenue, on February 7, 2000.

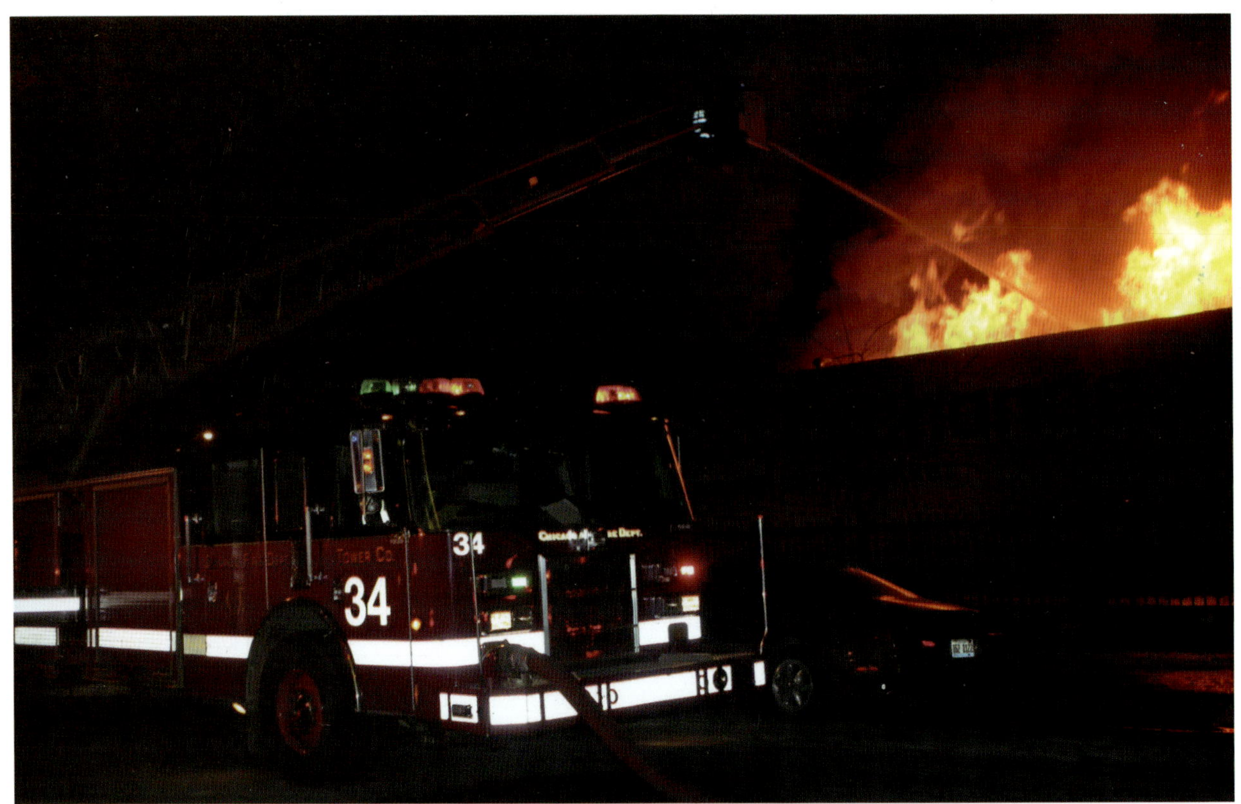

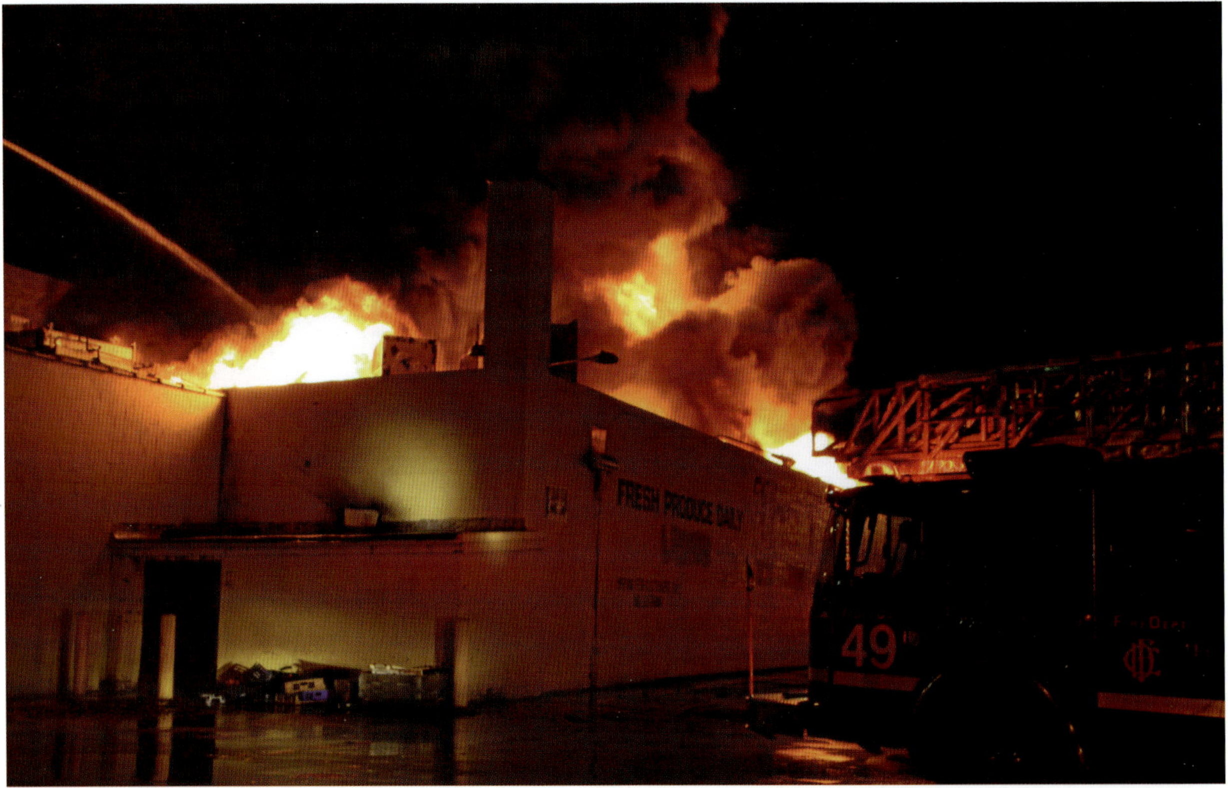

CHICAGO 3-11 alarm at 7162 S. Exchange, a large supermarket, on March 4, 2007.

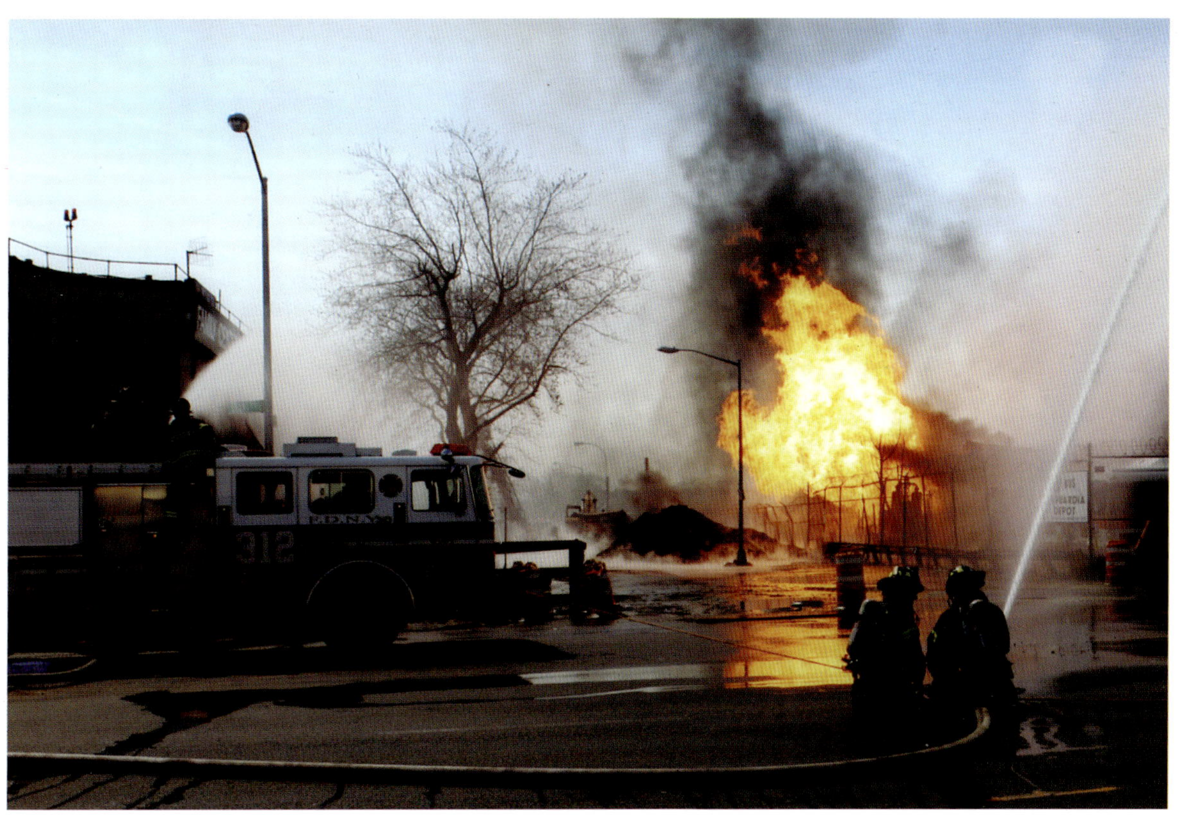

QUEENS, NY A high pressure gas line ruptured and ignited at the MTA LaGuardia Bus Depot on 23rd Ave. at 87th Street, on April 10, 2006.

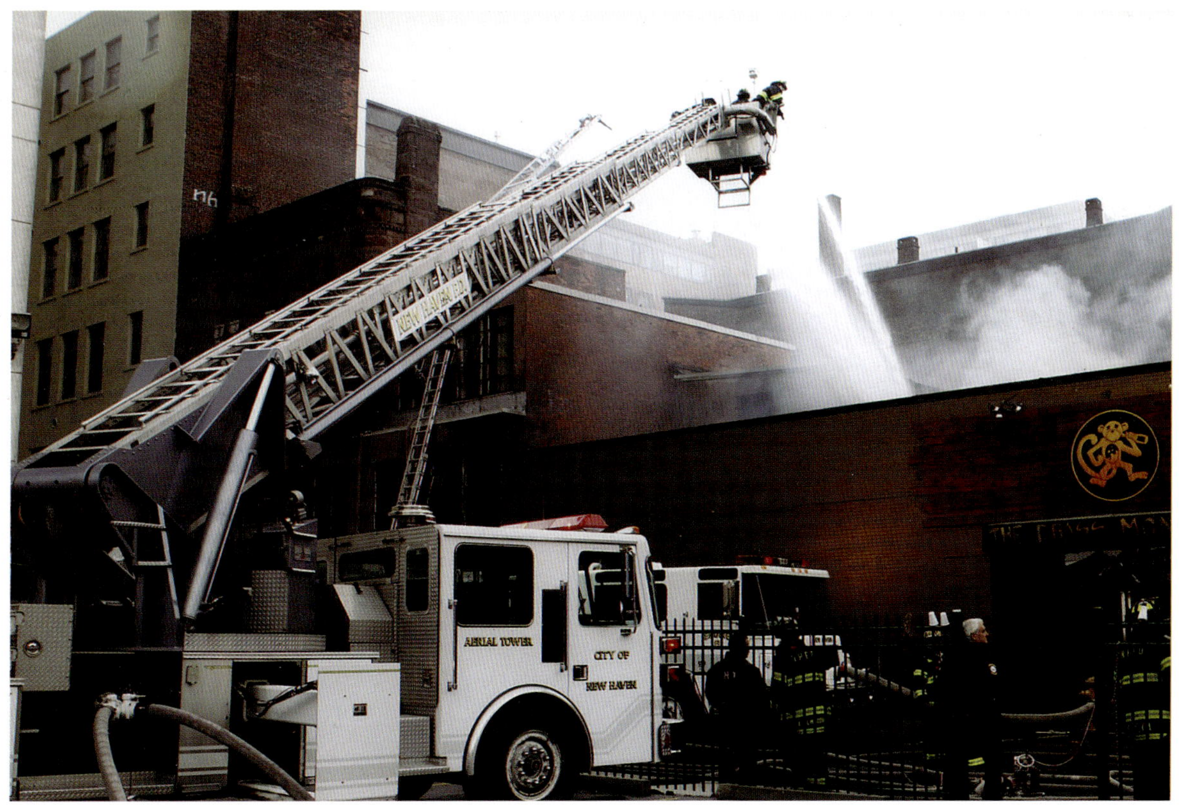

NEW HAVEN, CT 3 alarms in the 800 block of Chapel Street, on December 12, 2007.

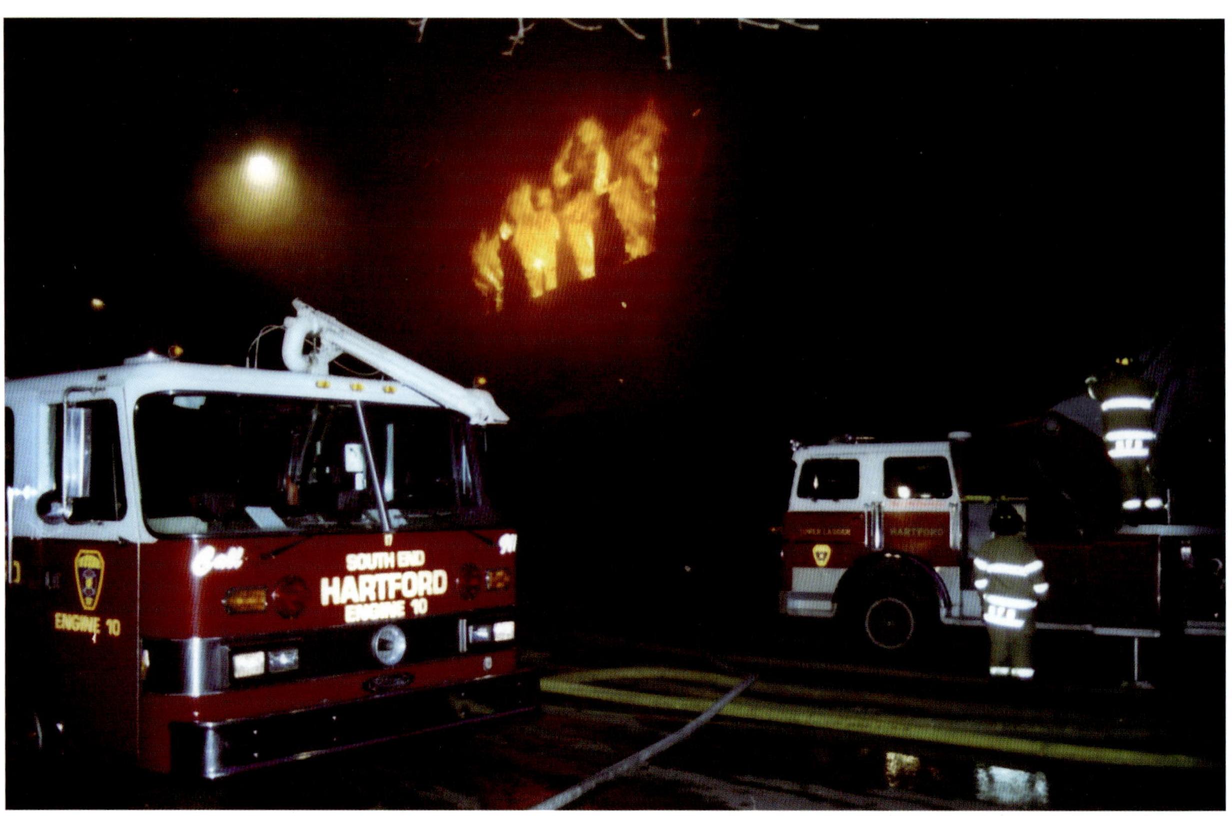

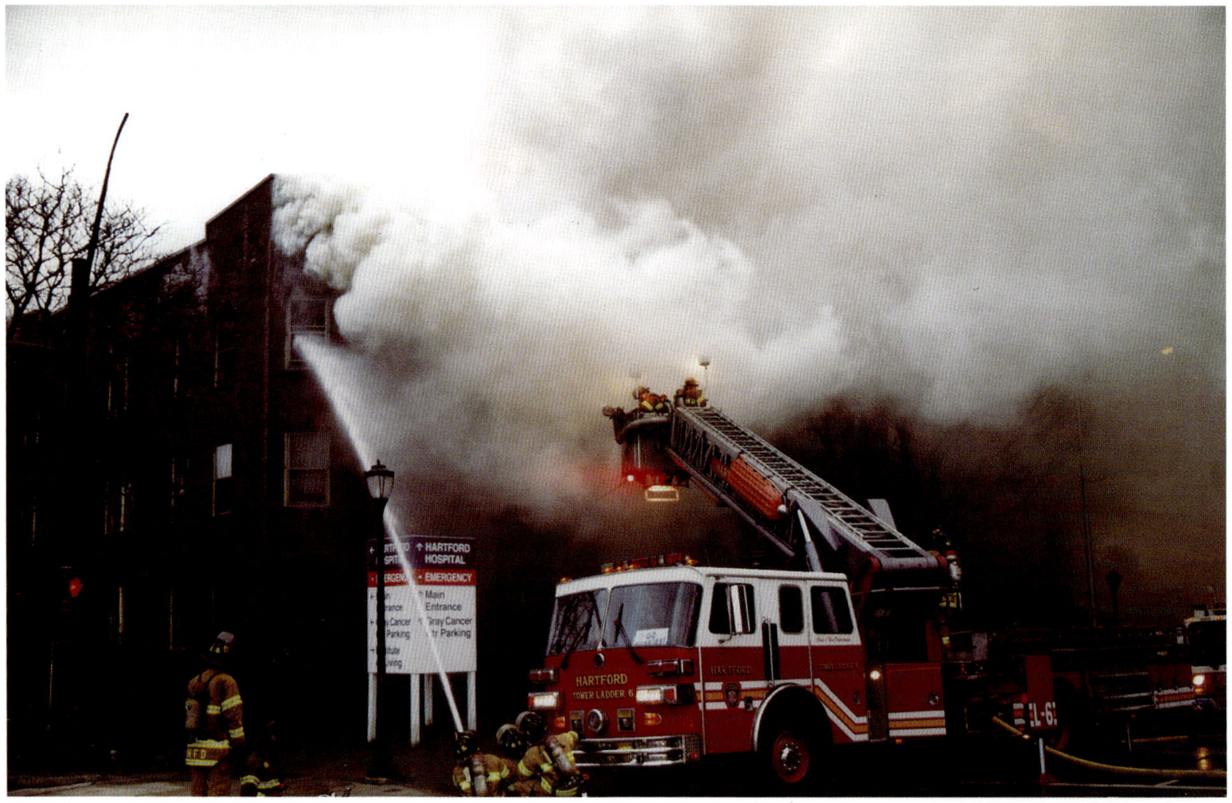

HARTFORD, CT 3 alarms in a vacant commercial building at 340 Washington Street. This fire burned all night and well into the next morning, on April 10, 1999.

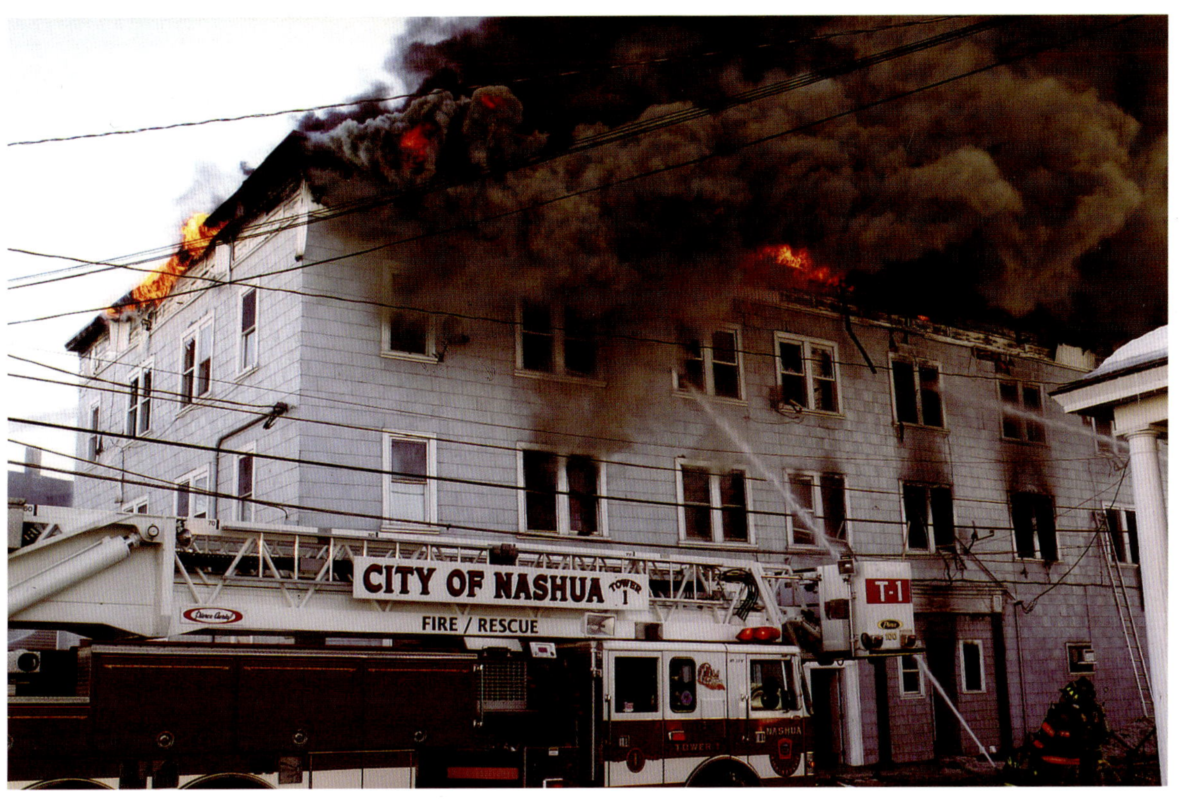

NASHUA, NH 5 alarms in an occupied block long rooming house at 126 Vine Street, on February 9, 2009.

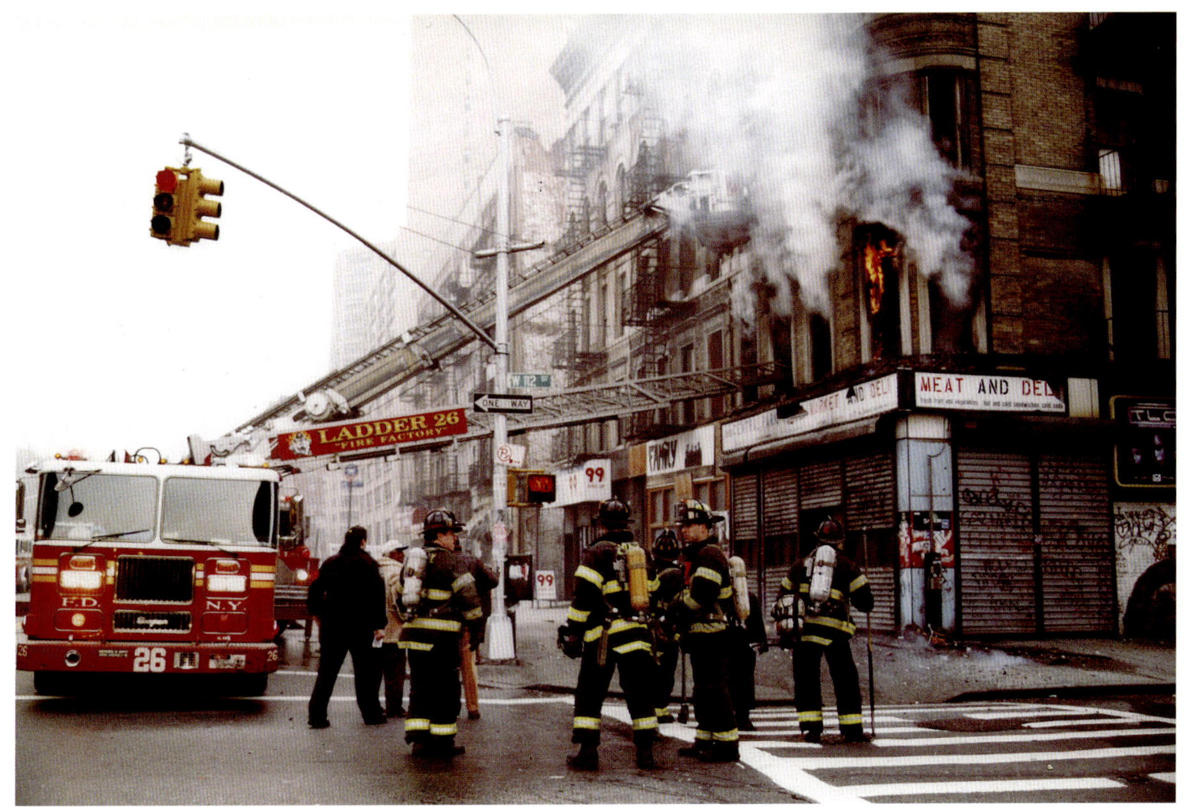

MANHATTAN, NY All hands are working at 2063 8th Ave., in Harlem, on February 22, 1999.

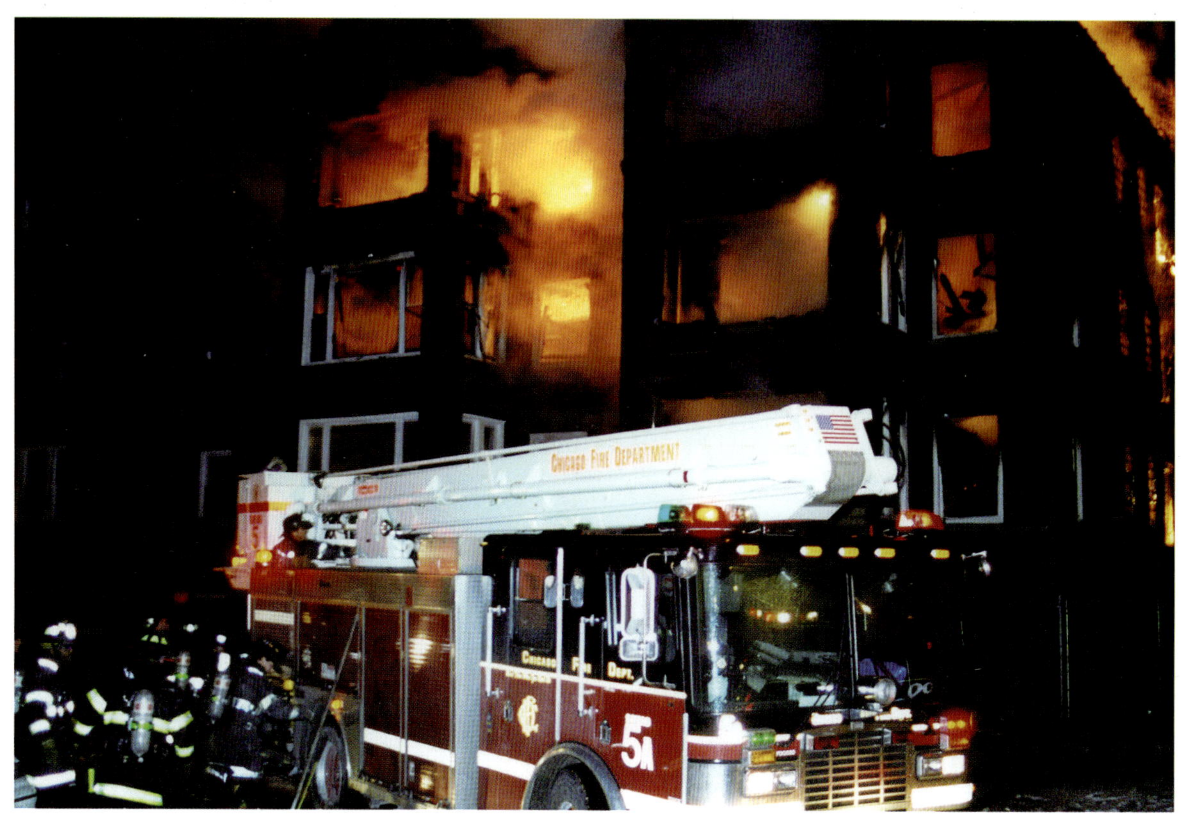

CHICAGO 2-11 alarm at 7220 S. Merrill, in single digit temperatures, on March 4, 2002.

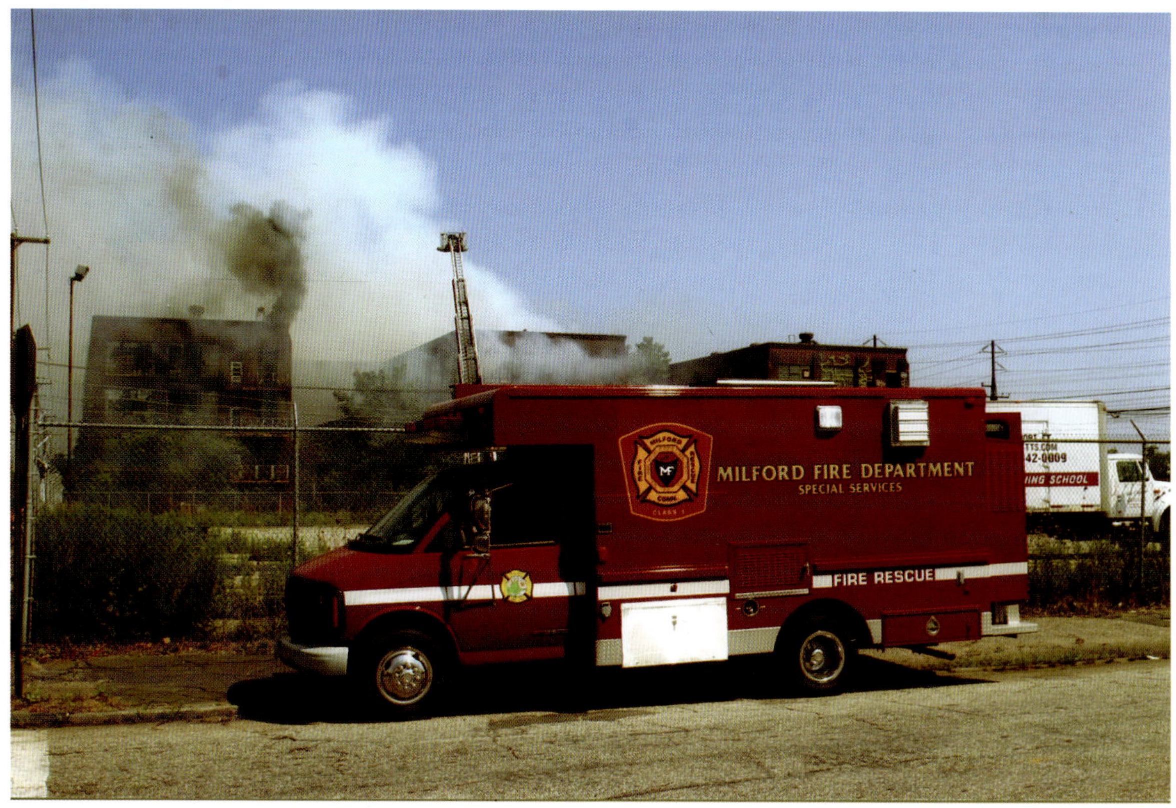

BRIDGEPORT, CT Milford, CT Special Services Rehab Unit, 1998 GMC G 3500 Series van, responds on mutual aid to the vacant Remington Arms Complex at 812 Barnum Avenue, on August 4, 2012.

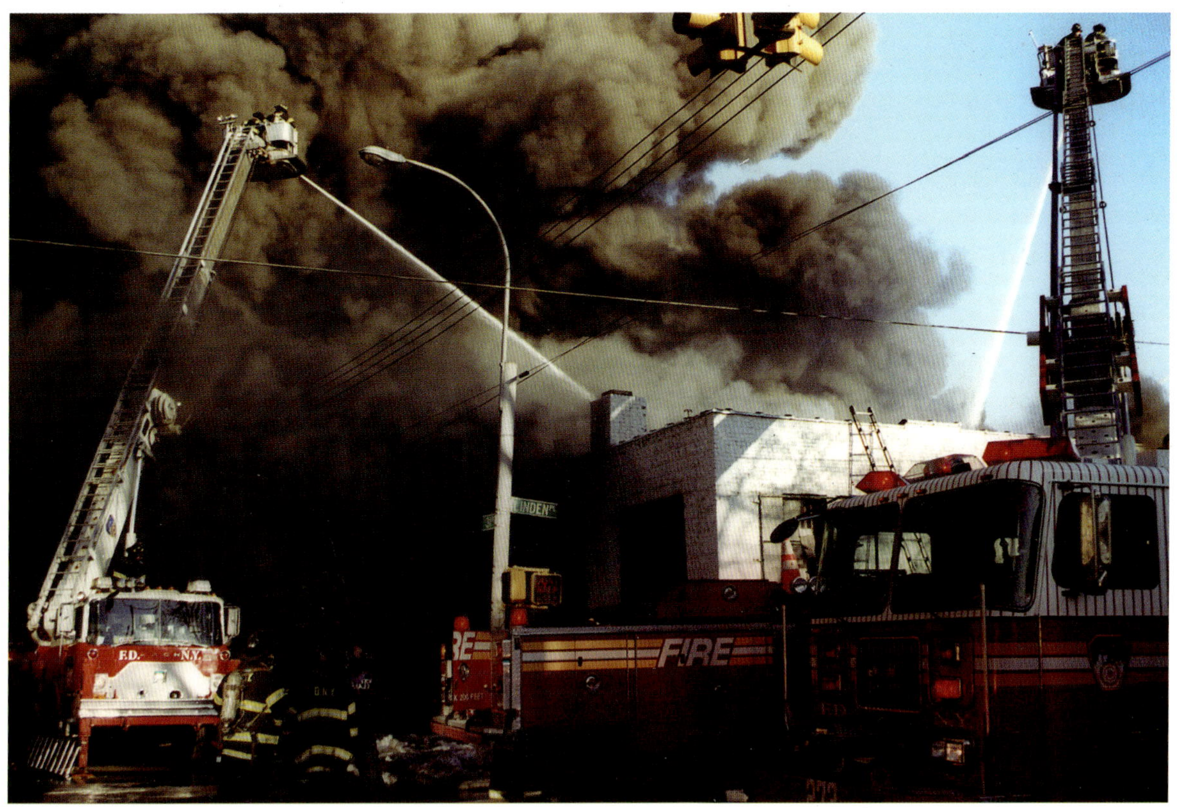

QUEENS, NY 3 alarm factory fire at 31-01 Linden Place, on January 13, 2001.

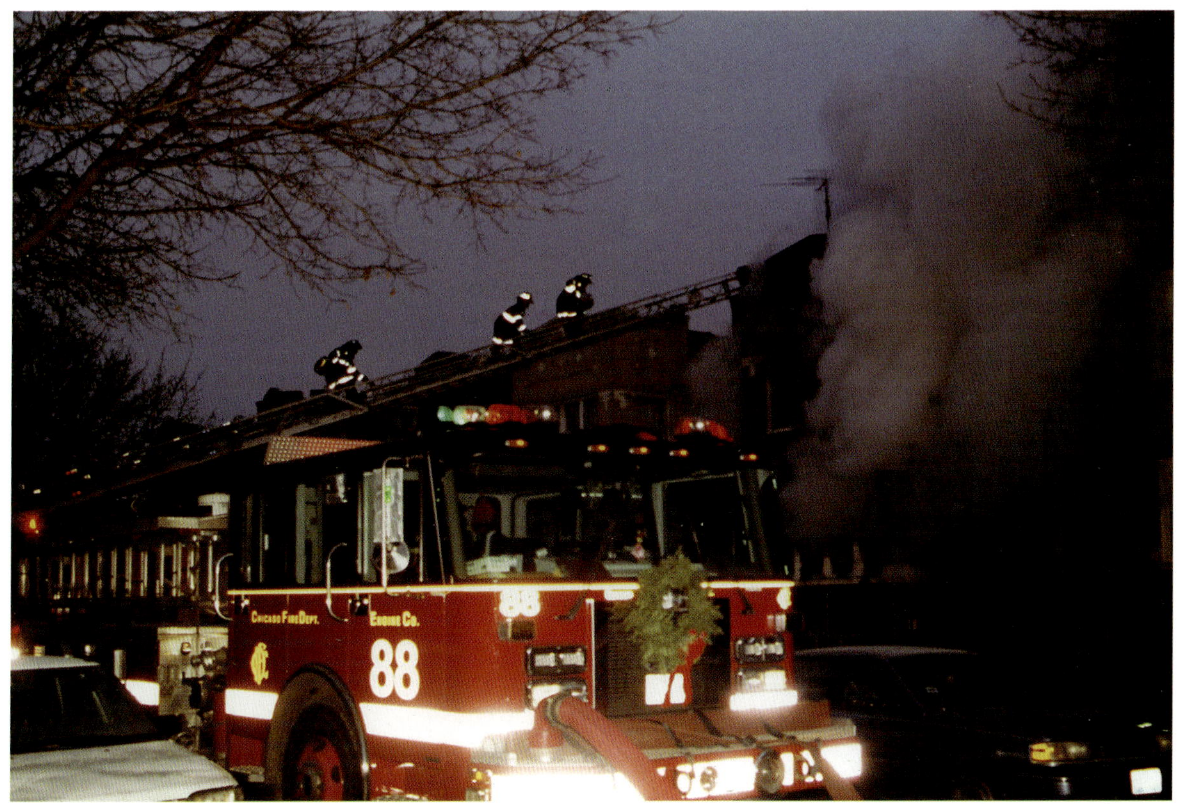

CHICAGO Still and box alarm at 6006 S. Albany, on December 13, 2003.

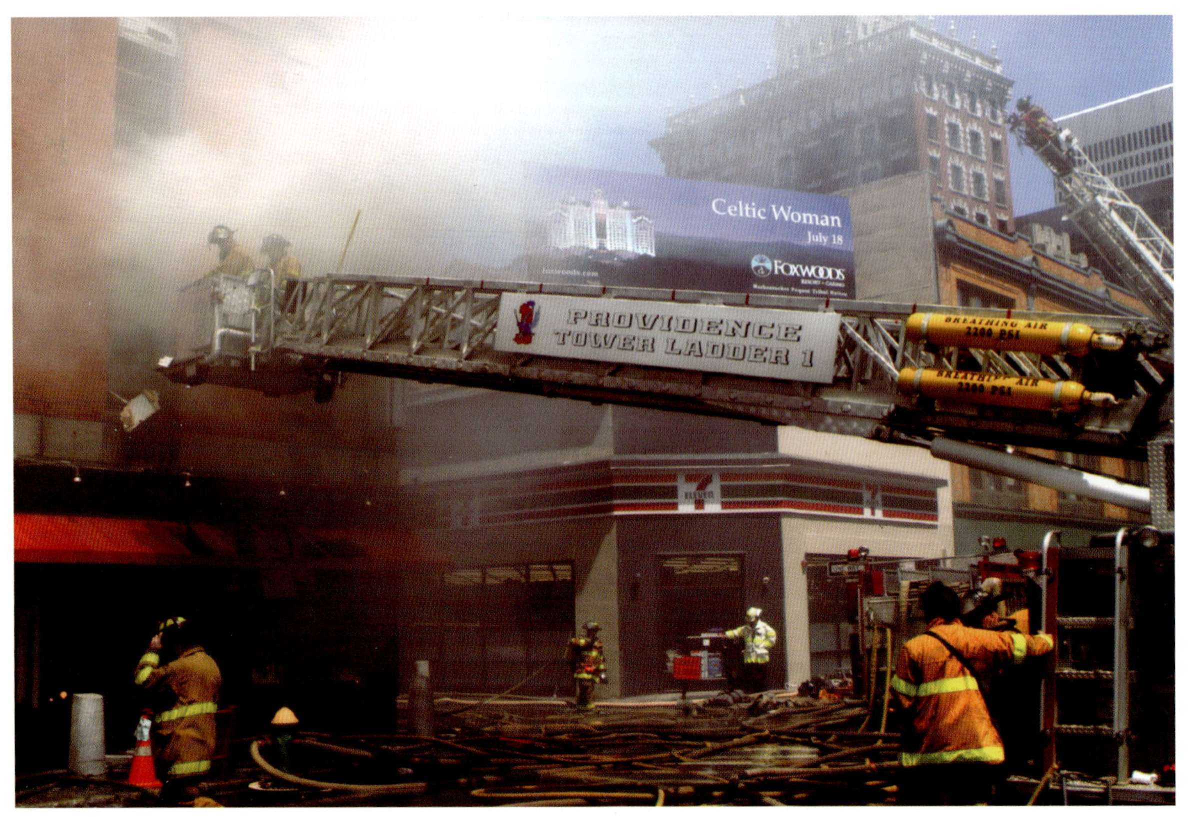

PROVIDENCE, RI 4 alarms in a commercial building at 151 Weybosset Street, on May 22, 2006.

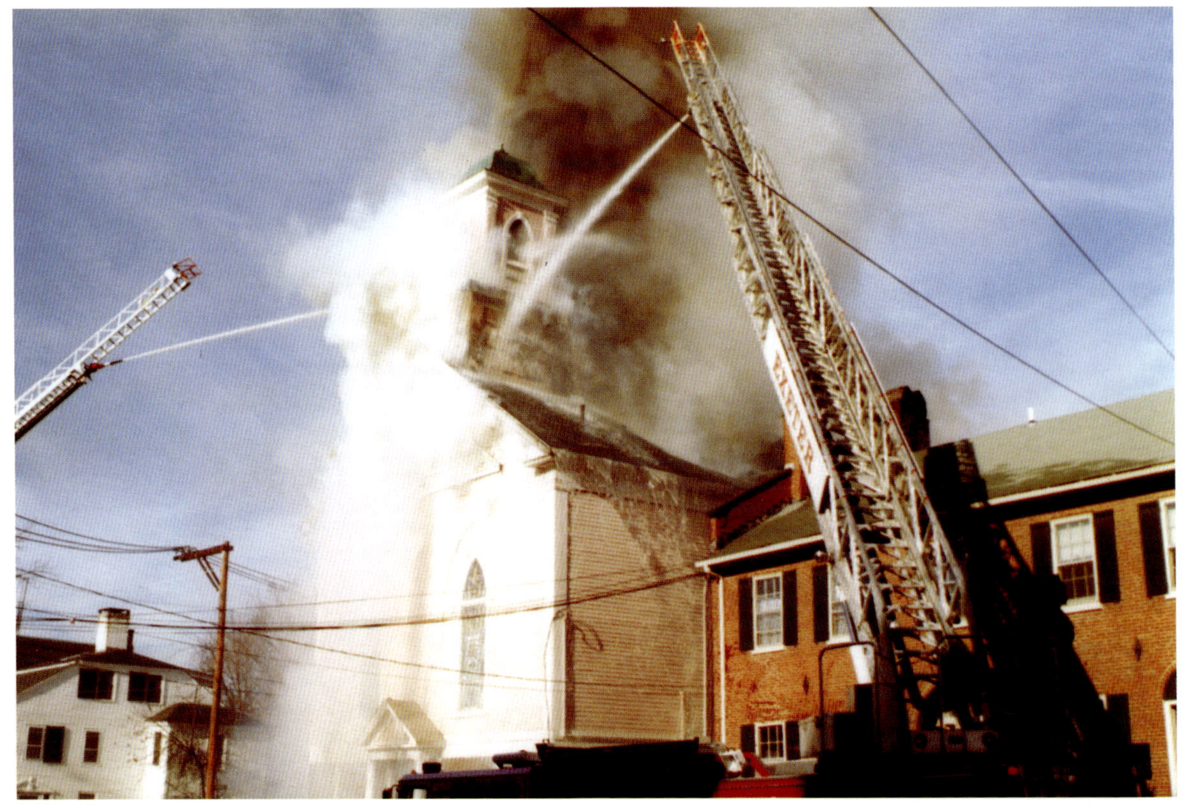

EXETER, NH The 158 year old Exeter Presbyterian Church at 29 Front Street, 6 alarms were sounded, on November 24, 2003.

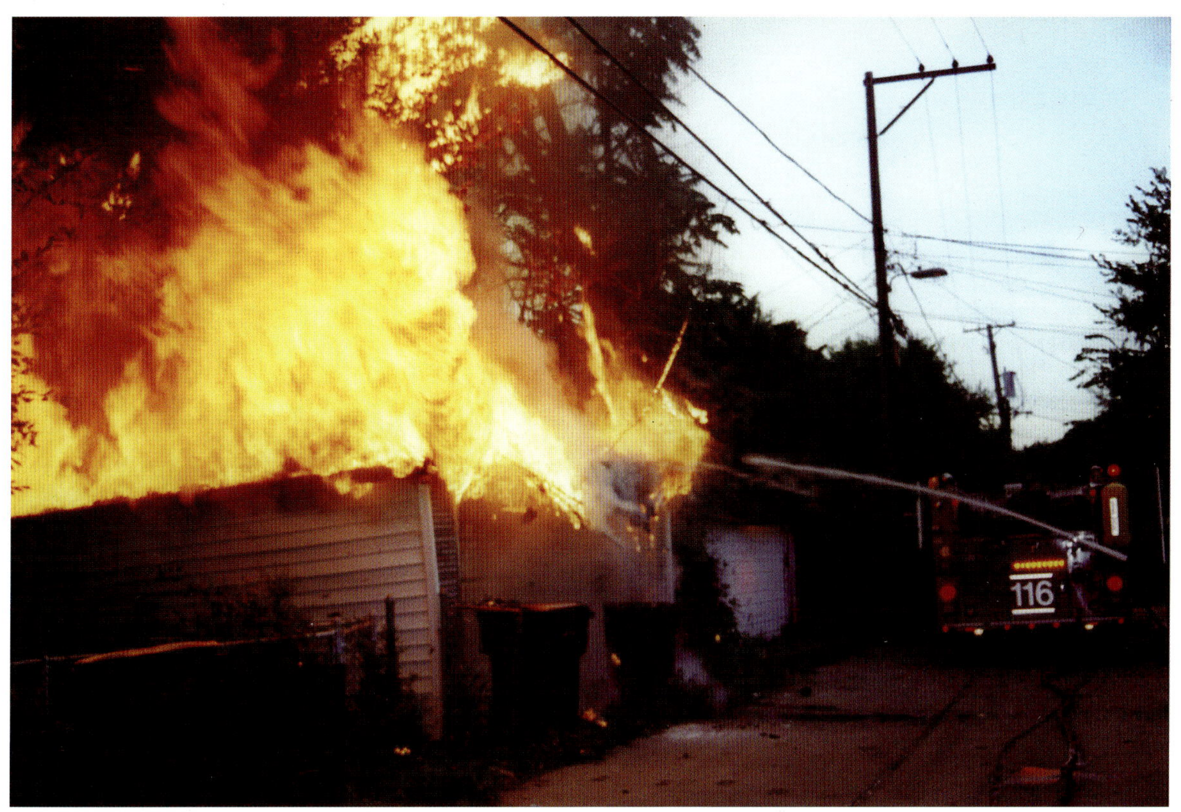

CHICAGO Still alarm at 5547 Hoyne Avenue, on July 23, 2004.

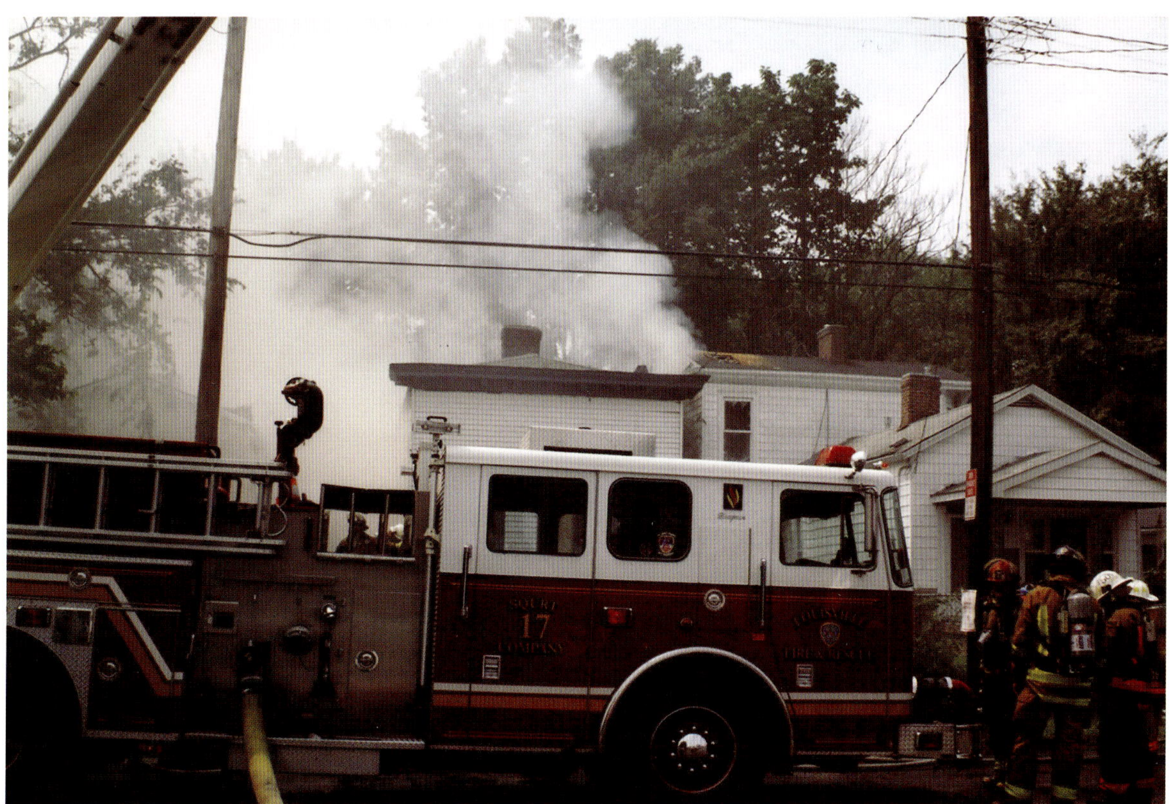

LOUISVILLE, KY Two houses are heavily damaged in a 2 alarm fire in the 2600 block of Muhammad Ali Blvd, on July 21, 2004.

WINTER FIREFIGHTING

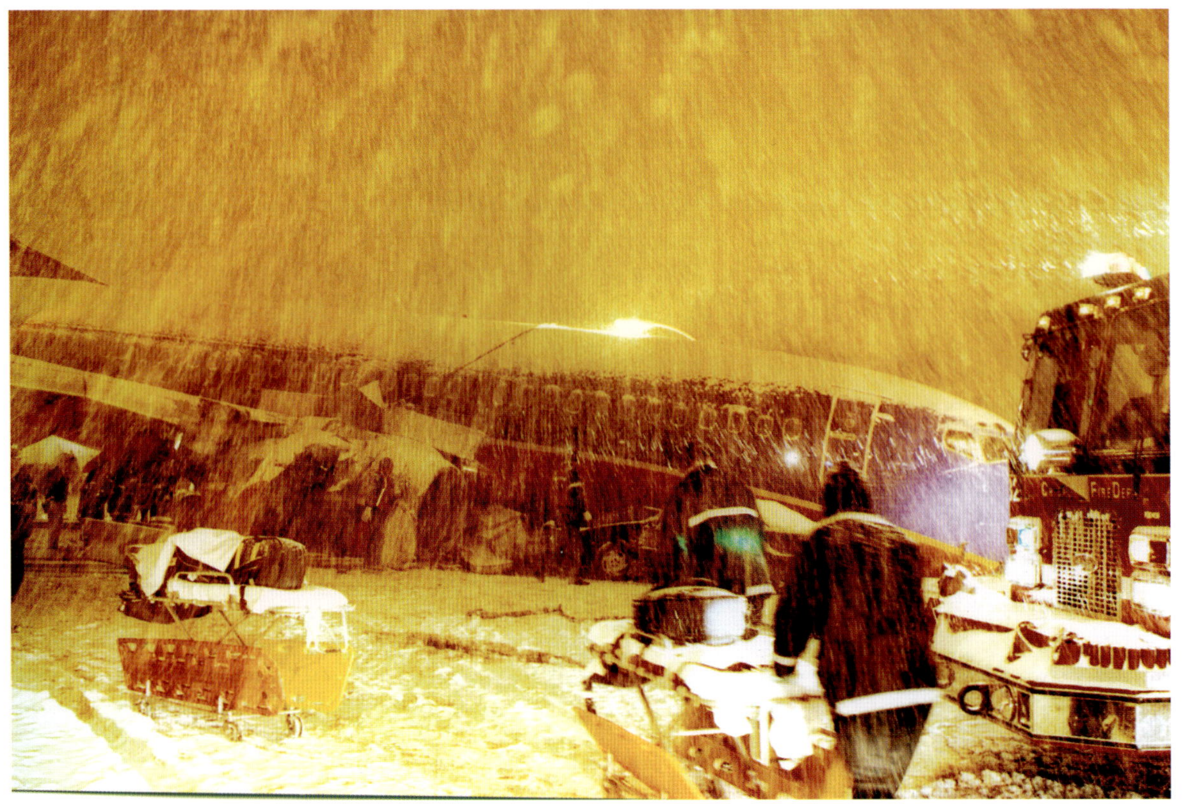

Chicago, Midway Airport.

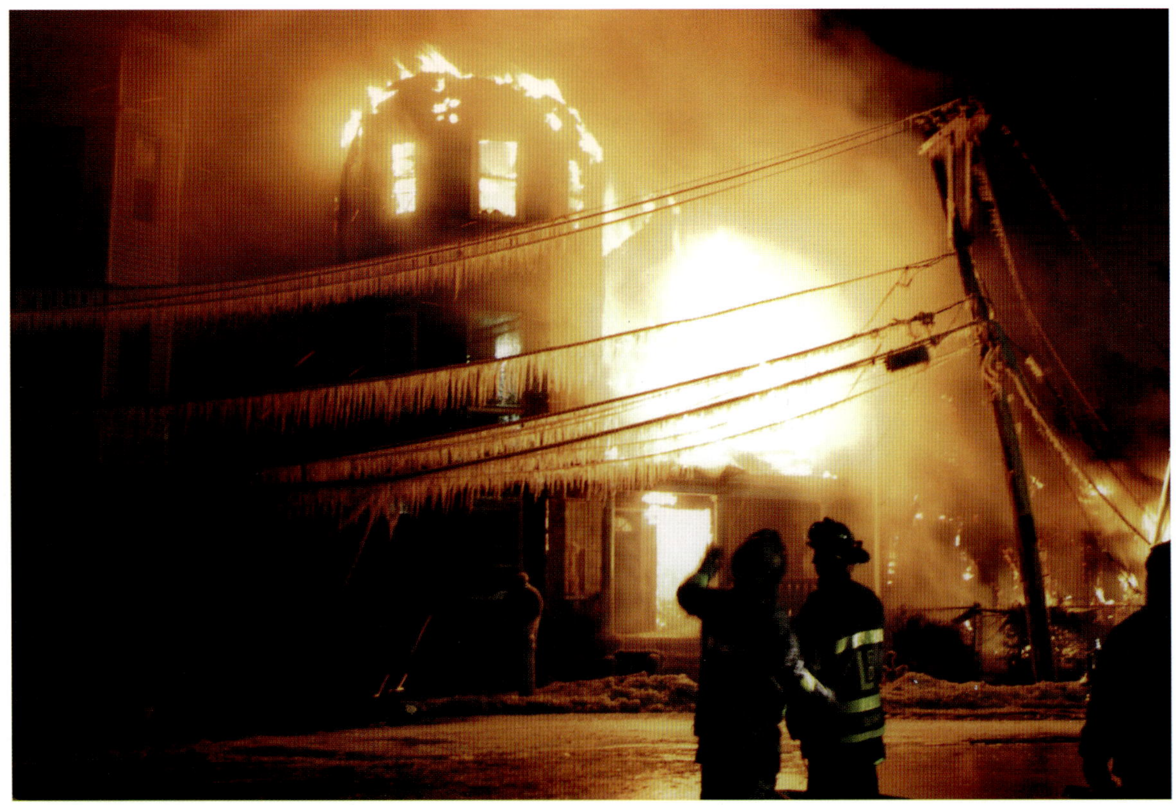

Lawrence, MA.

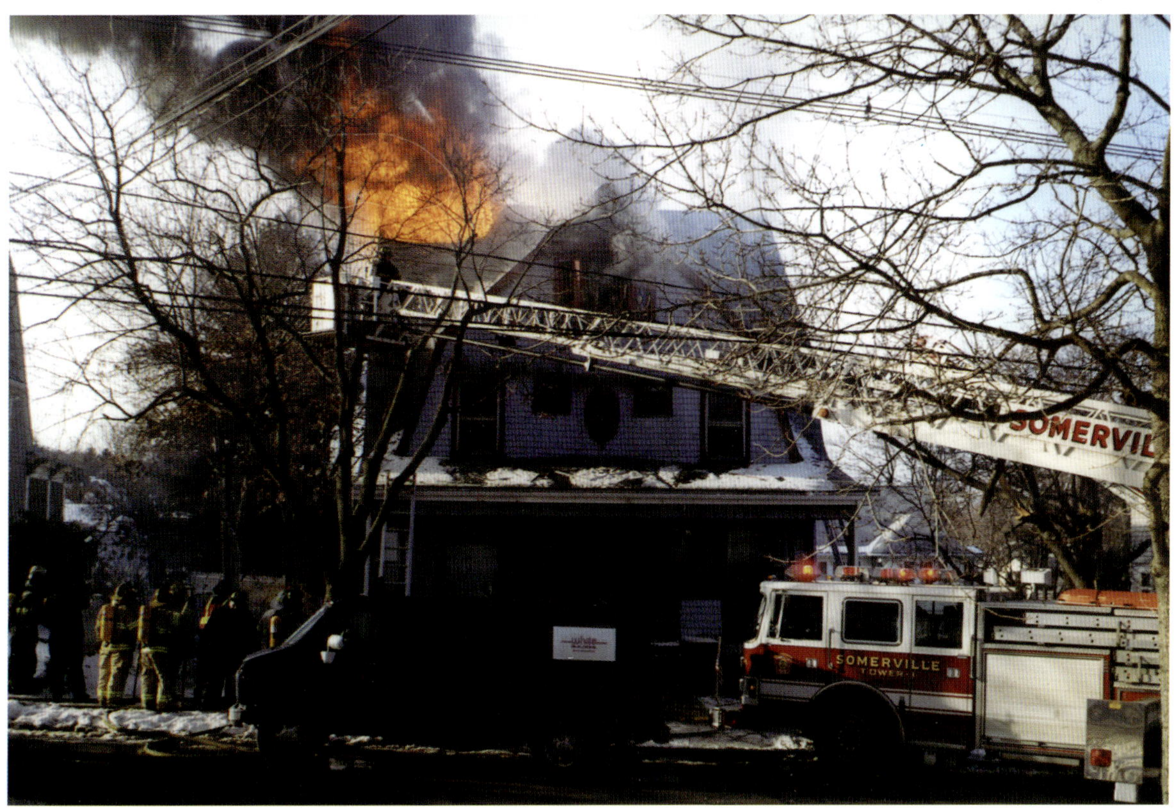

Arlington, MA.

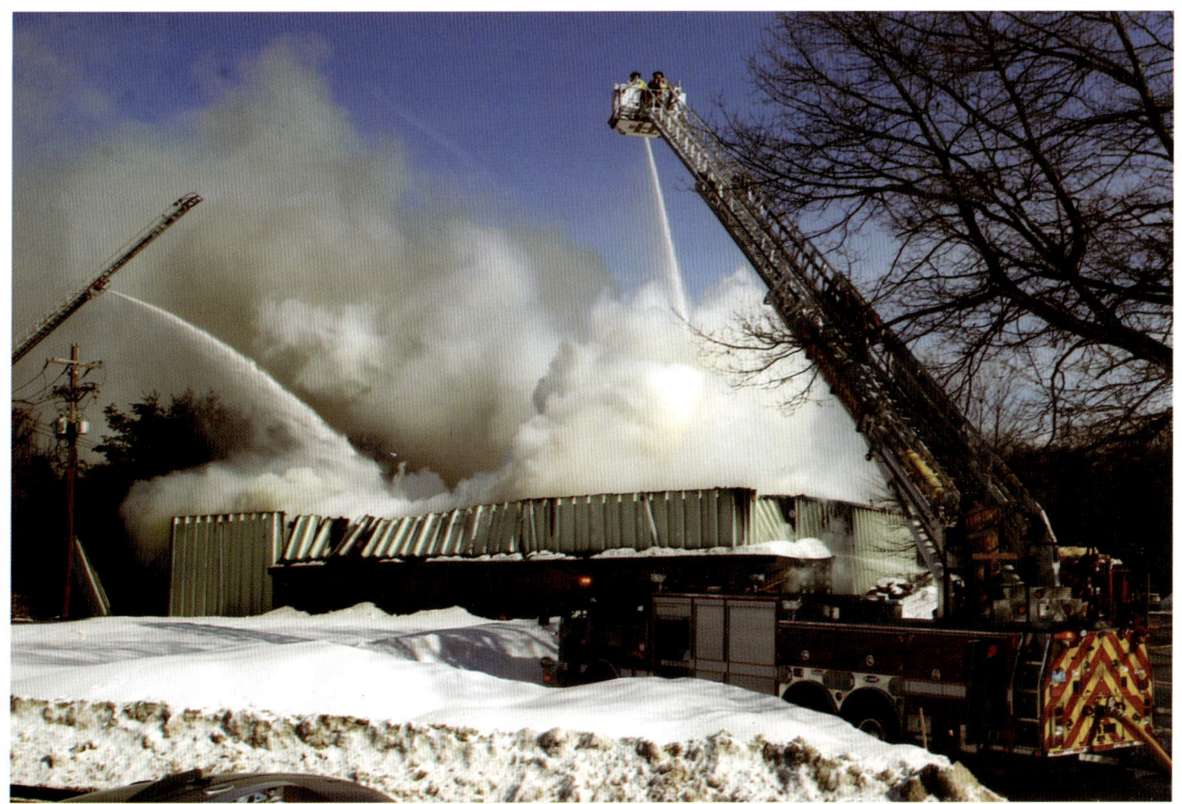

Wilmington, MA.

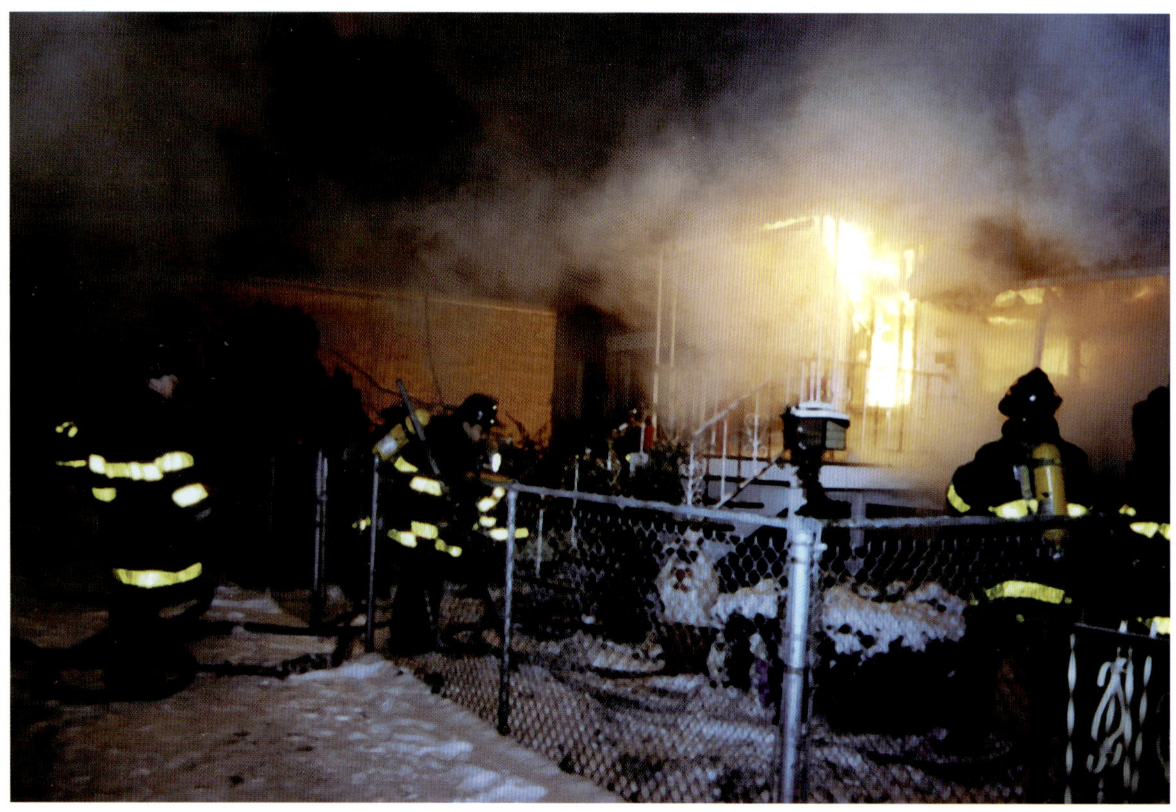

Chicago, Southside, below zero temperatures.

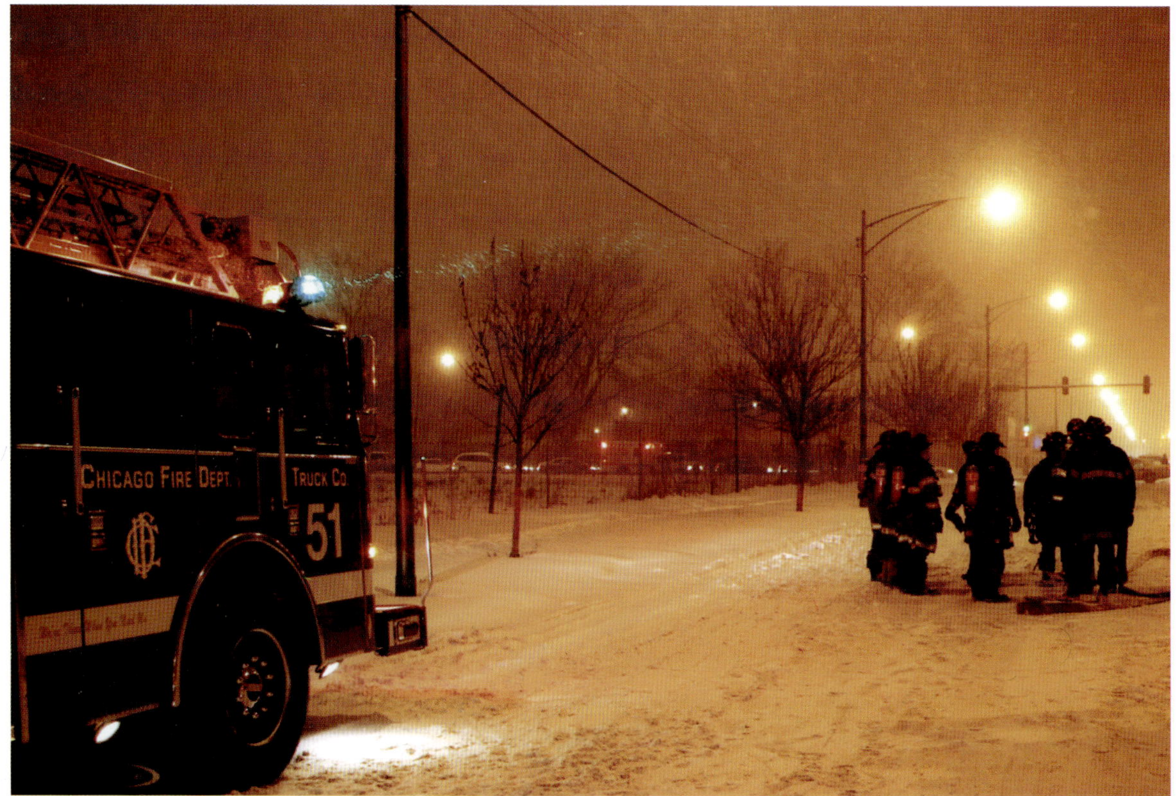

Chicago, Major gas leak, West Englewood.

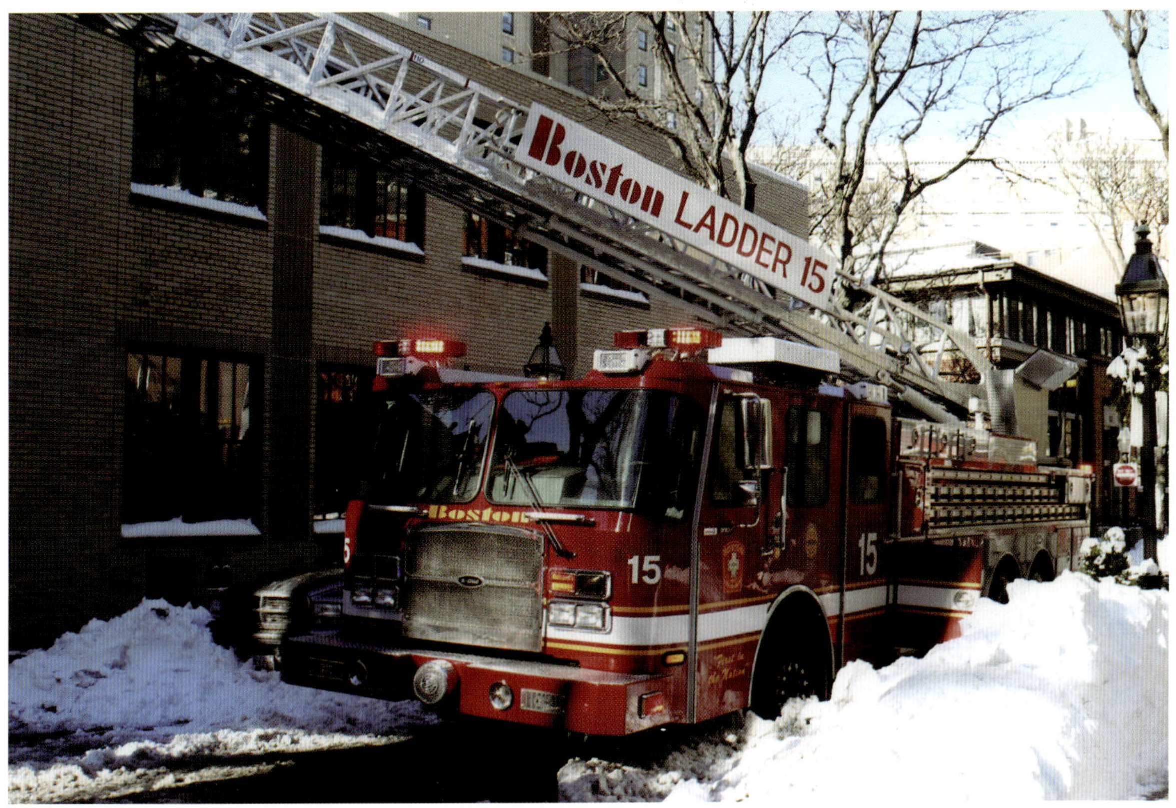

Boston, Bay Village.

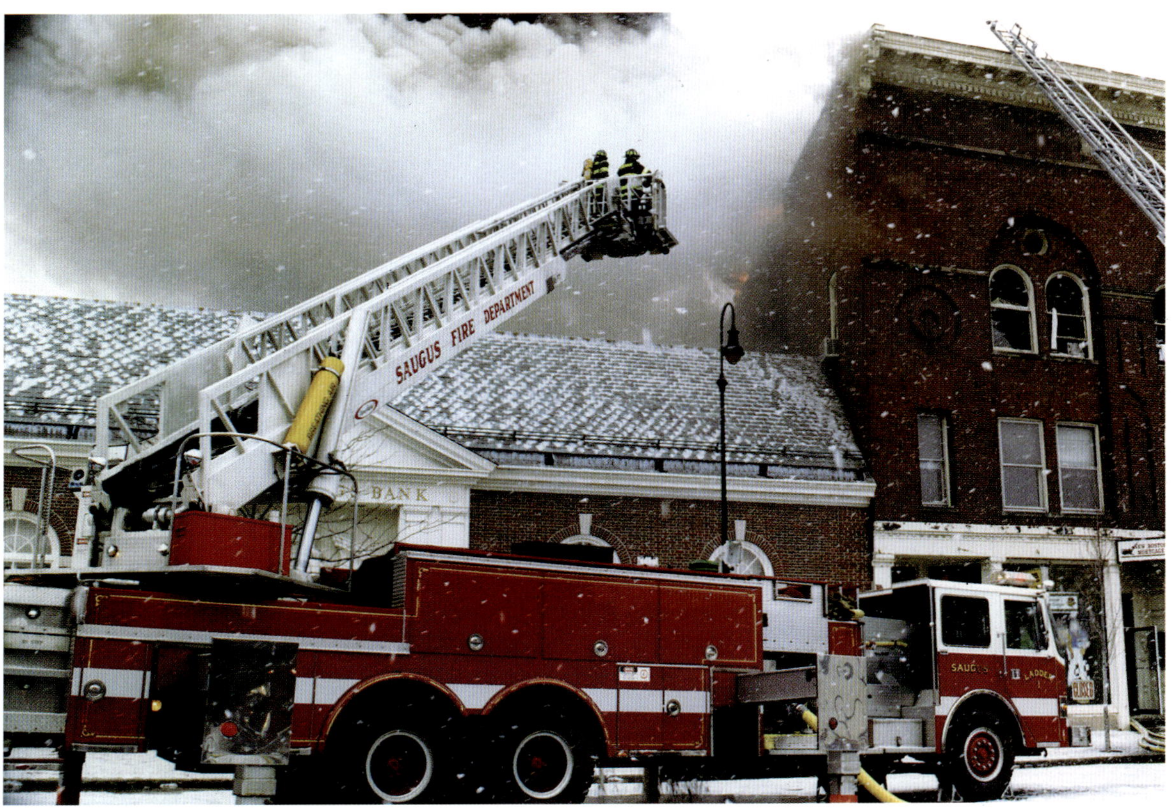

Wakefield, MA.

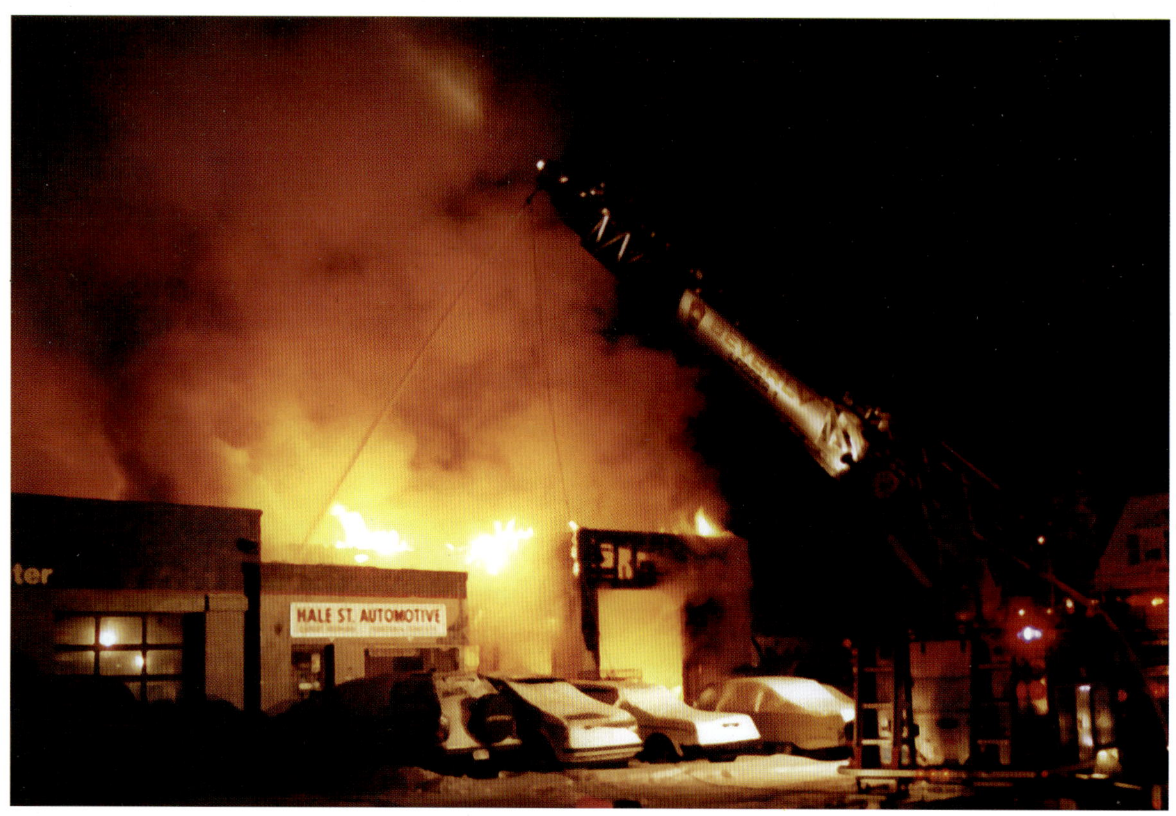

Beverly, MA.

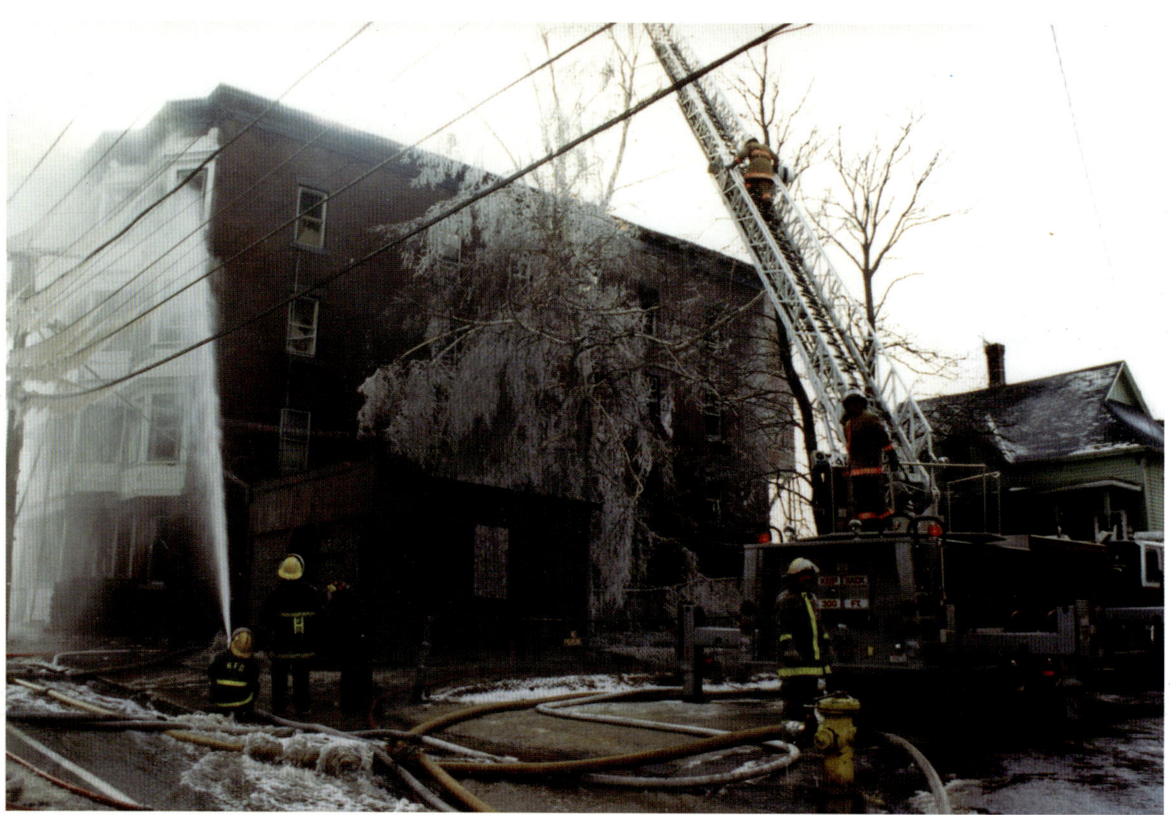

Gardner, MA.

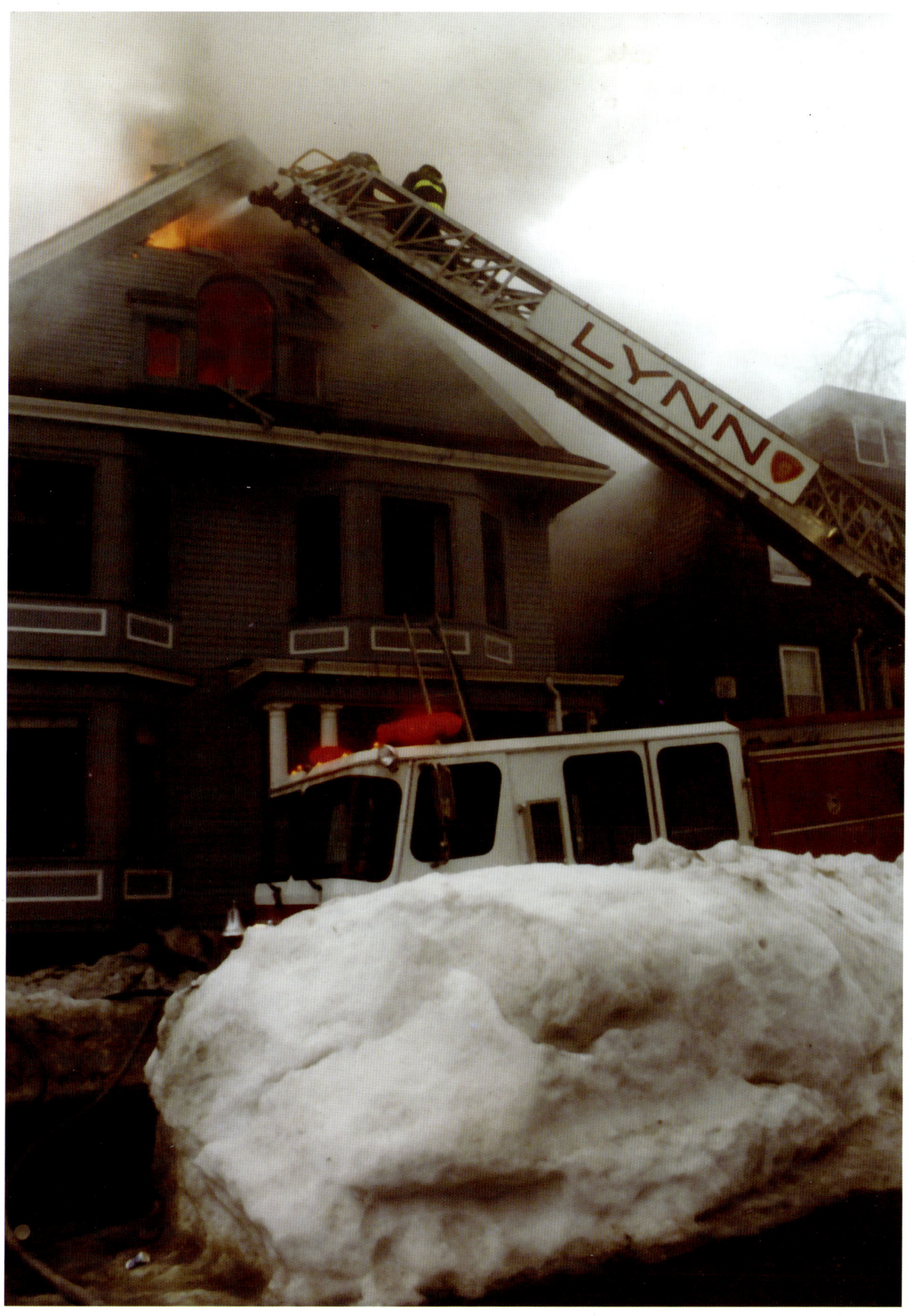

Lynn, MA.

TRUCK WORK

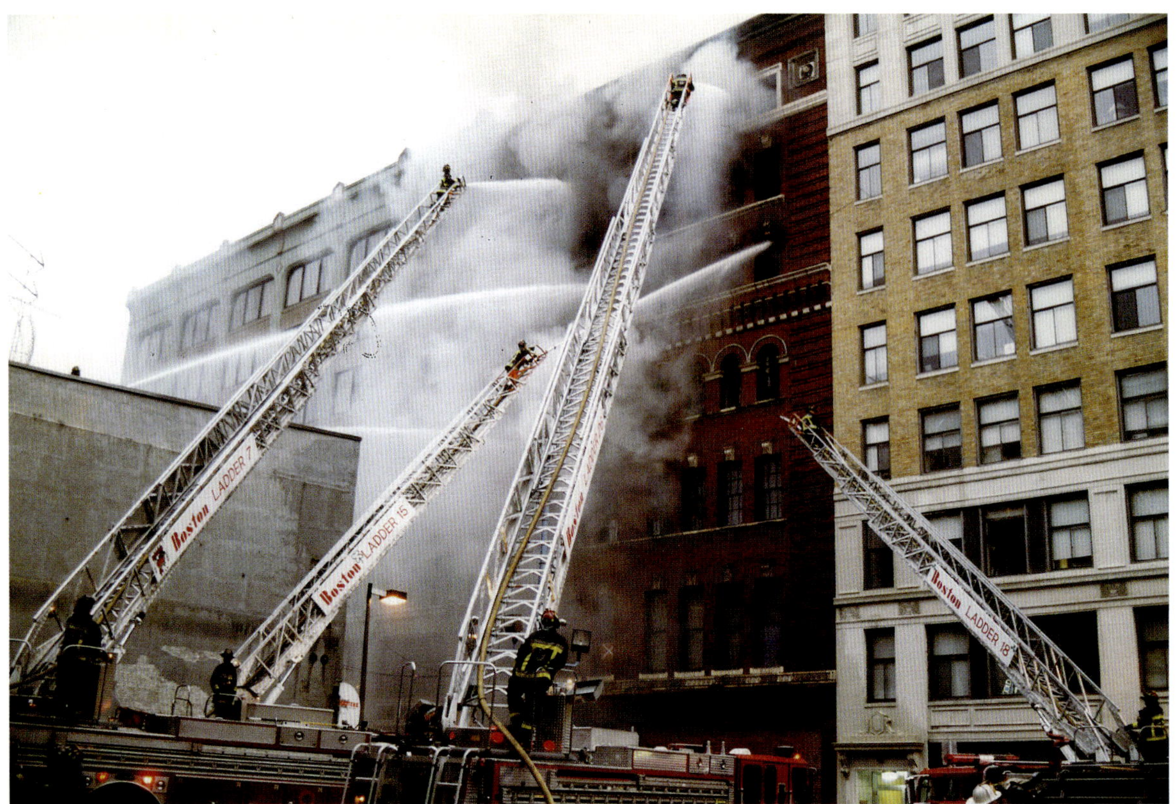

Boston, North Station.

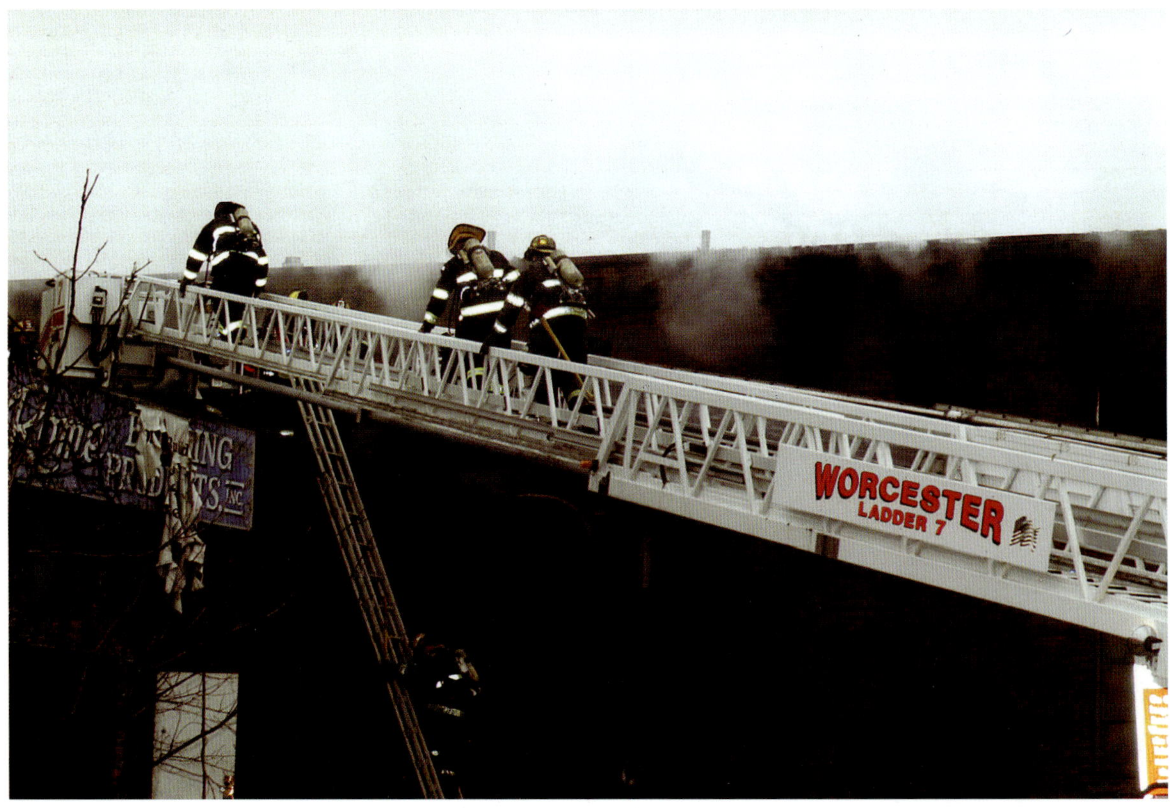

Worcester, MA.

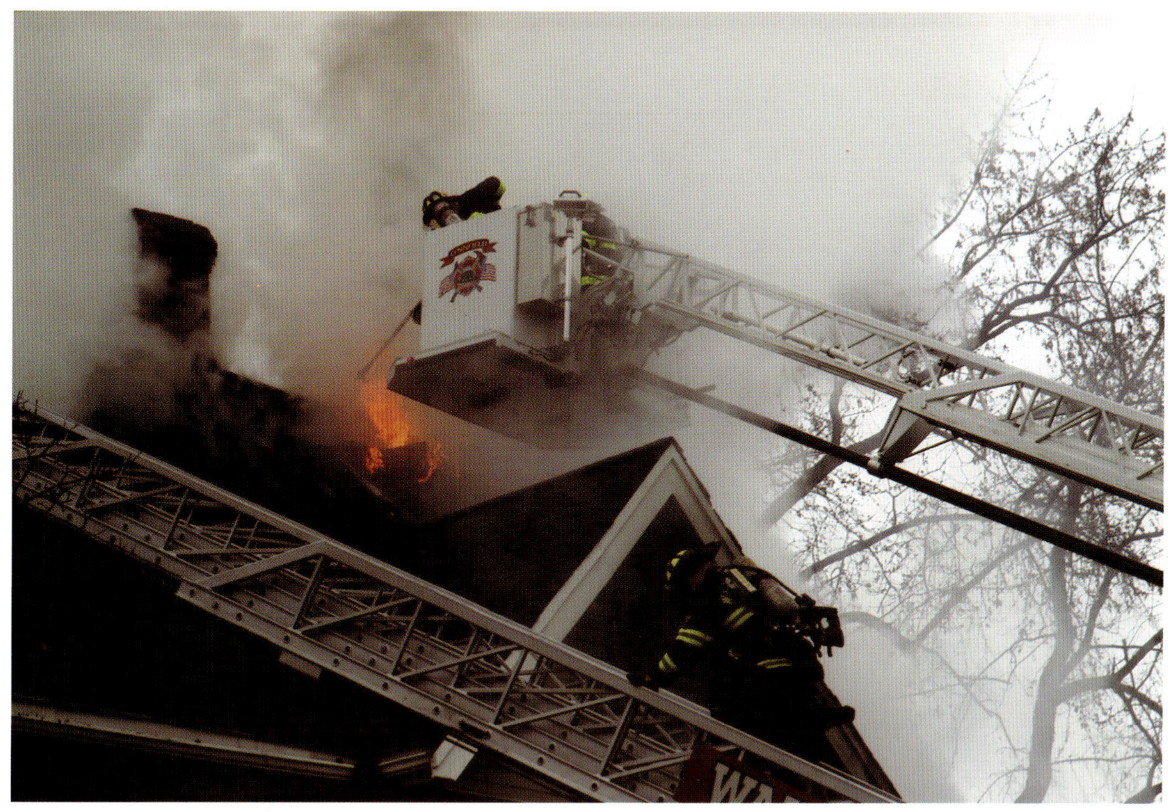

Wakefield, MA.

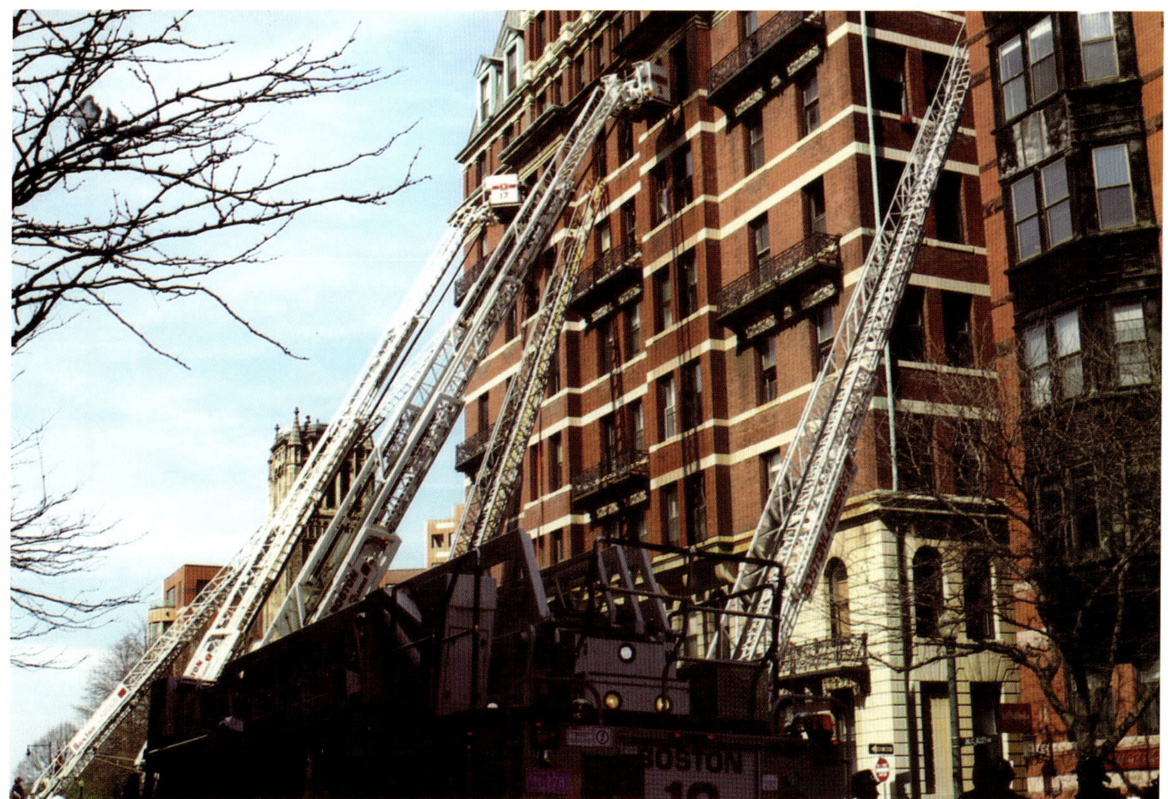

Boston, Back Bay.

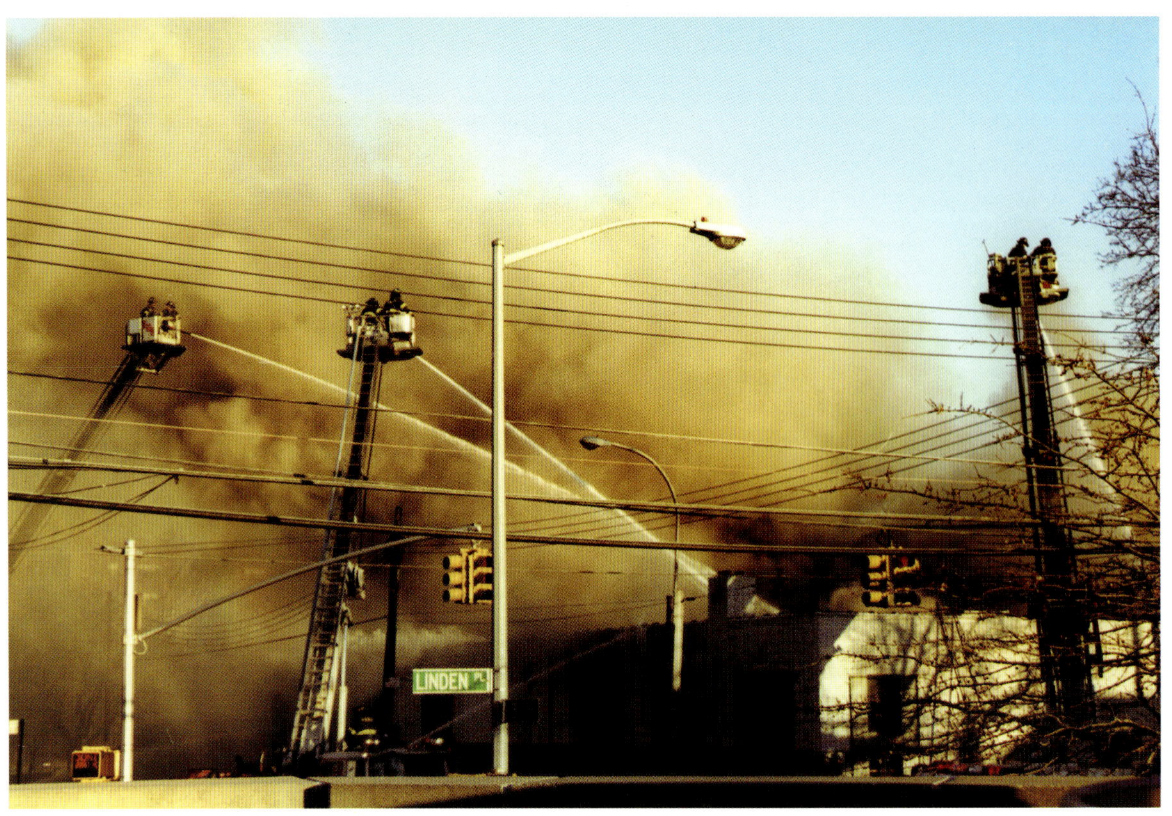

Queens, NY.

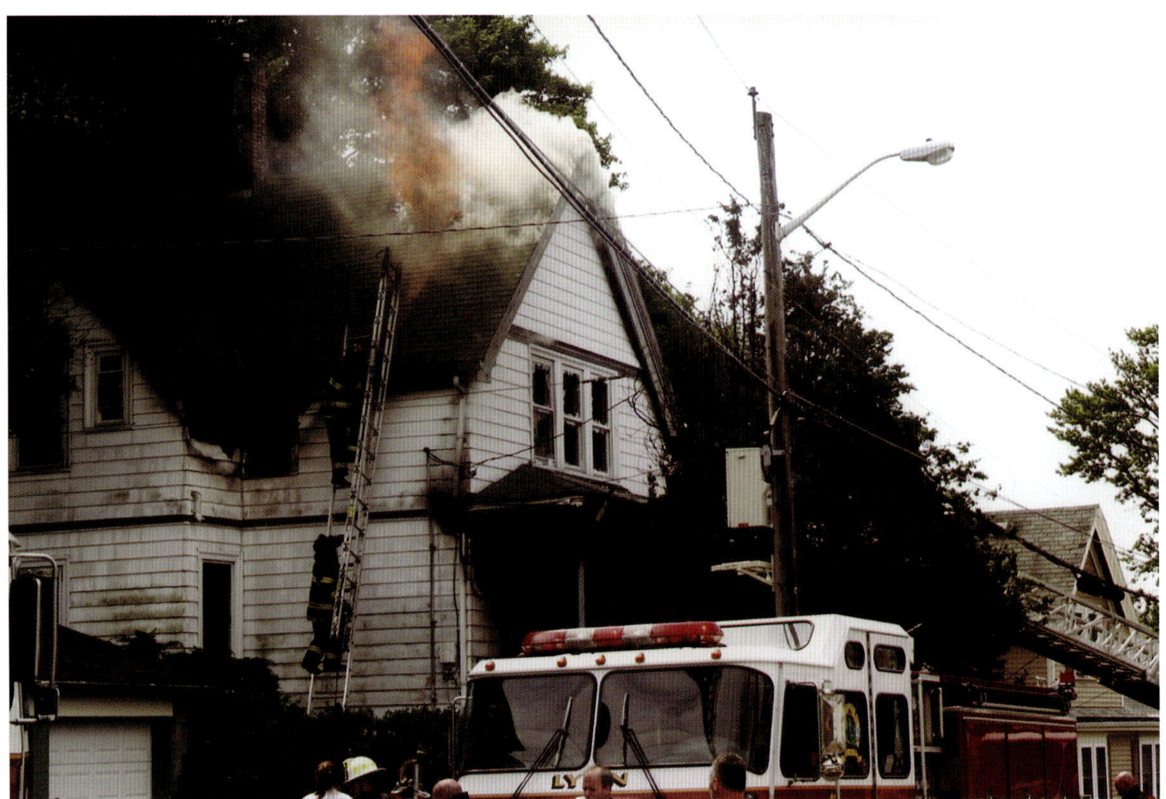

Lynn, MA.

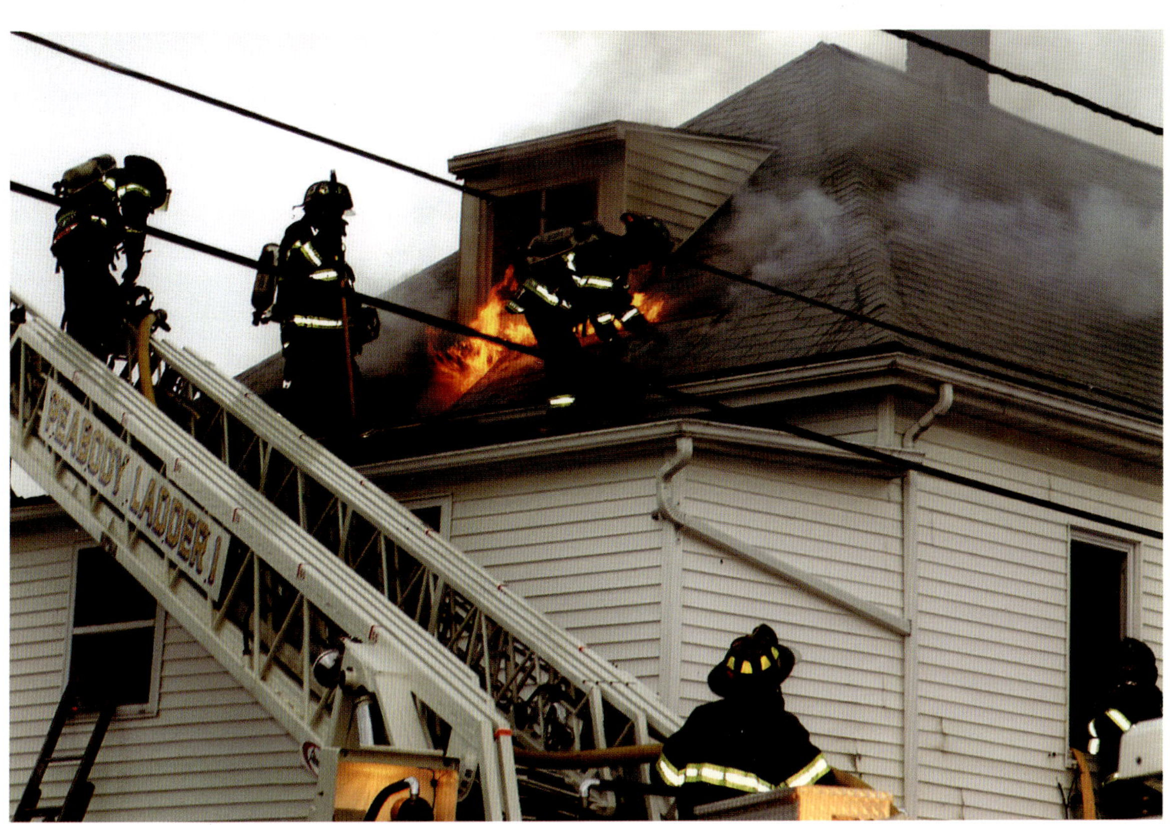

Peabody, MA.

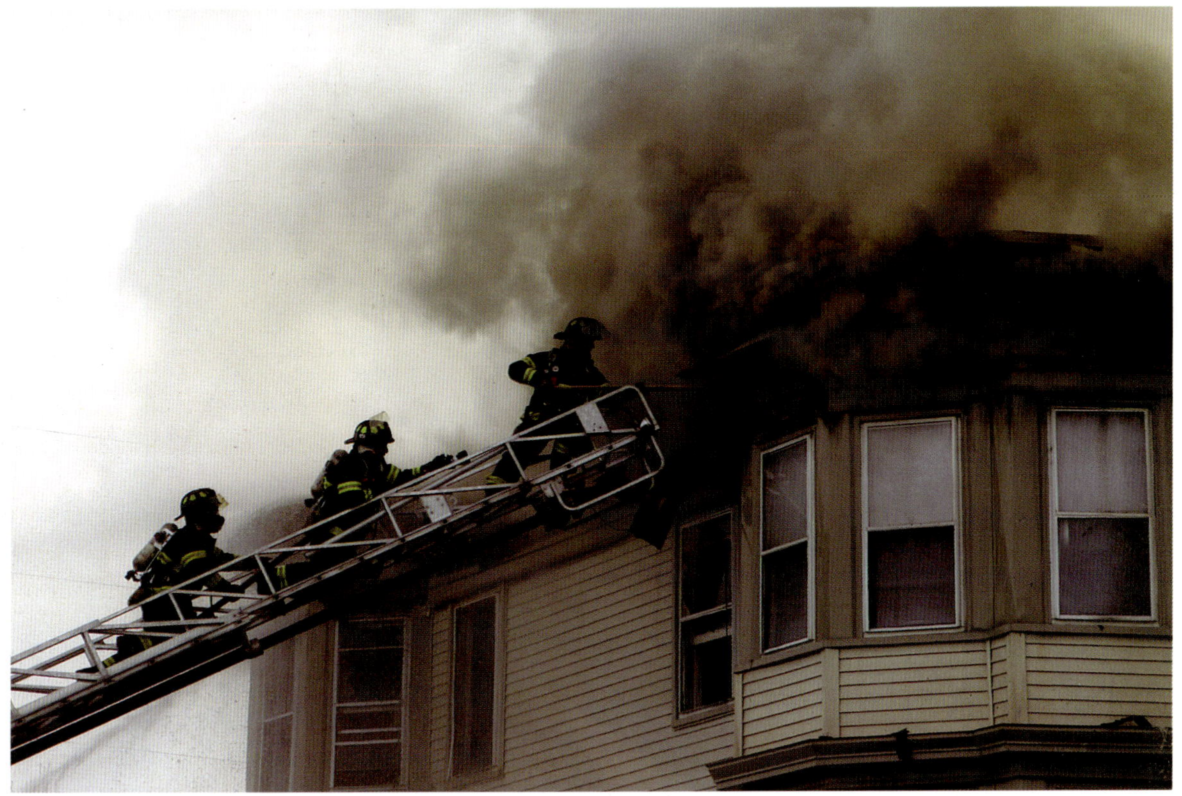
Beverly, MA.

GROUPS

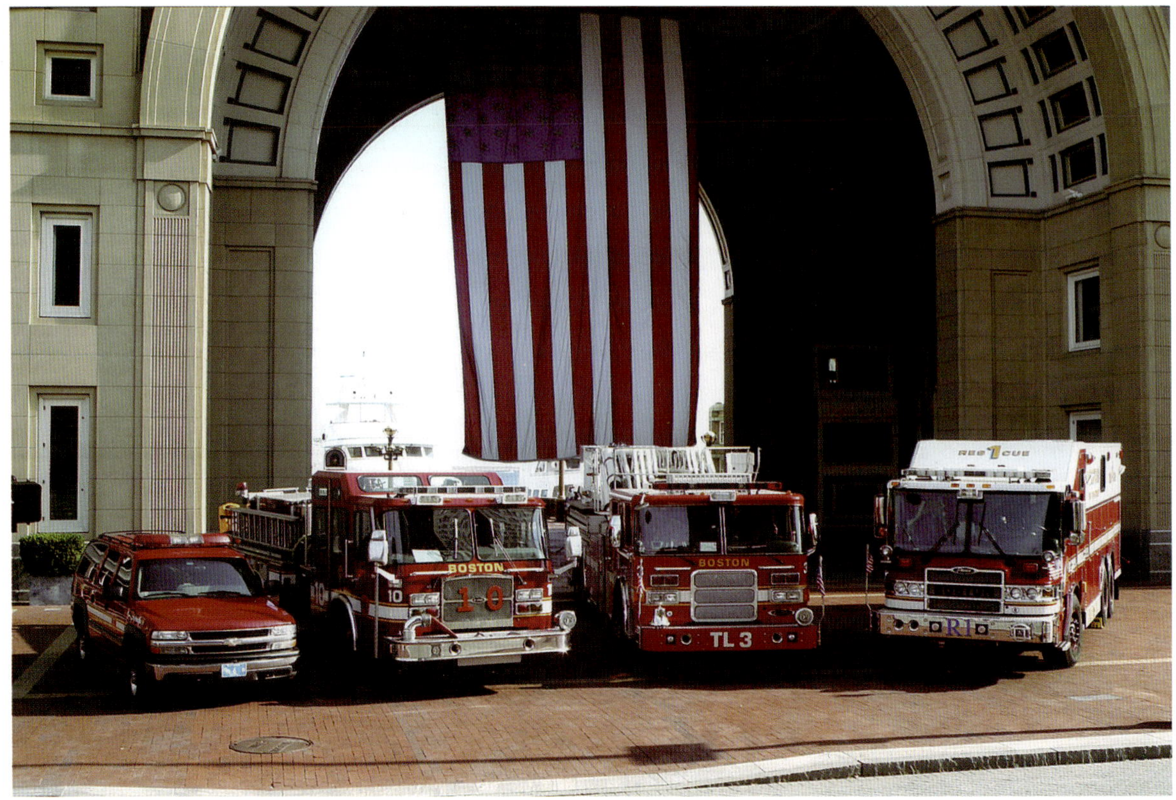

Boston Division One Headquarters Apparatus at Rowes Wharf.

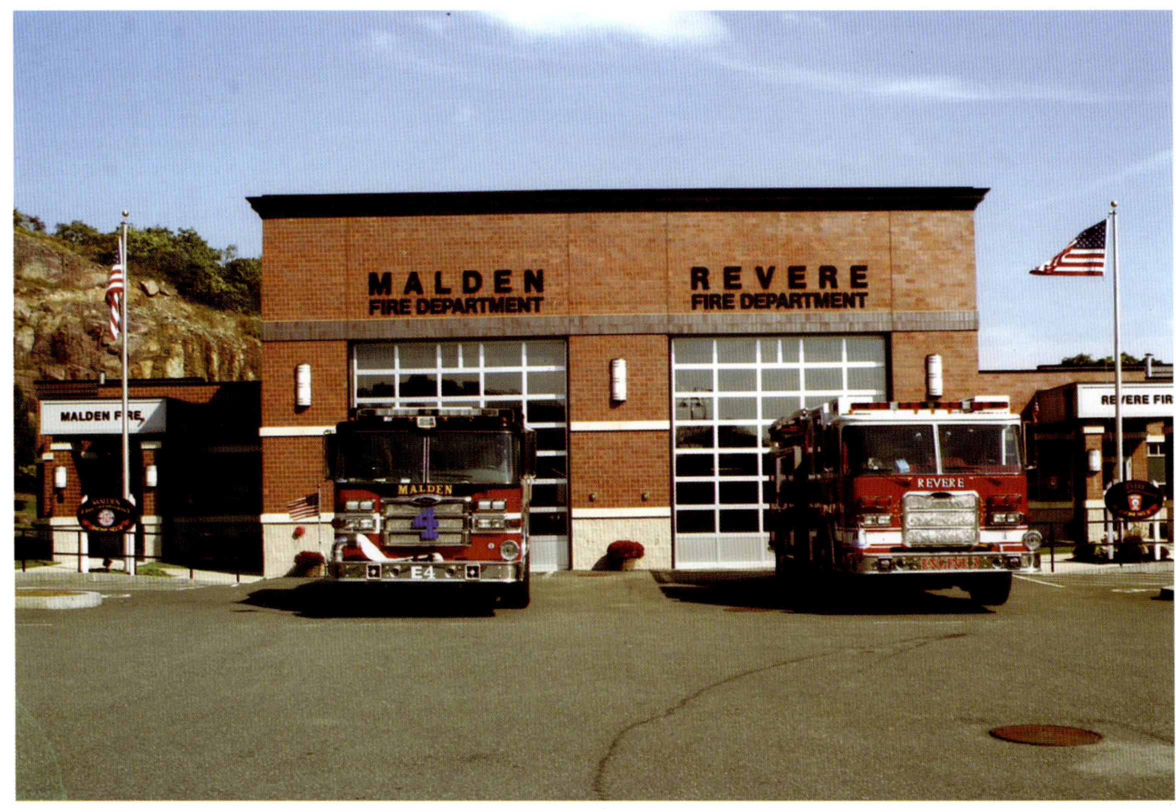

The developer of a large apartment complex built a firehouse in Revere, at the Malden line, and gave both cities 99 year leases. They each have their own entrances and separate facilities.

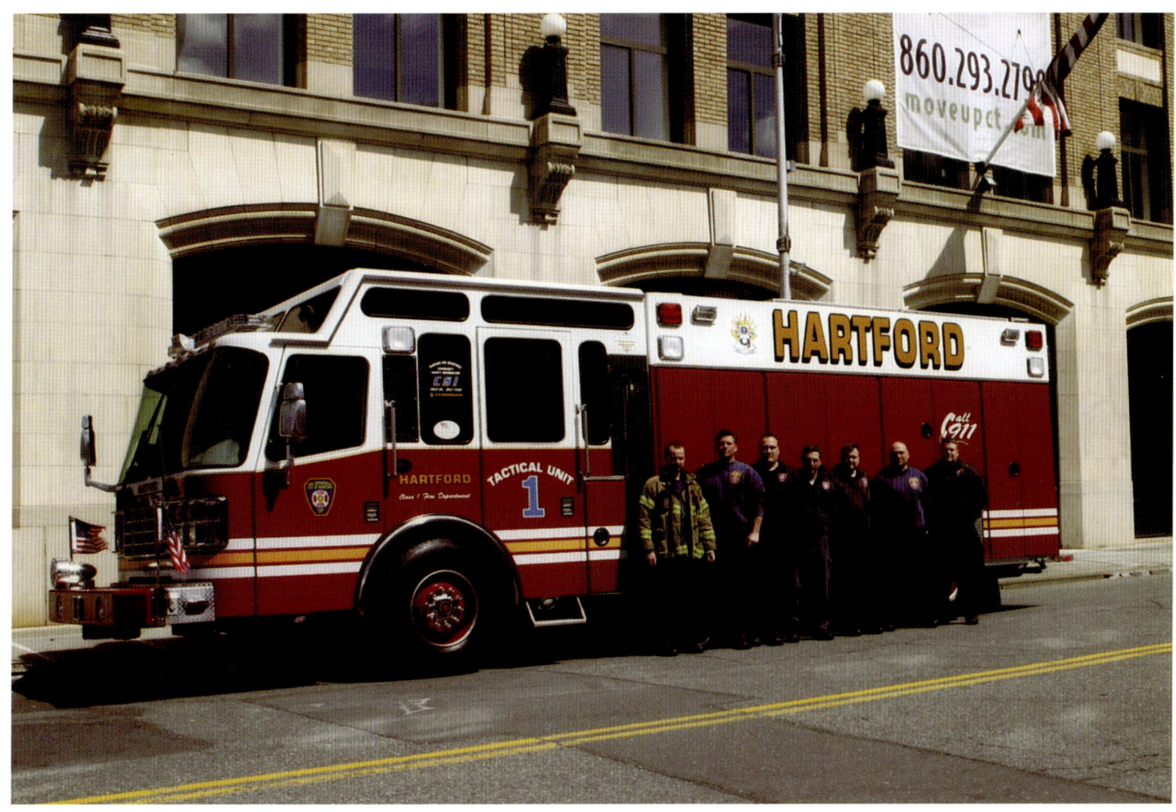

Tactical Unit 1, Hartford, CT.

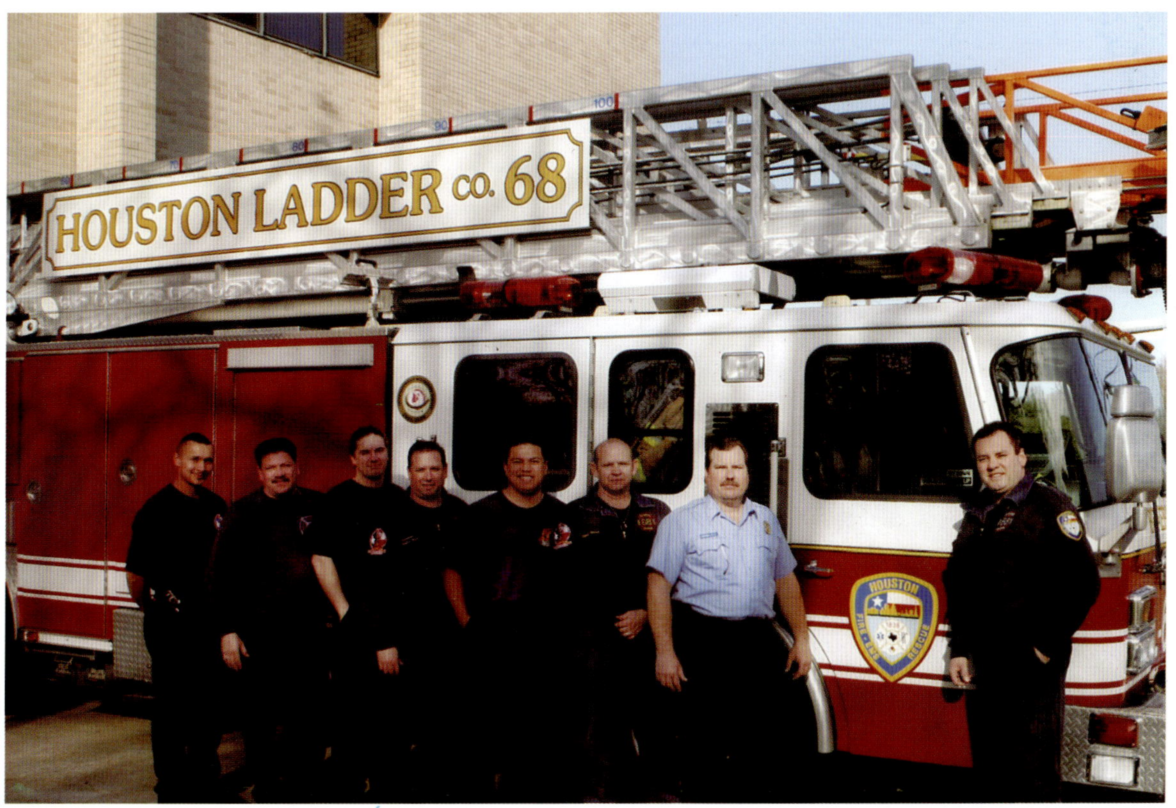

Ladder 68, Braeburn, Southwest, Houston.

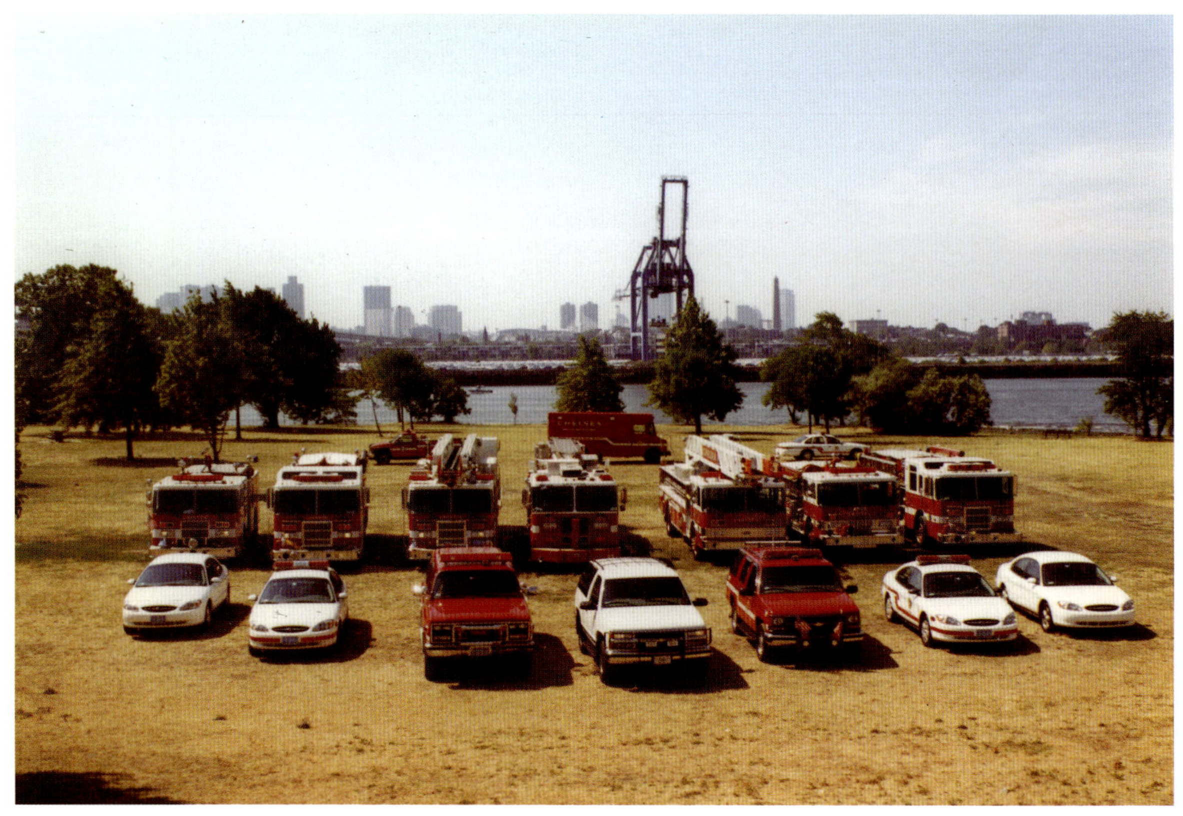

Chelsea, MA.

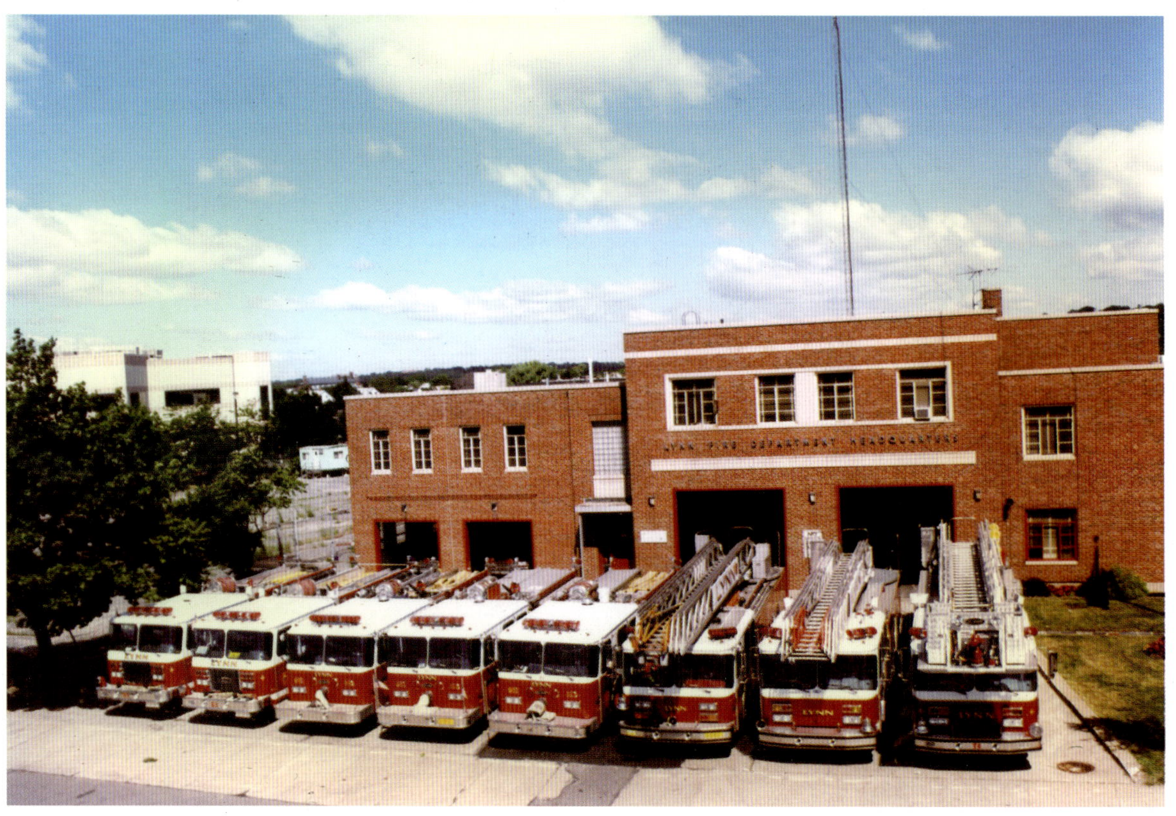

Lynn, MA.

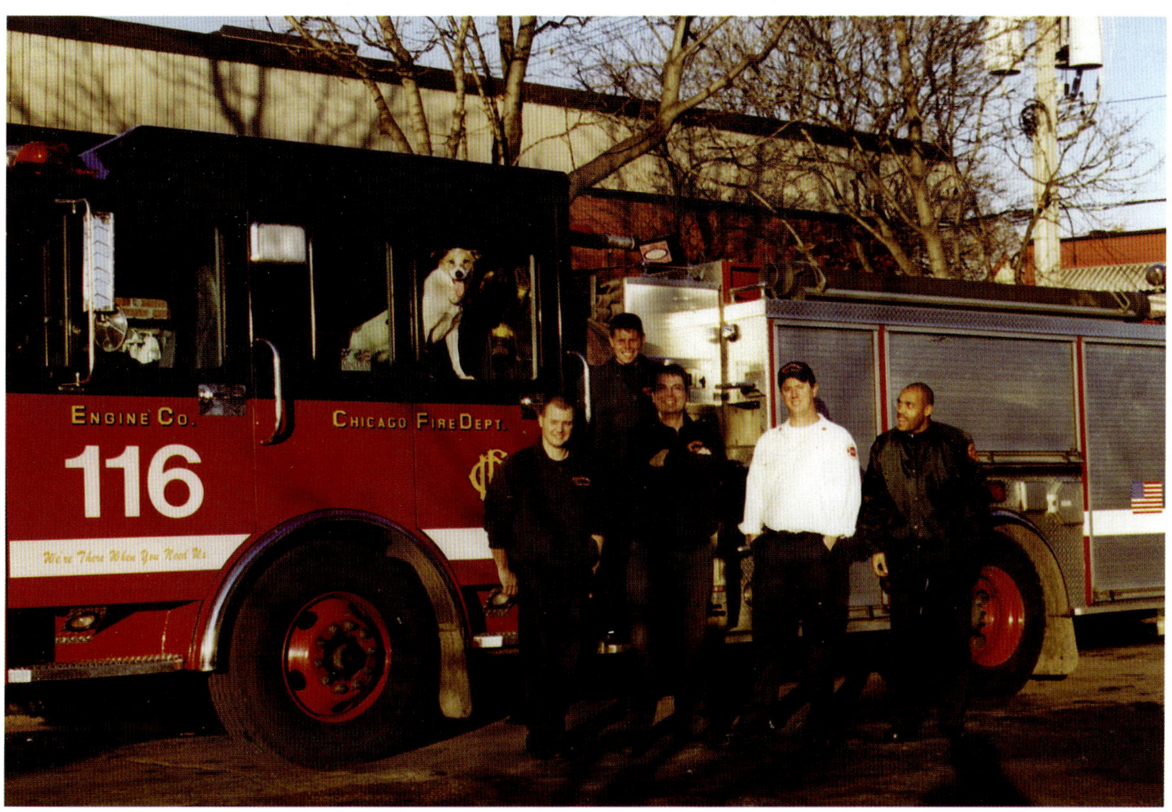

Chicago Engine 116 in West Englewood. "Salty" had been detailed across the floor from Squad 5.

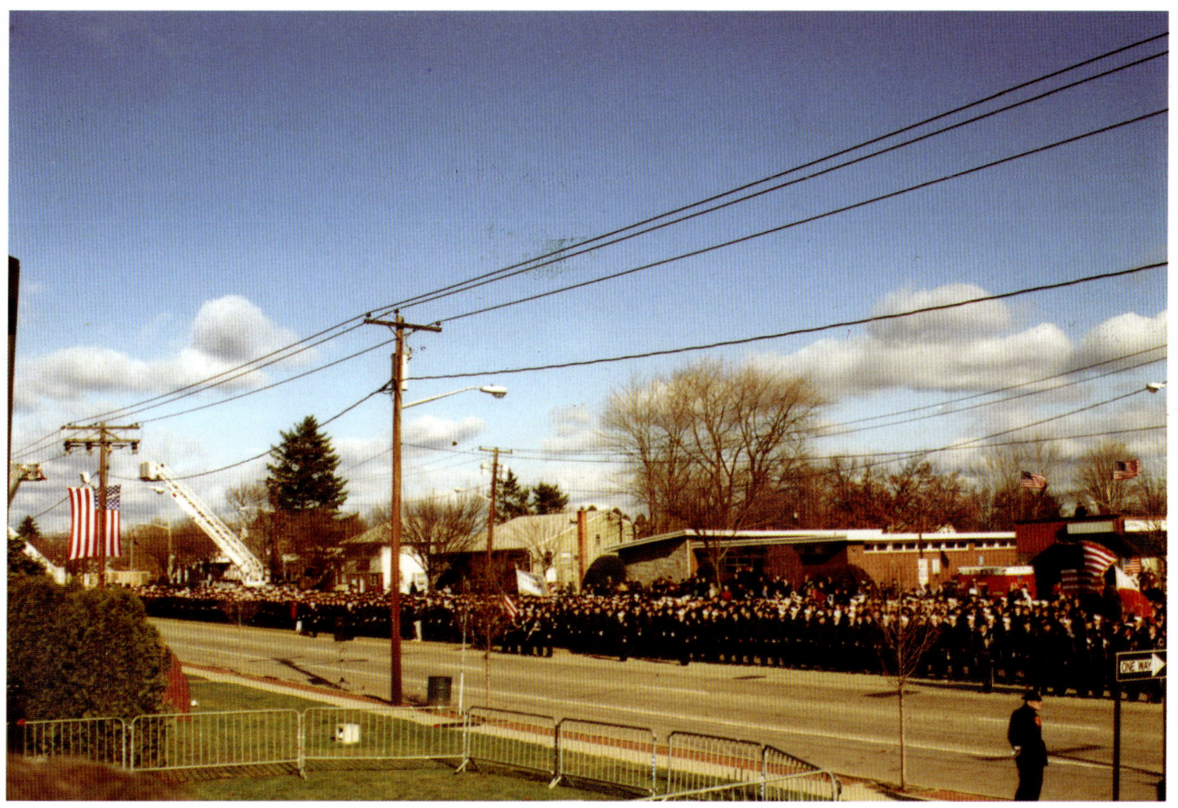

Deer Park, NY on December 15, 2001, thousands of firefighters from across the Country attend a memorial service for Deputy Chief Raymond M. Downey, Sr. who was killed on September 11, 2001.

MEMORIALS

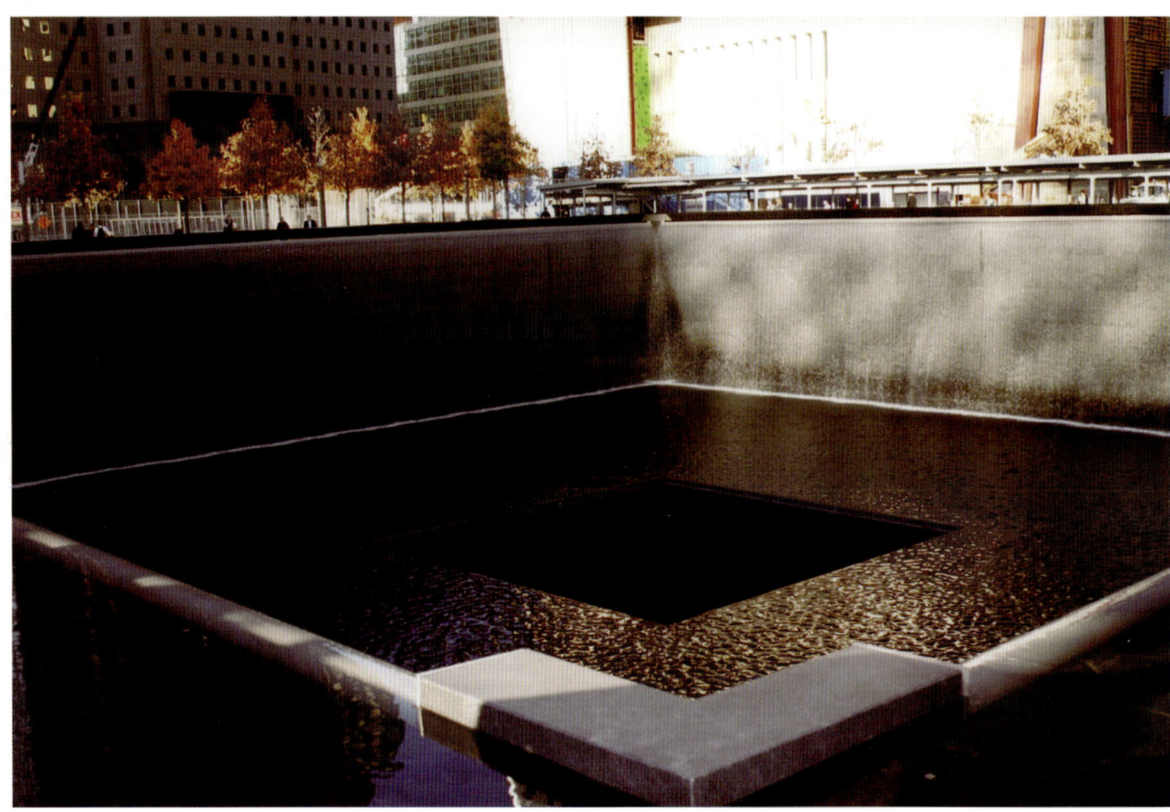

***SEPTEMBER 11 MEMORIAL PLAZA* -** The footprints of the original World Trade Center Towers consist of two thirty foot deep pools with water cascading down the sides of the granite walls. The names of all the victims of the 1993 bombing, the September 11, 2001 attacks, and those killed at the Pentagon, surround the memorial.

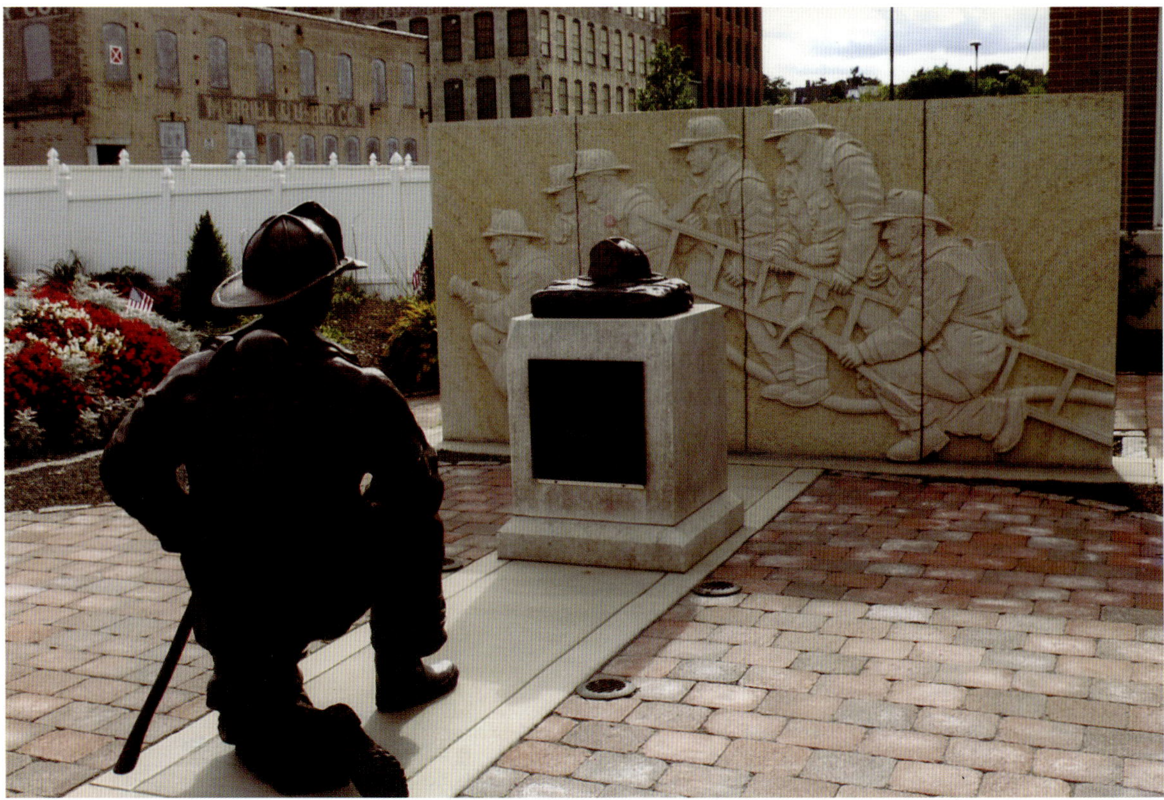

***WORCESTER COLD STORAGE MEMORIAL* -** Constructed in front of a new two million dollar firehouse at 266 Franklin Street, Worcester, MA, which was built on the site of the former Worcester Cold Storage Warehouse inferno which took the lives of six Worcester Firefighters on December 3, 1999.

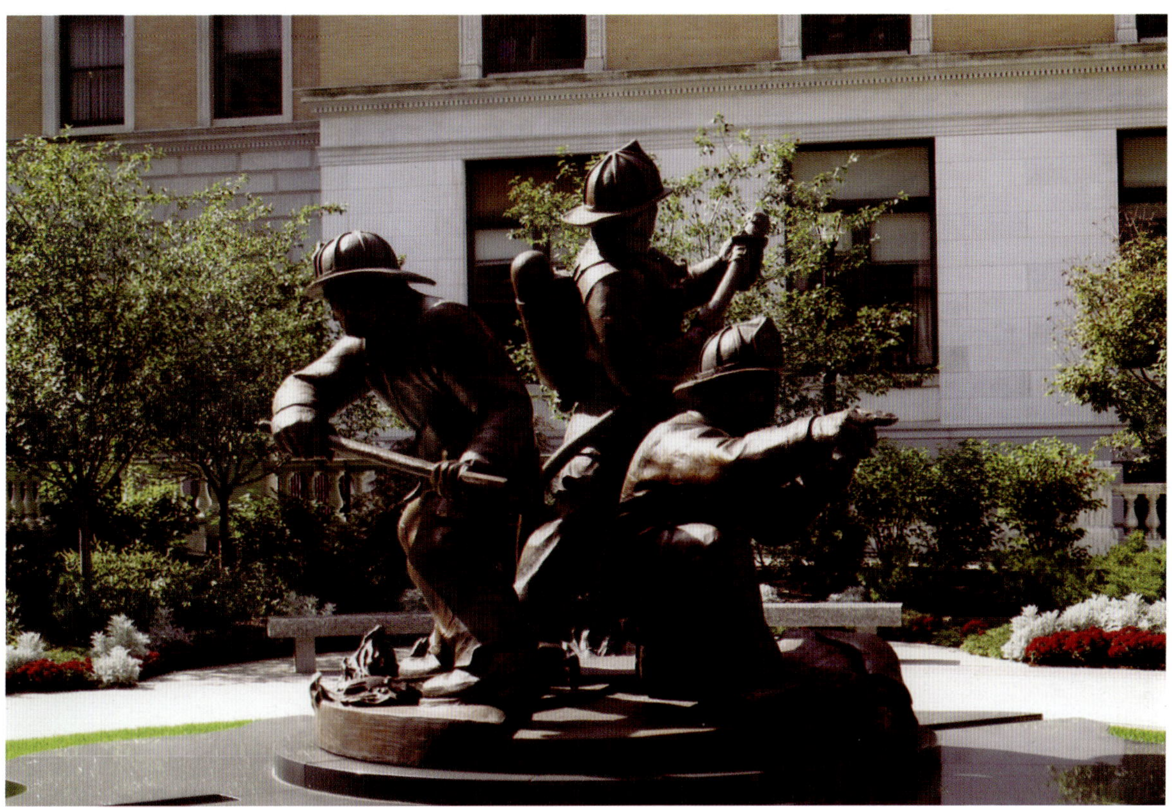

MASSACHUSETTS FALLEN FIREFIGHTERS MEMORIAL - Is located at the State House in Boston. The ten foot statue sits on a marble maltese cross, surrounded by a "Ring of Honor" which currently contains the names of 701 deceased firefighters.

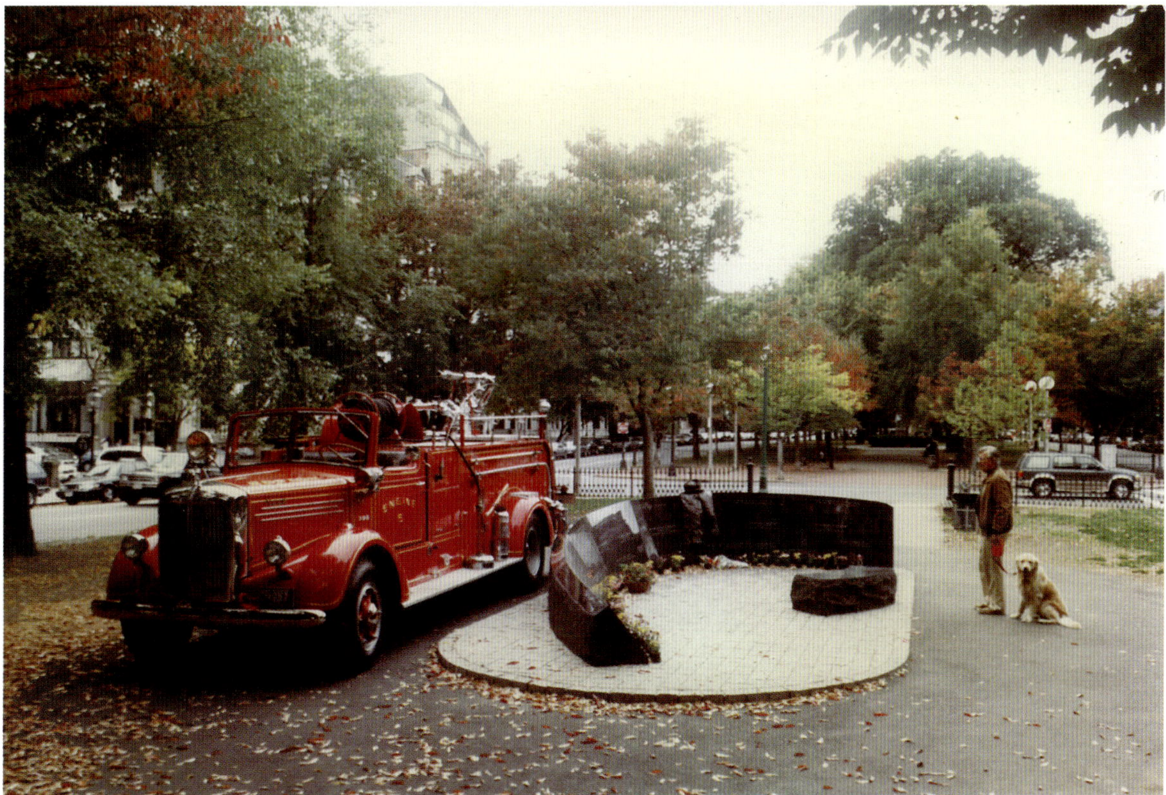

VENDOME FIRE MEMORIAL - To honor the nine Boston Firefighters who lost their lives in the Hotel Vendome collapse on June 17, 1972. It is located on the Commonwealth Avenue Mall at Dartmouth Street, across the street from the former hotel. Boston Engine 5, a 1948 Mack Hose Wagon, which has been completely restored, is the only remaining Boston apparatus which responded to the fire.

GONE BUT NOT FORGOTTEN

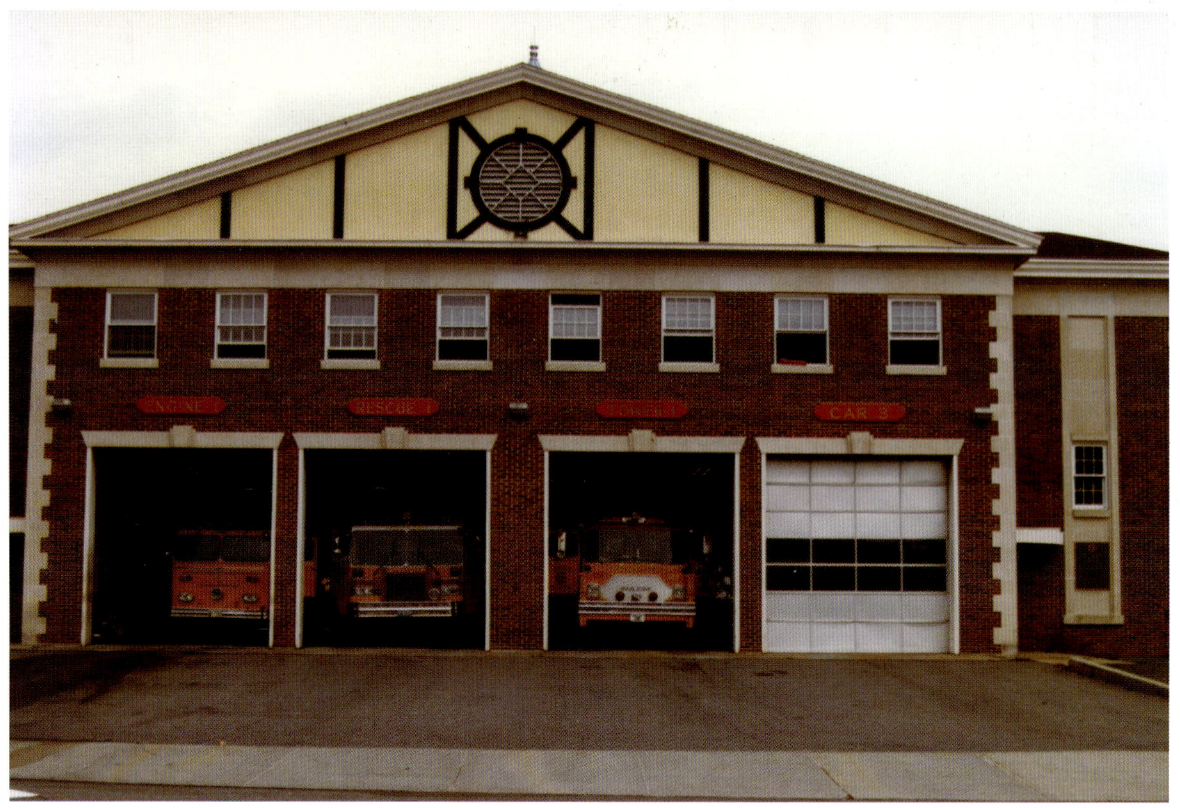

Worcester, MA Central Station, 70 Central Street, now a hotel.

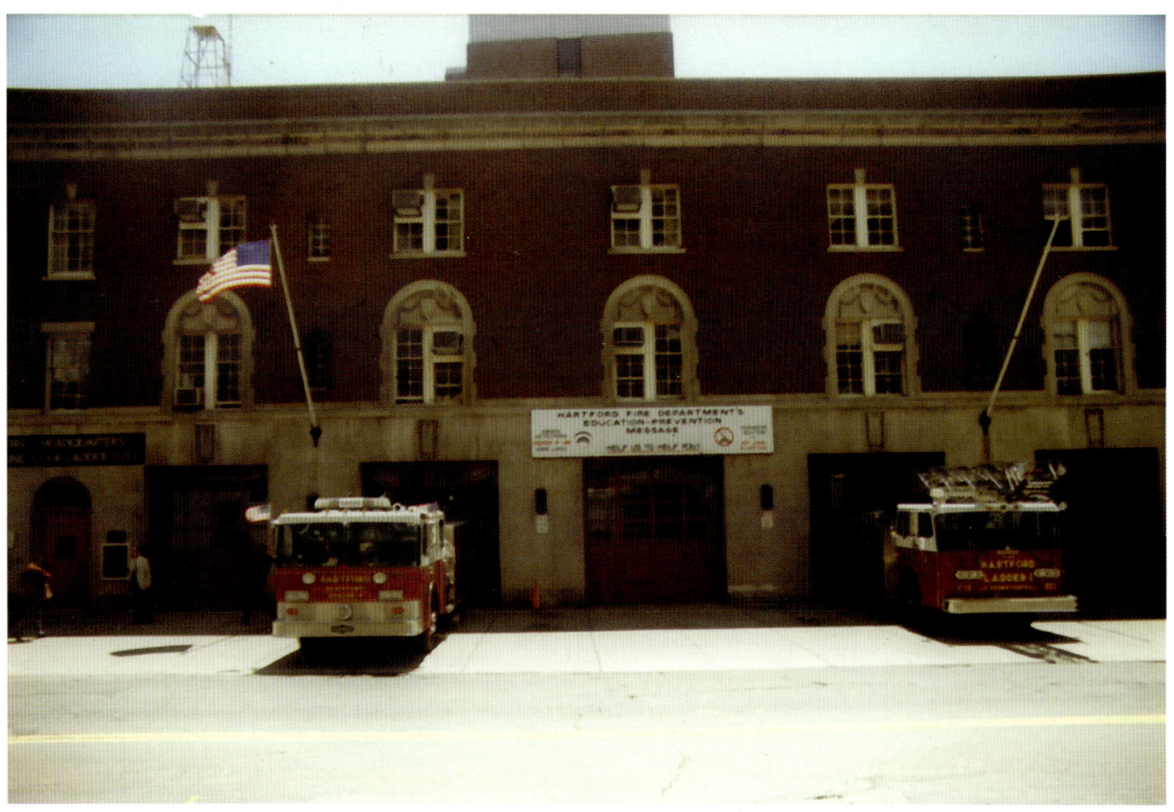

Hartford, CT Fire Administration Headquarters, 275 Pearl Street. Engine 4 and Ladder 1 were disbanded in the 90's and Headquarters moved into a new Public Safety Complex in November, 2012.

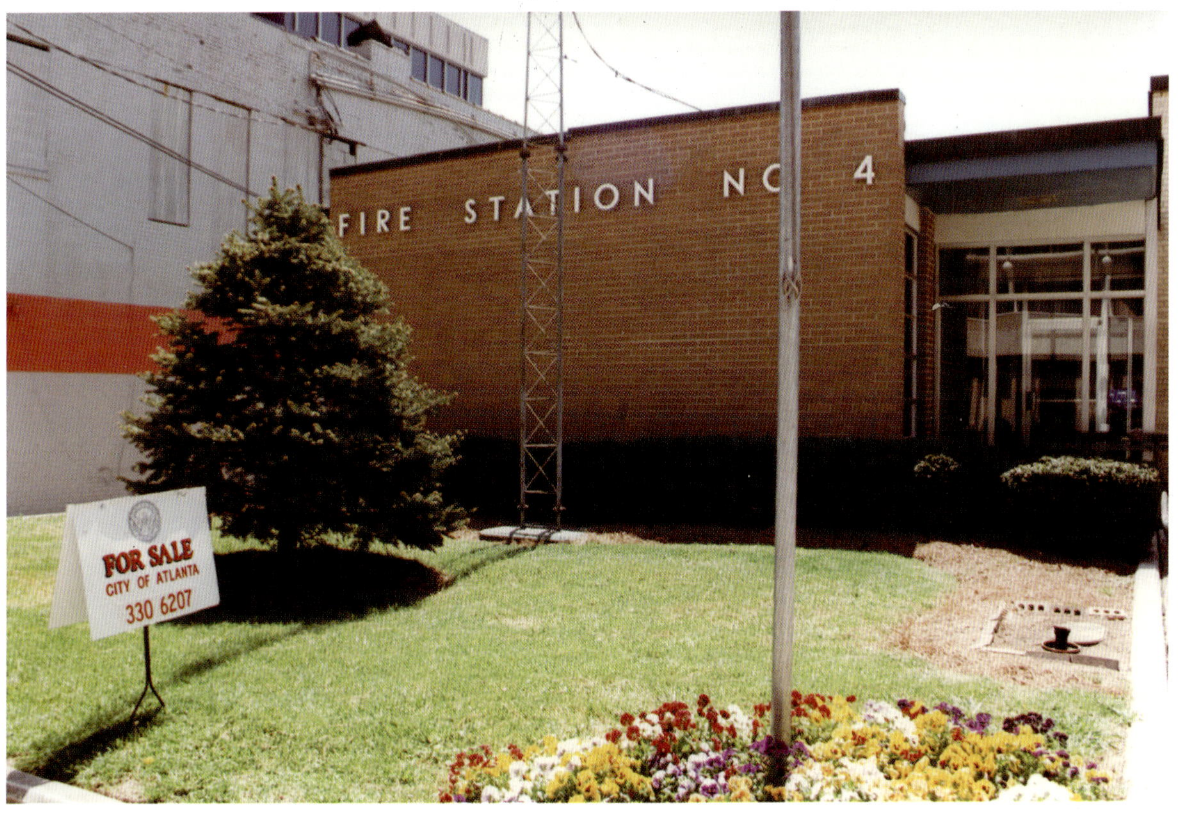

Atlanta, Station 4, 125 Ellis Street N.E. Now The First Congregational Church.

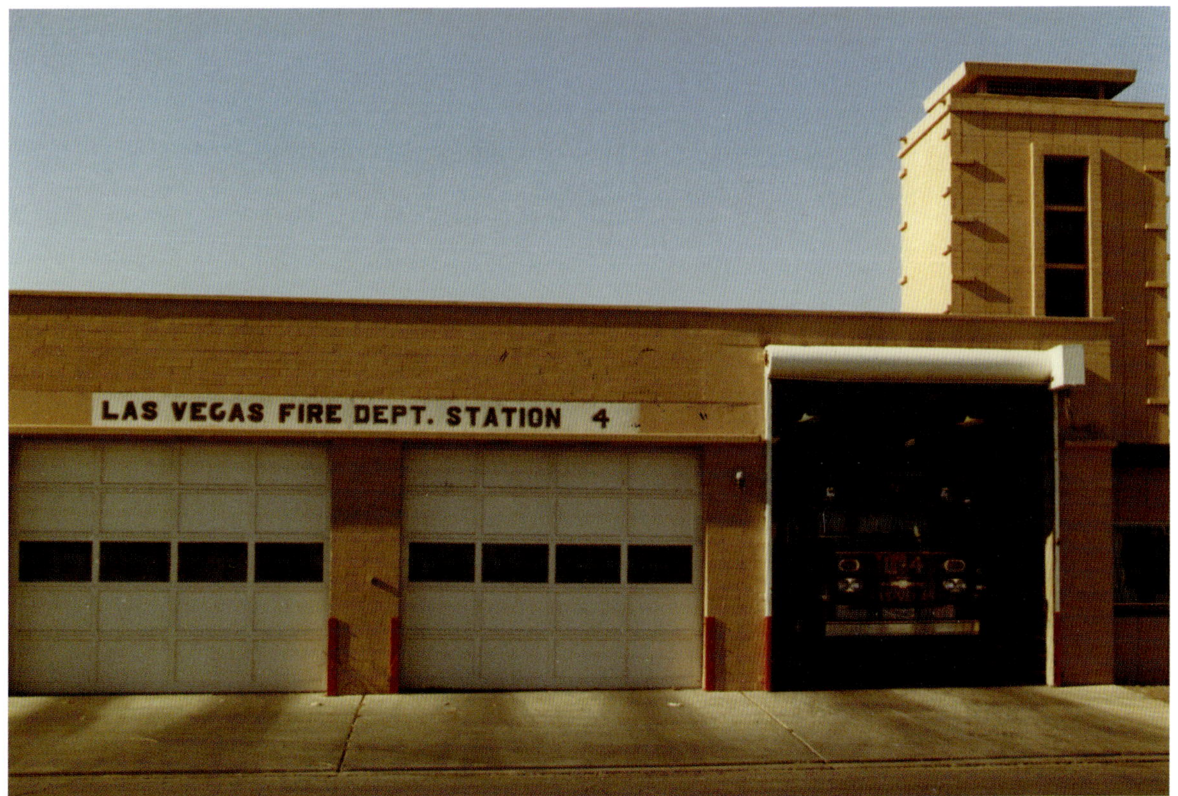

Las Vegas, Station 4, Industrial and Utah.

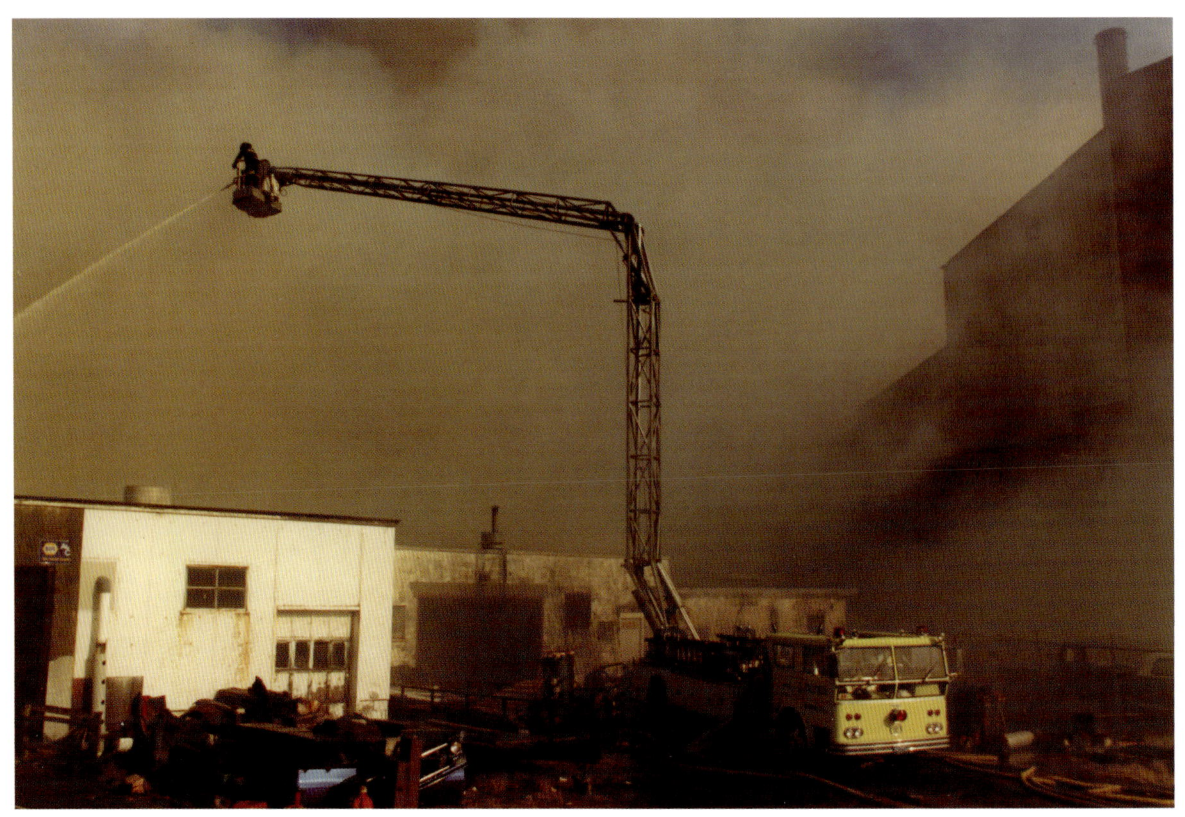

Ward LaFrance Hi-Ranger, Taunton, MA 1963, 85 foot snorkel.

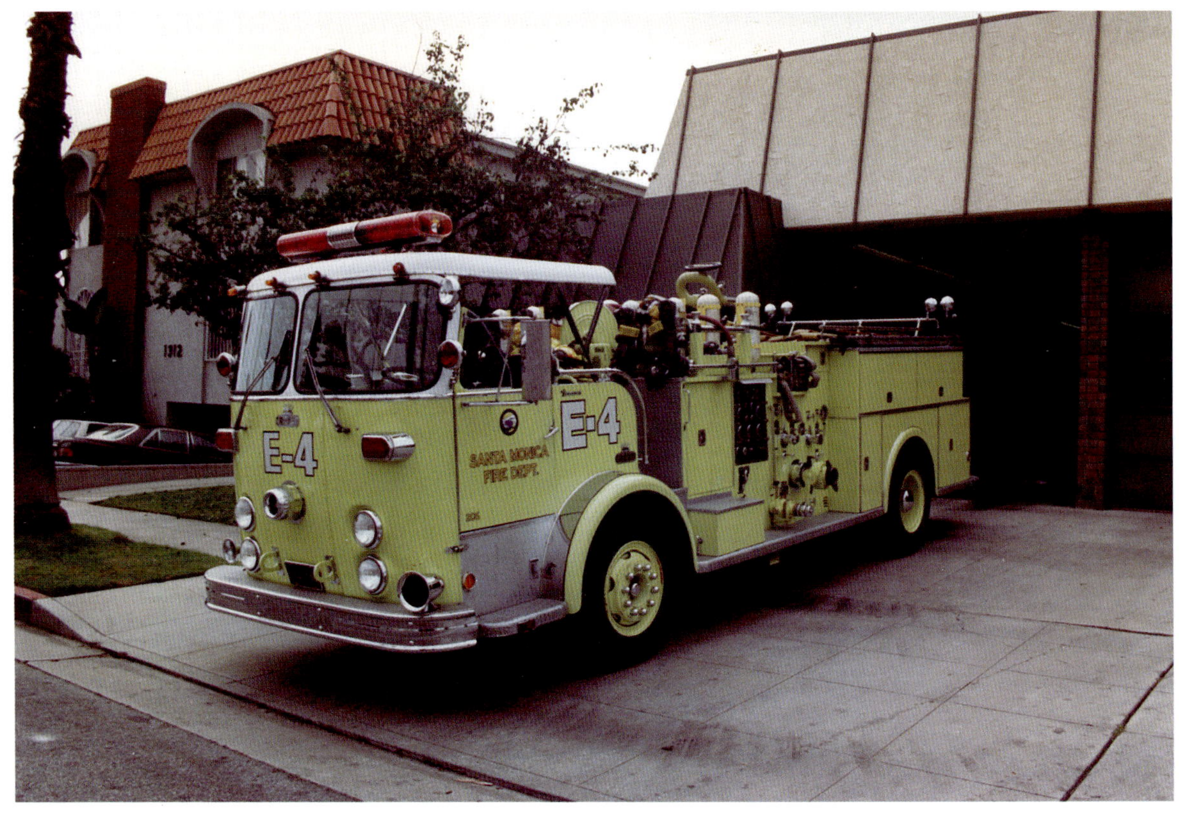

Crown Fire Coach (1951-1985) Santa Monica, CA.

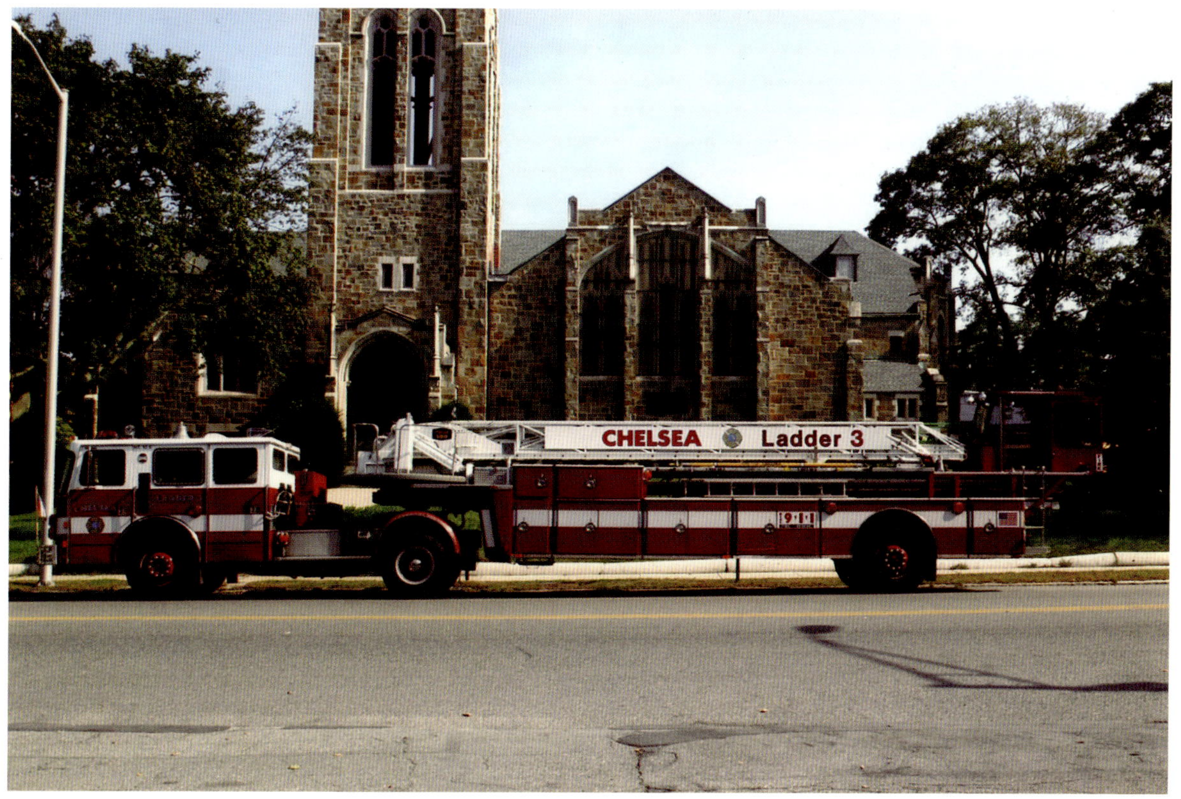

Maxim Motors, their next to last Tiller, manufactured, 1988 "F" Model, Chelsea, MA spare Ladder and formerly served Cambridge, MA as Ladder 3, 4 and 5.

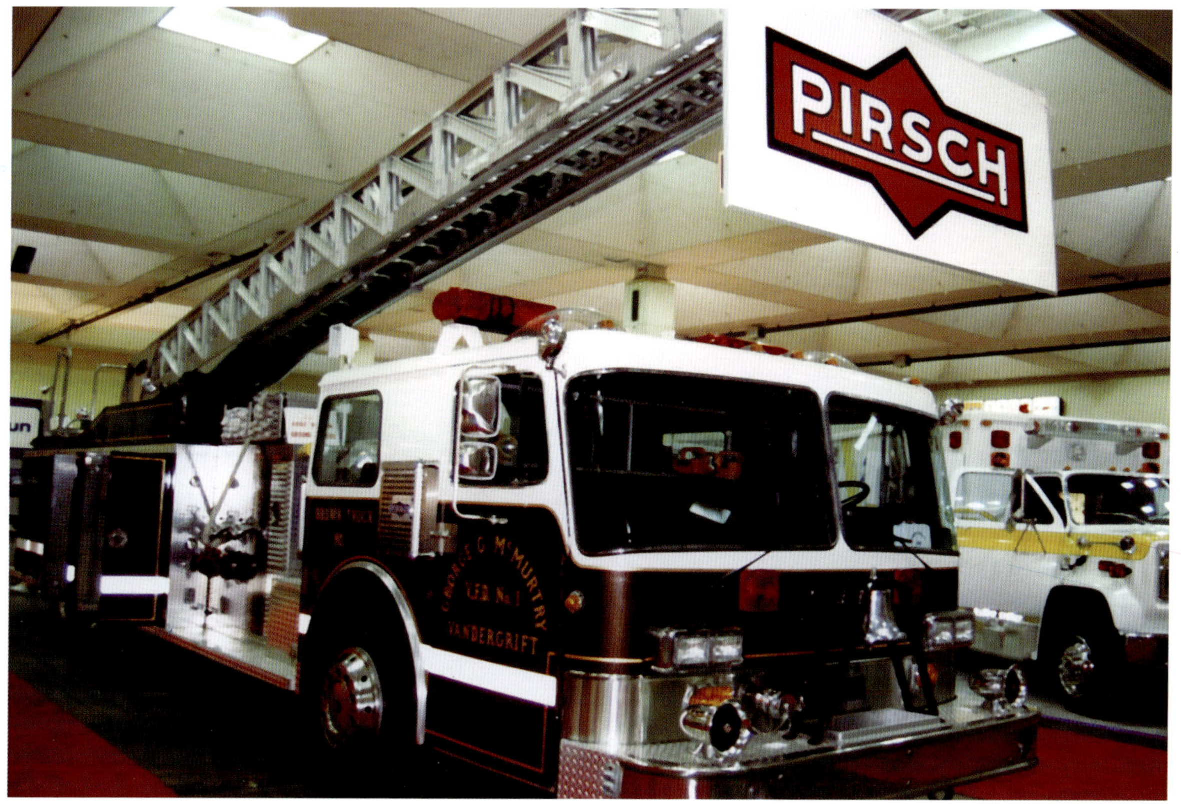

Peter Pirsch and Sons, established in 1857. One of the last trucks manufactured in 1988 was delivered to Vandergrift Borough, Westmoreland County, PA.

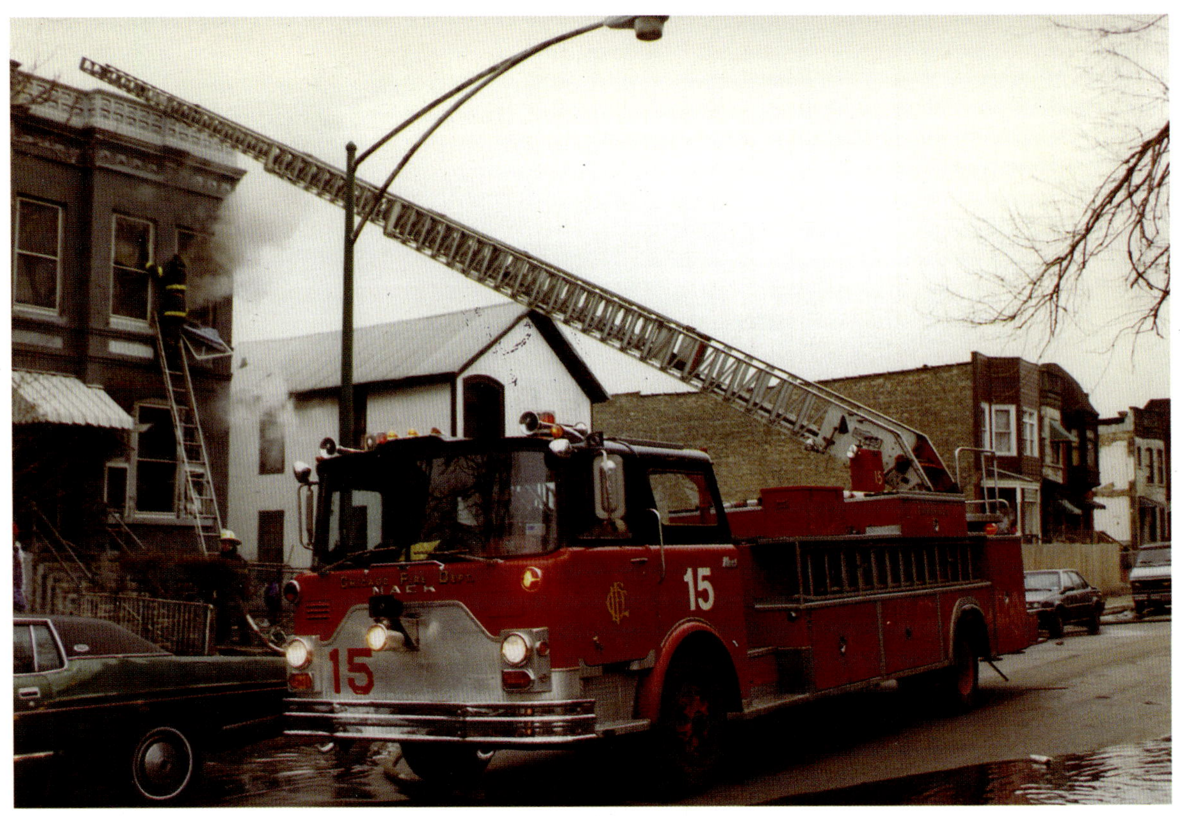

Chicago Truck 15, 1972 Mack/Pirsch. It's second career was in the movies, appearing in the *Fugitive and Backdraft.*

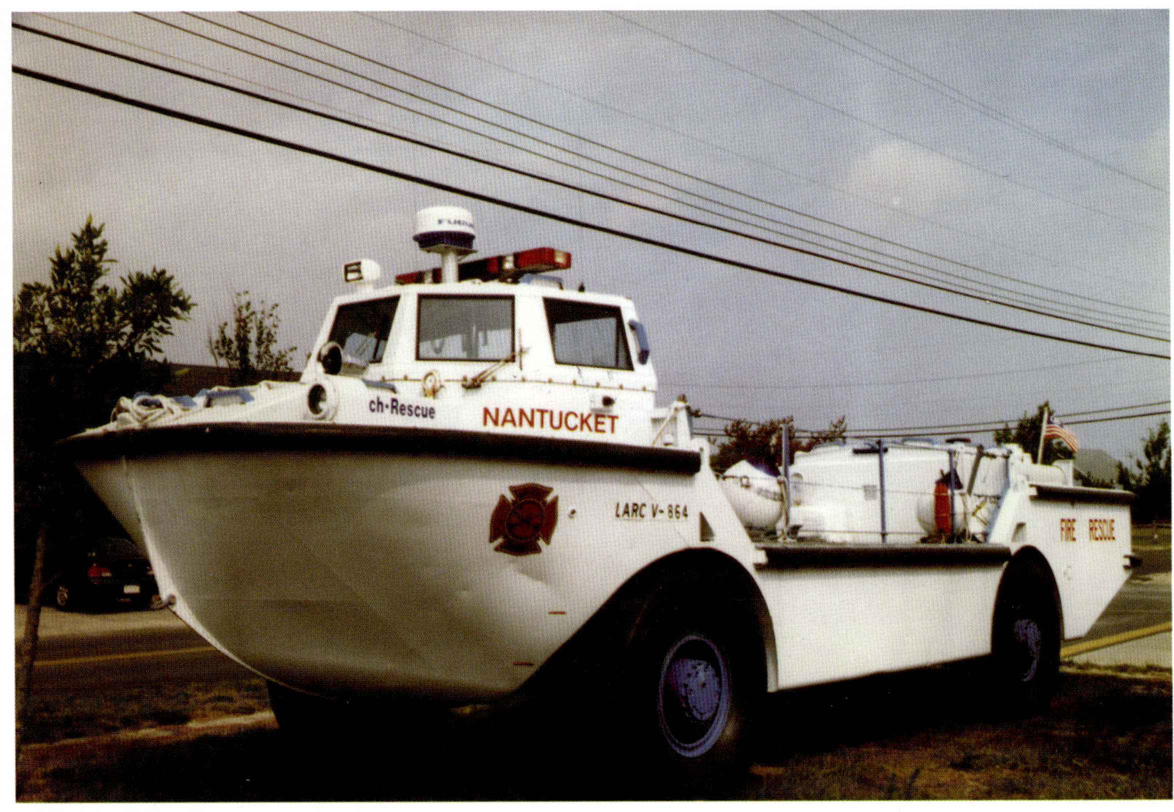

Nantucket, MA, Marine 5, 1971 LARC V 30 foot Amphibious Rescue Unit.

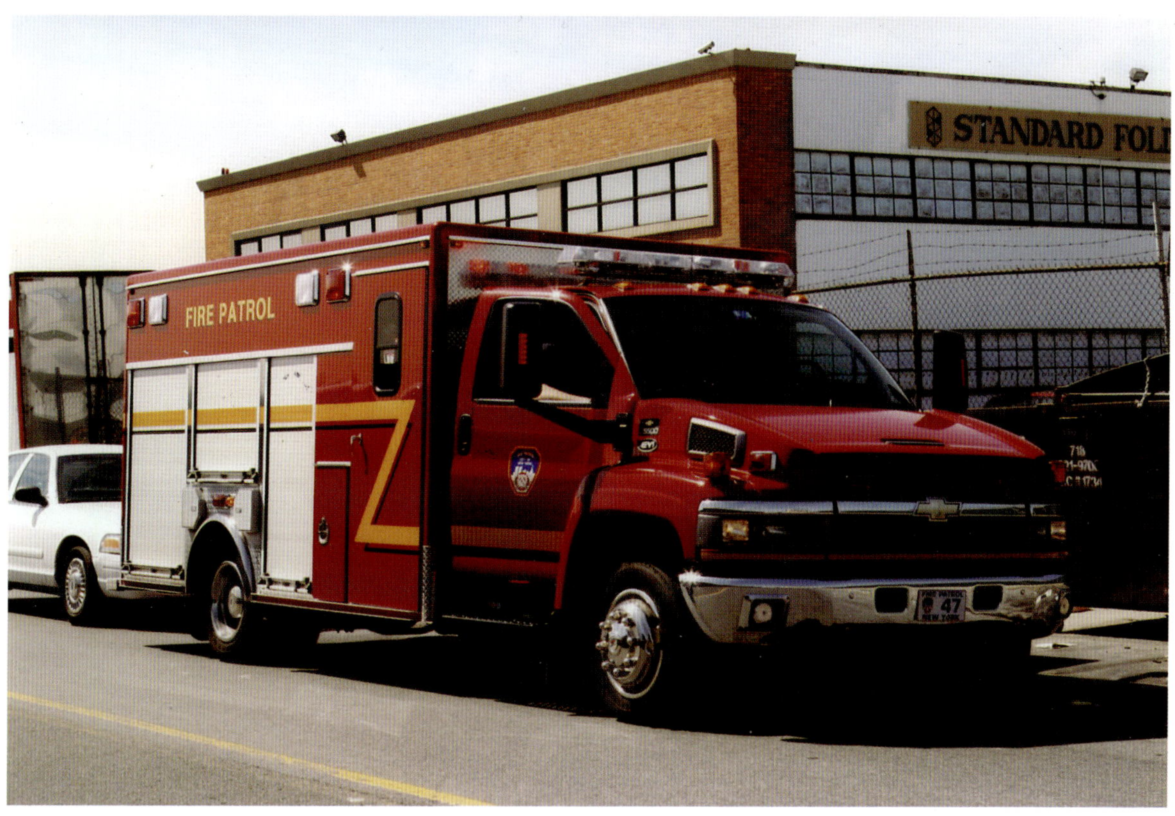

FDNY Fire Patrol, disbanded on October 26, 2006, by the New York Board of Fire Underwriters after 203 years, the oldest paid fire service in The United States.

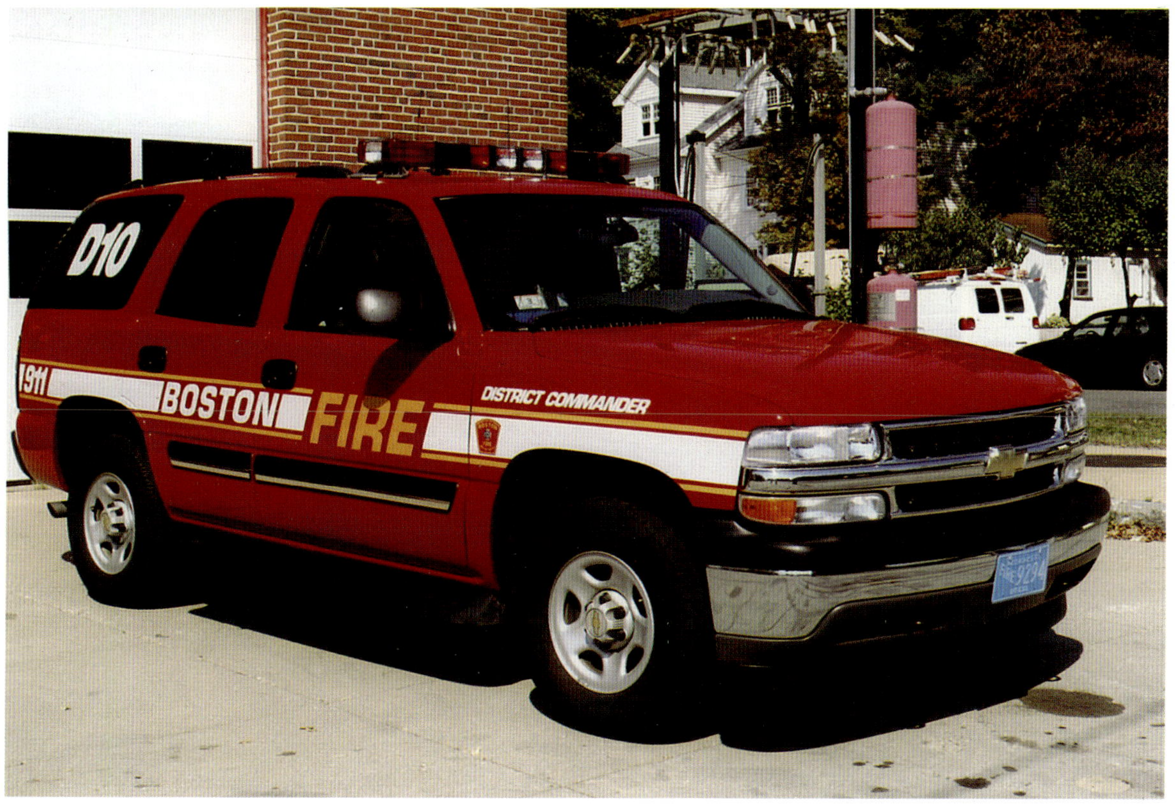

Boston District 10, West Roxbury, disbanded in 2009. West Roxbury is now part of District 12.

NO WORDS ARE NEEDED

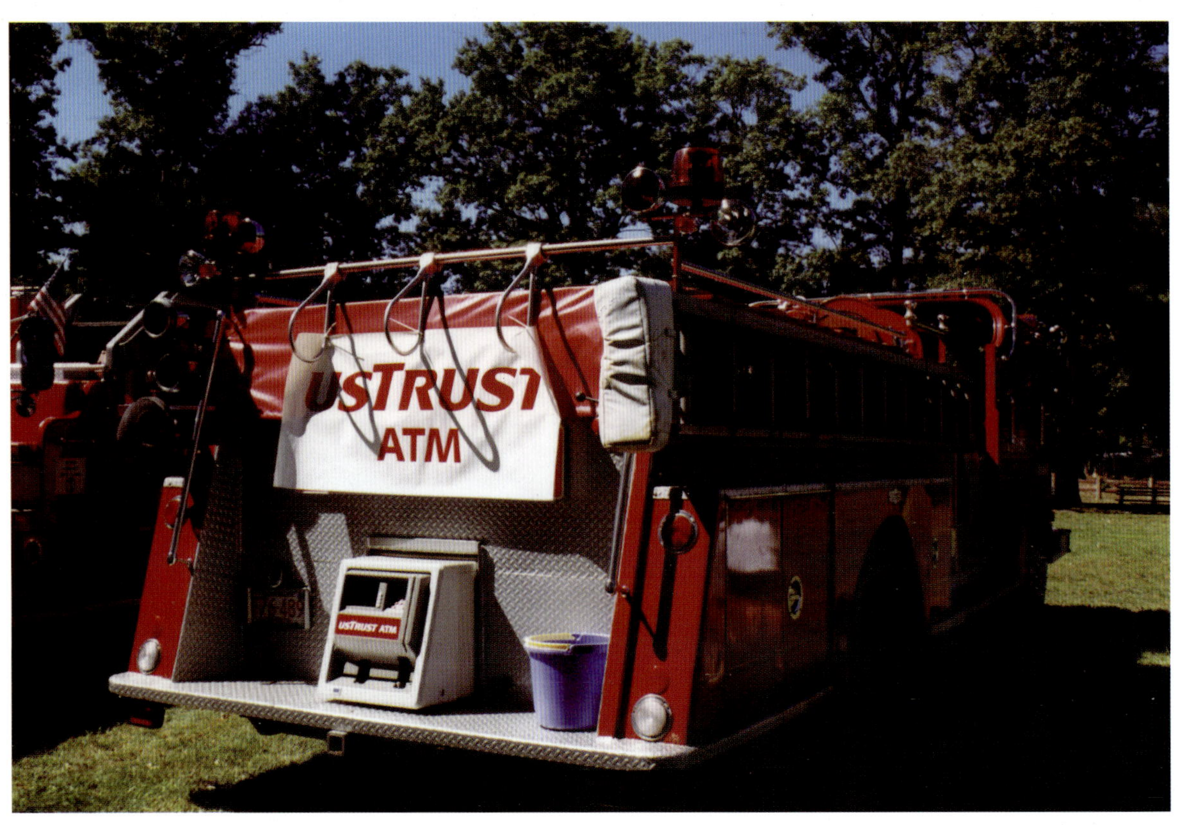

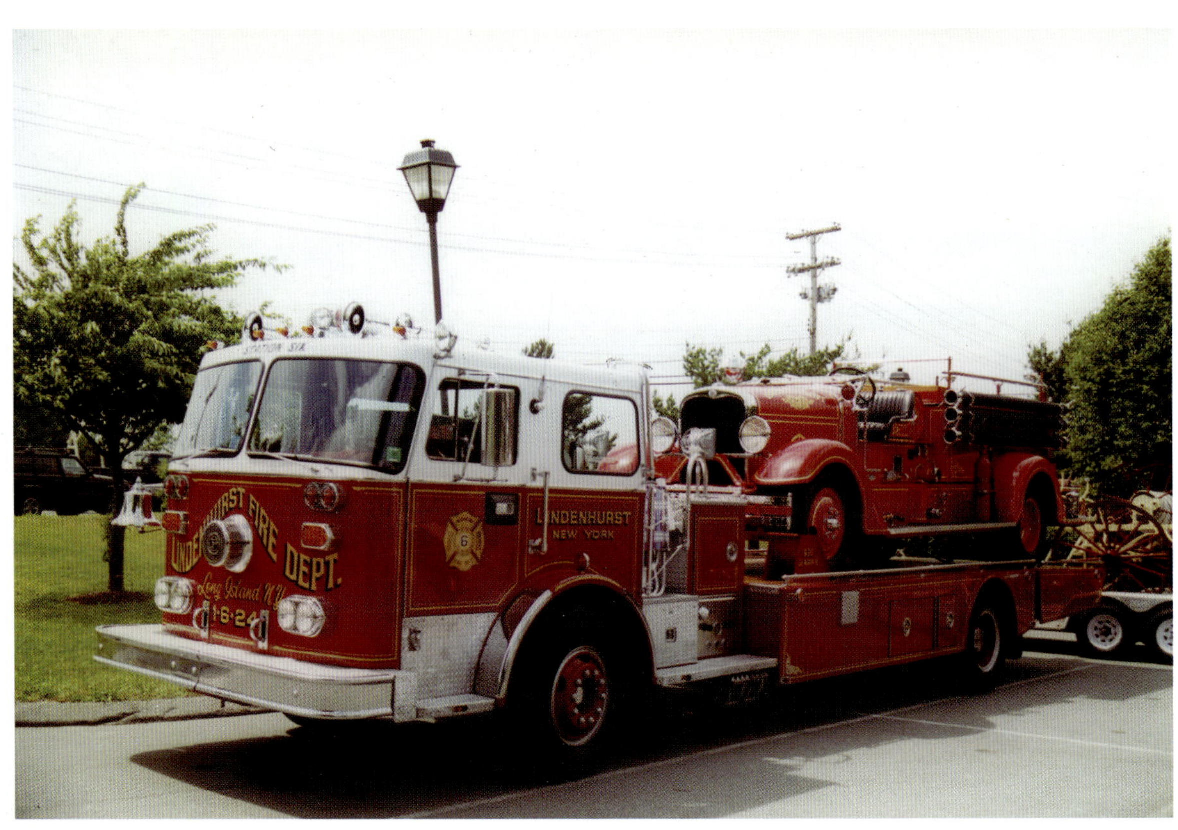

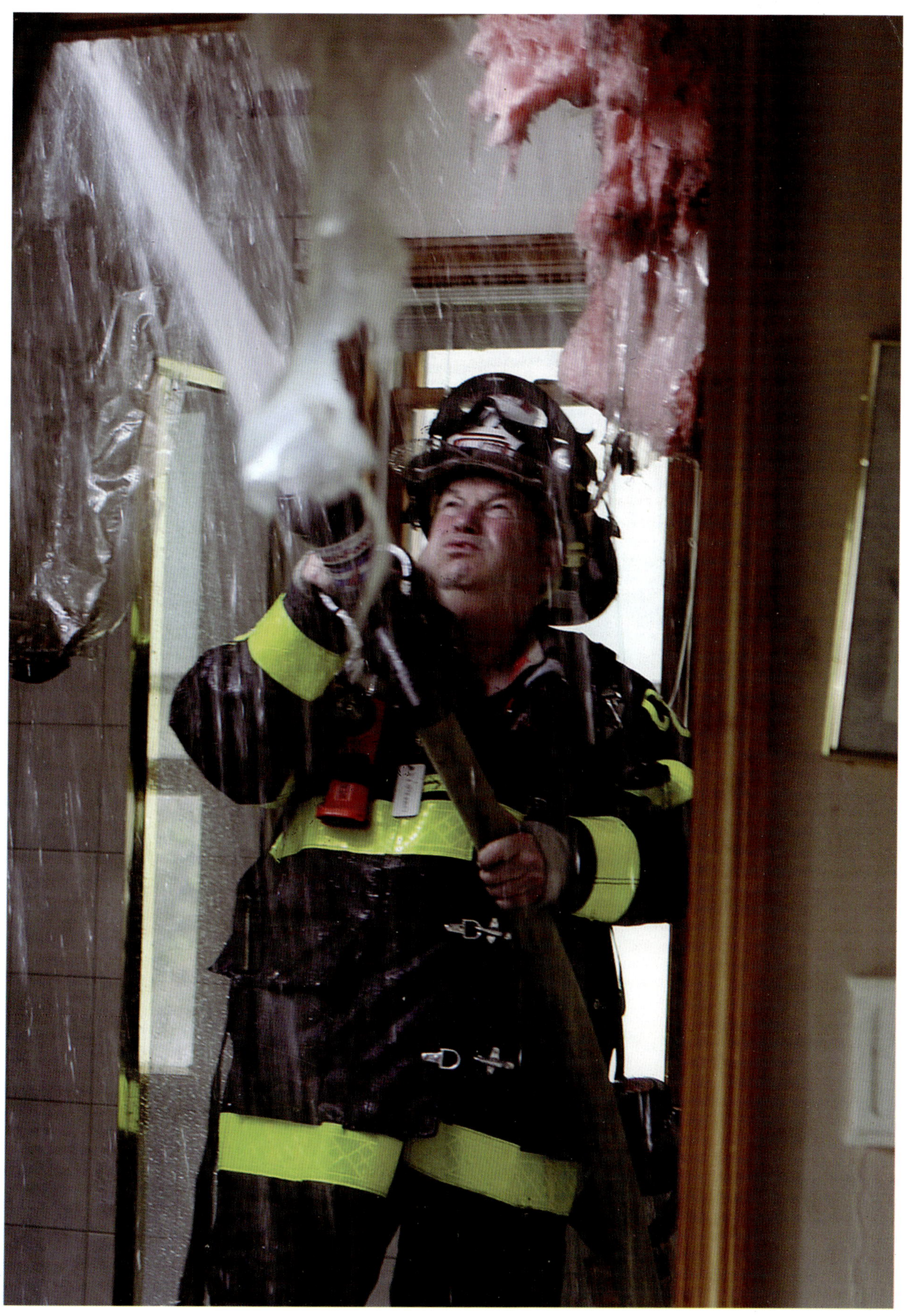